BRIDE'S all BOOK OF ETIQUETTE

BY THE EDITORS OF BRIDE'S MAGAZINE

A PERIGEE BOOK

Perigee Books
are published by
The Putnam Publishing Group
200 Madison Avenue
New York, New York 10016

Library of Congress Cataloging-in-Publication Data
Bride's all new book of etiquette / the editors of Bride's magazine. — 1st Perigee ed.
p. cm.
Prev. ed. published under title: Bride's book of etiquette. © 1989.
Includes bibliographical references and index.
ISBN 0-399-51834-7
1. Wedding etiquette. I. Bride's (The Condé Nast Publications Inc.)
II. Bride's book of etiquette.
BJ2051.B68 1993 93-4268 CIP
395'.22—dc20

Illustrations by Sharon Watts
Front cover photograph by Steven Klein, reprinted from *Bride's*;
copyright © 1992 by The Condé Nast Publications Inc.

First five editions by Grosset & Dunlop
Printed in the United States of America
2 3 4 5 6 7 8 9 10

This book is printed on acid-free paper.
∞

ACKNOWLEDGMENTS

BRIDE'S Magazine would especially like to thank Andrea Feld, Managing Editor, and Phyllis Richmond Cox, Art Director, for their extraordinary dedication and commitment to this project, and for the many hours spent bringing the text and design of these pages into the 90's. Thanks, too, to Laura Yorke, senior editor at Putnam, and her assistant, Eileen Cope.

BRIDE'S also acknowledges the contributions of its entire editorial staff, which is constantly reporting on the ways that people marry across the country and around the world. Specifically, we thank Wendy Caisse Curran, for her ace copy editing, and Denise Evans, for her computer wizardry. Thanks, too, to the following senior editors for critiquing these revisions: Millie Martini Bratten, Donna Ferrari, Sally Kilbridge, Cherylann Coutts, Rachel Leonard, and Renee Sheffey. Much appreciation to the following writers and researchers: Diane Botnick, Sarah Boyle, Julia Califano, Donna Christiano, Sue Bruskin Clarke, Wendy Caisse Curran, Paula Derrow, Wendy Marder, Julia Martin, Maria McBride-Mellinger, Kathy Mullins, Heather Twidale, and Antonia van der Meer.

Final acknowledgment is made to the many professionals who devoted their time as expert sources for the material in this book. Thanks to florist Bobby Wiggins of N.Y.C. and wedding consultant Gayle Labenow of You Are Cordially Invited in Babylon, NY.

Gratitude to the following individuals for reviewing the material on religious rituals: The Honorable Buck Allen, municipal judge in Vail, CO; Julie Parker Amery of the Unitarian Universalist Association, Boston, MA; The Rev. Yukei Ashikaga at the Buddhist Temple, Chicago, IL; Elisabeth Potts Brown of the Haverford College Quaker Collection, Haverford, PA; Lisa Cortez of the Baha'i National Center, Evanston, IL; The Rev. M. Dhammasri of the Vihari Buddhist Society, Washington, D.C.; Echi Ito of the Japan-America Hotline, Dial Service International Inc., N.Y., NY; Rabbi Irwin Fishbein of the Rabbinic Center for Research and Counseling, Westfield, NJ; James Golding, editor in chief of *Orthodox Observer*, Greek Orthodox Archdiocese of North and South America, N.Y., NY; The Rev. William Graham, Church of Saint Paul The Apostle, N.Y., NY; Dr. P. Jayaraman, Queens, NY; Maribel Kraybill, director of the Mennonite Information Center in Lancaster, PA; L. Don Le Fevre, Church of Jesus Christ of Latter Day Saints, Salt Lake City, UT; The Rev. John Wade Payne of The Park Avenue Christian Church, N.Y., NY; The Rev. Charles Scott of The National Episcopal Church in N.Y., NY; T. Muhammed Sherwani, Queens, NY; Dr. Raymond Smolover, Cantor of the Jewish Community Center of White Plains, NY; Lama Pema Wangdak of the Buddhist Studies and Meditation Center in N.Y.C.; M. Victor Westberg, Manager, Committees on Publication, The First Church of Christ, Scientist, Boston, MA; Rabbi Sherwin Wine, Farmington Hills, MI. And appreciation to The Rev. Roger Coleman of Clergy Services, Inc., Kansas City, MO, for sharing information on the Family Medallion and the Marriage Vessel and the Rose Service.

Thanks, too, to the following organizations: the General Council of the Assemblies of God, Springfield, MO; the Institute of Indian Culture in Queens, NY; the Islamic Center of Queens, NY; the Museum of American Folk Art, N.Y., NY; Wedding Service Watabe, Honolulu, HI.

Thank you to these musicians for sharing their knowledge of wedding music: Michael Assael of Michele & Papes, Forest Hills, NY; Mark Bani, organist of St. Vincent Ferrar, N.Y., NY; Dick Crest, San Francisco, CA; Dr. Gerre Hancock, N.Y., NY; Nick Jordan and Joseph Guadagne, San Francisco, CA; Lester Lanin, N.Y., NY; Kevin Walters, organist, Marble Collegiate Church, N.Y., NY.

And finally, many words of thanks to our readers, for the inspiration they give us daily through their phone calls and letters. This book is for them....

FOREWORD

As we prepared to celebrate the 60th Anniversary of BRIDE'S Magazine—which takes place *this* year, in 1994—we realized that the time had come for a revolution. This *all new* edition of *BRIDE'S Book of Etiquette* is not only expanded and updated for *today*, but it is sensitive to the needs of a juggernaut society that is changing before our very eyes, even as we read the morning newspapers or watch the evening news.

Marriage—that tender partnership of two people in love, two people who expect to build something bigger and more important *together* than either could create alone— is a fragile structure indeed. The respect of sacrament, the *will* to succeed, and the desire for a continuum and family are the driving forces that propel each couple from courtship to constancy, from private covenant to the public declaration of their commitment.

That public declaration is the wedding that occupies the dreams and fantasies of young girls, and the more serious thoughts of their older sisters. Is there a "perfect wedding" for everyone? The answer is yes. The trick is, know thyself.

When we find a partner we trust, someone with whom we believe we can reach our goals and create our future, we are eager to celebrate their existence with everyone we love. And today, we place an even greater emphasis on the importance of the family, on friendships that deepen with time and sharing. Inviting relatives and friends to the ceremony to have them witness our joy of discovery and the promise of our future is the ultimate Rite of Passage.

Contemporary couples, most of whom are older, wiser, and more mature than their siblings of several decades ago, *are* still choosing to have a traditional wedding—that is, the *elements* of tradition: sending invitations, wearing special clothes, choosing a beautiful site, flowers, music, and decorations to enhance the mood, breaking bread in the biblical sense (at any time of the day or evening), cutting a cake and toasting, and finally…going on a honeymoon. But all similarities stop there! Weddings now are as unique as the individuals who stand before us to say their vows. Brides and grooms *personalize* each element of the traditional ceremony, thus making it their own. Our multicultural society yields a rich tapestry of interfaith, intercultural, and interracial marriages that rejoice in the roots, the proud heritage, and the family histories of the participants. We have found many ways to make each wedding *unique* and yet comforting in its familiarity.

Everything you need to know is here, from announcing your engagement to planning your wedding and honeymoon. You'll learn all about the ceremony, who should attend you, what everyone should wear *when*, how to handle invitations and announcements, prewedding parties, uninvited children, and unexpected situations. There's a special chapter on remarriage for the *almost 40 percent* of the population who are marrying again. Other chapters spell out details about religious requirements, transportation, photography and videography. We have the answers to *years* of readers' questions, the solutions to *decades* of engaged couples' problems.

What's *brand*-new is...MORE. *More* about wedding gifts (to give and to receive); *more* about the responsibilities of wedding guests (*plus* how to treat them courteously); *more* about the reaffirmation ceremonies so popular today; plus *special* weddings—from Renaissance to Art Deco, Military to Holiday—that will inspire every couple to design a celebration that is uniquely theirs.

Enjoy this book as you leaf through its pages, quick-read the sidebars, and discover not what is *proper* per se, but what is right for *you*, your fiancé, and your family. Your most important goal *now* is to have a wedding that sends you out into the world as husband and wife with joyful hearts and a lifetime of memories. We hope this book will make that happen.

With all best wishes for happiness and contentment,

Barbara Tober
Editor-in-Chief
BRIDE'S Magazine

CONTENTS

YOUR ENGAGEMENT

1

Whether you've known each other for five years or five months, getting engaged is one of the most exciting—and one of the busiest—times of your life. First, you'll want to share your excitement with family and friends. You might call or visit them spontaneously, invite them over for a small celebration, or break the news on a special occasion. Some couples have even printed the message on a cake, or enclosed it in fortune cookies! Once the news is out that you're going to be married, parties and decision making will follow. During the engagement period, the way that you and your fiancé negotiate with each other and with your families to plan your celebration, honeymoon, and new home is the best "rehearsal" you could have for marriage.

Sharing the News

Your families should be the first to hear the news of your engagement. How you go about letting them know of your decision is up to you.

If your parents know your fiancé extremely well, and he's visited their home often, you might choose a time when you're all together. Living far away from your parents, however, means you may not be able to wait to see them in person. In this case, arrange a conference call; make arrangements to see them as soon as possible.

If your parents aren't acquainted with your fiancé, you might ask them if you can bring him to visit for a weekend or holiday. You two needn't break the news until your fiancé feels comfortable with your family, perhaps a day or two into your visit.

If your fiancé's schedule doesn't permit a visit to your parents, or you're not sure how they'll react to your decision, then you may want to tell them yourself of your upcoming marriage. No matter what your situation, speaking with your family alone gives them—and you—the opportunity to express yourselves freely.

Your fiancé may want to speak privately with your father. Some fathers appreciate the old-fashioned courtesy of the groom-to-be asking for your hand. Your fiancé will also probably receive congratulations, some loving reminiscences about you, and a warm welcome to the family. If your father is no longer alive, your mother, stepfather, guardian, or whoever raised you may talk with your fiancé. If your parents are divorced, he can visit one parent first, then the other. Expect that your parents may have questions about your fiancé's career goals, where you two will live, how you'll deal with education, religion, nationality, or race differences. If you sense conflict over your choice of a partner, urge your parents to talk to your clergymember or a family member who thinks highly of your fiancé. Seek out a premarital-counseling program (see Chapter 4, "Planning Your Wedding," and Appendix, under Chapter 4).

Your fiancé should tell his own parents the good news. They, too, may appreciate hearing the news privately first, so they can express excitement and any possible reservations. His parents will want to get to know you (if they don't, yet), and be reassured that you're both making a carefully considered decision.

If one of you is divorced, the other's parents may be uneasy about what went wrong with the first marriage. Offer them a simple, reassuring statement (*We were much too young when we got married. . . .*). If one of you has children, the other's parents may be apprehensive about their son or daughter becoming an instant parent. Help them get to know the children before the wedding.

Once your fiancé tells his parents, they traditionally call on your parents so everyone can get acquainted. His mother might drop your mother a note, or phone to invite your parents for drinks, brunch, or dinner. Any way his parents usually entertain their friends is a good way for them to get to know your parents. If your parents are divorced, your fiancé's family might first extend their invitation to the person who raised you. If your families live in different towns, a note from your fiancé's mother to your mother saying how pleased she is that you'll be a member of the family is a thoughtful gesture. Even if your parents and his are old friends, this is the perfect excuse for them to have dinner together and toast the occasion (you two—and your brothers and sisters—may or may not be included). Your fiancé's parents haven't contacted your parents? Then your parents might make the first move, inviting them over for a drink. Or, you and your fiancé might get everyone together.

If one or both of you have children, make telling them a top priority; you certainly

engagement checklist

- ☐ **Shop for a ring.**
- ☐ **Tell your family.**
- ☐ **Tell your friends.**
- ☐ **Tell your boss/co-workers.**
- ☐ **Send newspaper engagement announcement(s).**
- ☐ **Ask friends/family members to be attendants.**
- ☐ **Have an engagement portrait taken.**
- ☐ **Register for china, crystal, silver, other gifts.**

don't want them to hear the news from someone else. Tell them far in advance of the wedding, so you'll have time to discuss their concerns. Make the announcement time as comfortable as possible and encourage your children to air troubled feelings. Keep in mind that each child, partly depending on his or her age, may react differently. Anticipate worries they may have: Will you still have time for them? Will they still see their own father? Do they have to change their name? Will their stepfather make curfew rules? Will their father still pay for college? Will the family have to move? Don't be hurt if your children are less than overjoyed. Time will help work things out.

There may be other special people to tell personally, such as your bosses and co-workers. Reassure everyone that you'll use lunch hours for wedding chores (schedule vacation days for planning if you feel you'll need them).

Tell your ex-spouse, if you are on speaking terms. You might write a note or telephone to say that you're remarrying. It is best if the news comes directly from you. If there are children involved, it is very important that you and your ex-spouse speak to discuss your children's needs and concerns, as well as his or her concerns (e.g., Will you be moving to another state? Will your son have to share a room with your new husband's son?). Don't create a situation where your children must answer questions from your ex-spouse about your relationship with your new partner.

Length of Engagement

You can consider yourselves engaged as soon as you decide to marry and to inform your parents. Today, there is no traditional or expected engagement length. Many couples wait to announce their engagement until they begin making wedding plans (often at least twelve months before the wedding date, in major cities). It is not unusual for couples to be engaged longer than a year, during which time the bride and groom finish school, complete military service, and save for the wedding. Some couples, due to new job commitments or a military relocation, may speed up their wedding plans so that the engagement lasts just a few months, weeks, or even days.

Sticky Engagement Questions

Engagement often brings a flood of unexpected inquiries, some of which you may find intrusive. Knowing why a friend or family member is asking these questions will help you come up with tactful replies.

"Why do you want to get married?" Today, women have many options and no longer rely on marriage for financial support. The asker may just be curious about your views. Did you once announce to college friends that you never wanted to marry? They may want to know what changed your mind.

"Why did you choose him?" If this question is coming from family members or close friends, it may signal that they have reservations about your fiancé. Remember that these people care about you and want to make sure you're happy. Invite them to air concerns; be as reassuring as you can. If that doesn't work, don't worry—in most cases their worries will be calmed near or soon after wedding day. Finally, remember it is *your* choice to make.

"When are you going to have a baby?" This is most likely to come from hopeful future grandparents. If so, you may wish to acknowledge their longing. Then politely—but firmly—tell them that when the time is right for you two to start a family, they'll be among the first to know. Coming from people who aren't so close to you, this question may seem like an invasion of privacy. Humor can often diffuse tense moments; you might simply laugh and say, "That's a very good question!" leaving it unanswered, or turn the question around and say, "I don't know. When are *you* going to have a baby?"

"Who's paying for the wedding?" Although this may seem like a rude question, wedding expenses today are shared in many ways. People may be exploring options for future reference. If this question makes you feel very uncomfortable, you may have to work on discussing money matters with your fiancé—essen-

tial to a healthy marriage. Remember, of course, you don't have to answer. Whenever a question seems impertinent, it's fine to respond, "Why do you ask?"

"Why are/aren't you changing your name?" People may just be curious. Or, a friend may be looking for confirmation of her own decision. If you choose not to take your husband's name and you sense that his family members are uncomfortable with your nontraditional choice, reassure them that your decision is not meant as a rejection of his family. Perhaps explain that you have established a professional identity already with your own name. If you've decided to use only your surname professionally, tell his family that you will be "Mrs. Jones" socially. You also might reassure them that any grandchildren will take your husband's surname (if that decision makes you comfortable).

"How will the two of you survive financially?" "Why, do you want to contribute?" is the perfect answer to anyone asking this question—except a parent with a specific concern (e.g., your fiancé is unemployed). By now, you two should have discussed all major issues, including finances.

"Am I invited to the wedding?" Who gets invited depends on the type of celebration you want and what you can afford. If the person asking is someone who probably won't be invited, respond, "I'm so flattered that you want to attend." Then, fill in an appropriate excuse ("Unfortunately, we're having a small reception"; "I have a huge family," etc.). If this is someone you wish you could invite, follow up with a post-wedding invitation to dinner, where you share anecdotes and photographs of your wedding and honeymoon, and perhaps show your wedding video.

Publishing the News

Once you've told close friends and relatives personally about your plans to marry, your engagement may be announced in newspapers in your hometowns and in the cities where you work, in alumni magazines and organization newsletters.

Announcement styles vary by publication. Call each newspaper's lifestyle department and ask for the correct spelling of the lifestyle editor's name; address all correspondence to her or him. Find out if there is a standardized form that can be mailed to you. If not, read the paper's announcement section to familiarize yourself with their style. Most engagement and wedding announcements include career information for bride, groom, all parents; offices held by the couple in professional associations; military service; academic honors; schools attended. Although you might mention the month of the wedding, listing the specific wedding date and your street address may invite theft. (For submission tips, see the box, "Preparing Your Announcement.")

Ask about the publication's photo policy. Will the editors publish wedding photographs only? Will they accept photos of the bride only, or of the couple, if preferred? Most newspapers require 8x10-inch or 5x7-inch glossies.

Inquire about deadlines. What are the publication deadlines for engagement and wedding announcements? Some newspapers accept information over the phone, others require that their standardized form be submitted at least ten days prior to publication. Is there a fee?

Keeping your surname? Include a line such as, *The bride will keep her name* or *The bride will keep her name professionally.*

Divorced or widowed? There is no need to mention it in the announcement. Some newspapers, however, will insist on printing a line such as, *The bride's/groom's previous marriage ended in divorce.* Recently divorced or widowed? Wait and announce your wedding only.

Illness in the family? You may find that a close relative or friend who is ill will be anxious to share your happiness at once, and eager for you to make your engagement announcement. Don't delay.

---

preparing your announcement

If your newspaper doesn't supply announcement forms:

- Type the announcement, double-spaced, on one side of an 8½ X 11-inch sheet of paper.

- In the upper-right corner type the name, address, home and office phone numbers of your parents or someone to contact to verify the information.

- Include the date on which you would like the announcement to appear. Note: Sunday is a popular day for weddings and your news might not get in the paper then; consider typing: *For release Monday, May 26.*

- Protect your 8x10-inch or 5x7-inch photo with a stiff piece of cardboard. Write name, wedding date, and phone number on back, lightly in ink (pencil or felt-tip pen might blur). Note: Photo may not be returned.

- Send the announcement to the lifestyle editor, by name.

Announcement Wording

Traditional

Mr. and Mrs. Dennis Brown announce the engagement of their daughter, Ann Marie, to John Smith, the son of Mr. and Mrs. Thomas Smith of St. Louis. No date has been set for the wedding. [Or, The wedding will take place in December.]

The city is mentioned only when it is not the same as where the paper is published. If your mother uses her maiden name, write *Mr. Dennis Brown and Ms. Ann Hoyt.*

Divorced parent, announcing alone

Mrs. Hoyt Brown announces the engagement of her daughter, Ann Marie, to John Smith, the son of Mr. and Mrs. Thomas Smith of St. Louis. Miss Brown is also the daughter of Mr. Dennis Brown of Tulsa.

If your parents are divorced, the announcement is made by the parent with whom you've lived, but both parents are mentioned. (A divorced mother's name is traditionally a combination of her maiden and married surnames: *Mrs. Hoyt Brown.* She may prefer the contemporary pairing of her given name and married surname: *Mrs. Ann Brown*).

Divorced parents, announcing jointly

If your parents are divorced but friendly, they might jointly announce the news:

Mr. Dennis Brown of Tulsa and Mrs. Hoyt Brown of Chicago announce the engagement of their daughter, Ann Marie, to John Smith, the son of Mr. and Mrs. Thomas Smith of St. Louis.

Remarried mother

Mr. and Mrs. Raymond Jones announce the engagement of Mrs. Jones's daughter, Ann Marie Brown, to John Smith, the son of Mr. and Mrs. Thomas Smith of St. Louis. Miss Brown is also the daughter of Mr. Dennis Brown of Tulsa.

If your mother has remarried, she uses her current married name: *Mrs. Raymond Jones.*

One parent deceased

The engagement of Miss Ann Marie Brown, daughter of Mrs. Dennis Brown and the late Mr. Brown, to Mr. John Smith, the son of Mr. and Mrs. Thomas Smith of St. Louis, is announced by the bride's mother.

Both parents deceased

If both parents are deceased, the announcement is usually made by an older brother or sister or any close relative—even a close friend:

Mr. Jason Hoyt of Pittsburgh announces the engagement of his niece, Miss Ann Marie Brown, to Mr. John Smith, the son of Mr. and Mrs. Thomas Smith of St. Louis. Miss Brown is the daughter of the late Mr. and Mrs. Dennis Brown.

Should your fiancé be the one whose parents are deceased or divorced, you can adapt the appropriate wording to suit his situation.

Bride and groom sponsoring wedding

If you are sponsoring the wedding, you might still have your parents announce the engagement, or you can announce it yourselves:

Susan Elizabeth Scott, newscaster for WBIX-TV, is to be married in June to

James J. Sampson, vice president, trust accounts, for First National Bank of Denver. Ms. Scott is the daughter of John Z. Scott of Atlanta, Georgia, and Sarah Newberry Scott of New York, New York. Mr. Sampson is the son of Mr. and Mrs. Dudley P. Sampson of Cleveland, Ohio.

Remarriage

Word the announcement in the traditional style, using the bride's legal name:

Mr. and Mrs. Alvin G. Dunlap announce the engagement of their daughter, Anne Dunlap Crosby, to Joseph G. Riggs, son of Mr. and Mrs. G. Denton Riggs.

Engagement Parties

Anyone may give a party in your honor, but your parents should have the opportunity to be the first ones to celebrate your engagement. It may be held shortly before, after, or perhaps on the very day your engagement announcement appears in the paper, if you have chosen to publish the news.

Any style of party is appropriate: a buffet, cocktail party, picnic. On the invitations, you might write: *in honor of Howard and Carol.* You and your fiancé—along with your parents and his parents—might greet guests in an informal receiving line.

Gifts are optional at an engagement party and should not be expected. However, since some guests *will* want to mark the occasion with a gift, it's wise to list your gift choices and patterns at a Wedding Gift Registry (see Chapter 17, "Wedding Gifts").

At the gathering, your father might propose a toast to you and your fiancé. (Remember: Whenever a toast is proposed to you, remain seated and refrain from raising your glass or drinking.) After your father's toast, it's customary for your fiancé to rise and respond by toasting you and your parents, then his parents. You might also choose to rise and make a toast to your fiancé and both sets of parents.

Surprise guests with your news sometime during the party. Some couples prefer to invite guests to a cocktail party, then announce the news of their engagement sometime during the celebration. It's a perfect occasion to break the news, since so many friends and relatives will be gathered in one place.

Your fiancé's parents may also host a party to introduce you to their family and friends. This might be a luncheon, cocktail party, or dinner, but it shouldn't be a shower. (Since the hosts are members of the groom's immediate family, it should not appear as if they are asking for gifts.)

Thank anyone who entertains you, even if it was a family brunch. Send a sincere note, perhaps accompanied by flowers, to express your gratitude.

Engagement Presents

Your first engagement gift will probably be a ring given to you by your fiancé (although you can be engaged without having a ring). A single diamond (symbolizing love and fidelity) is the classic choice, but other precious and semiprecious gemstones—perhaps opals, sapphires, rubies, or emeralds, alone or paired with diamonds—are also appropriate. Some couples choose engagement rings that they will wear as wedding rings, as well. Or, if you plan to wear your engagement ring on the same finger as your wedding ring, or you want your wedding ring to match the groom's, shop for matching sets together. Your fiancé's family may present you with an heirloom ring, instead, or you may have stones belonging to your family placed in a new setting.

In addition to your ring, your fiancé may give you another gift, such as a bracelet or necklace—perhaps a watch—in honor of the engagement, or later for the wedding. You may also wish to give him a present—perhaps a watch (see "Engagement Gifts to Give Each Other" box and Appendix, under Chapter 1, "Your Engagement").

An engagement need not be a gift-giving occasion. Those particularly close to you, however, may surprise you with household or trousseau items. Whatever you receive, respond promptly with a written note of thanks, even if you expressed your gratitude in person (see Chapter 17, "Wedding Gifts").

*engagement
gifts
to give
each other*

- engagement rings
- wedding rings
- wristwatch
- pocket watch
- pearls
- gold bracelet
- necklace
- locket
- cuff links
- jewelry box
- money clip
- leather-bound edition of a favorite book
- two champagne flutes

Engagement Customs

Your engagement brings with it a host of customs that have been practiced for centuries by couples throughout the world. Here are some popular traditions.

The engagement ring

The *betrothal ring* dates back to the days of marriage by purchase, when it served as both partial payment for the bride and as a symbol of the groom's honorable intentions. The *gimmal ring* had three parts, and at betrothal the woman, the man, and their witness each donned a portion to wear until wedding day, when the pieces were reunited as a single ring for the bride. In the fourteenth and fifteenth centuries, *posy rings* were popular (a posy, or endearing saying, was inscribed on the outside of the ring). A *regard ring* spelled out a message of love (DEAR) with precious stones such as di-amonds, *e*meralds, *a*methysts, and *ru*-bies. The diamond, first incorporated into engagement rings in medieval Italy, was chosen to stand for enduring love, because of its hardness. Now that men and women are enjoying equal roles in their relationships, a bride may also give a ring to her groom.

Love tokens

Welsh and Pennsylvania Dutch couples often gave each other handcrafted gifts, useful for their future home. Such things as cake molds, butter prints, and carved spoons were covered with symbols and statements of love. In Wales, a young man carved a wooden spoon for his lady to wear as a "locket" around her neck, signifying engagement (the origin of the term *spooning*). Today's versions are equally romantic. Or, borrow an English custom: Hang a painted porcelain rolling pin over the kitchen door to use only for baking on special days (your anniversary, the day you met).

Wedding gifts

A Finnish bride-to-be was considered snobbish if she did not *go collecting*— door-to-door—to receive her gifts in a pillowcase. An older married man (symbolizing long-lasting marriage) in a top hat, carrying an umbrella (representing shelter), accompanied her and was given a drink at each door! A contemporary bride is more likely to travel to a store's Wedding Gift Registry to list preferences and make shopping easier for her guests. She receives gifts at a bridal shower, where an umbrella is often a decoration, still symbolizing protection, shelter, and good luck.

A hope chest

In Europe and later in America, the bride's family began preparing for her marriage when she was born. They collected, embroidered, and crafted items to store in a striking piece of furniture, called a *marriage chest*. Today, the bride's or groom's family might purchase a hope chest which can be used as a place for the bride and groom to store gifts and purchases before the wedding, and, later, in the couple's home.

Engagement parties

In Guernsey, England, a betrothal party,

called a *flouncing*, was held for the engaged couple to meet friends of both families. The flouncing established a formal contract and marked an abrupt change of status. Afterward, the couple could not be seen with or talk to other suitors. Following this formal declaration, if either changed his or her mind about the marriage, the other could lay claim to half of his or her property.

Formal engagement ceremonies or parties, common in many cultures, bestowed responsibilities (a concept that grew into breach-of-promise lawsuits). For instance, in China, betrothal was a family obligation. If an engaged man died before the wedding, his intended bride was treated like a widow.

Today, your parents will probably want to schedule their own contemporary version of flouncing—a chance to get together to meet each other.

The bridal shower

Legend has it that the first bridal shower took place in Holland when a maiden fell in love with a poor miller. Hoping to discourage the marriage, the maiden's father denied her the customary bridal dowry. To help the young couple set up housekeeping, the miller's friends showered the bride with gifts. Today, there are many kinds of showers (see Chapter 3, "Prewedding Parties").

A matchmaker

In countries where marriages are arranged, *go-betweens* play a respected role. In China, a matchmaker must determine if birth signs are compatible. In Uganda, the bride's elder brother and paternal uncle speak to prospective

what to call in-laws:

Is it time to be more familiar than "Mr. and Mrs. Jones?" Have your fiancé ask his parents in private what they prefer to be called. Or, during a visit with his mother, say, "You've really made me feel a part of your family. Rick calls you Mom—may I call you Mom, too?" Your options:

- "Mom," "Dad"
- "Mother," "Father" (*not* what you call *your* parents
- "Mother B," "Father B"
- their first names
- whatever your fiancé calls them

what to call step-parents:

- A divorced and remarried in-law? Call the new partner what your fiancé calls him or her (probably by their first name).
- Fiancé has children? See what they are comfortable with (perhaps you'll be "Mom," his or her real mom, "Mommy").
- Give children the option to be more affectionate in the future (say, "You can call me Ann now, but I'll answer to 'Mom' if you ever feel like calling me that."

grooms and barter for the family. You may want to pay tribute to the person who introduced you to your fiancé with a seat of honor at the reception (at the head table?), a corsage, or a toast.

The phrase *tying the knot*

Tying the knot, a phrase associated with getting married, refers to an ancient Babylonian custom. Threads were taken from the clothes of both the bride and the bridegroom and tied together in a knot to symbolize the union of the couple. In some cultures today, the couple's hands are loosely bound during the ceremony (with plaited grass in Africa, with a rosary in Mexico). (See Chapter 2, "Wedding Customs.")

Broken Engagements

Sadly, not all engagements endure, for a variety of reasons. During this period of planning, the bride or groom may experience cold feet, feel they are not ready to make a lifelong commitment, or realize that there are irreconcilable differences. If you decide to call off your engagement:

Return any gifts that you were given to celebrate the occasion. Legally, whoever initiated the breakup has no claim to the engagement ring. If the bride received a family heirloom, however, it is honorable to return it to the groom's family. You may keep any birthday or holiday presents received from the groom and his family.

If it's a last-minute decision, wedding invitations will have to be recalled via notes, telephone calls, or telegrams (see Chapter 5, "Invitations & Announcements"). Write a brief personal note to close friends and relatives; there is no need to go into detail.

Send a release to every newspaper that

published your announcement, simply stating:

The engagement of Miss Ann Marie Brown and Mr. John Smith has been terminated by mutual consent.

In the unfortunate case of a partner's death before the wedding, gifts also must be returned. Someone in the bride's family or a close friend may assume this task, in consideration of the feelings of the survivor and the couple's parents.

You might also send a release to every newspaper that published your announcement, simply stating:

The wedding of Miss Ann Marie Brown and Mr. John Smith will not take place due to the death of Mr. Smith.

WEDDING CUSTOMS

Today, couples are choosing to observe centuries-old traditions, updating them to reflect their own personalities. And, more couples than ever before are including ethnic customs from their heritages in wedding celebrations.

Contemporary Customs

Here are the meanings behind many of the traditional marriage customs that are commonly practiced today. (For more on rituals and customs, see Chapter 9, "Religious Rituals & Requirements," and Appendix, under Chapter 2, "Wedding Customs.")

Why a wedding ring? The circular shape of the wedding ring symbolizes never-ending love. According to folklore, the ring protected the bride against evil spirits; if the bride or groom dropped it during the ceremony, bad luck would follow. Originally, rings were made of rushes, hemp, or braided grass, which had to be replaced every year. Early Romans chose more durable iron to symbolize the permanence of marriage. Gold has always been a popular, but more expensive, choice, symbolizing lasting beauty, purity, and strength. In ancient Egypt, before coins were minted, gold rings were used as currency and as a symbol of the groom's wealth and his intention to wed. To show that he trusted his wife with his money, the Egyptian husband placed a gold ring on the third finger of her left hand.

Only one ring was worn, until the thirteenth century. The declaration of Pope Innocent III that a waiting period was to be observed between betrothal and marriage led to separate betrothal and wedding rings. The first recorded account of a diamond engagement ring was in 1477, when Maximilian I, King of Germany, proposed to Mary of Burgundy and offered her a diamond ring to seal his vow.

Why the third finger, left hand? Ancient peoples believed that the vein in the third finger of the left hand ran directly to the heart. Medieval bridegrooms placed the ring sequentially on three of the bride's fingers to symbolize the trinity—first on the bride's thumb ("in the name of the Father"), then on the index finger ("and the Son"), then the middle finger ("and the Holy Ghost")—before sliding it onto the third (ring) finger, saying "Amen." The ring remained on the third finger throughout the marriage. This has since become the customary ring finger for all English-speaking cultures. However, in many European countries, the wedding ring is worn on the right hand. A Greek woman wears her ring on her left hand while she is engaged, moving it to her right hand when she is married.

Why does the bride wear a veil? Originally, the bride's veil symbolized her youth and virginity. Bridal veils helped brides remain modest and hide themselves from jealous spirits. Even today, in Muslim countries (in the Middle East, Africa, Eastern Europe), a young man is bound by the constraints of religious modesty to conduct his entire courtship with his bride-to-be veiled, never being permitted to see her face until after the wedding.

In early days, veils were worn to confuse the devil and protect the bride from the evil eye. Veils were often red (the color of defiance), blue (meaning constancy), or yellow (the classic color of Hymen, god of marriage). Early Greek and Roman brides wore flame-yellow or red veils. The yellow (probably representing fire) was thought to ward off demons. Sometimes, Roman brides swathed their entire body with a long red veil to shield themselves from malicious spirits. Early Christian brides wore white (indicating purity, celebration) or blue veils (a symbol of the Virgin Mary's purity). Martha Washington's granddaughter, Nellie Custis, is said to have started the custom of wearing a white lace veil. She covered her head with a long lace scarf on her wedding day after her fiancé, Major Lawrence Lewis, President Washington's aide, complimented her as she stood behind a lace window curtain.

Why does the bride wear white? White has been a symbol of celebration for some two thousand years, since Roman times. In nineteenth-century Victorian times, white was a sign of affluence—since it was assumed that a woman would only be able to wear a white dress once or twice, until it was soiled. At the beginning of the twentieth century, white became synonymous with purity. Today, white once again symbolizes the color of joy on wedding day; women who are remarrying may choose among many shades of white—from ecru and eggshell to cameo.

Why does the bride carry flowers? Flowers have long represented a variety of emotions and merits—lilies symbolize virtue; roses, love; and so on. Early Roman brides carried bunches of herbs under their veils to symbolize fidelity and fertility, and to ward off evil. The Greeks used ivy as a sign of indissoluble love. Orange blossoms were originally chosen by the ancient Saracens to represent fulfillment and happiness, as the orange tree blooms and bears fruit at the same time. Today, pretty wedding blooms convey a message of fertility, "flowering," and bounty.

Why do the bridesmaids and the groom have flowers, too? Early bridesmaids' bouquets were made of pungent herbs such as rosemary and garlic—not flowers. The smell was supposed to drive away any evil spirits eyeing the bridal party. Even the groom wore a few sprigs.

Why does the bride carry a handkerchief? Not all brides do, but if you choose to, it is considered to be a lucky sign. Early farmers thought a bride's wedding-day tears were lucky and brought rain for their crops. Later, it was believed that a bride who cried at her wedding would never shed another tear about her marriage.

Why is it traditional to have bridesmaids and ushers? Long ago, marriage by capture was the norm. A groom's friends helped him kidnap his mate and defended him against anyone who might try to steal the bride—including her family! The best man and ushers represent the warriors. At the altar, the groom always stood on the bride's right side, leaving *his* right hand—his sword hand—free to defend her.

In later years, it was customary for the bride to travel to her groom's village accompanied by escorts, her "bridesmaids," who would defend her and her dowry against suitors and robbers. In England, the bride was escorted to the church by boys, or "bride knights," symbolizing her innocent status; on the way home, she was escorted by married men, or "bridegroom men."

Why do wedding attendants all dress alike? Under Roman law, ten witnesses were required to make a wedding legal. To confuse the nether world and the evil spirits that lurked at the altar, several witnesses dressed exactly like the bride and groom. Another reason: In Europe, it was common for the bride, groom, and all their friends to walk together to the church. Afraid that someone—perhaps a rejected suitor—would spot the happy couple and put a curse on them, the groom's friends wore clothes almost identical to his, and the women costumed themselves like the bride, thus tricking evil-wishers.

Why does a bride shop for a trousseau? Derived from the French word *trousse*, meaning bundle, the trousseau originated as a bundle of clothing and personal possessions the bride carried to her new home. This was later expanded into a more generous dowry that enhanced the value of an unmarried daughter in the eyes of prospective suitors. Today, the trousseau encompasses all of the new things—for the household and for the couple themselves—that help make the transition to a new stage of life.

Why is it bad luck for the groom to see his bride before the ceremony? Once, it was considered bad luck for the groom to see his bride *and* for the bride to see *herself* in a mirror in her wedding clothes before the wedding. Because the wedding ceremony marked a break between old and new, never to overlap, people thought that if the groom saw the bride before the ceremony, she would not be pure and new. If the bride saw herself in a mirror before the wedding, she would leave some of herself behind in the reflection.

Why is a white or red aisle runner used? This is not just a decorative detail. In times past, women were carried to a wedding, in part to show respect, but also to protect them from evil spirits that lurked in the ground. The "red-carpet treatment" is a way to honor someone; the white runner, a pure pathway. Rose petals in the bride's pathway lead her to a sweet, plentiful future.

Why does the bride wear something old and something new? This custom stems from an Old English rhyme, "Something olde, something new, something borrowed, something blue, and a sixpence in her shoe...." Brides throughout the decades have taken care to include these touches in their bridal outfit, a nod to tradition and superstition. The symbolism: continuity, optimism for the future, borrowed happiness, fidelity, and good fortune.

Why does the bride wear something blue? Brides of ancient Israel wore a blue ribbon on the border of their fringed robes to denote modesty, fidelity, and love—ideals still associated with that color. Blue is also the color that represents the purity and innocence of the Virgin Mary.

Why is it good luck to put a coin in your shoe? This custom originated in England. Coins were given to young ladies as love tokens. A gentleman burnished the reverse side of a coin, then engraved the initials of his beloved. In Sweden, the bride's father places a piece of silver in her left shoe; her mother, a piece of gold in her right, so that she may never lack in luxuries. Royal brides traditionally have a tiny silver horseshoe sewn in the hem of their gown, for good luck.

Why is the bride given away? She isn't always. Nowadays, although many brides are escorted to the altar by their father, they are no longer "given away." In earlier times, when women were granted fewer personal rights, the bride was literally given to the groom in an arranged marriage. A vestige of that practice can be found in the question in the marriage service, "Who gives this woman to be married to this man?" The bride who keeps the "giving away" in her marriage service often sees it as symbolic of her parents' support for her union and their promise of continued trust and affection. A popular alternative found in ceremonies today is the question, "Who supports this man and this woman in this marriage?" Both parents might respond, "We do." Or, all parents and guests might join in the response.

Why does the ceremony end with a kiss? From the days of ancient Rome, the kiss was a legal bond which sealed contracts, and thus, the betrothal. Christianity incorporat-

---

something old, something new...

- Something old: a family heirloom—a Bible, antique lace on the gown, jewelry—for continuity.

- Something new: the bride's clothes, lingerie—for optimism.

- Something borrowed: a lacy handkerchief, jewelry borrowed from a happily married relative (happiness rubs off!).

- Something blue: blue ribbon threaded through lace, slip, in garter—for purity, fidelity, love.

- Penny in your shoe: a sixpence in England, a quarter in Canada, a penny in the U.S.—to ensure a life of fortune.

ed the betrothal ceremony into the marriage ritual. It was also believed that when a couple kissed, part of each of their souls was left behind in the other when their breath was exchanged. Occurring at the end of the rites, the kiss announces a new status.

Why do couples receive wedding gifts? Once, a bride prepared for marriage by filling a hope chest with handsewn linens and other household furnishings. Families endowed offspring with dowries. Today, family members and friends help furnish the couple's new home and lifestyle with shower and wedding gifts (see Chapter 17, "Wedding Gifts"; Chapter 3, "Prewedding Parties").

Why is there a wedding cake? A symbol of good luck and fertility, cake has been a part of wedding celebrations since Roman times, when a small bun was broken above the bride's head at the close of the ceremony. Wheat, the main ingredient, symbolized fertility; crumbs were eagerly sought by guests as good-luck charms. During the Middle Ages, custom required the bride and groom to kiss over a pile of small cakes donated by wedding guests. In Elizabethan times, bridesmaids baked small, sweet buns with currants, the centerpiece for the wedding feast. In the seventeenth century, it was an innovative visiting French baker who frosted the stack of buns so that they'd stand upright—creating the first tiered and frosted wedding cake! The Chinese originated the custom of serving each guest a slice of cake to spread the good luck.

What is the groom's cake? The groom's cake is often a rich, solid fruitcake topped with marzipan and white icing (the traditional wedding cake in England and Ireland) or a cake in the groom's favorite flavor. According to custom, the groom's cake is either served at the reception along with the bride's lighter cake, or packed in decorative boxes for guests to take home—a way to share the couple's good fortune and the sweetness of married life. Custom holds that single guests who put a sliver of groom's cake under their pillows that night will dream of their future spouses (see Chapter 13, "Your Reception," "The Groom's Cake" section).

Why are toasts made at the reception? Raising a glass together is a way for everyone to share in wishing health and happiness to the newlyweds. The term *toast* comes from the old French custom of placing a piece of toast at the bottom of the wine cup. The cup was then passed from hand to hand until it reached the recipient of the good wishes—who drained the goblet and also got the lucky morsel. Toasts may be offered with any beverage, but champagne is a wedding favorite.

Why are there wedding favors? The bride and groom were considered to be lucky—as were any of the things they touched. In times past, guests helped themselves to lucky souvenirs by tearing off ribbons and bits of lace from the bride's dress, or snatching flowers from her bouquet. Now, probably out of a sense of self-preservation, the bride offers guests boxed pieces of wedding cake, candy, almonds, souvenirs—and even more expensive favors—to thank them for sharing their happiness and to impart a little wedding magic.

Why is rice thrown? In the Orient, rice means, "May you always have a full pantry." In other cultures, grains such as rice and wheat symbolize fertility, prosperity, and bounty. In some countries, the bride wore or carried sheaves of grain. Other societies literally sprinkled the newlyweds with grains or nuts, wishing a large harvest for themselves, abundance and a large family for the newlyweds. In Italy, wedding guests flung coins, dried fruit, and candy, called *confetti*. Eventually, shopkeepers sold imitation candies—or colored pieces of cardboard—to throw at newlyweds, later called confetti. Today, rice remains a token of a life of plenty, but guests may also throw rose petals, ecologically disposable paper, potpourri, wheat, millet seed, safflower seed, or birdseed (see Appendix, under Chapter 2, "Wedding Customs").

Why is the bouquet tossed? As the bride left the festivities, she tossed her bouquet to a friend—so that the friend would have luck and protection. The custom evolved to imply that whoever caught the bouquet would be lucky and wed next! Flowers were also believed to be pungent enough to ward off evil spirits.

Why is the bride's garter tossed? Since guests in olden times would literally rip off pieces of the bride's gown as good-luck tokens, eventually, in self-defense, the bride simply threw her garter to the crowd. Another custom from early England: Friends would follow the newlyweds to their wedding chamber, where the groom's friends would take off their stockings, then hurl them at the groom. The thrower who first hit the groom in the nose would be next to wed!

Why are shoes attached to the getaway car? Shoes represent power. They have been associated with the transfer of authority since early Hebrew times. In ancient cultures, sandals were often exchanged as evidence of good faith in the sale of property. An Anglo-Saxon father transferred his authority over the bride by giving the bridegroom one of her shoes. Tied to the back of the wedding car (as is the custom in England), shoes signify the creation of a new family unit; they also cause a noisy clatter once intended to drive off evil spirits that lurk in the ground.

Why do newlyweds go on a honeymoon? In ancient marriages by capture, the groom kept his bride in hiding for a month to prevent searching relatives from finding her. The term *honeymoon* has its origin in an early Teuton custom: Couples drank a fermented honey drink, known as mead or metheglin, for thirty days after their wedding or until the moon waned. An intoxicant, it might have eased sexual inhibitions. Honey is an ancient symbol of life, health, and fertility; the couple's "month of sweetness" was a time alone—a month of happiness (and, they hoped, of fertility!) before taking up the everyday responsibilities of marriage.

Why is the bride carried over the threshold? The Roman bride, demonstrating her reluctance to leave her father's home, had to be dragged over the threshold to her new house. It was also believed that evil spirits hovered at the threshold of whatever house the newlyweds would enter. The bride was lifted over the entrance to keep the evil spirits from entering through the soles of her feet.

American Customs

Each region of the country has customs uniquely theirs. Below is a sampling.

Native American

● Hopi Indian weddings still may involve the whole tribal village. The groom's clan may withhold approval of the marriage until the bride proves herself by grinding corn with the groom's female relatives. As a sign of approval, the whole community may spin cotton to weave a fine set of wedding garments, really blankets, which become the bride's treasured possessions.

● The bride goes to stay at the groom's house before the wedding. There, she bakes cornbread. In a cleansing ritual, both mothers wash the bride's and groom's hair in a stream.

● On wedding morning, Hopi couples greet the rising sun, praying for a good life together, for children, and for faithfulness to each other.

● Navajo Indian brides traditionally marry while facing East, in the direction of the rising sun.

● A Navajo marriage is symbolized by combining corn ground by each family—white by the groom's family, yellow by the bride's—in a corn pudding, which is carried to the wedding in a Navajo wedding basket. The couple share a taste of pudding—symbolizing the first of many meals they'll share in their marriage.

Early American

● In the 1800s in Georgia, if a bride-to-be brought her blanket to the groom-to-be's home, placed it beside his, and spent the night there, she woke up as good as "married."

● Young Amish boys in the Midwest playfully tossed the groom over a low fence to symbolize his passage into a new life.

● Friends serenaded the couple with a "shivaree" on their wedding night by "playing" pots and pans, sometimes shooting off their guns.

● In rural Pennsylvania, a centuries-old tradition lives on: Older single siblings of the bride and/or groom do the "Hog's Trough Dance." They dance in an empty wooden hog's trough until it breaks, ensuring future good luck.

● For summer weddings, nineteenth-century brides often carried fans, usually made of lace, instead of a bouquet. The honor attendant held the bride's fan and scent bottle during the ceremony, in case the bride fainted from the heat! Brides often gave their fans to bridesmaids as favors.

● Victorian brides wore gloves, symbols of modesty and romance; without the "g," they were a pair of *loves*.

International Customs

Today, couples are honoring their heritages by including traditional wedding customs from their countries of origin or adopting others that seem especially meaningful.

Africa/African American

● *Koala Nut*—Before a betrothal, the hopeful groom's family visited the bride-to-be's home to propose the marriage. If her family agreed, a small amount of money and a koala nut were offered to the bride. She accepted the nut, opened it, and shared it with her groom, then with the family representatives present. A messenger, bearing a small piece of the same koala nut, was sent to other families to announce the engagement.

● *Crossing Sticks*—In the early 1900s, African-American couples demonstrated their commitment to each other by leaning long sticks or staff-like branches on the ground and crossing them against each other in the middle. The sticks represented the vitality and strength of trees. The custom blessed their new life together. (In Kenya, a Samburu groom used sticks during the wedding festivities to brand the cattle he would give to his bride to finalize their vows.)

● *Jumping the Broom*—In the times of slavery in this country, African-American couples were not allowed to formally marry and live together. To make a public declaration of their commitment, a man and woman jumped over a broom into matrimony, to the beat of drums. (The broom has long held significant meaning for various Africans, symbolizing the start of homemaking for a newlywed couple. In Southern Africa, the day after the wedding, a Kgatla bride assisted the other women in the family in sweeping the courtyard, indicating her dutiful willingness to help her inlaws with housework till the newlyweds could move to their new home.) Some African-American couples today are choosing to include this symbolic rite in their wedding ceremony, directly before the recession.

● *Binding Wrists*—Some tribes still perform the ancient rite of binding the bride's and groom's wrists together with plaited grass.

● *Hairstyles*—On special occasions, it was traditional for women in most African countries to braid their hair, perhaps cover it with a deep-red ocher dye and animal fat. Today, many African-American brides are choosing to braid their hair on wedding day.

● *Wedding Dresses*—Nigerian brides wear traditional *asooke* cloth (with a textured, pointillistic, geometric pattern); Ghanaian brides and grooms wear the customary *kente* cloth (in colorful, bold, geometric patterns) made into a four-piece *bubah*. Today, some African-American grooms may wear black trousers under a sport jacket made of *asooke* or *kente* cloth, traditional formalwear with an *asooke* or *kente* vest, cummerbund, bow tie, pocket handkerchief.

● *Cowrie Shells*—Smooth cowrie shells, which encourage fertility, are worn in bridal necklaces or used to trim gowns, jackets, and headpieces in silver and white—as decorative accents. Cowrie shells, found off the coast of West Africa, were once used as money and today are used for purification. The shell is also a symbol of beauty and power.

● *Rings*—Some African-American couples today are choosing wedding bands that are designed with Khamitic symbols. The Khamites were ancient, pre-Egyptian peoples from the Nile Valley. Cast in silver and gold, the rings have carvings that symbolize truth, love, fertility, or eternal life.

● *Wooden Stools*—The Asante tribe in West Africa cherished wooden stools, each carved out of one piece of wood. The stools and the symbols on them bore the lore and history of each clan and their ancestors. They were considered the receptacle of the owner's soul, and were seats of honor and power for women. Today, at African-American weddings, some couples set Asante stools in the front row—designated as seats of honor for their parents.

● *Corn Kernels*—African couples are showered with kernels of corn (symbolizing fertility) as they exit from the wedding festivities.

Armenia

● Two white doves may be released to signify love and happiness.

● The bride may dress in red silk and may wear cardboard wings with feathers on her head. Small coins may be thrown at her.

● The bride may wear valuable rings with precious stones on each hand, and a necklace of fine turquoise.

Austria

● Brides may crown their veils with myrtle, the flower of life.

Belgium

● The bride may still embroider her name on her handkerchief, carry it on wedding day, then frame it and keep it until the next family bride marries.

Bermuda

● Islanders top their tiered wedding cakes with a tiny sapling. The newlyweds plant the tree at their new home—where they can watch it grow—as their marriage grows.

Bohemia

● The groom gives the bride a rosary, a prayer book, a girdle with three keys (to guard her virtue), a fur cap, and a silver wedding ring.

● The bride gives the groom a shirt sewn with gold thread blended with colored silks and a wedding ring.

● Guests each receive a handkerchief at the wedding breakfast.

● Before the ceremony, the groomsman wraps the groom in the bride's cloak to keep evil spirits from creeping in and dividing their two hearts.

● The bride's mother-in-law greets the bride outside her new home with a cup of coffee or glass of wine. After drinking, the bride hurls the glass over her shoulder; it is considered a good omen if it does not break.

Caribbean

● A rich black cake baked with dried fruits and rum is especially popular on the islands of Barbados, Grenada, and St. Lucia. The recipe, handed down from mother to daughter, is embellished by each. It is considered a "pound" cake—with the recipe calling for a pound each of flour, dark brown sugar, butter, glacé cherries, raisins, prunes, currants, plus a dozen eggs, and flavorings. The dried fruits are soaked in rum and kept in a crock anywhere from two weeks to six months.

China

● Chinese brides receive pocketbooks filled with gold jewelry from female relatives, which bestows status on the bride.
● In old China, the color of love and joy is red, which is the favorite color choice for the bride's dress, candles, gift boxes, and the money envelopes that are presented to the bride by the guests.
● During the ceremony, the couple drink from goblets of wine and honey, symbolically tied together with red string.
● The bride is given chestnuts and jujubes in a wish for a son as soon as possible.

Croatia (once part of Yugoslavia)

● Married female relatives remove the bride's veil and replace it with a kerchief and apron, symbols of her new married status. She is then serenaded by all the married women.
● Following the wedding ceremony, those assembled walk three times around the well (symbolizing the Holy Trinity), and throw apples into it (symbolizing fertility).
● The bridal car and guests' cars are all decorated with flowers.

The Czech Republic

● Friends would sneak into the bride's yard to plant a tree, then decorate it with ribbons and painted eggshells. Legend said she would live as long as the tree.

● Brides in the countryside carry on the very old custom of wearing a wreath of rosemary, which symbolizes remembrance. The wreath is woven for each bride on her wedding eve by her friends as a wish for wisdom, love, and loyalty.
● Three symbolic dishes are set before the bride on her wedding day: wheat, symbolizing fertility; ashes mixed with grains of millet—which the bride picks out to demonstrate her patience; and a sparrow under a covered dish, which flies out when she lifts the lid.
● Peas are tossed at the newlyweds as they exit, not rice.

Denmark

● The traditional wedding cake is the cornucopia cake or Danish marzipan ring cake, made of almond cake, pastilage, and marzipan and beautifully decorated with sugarwork. It is filled to the brim with the good things in life: candies, almond cakes, perhaps fresh fruit and sorbet. The cake may also be decorated with marzipan medallions bearing portraits of the bride and groom.

Egypt

● Families, rather than grooms, propose to the bride. In Egypt, many marriages are arranged.
● The *zaffa*, or wedding march, is a musical procession of drums, bagpipes, horns, belly dancers, and men carrying flaming swords; it announces that the marriage is about to begin.

England

● Traditionally, the village bride and her wedding party always walk together to the church. Leading the procession: a small girl strewing blossoms along the road, so the bride's path through life will always be happy and laden with flowers.

● If the bride meets a chimney sweep on her way to the church and he kisses her, it's good luck! (Chimney sweeps kept the home fires burning safely.)

● Brides sew a good luck charm, such as the silver horseshoe worn by royal British brides, to the hem of their wedding gown.

● The traditional wedding cake of England (see "Ireland," as well) is a rich fruitcake with golden raisins, ground almonds, cherries, and spices (sometimes liquor-laced).

Fiji

● The groom presents the bride's father with a *tabua*—a whale's tooth, which is a symbol of status and wealth.

Finland

● Brides wear golden crowns. After the wedding, unmarried women dance in a circle around the blindfolded bride, waiting for her to place her crown on someone's head. It is thought that whoever she crowns will be the next to wed.

● The bride and groom have seats of honor at the reception. The bride holds a sieve covered with a silk shawl; when guests slip money into the sieve, their names and the amounts given are announced to those assembled by a groomsman.

● After the wedding, brides have their braids cut off and thereafter wear a white linen cap.

France

● During the reign of Louis XVI, the bride gave her bridesmaids her fans, decorated with mythological paintings, as wedding presents.

● Many couples drink the reception toast from an engraved two-handled cup (the *coupe de mariage*), as did newlyweds from days past. This cup will be passed on to future generations.

Germany

● To mark their betrothal, a couple give each other gold bands, worn on their left hands. Throughout their engagement, the couple are referred to as bride and bridegroom.

● Both bride and groom hold candles trimmed with flowers and ribbons.

● During the ceremony, when the couple kneel, the groom may kneel on the bride's hem to show that he'll keep her in line. The bride may step on his foot when she rises, to reassert herself.

● In Hanover and elsewhere, crockery is thrown against the bride's house on wedding day to bring good luck.

● On wedding day, the bride carries salt and bread in her pocket; the bridegroom, some grain, for wealth and good fortune.

Greece

● The *koumbaros*, traditionally the groom's godfather, is an honored guest who participates in the wedding ceremony. Today, the *koumbaros* is very often the best man, who assists in the crowning of the couple (with white or gold crowns, or with crowns made of everlasting flowers such as orange blossoms, or of twigs of olive and vine wrapped in silver and gold paper), and in the circling of the altar three times. Other attendants may read Scripture, hold candles, pack the crowns in a special box after the ceremony.

● To be sure of a "sweet life," a Greek bride may carry a lump of sugar in her glove on wedding day.

Holland

● Dutch families used to plan a party prior to the wedding. Bride and groom sat on thrones under a canopy of fragrant evergreens. One by one, the guests came up to offer their good wishes.

● Dutch weddings traditionally include heavy eating, including a sweetmeat called "bridal sugar" and spiced wine called "bride's tears."

Hungary

● The couple exchange betrothal rings. The groom also gives the bride a bag of coins; the bride gives the groom either three or seven handkerchiefs (believed to be a lucky number).

● Guests dance with the bride at the reception, and give her a few pence in exchange for a kiss.

● Guests give the bride pigeons, chickens, fruit, as well as other edibles—in exchange for a dance.

Iceland

● The wedding cake indigenous to Iceland is *kransakaka*. It consists of rings of almond pastry of various sizes piled on top of one another to form a pyramid. Swirls of white icing decorate each ring and fine chocolates or decorative candies fill the hollow center.

India

● The groom's brother sprinkles flower petals (to ward off evil) on the bridal couple at the end of the ceremony.

● To banish evil spirits, a coconut may be held over the couple's heads and circled around them three times.

● As in other Muslim countries (see "Morocco"), five days before the wedding, the bride has a ceremonial bath for ritual cleansing, then is painted with henna swirls on her hands and feet, and adorned with makeup and jewels by other women.

● The *tali*, a jewel set in gold and fastened on a yellow string (gold is the color of good fortune and approval) is tied around the bride's neck. Worn throughout the marriage, the *thali's* three knots remind her of her duty to her parents, husband, and sons.

Indonesia

● During an engagement period that may last for years, many ceremonies involving gift exchanges bring the two families together and strengthen their ties.

● During a ceremony on the Indonesian island of Java, the bride and groom sit on the lap of the bride's father, seated on a ceremonial wedding couch. The bride's mother asks the bride's father if the bride or the groom is heavier. The father replies that they are the same weight, signifying that from then on, the bride and groom will be loved and treated equally by the parents.

● A Javanese bride is secluded after the marriage blessing and is visited by an angel, which stays with her throughout the six-day ritual that blends Muslim customs with local folklore.

● The Javanese bride and groom are each served from a bowl of yellow and white rice, then eat from each other's plates—to blend their lives.

● Young people on Bali, who have not already done so, have their canine teeth filed before marriage to reduce "animal passions" such as anger and jealousy. The ritual is conducted by a member of the Brahmana caste and accompanied by beautiful displays of food.

Iran

● When this country was called Persia, the groom bought the wedding dress—ten yards of sheeting—to wrap around his bride.

● Happily married women hold a sheer cloth over the heads of the wedding pair during the ceremony. Later, the women scrape crumbs from two beautifully decorated sugar cones, known as *kaleh-ghand*, over the couple's heads for luck.

Ireland

● The traditional wedding cake of the Emerald Isle is a rich fruitcake (see "England," as well). In true Irish spirit, the recipe is laced with brandy or bourbon.

● A lucky horseshoe is given to the bride and groom to keep in their home.

Italy

● Ribbons signify the tying together of two lives. A ribbon is tied across the front of the church door to symbolize the wedding bond.

● Wedding guests have for centuries tossed *confetti* (sugared almonds, not small pieces of paper!) at the newlyweds. Sometimes, these decorate each place at reception tables—in pretty little porcelain boxes or tulle bags called *bomboniere*, which are personalized with the couple's names and wedding date—to symbolize the sweet (sugar) and bitter (almonds) in life.

● The newlyweds lead the guests in dancing the *tarantella*.

● After a line dance called "The Grand March" (see Chapter 13, "Your Reception," under the "Reception Dancing" section), the reception may end with a second sweet receiving line, where guests may receive their *bomboniere*—and give the couple money envelopes in exchange. The couple then dance their last dance.

Jamaica

● Slices of dark wedding fruitcake laced with rum are mailed to all friends and relatives unable to attend the reception.

Japan

● Many weddings are held in front of a Shinto shrine in Japan, even though a marriage is not considered a religious service. A Shinto priest officiates, but there are no vows. The ceremony brings the bride into the groom's family. Ancestors are honored in the ritual with bows, the ringing of bells, and offerings of food before ancestral shrines. The bride wears a ceremonial kimono. Bridal couples take nine sips of *sake* (rice wine)—the essence of the ceremony—becoming husband and wife after the first sip. Later, sips are exchanged with the parents, both to honor them and to mark their formal acceptance of the marriage.

● On her wedding day, the bride and her parents visit the groom's house. Traditionally, she wears a triangular band on her head, known as a *tsunokakushi*, or horn cover, to hide the horns of jealousy, which supposedly all women possess.

Korea

- The groom once traveled to the bride's house on a white pony, bearing fidelity symbols—a gray goose and gander (fowl that mate for life).
- Friends of the groom deliver a "ham," a box containing gifts for the bride and her new home, several days before the wedding. The ham often contains the red and blue fabric needed to make her ceremonial dress.
- Ducks are included in the wedding procession because they mate for life.
- After the ceremony, the couple change into Korean ceremonial clothes for the *p'yeback* ceremony, where families are introduced. Dates, chestnuts, and candies are thrown by the groom's mother into the bride's lap. The number caught is supposed to foretell the number of children she'll have.

Latin America

- *Padrinos* and *madrinos* are the wedding sponsors, who promise financial and spiritual aid. There may be several sponsors, a pair for each wedding part (e.g., music, food, church).

Lithuania

- The wedded couple are served a symbolic meal by their parents—wine for joy, salt for tears, and bread for work.

Malaysia

- The groom's gifts to the bride are delivered to her home by costumed children in a noisy procession, carrying lavish trays of food and currency folded into animal or flower shapes.

- The groom's family pays for the expensive brocade cloth used to make the wedding clothes.
- Although the groom travels with much fanfare to the bride's house for the wedding, he is often denied entry until his best man wages a mock battle against the bride's relatives.
- Each wedding guest is given a beautifully decorated hard-boiled egg, a symbol of fertility.

Mexico

- Guests at many Mexican weddings gather around the couple in a heart-shaped ring at the reception, perhaps before the first dance.
- A "lasso," a very large rosary, is wound around the couple's shoulders and hands during the ceremony to show the union and protection of marriage.
- Six sets of godparents, known as *padrinos*, sponsor and participate in aspects of the wedding, such as providing the kneeling pillows to show the comfort of marriage. They also give the gift of thirteen gold coins representing hope for a successful life, and Jesus Christ and his twelve apostles; the bride carries the coins in a purse, or a young girl holds them on a pillow or handkerchief.

Morocco

- As in other Muslim countries (see "India"), five days before the wedding, the bride has a ceremonial bath, then is painted with henna swirls on hands and feet, and adorned with makeup and jewels by other women.
- Before becoming guardian of her hearth, the Moroccan bride circles her marriage home three times.

Norway

● After a reindeer-kabob dinner lit by the midnight sun, nomadic tribes danced, ate, and feasted the night away.

● The folk bridal costume is not complete without sterling-silver jewelry and a gold-and-silver crown edged with small silver spoon-shaped bangles, whose tinkling sounds were thought to ward off evil spirits. The bride "dances off" this crown at the wedding feast (see "Finland").

● Bridesmaids wear green, which is considered unlucky in some countries.

● Traditional wedding gifts are eiderdown beds and pillows.

● Two small fir trees are set on either side of the door to the couple's house until they are blessed with a child.

Pakistan

● A bride and groom traditionally saw each other for the first time in the reflection of a mirror—during the ceremony. The couple held the mirror between them, allowing the bride to keep her eyes lowered modestly. The custom dates to a time when all marriages were arranged.

● The bride's family strings hundreds of brightly colored lights around the house in anticipation of the wedding.

● The groom wears a long silk coat and is adorned with flowers.

● The bride leaves her family to join her husband's family with the Holy Koran held over her head.

Philippines

● Following the couple's engagement, the groom's parents call on the bride's parents to collaborate on wedding plans.

● A white silk cord is draped around the couple's shoulders to indicate their union.

● The "sponsor" of the wedding is an honored person who stands beside the couple and signs wedding papers as a witness.

● A bell-shaped cage housing white doves (symbolizing peace) is a favored wedding decoration. At a well-timed moment, the bride and groom pull on ribbon streamers to release the birds, a send-off into their new lives.

Poland

● For village weddings, friends weave a wedding crown of rosemary leaves (symbolizing remembrance) for the bride. Long white beaded ribbons—family heirlooms passed from mother to daughter—were tied to the crown.

● Reception guests customarily buy a dance with the bride by pinning money to her veil or tucking bills into a special bridal purse (perhaps of white satin embroidered with the couple's names, the wedding date), to build a honeymoon fund.

● Luck comes to the bride who drinks a glass of wine at the celebration without spilling a drop.

Puerto Rico

● A bridal doll, in a dress that replicates the bridal gown, is placed on the head table at the reception. It might also be placed on the cake table if the wedding cake is decorated with flowers and colors that echo the bride's gown.

Romania

● Girls begin making things for their

trousseau as young as age six. The trousseau is carried by a cart drawn by oxen to the annual "maiden market" on June 29; the families camp on a mountain.

● Crowns are placed on the newlyweds' heads; sweets and nuts are thrown at them after the ceremony (symbolizing fertility).

● Guests toss sweets and nuts at the new couple to wish them prosperity.

Russia

● The groom comes to claim his bride on wedding day. She kneels before her parents and asks their forgiveness for all offenses she may have committed toward them. They lift her up and kiss her, then offer her bread and salt—so that she may never want for food as long as they are alive. When the bride leaves, the door is left open—so she may never lack shelter if she wishes to return.

● Wedding guests don't only give presents—they get them! The bride gives friends and relatives favors of sweets. They give her money after the wedding.

● Couples often tour the city in commercial wedding taxis on a mini-honeymoon, visiting important monuments and having their photos taken. These special nuptial cars are decorated with rings on top, a bridal doll on the front, and streamers. The groom gives out bottles of wine to keep his friends from blocking the way.

● After the couple are crowned in a Russian Orthodox wedding ceremony, they race to stand on a white rug. It is believed that whoever steps on it first will be the master of the household. (The rug can become a wedding keepsake after the ceremony.)

Samoa

● The bride wears a dress of tapa cloth, made from mulberry bark.

● The bride wears fresh flower leis and a mother-of-pearl crown.

Scotland

● A bridegroom once traveled to the goldsmiths of Edinburgh to purchase a silver teaspoon, called a *wedding spune*, engraved with the couple's initials and wedding date, to give to his bride. Today, Scottish couples might still observe this tradition to honor their heritages.

● Friends carry on an old good-natured custom: They wash the feet of both the bride and groom, preparing them to set off on a new path.

● The sword dance, similar to an Irish jig or a Highland fling, is usually performed at a Scottish wedding gathering.

Spain

● Peasant brides once wore a black silk dress to symbolize devotion until death. They also wore a mantilla, with orange blossoms in their hair. (Orange blossoms symbolize fertility and happiness.)

● Grooms wear a tucked shirt hand-embroidered by the bride in a design of her choosing.

● The groom gives thirteen coins (the giving of *monedas* or *arras*) to the bride, symbolizing his ability to support and care for her. During the ceremony, she carries them in a special purse, or a young girl carries them on a pillow or handkerchief.

● Wedding guests dance a *seguidillas manchegas* at the reception, during which each guest presents the bride with a gift.

Sweden

- To frighten away trolls (imaginary beings who were once thought to bring misfortune), bridesmaids carried bouquets of pungent herbs and the groom sewed thyme (symbolizing activity—perhaps of a sexual nature?) into his clothes.
- The groom-to-be gives the bride-to-be a goblet of precious metal, filled to the brim with coins which are wrapped in white tissue paper.
- The bride may place a silver coin from her father in her left shoe; a gold coin from her mother in her right shoe, so she'll never do without. Her shoes are unfastened—symbolizing easy childbirth in the future.
- The bride gives her lover a shirt made of fine material to wear on wedding day; he never wears it again until he is buried in it.
- Swedish wives wear three wedding rings: for the betrothal, for the marriage, and for motherhood.
- Wedding picnics are held outdoors. Carpeting and tableware are laid down on the forest floor, and frolicking games are played.
- The bride keeps a portion of every food from the wedding feast and gives it to the poor of the district.

Switzerland

- The junior bridesmaid leads the procession to the reception with handfuls of colored handkerchiefs for the guests. Whoever wants a "lucky" handkerchief contributes a coin toward the newlywed nest egg.
- After vows, the bride's floral wreath, which symbolizes her maidenhood, is removed and set afire by the mistress of ceremonies. It's considered lucky if it burns quickly.
- A pine tree, which symbolizes luck and fertility, is planted at the couple's new home.

Thailand

- An old custom, still practiced in rural areas, is to have an older couple prepare the bridal bed and leave behind lucky talismans—such as bags of rice, sesame seeds, coins, and a tomcat—to wish both fertility and happiness.
- On the morning of their wedding, the couple go to feed the monks (who have taken a vow of poverty), in order to obtain a blessing.
- The timing of the joining is determined by astrologers.
- Weddings are not religious and do not include vows, but the ceremony of *sai monkon* (white thread) is a sacred ritual. The head of each partner is encircled with the thread, which is then joined together to unite them. A respected elder pours sacred water over their hands to bless them.

Ukraine

- A mock capture of the bride is carried out at wedding receptions to remind everyone present of the many times their homeland was invaded.
- Instead of a cake, Ukrainian couples share *korovai*, a sacred wedding bread decorated with symbolic motifs that represent eternity and the joining together of two families.

Vietnam

- There are two wedding celebrations, one party given by the bride's family and the other by the groom's.

● The mother of a Vietnamese groom visits the bride's home on the wedding day to deliver betel (a plant that is used to pay respect) and pink chalk (the color chosen to wish for a rosy future).

● The groom's procession arrives at the bride's home carrying gifts: clothes, jewelry, and money. Friends and relatives join the parade, but the groom's mother does not, to symbolize her wish that there be no rivalry between her daughter-in-law and her.

Wales

● Here, and throughout the British Isles, the bride gives her attendants cuttings of myrtle (symbolizing love) from her bouquet. According to custom, if the plant roots and blooms—they'll marry soon!

● The churchyard gates are only opened after the village children are bribed with a shower of coins.

● Attendants race home from the ceremony with news of the marriage; first to arrive wins a pint of ale.

West Indies

● The traditional rum-flavored wedding cake is covered with a fine white tablecloth. Guests pay for a lucky peek.

● Guests are served curried goat and white rice.

Yemen

● The elaborate costumes worn by the bride and groom may be of gold cloth—indicating their "royal" status. The bride's hair is completely covered by a jewel-adorned headdress and woven braids, signifying strength and fertility. The groom wears a necklace of gold coins, a talisman for prosperity.

● The whole community is invited to join the celebration. Playing music to "gladden the bride and groom" is a sacred duty, and professional musicians, performers, and guests take turns with cymbals, drums, and other instruments.

● The bride's female relatives prepare the food, including small sweetened fritters, which promise a sweet life for the newlyweds and all who partake.

American Wedding Trends

America has a rich heritage of regional wedding traditions. In many places, a wedding is a community event, in keeping with the centuries-old understanding of marriage as a public rite of passage. Here are some of the contemporary customs you may encounter today at weddings throughout the United States. To research more old-country traditions, consult your librarian, older relatives, or leaders of cultural associations (see Appendix, under Chapter 2, "Wedding Customs").

Prewedding customs

● At some prewedding showers today, friends circulate a beautifully bound blank book so married women can write in their "recipe" for a happy marriage.

● Even if families are separated by distance, they get to know each other through conference calls, exchange of videotapes, photographs, and letters.

● To express their commitment, couples

talk about feelings and deal with marriage issues before the wedding with a counselor, clergy, family members, or through organized programs such as Engaged Encounter (see Chapter 4, "Planning Your Wedding," the "Visiting Your Clergymember" section).

● It's a Southern custom for guests to drop by anytime during the prewedding teas, often hosted by female friends and relatives of the bride, and leave a gift.

● To get to know the bride's father, many fiancés are making dates for lunch, tennis, and ball games.

Ceremony Customs

● The custom of "open church" is popular in small communities; it means everyone's invited to the wedding.

● A floral wreath is often hung on the door of the house of worship to announce a wedding is in progress.

● Weddings are being held at historic sites—such as a turn-of-the-century mansion, a museum, a battlefield, or a national monument—giving brides and grooms an opportunity to re-create decades and eras past, using replicas of the wedding costumes, accessories, and transportation of the period.

● Ceremony sites are being chosen to reflect the couple's interests: a ski slope, a baseball stadium, an underwater reef.

● Grooms may get to the church on time in stylish transportation—a horse and carriage or antique roadster. (Allow extra travel time for antique motors.)

● In the Southwest, Western attire is almost always worn in some form—perhaps a traditional string tie or cowboy boots. Surreys with a fringe on top, horse-drawn wagons, are favorite forms of wedding-day transportation.

● One of the most well-known Southern traditions is for grooms to ask their fathers to be their best man. Today, grooms may choose a best woman; bride's sometimes select a man of honor or a bridesman (see Chapter 6, "The Wedding Party").

● Wedding programs list the participants, explain customs, describe events in other languages. They become treasured mementos.

● Nosegays, pocket posies (for suits), symbolic bouquets, are being given to mothers, grandmothers, aunts, other female guests of honor.

● Family members, friends, and members of the wedding party take part in the ceremony by reading Scripture, holding candles, leading prayers.

● Wine or sake is being sipped from an heirloom silver goblet at the altar; some couples are registering for or buying and engraving their own to keep.

● Some couples are saving a ceremony taper used at the altar and relighting it for a romantic first-anniversary dinner.

● Couples are demonstrating family togetherness and the creation of a new family during the wedding ceremony by lighting a Unity Candle. At the altar, three candles are lit in turn: The bride's parents light a candle on one side of the altar; the groom's parents light a candle on the other side; the bride and groom pick up each of their families' candles and jointly set the center taper aflame. And so two become one.

● Some couples are arranging for church bells to peal after the vows are said—loud noises were once thought to scare away evil spirits lurking at the altar!

trends for the bride

● Instead of a traditional long veil, fresh (or silk) flowers are caught with a wisp of veiling; a hat is tied with tulle, banded with fresh flowers.

● Instead of a headpiece, African-American brides may braid their hair in Goddess Queen N'zinga braids (piled tall on top of the head).

● Initials and wedding date are embroidered on handkerchiefs by brides, then passed to the next woman in their family to wed.

● Traditional clothing is worn by brides to reflect their heritage (see "International Customs" section).

● Good-luck symbols—small silver charms—are sewn into the hems of brides' gowns. Some brides sew a small pouch filled with a tiny piece of bread, a bit of cloth, a sliver of wood, and a dollar bill—to protect against future shortages of food, clothing, shelter, and money—into the hem of their petticoat.

● Symbolic bridal bouquets—composed of flowers with special meanings, or flowers whose first letters spell out a message—are carried. Some brides carry the first flowers the groom ever sent them, or wildflowers from a family garden.

● Instead of rice, guests at weddings in the Northwest may throw kernels of wheat—which thrives in the state of Washington—to wish the couple good luck, fertility. Across the country, many brides make up packets of birdseed, millet seed, or safflower seed. (For information on symbolic dried herbs and flowers, see Appendix, under Chapter 2, "Wedding Customs.")

● Some couples are decking their dog in flowers and slipping a small sashed ring pillow around his or her neck; flower dogs are the new attendants.

● The bride's father may no longer answer the question, *"Who gives this woman in marriage?"* Instead, he might be asked, *"Who supports this man and this woman in this marriage?"* Both parents, or all parents (and guests?) respond, *"We do."*

● Many couples share their joy with family and friends by passing the "kiss of peace"—a friendly handshake or hug passed through the congregation.

Reception Customs

● Many couples schedule their wedding during a family reunion or anniversary reaffirmation ceremony. Everyone in the groom's family is included, too.

● Traditional potluck suppers become something special if parents and relatives bring festive ethnic dishes to the reception.

● Long Weekend Weddings (see Chapter 10, "Special Weddings & New Ways to Wed") allow the celebration to last longer, and include a variety of different festivities—a welcome cocktail party, a museum tour, a picnic, a bride's-vs.-groom's-team softball game, a pool party, a postwedding brunch.

● Some couples plan a Honeymoon Wedding (see Chapter 10, "Special Weddings & New Ways to Wed") at their honeymoon destination, inviting a group of friends and relatives to join them.

● When families and friends are far-flung, some couples plan a Progressive Wedding (see Chapter 10, "Special Weddings & New Ways to Wed")—which means there will be a second reception in another town. They invite those friends and relatives who were unable to travel to the wedding.

● Theme weddings (see Chapter 10, "Special Weddings & New Ways to Wed") are being woven subtly around a national holiday.

● For African-American couples the vestibule and stairway of the house of worship may be festooned with African *kente* or *asooke* fabric to emphasize the meaning of the day.

● Church pews, pulpits, the ring bearer's pillow, the guest-book table are made of *kente* cloth. Even the minister might wear a traditional African robe.

● Culturally rich foods celebrate the couple's heritages, combining two cultures for a lavish feast.

● Couples are walking to their reception site while young friends (or the couple's children) head the parade—symbolizing bounty, fruitfulness, and fertility.

● In Louisiana, jazz musicians often lead a procession from the church to the reception site, with bridesmaids twirling ribbon- and flower-bedecked umbrellas.

● The groom's cake may be served at the reception along with the wedding cake, it may be cut ahead of time by the caterer and packed in small decorative boxes for the wedding guests to take home—or both!

● Couples are giving ecologically sound favors to guests—packets of seeds, tree saplings to be replanted (see Appendix, under Chapter 2, "Wedding Customs"). Or, they're setting engraved notes at each guest's place setting, noting that in lieu of favors, a donation has been made to a favorite charity.

● Reception tables are being adorned with state flowers or regional favors (e.g., a breakaway arrangement of potted cacti, if wedding is in Arizona; pewter key rings from Williamsburg, Virginia) for guests to take home.

● Couples are sending favors, programs, photos, and wedding announcements to guests who could not attend.

● Couples appreciate a donation to a charity in honor of their wedding.

● Invitations are being printed on recycled paper.

● It's a Southern custom, borrowed from the bridesmaids' tea (a tradition in England), to tie tiny charms (an anchor, symbolizing adventure; a ring, symbolizing marriage; a horseshoe, luck; etc.) to a ribbon. These ribbons are nested between the layers of the wedding cake. Each bridesmaid pulls out a ribbon with an attached charm before the cake cutting. This custom may be observed at a shower, a bridesmaids' luncheon, or at the wedding reception.

● Today, wedding cakes are being cut with a great-grandmother's sterling-silver cake knife. Or, couples are starting a new tradition: having their initials engraved on a Heritage Cake Knife; when their children wed, they'll add their initials, and so on....

● Couples cherish heirlooms. Punch is being served with an antique ladle, or the wedding cake is being topped with the cake topper from the wedding cake of the bride's or groom's parents.

● Older unmarried siblings of a Cajun bride or groom (from a region west of New Orleans, Louisiana) playfully dance with a broom at the wedding reception—to mock their single status.

● In rural Pennsylvania, the bride and groom dance first to the "Buck and Doe Dance." Guests pay to cut in on them. The maid of honor collects the bucks and dough for the privilege!

● In the Midwest, there's often a "Dollar Dance" (see "Poland").

● Midwest receptions often include the "kidnapping" of the bride by the ushers, who carry her to a public event to show off her wedding finery, then deliver her back to the reception.

● African and Caribbean food is being served, tropical flowers are decorating the tables, and guests are being asked to remove their shoes before entering the reception site (an African custom).

● African-American couples are hiring traditional African drummers (there are different drumming styles for each region in Africa) for their reception, or for the ceremony when the couple Jump the Broom. Contact a local black newspaper or music school (see Appendix, under Chapter 2, "Wedding Customs") for referrals to African-American entertainment sources.

● Ethnic music and dances are being played at the reception (see Chapter 13, "Your Reception," under the "Reception Dancing" section).

● Brides plan a special dance with their

trends for the groom

● Some grooms are wearing outfits that reflect their heritages (see "International Customs" section).

● Most grooms are choosing to wear a wedding band. The rings are of gold or platinum, some studded with diamonds, or other gemstones.

● Grooms are wearing a boutonniere that makes a meaningful statement: a bachelor's button (celibacy), a red chrysanthemum ("I love you"), a myrtle sprig (love), a white rose ("I am worthy of you"), sweet william (gallantry). The bride might pin this blossom from *her* bouquet to his lapel at the altar.

● Grooms are having bachelor parties that they and their friends enjoy, where they can talk to each other: dinner at a favorite restaurant, a baseball game, a ski weekend with old friends.

● Grooms are selecting their own groom's cake, baked in their favorite flavors (banana, chocolate), in a clever shape (top hat, golf course, tennis racquet).

father at the reception; grooms also have a special dance with *their* mother.

● Couples are honoring their parents at their wedding. The band is playing the first dance the parents chose for *their* wedding.

● Talented guests are being asked to entertain at wedding receptions—after the structured festivities are over.

● Couples are sending joyous wishes skyward—airborne skywritten messages, helium-filled balloons, and fireworks are entertaining guests and bringing a cheer of congratulations.

● Disposable cameras are being set on each reception table so that guests can take candid shots throughout the wedding, then leave the film for the couple to develop later.

● Friends are joining together and presenting couples with a handmade communal gift, such as a wedding quilt. The quilt might consist of commemorative squares, each individually embroidered or appliquéd to remember a meaningful event or thought. The squares are then pieced together. Or, it might re-create traditional quilting patterns—Bride's Quilt, Bridal Wreath, or Double Wedding Ring. The gift quilt may be displayed as the cover for the seating-card (escort-card) table, then later grace the marriage bed.

● Blankets are practical and traditional wedding gifts, which symbolize the new married state.

● Couples are saving wedding mementos: a porcelain-figurine cake topper, an artistic picture created with pressed flowers from the bride's bouquet.

● Many couples, caught up in the spirit of generosity that surrounds weddings, arrange to donate leftover food to needy organizations, extra floral arrangements to local hospitals.

● Some couples are creating a time capsule that is saved for a future daughter or granddaughter. In a decorative box, they store wedding mementos, such as wedding checklists; florist, formalwear, gown, and photography orders; the cake topper; an invitation; the bride's garter; potpourri made from the dried petals of the bride's bouquet.

PREWEDDING PARTIES

For the bride and groom, the engagement has traditionally been a whirlwind of teas and cocktail parties hosted by family and friends. Today, however, the celebrations are anything *but* traditional. Whether you're hosting a spa day for your bridesmaids or being toasted at a prewedding breakfast, expect the unexpected! Showers and "bachelorette bashes," for instance, are no longer for women only—and gifts are as likely to include cross-country skis and scuba gear as lasagne pans and lingerie.

The Shower

The shower, a vestige of the dowry that a woman once brought to her marriage, helped a couple outfit their new home or assemble a trousseau. It was traditionally an all-female afternoon tea or luncheon. Not anymore!

Who hosts? Today, friends, bridesmaids, the honor attendant, or the best man might throw a single-sex or coed bash for the bride *and* the groom.

When is it held? There may be more than one shower during the engagement. All showers should be scheduled a significant amount of time after the engagement parties, but at least two weeks before the wedding. (They should also be after the couple have registered at a Wedding Gift Registry.) If the bride lives far away, a shower might be scheduled for when she's in town for a dress fitting or to get the marriage license, so she won't have to make an extra trip. (See "Long-Distance Shower" question.)

How to celebrate? Showers tend to be informal, whether planned at home or in a restaurant, hotel, or at another site. They are most often a luncheon, but might be a brunch, barbecue, pool party, or coed cocktail party. They may or may not be a surprise.

guest- of-honor tips

- Urge your mothers, sisters, aunts, *not* to cohost your shower; it shouldn't seem like they are asking for gifts! (This *may* be the custom, however, in some parts of the country.)

- Ask your maids *not* to plan the shower closer than two weeks to the wedding (you'll be busy!), *unless* they or you are arriving from a distance. (See "Long-Distance Shower" question.)

- Urge friends to group together to cohost prewedding parties. Too many activities will wear everyone out.

- Urge friends not to invite guests to showers who will not be invited to the wedding. The shower's purpose is to shower the bride with gifts *and* make guests feel part of the wedding-related festivities.

- Have your groom ask his best man *not* to schedule the bachelor party during the week before the wedding. If the groom is arriving from a distance, ask the ushers *not* to schedule it the night before the wedding. He'll need rest, too.

- Don't put the same friends on every guest list. Too many parties may make them feel pinched for time and money.

- Reserve the last week or so before the wedding for private time for yourself and your groom.

- Express your appreciation afterward to your hosts with notes of thanks and flowers.

What happens at a shower? Usually a surprise, the host/hostess should ask guests to arrive about thirty minutes early to help set up a display of wrapped boxes, perhaps under a shower umbrella (symbolizing good luck and shelter). Serving the food and opening the gifts are the main activities. As the bride or couple unwrap each gift, someone should write down who gave what (to assist the bride with thank-you notes). Another guest might collect all of the ribbons and make a "rehearsal bouquet" by taping or stapling them to a paper plate, or tie them together into a long boa; traditionally, the bride carries it during the ceremony rehearsal. The host and/or hostess might also plan several creative party games (see "Shower Games" box).

Who is invited? Usually, shower guests are those who will also be invited to the wedding, unless it is an office shower (see "office shower" question). The guest list should include your honor attendant and bridesmaids (groomsmen, too, if men will be included), the mothers and sisters of the bride and groom, other close relatives and friends. People who you don't know may be left off the guest list, even if they *are* friends of your parents. The host or hostess issues invitations most often by mail, at least two weeks before the shower.

How is an office/school/club shower planned? This type of shower is often hosted by office coworkers, club members, or school friends who are not necessarily invited to the wedding. It is usually planned for one of the final days or meetings for which the bride will be pre-sent before her wedding. Usually a surprise, the bride's colleagues gather together with refreshments (cake, cookies, fruit, tea, soft drinks) and present a group gift.

How can a Long-Distance Shower be planned if the bride and her attendants live in different cities? If the bride lives far away from the site of the wedding, her attendants or friends living there may gather together with unwrapped gifts for a Long-Distance Shower. While sharing anecdotes about the couple, the guests wrap their gifts (the hostess provides paper and bows), then pack them for shipping. During the party, guests might call the bride to let her know she's missed. *Other options*: 1) The attendants might schedule a shower for a long-distance bride once she is in town, days before the wedding. In this instance, a surprise is not a good idea, since the bride's schedule will be tight. 2) If the couple will be returning to the wedding town after the honeymoon, before traveling home, it is perfectly acceptable to schedule a shower (traditional or coed) then. Again, a surprise may be risky.

Can a remarrying bride have a shower? In the past, remarrying brides didn't have showers or other prewedding parties. Now, they're very much a part of the wedding festivities. Guests may include children, coworkers, parents, relatives, couples, and friends. Since an older bride and groom have probably already established their homes, they may not need the basic gifts. Friends may chip in for lifestyle gifts (see "Remarrying Shower Gift Ideas" box).

Ten Shower Themes

1. Kitchen Shower—Throw a party designed to broaden the bride's and groom's culinary skills. Ask guests to write down their favorite recipes—and buy gifts that are needed for the preparation (e.g., rolling pin, pie dish, baking apples, flour, with an apple pie recipe). Couples should register for kitchen tools in a wide price range—from whisks, wastebaskets, mops, brooms, and sponges to food processors and pots and pans. Decorate with luscious food photographs from magazines.

2. Home Shower—Ask each guest to bring a gift for a particular room of the home. More guests than rooms? Double up on living areas: hallway, kitchen, bathroom, bedroom, living room, garage, garden. Gift ideas range from linens for bed and bath (include the couple's color scheme on the invitations), garden tools, and basement-workroom tools to an umbrella stand for the foyer. Place wrapped gifts in the appropriate rooms, then ask guests to travel from room to room as each is opened, snapping photos along the way.

3. Pampering Shower—Harried brides always appreciate a little tender loving care. Ask guests to bring something soothing: a gift certificate for a massage, flannel pajamas, New Age CDs. Present the bride with a robe and slippers, prop her feet up, have a manicurist on hand to do her nails. Serve comfort foods: tea sandwiches, baked potatoes with assorted toppings, chocolate-chip cookies, and hot chocolate with marshmallows.

4. Travel Shower—Treat a couple about to leave on a honeymoon to gifts that are meant to be stashed in a suitcase: a mini–blow-dryer, a leather-bound trip diary, beach gear, a travel alarm clock, a restaurant guide and map of their destination city or island, a frame for a favorite honeymoon photo. Tack maps and travel posters of their destination to the walls; use luggage tags with each guest's name as place cards. Decorate the shower cake with a palm tree, the Eiffel Tower, or some other symbol of their trip.

5. "That's Entertainment" Shower—The newlyweds will love curling up in front of their own entertainment center in their new home. Ask guests to chip in for a VCR or CD player. Gifts ideas include CDs, videocassettes of favorite films, bestselling books, and magazine subscriptions. Decorations and activities should celebrate leisure time: Stretch a flower-entwined table-tennis net across the buffet; put out a variety of favorite board games. Mount posters of old TV shows (*Leave It to Beaver*, *All in the Family*, *The Brady Bunch*, *Family Ties*) on the walls.

6. Calendar Shower—After the wedding, the newlyweds will still want to see their friends and plan an active social life. Assign each guest a month of the year (or a

creative shower games

- **Pin the Boutonniere on the Groom**—Using a blown-up photograph of the groom, guests are blindfolded and asked to pin a paper flower on him. The one who comes closest to the left lapel wins!

- **Bridal Jeopardy**—The hostess compiles a series of trivia answers relating to the bride and groom, then asks the guests to phrase the questions (e.g., ANSWER: "The canoe capsized." QUESTION: "What happened on Bob and Sue's first date?").

- **Wedding Charades**—The hostess passes out squares of paper on which are printed wedding-related phrases or superstitions (e.g., "Happy is the bride the sun shines on"). Guests are divided into two teams, and take turns acting out the phrases.

- **Bridal Mad-Libs**—The hostess writes, in advance, a humorous story about the couple, leaving out key words. She asks the guests to call out the needed nouns, adjectives, and adverbs, then reads the story aloud, plugging in the words they've suggested. The results may be hilarious!(See Appendix, under Chapter 3, "Prewedding Parties," for more ideas.

remarrying shower-gift ideas

- ☐ a videocassette recorder (VCR)
- ☐ a compact-disc (CD) player
- ☐ new sheets and towels
- ☐ matching pajamas
- ☐ gift certificates for a health spa
- ☐ a donation to a charity
- ☐ an espresso maker and fresh coffee beans
- ☐ a pasta maker and pasta cookbook
- ☐ everything for afternoon tea: tea set, teabags, strawberry jam, scones, etc.
- ☐ blank thank-you notes in envelopes already stamped, addressed to shower guests

week, if you're inviting more than twelve). Then, fill the couple's calendar with events they'll both enjoy: Tickets to the opening game of the baseball season or an invitation to a mid-summer barbecue. Mount an oversized calendar on the wall. Have the bride open gifts chronologically, by week and month; fill in her dates.

7. Memory Shower—Ask guests to bring photographs—preferably ones that include both the guest and bride; arrange in a montage. Note on the back of each photo where and when it was taken. Enlarge the best ones to poster-size and mount on the walls. You might also ask guests to submit a written favorite memory shared with the bride. Compile a memory book of these reminiscences for the bride; ask each guest to read theirs at the shower, before gifts are opened.

8. "Honey-Do" Shower—Invite each guest to bring a gift that the bride can later hand over to her fiancé with the simple request, "Honey, do this." Possibilities range from the practical (a comforter might prompt the request, "Honey, *do* make the bed") to the private (a request accompanying a gift of lingerie!). For a coed bash, have men bring "Honey dos" for the bride; have women bring "Honey dos" for the groom. *Variation*: Have guests pledge a service (e.g., two hours of grass cutting).

9. Garden Shower—Guests might bring bulbs to plant, gardening tools and how-to books, even a birdhouse. The festivities should be held outdoors, of course! Serve salads in clay pots, dressing in watering cans. Dish out desserts with trowels; "plant" cupcakes on beds of moss.

10. Bar Shower—Ask guests to give bottles of liquor and wine, stemware, a blender, coasters, a corkscrew, a wine rack, other barware equipment. Another idea: Give the couple a gift certificate for a bartending course.

Bridesmaids' Parties

Bridesmaids' parties are the perfect time to introduce out-of-town attendants, schedule final dress fittings, display wedding gifts, and distribute presents to thank attendants for being in the wedding. (The couple may prefer to give all attendants their gifts at the rehearsal dinner.) Bridesmaids might also want to give their gifts to the bride at the bridesmaids' party (see Chapter 17, "Wedding Gifts").

Who hosts? It's customary for the bridesmaids—individually or together—to entertain for the bride (if they are not co-hosting the shower). Or, the bride may want to treat her bridesmaids to a party—traditionally a luncheon or afternoon tea, but today, possibly a chili-and-beer supper at a local pub.

When is it held? More-formal gatherings

should be held at least two weeks before the wedding (unless bridesmaids will not arrive until the week of the wedding). Informally, the bride might spend time alone with her bridesmaids throughout the days leading up to the wedding. The bride might also treat her attendants to lunch after a dress fitting or invite them to a breakfast on wedding morning.

Is this when bridesmaids find the "ribbon pulls" in a cake? There is a delightful Southern custom that began at a bridesmaids' tea. The baker prepared a traditional pink-iced cake for dessert, with a thimble baked into the layers. Whichever maid found the trinket in her piece would be the next to wed. Today, bridesmaids may gather at a bridesmaids' party or before the cake cutting at the wedding reception to pull ribbons trimmed with tiny charms from between the cake layers: a horseshoe and four-leaf clover mean "good luck"; a fleur-de-lis, "love will flower"; a heart, "love will come"; an anchor, "hope, adventure"; a thimble and button, "old maid"; a tiny wedding ring, "next to marry."

The Bachelor Party

The bachelor party is an optional custom that gives the groom and his attendants a chance to release prewedding tension, celebrate the groom's final night out as a single man, and spend time with close friends and relatives.

Who hosts? A friend or relative of the groom (usually the best man) and perhaps all of the ushers.

When is it held? At least a week (preferably two weeks) before the wedding. Too many ushers and grooms have almost missed the wedding while oversleeping after a late night on the town—so don't celebrate the night before!

What is the purpose? It was once thought that bachelors needed to get philandering out of their system before wedding day. Card playing or gambling was often part of the evening, the winnings going to the groom-to-be. Why? So that he could afford another night out with the boys once his wife took control of his money! Today, the bachelor party is an occasion for the groom's close male friends and relatives to reminisce with him about the past, toast his future, and bid farewell to his days as a single man.

What happens at a bachelor party? While some bachelor parties carry on the tradition of visiting burlesque shows or casinos, others gather male guests together for a softball game followed by a keg of beer, a day at the racetrack, or a weekend camping trip. Most grooms say that friendship and camaraderie are key, not drinking and carousing.

Who is invited? The groom's attendants, college friends, current friends, brothers, and close cousins. The groom's father and the bride's father and brothers may also be included.

During the wedding-planning months, the bride and groom may gather their attendants together for some fun—and needed assistance. Plan the following theme parties:

- **Inviting Ideas**—Address invitations and announcements, stuff and stamp envelopes. For inspiration, play songs with a letter theme (e.g., "Please Mr. Postman," "P.S. I Love You").

- **Seating Solutions**—Help work out the seating plan for the rehearsal dinner, reception. Afterward, play a game of musical chairs.

- **Who Goes Where?**—Write out place cards for guests. Later, write ideas for charades on similar slips of paper. Divide into two teams and act them out!

- **Cake Tasting/Hors d'oeuvre Sampling**—Taste the best menus, recipes, of several bakers and caterers, with attendants. Most will make mini-portions.

- **Wine/Champagne Tasting**—Ask attendants to help you choose your reception spirits.

- **Battle of the Bands**—Invite bridesmaids and ushers to go with you to clubs, reception sites, to "audition" bands live, at weddings or similar events.

- **Treats for Guests**—Make wedding favors for the reception (e.g., rice packets, bags of almonds). Treat your attendants to a make-your-own-sundae party when the work is finished!

The Bachelorette Bash

These days, prewedding revelry is not for men only. The bridesmaids, along with close friends and relatives, may want to take the bride out for one final night alone with them, as a single woman.

Who hosts? A close friend (often the honor attendant), or all of the bridesmaids, may plan this celebration, although it may also be hosted by college roommates, sisters, or cousins.

When is it held? *Not* the week or night before the wedding. It may be scheduled for the same night as the bachelor party.

Who is invited? Anyone whom the hostesses feel the bride would want in attendance. The guest list should include only those individuals who will be invited to the wedding.

How to celebrate? Rent a limousine to chauffeur the group to favorite pubs. Or, dress formally for an elegant champagne party at home. Feeling adventurous? Escape for the weekend to a seaside house, or rent a great hotel suite. Perhaps plan a make-over day at a nearby spa or image-consulting firm.

Wedding Work Parties

Getting organized for wedding day doesn't have to be hard work. One way to lighten the load? Invite your wedding party and closest friends to enjoy a buffet supper (or, order take-out food) while they help get important tasks done.

Who hosts? Usually the bride, at her home.

When is it held? Throughout the wedding engagement, to coincide with each wedding-planning deadline.

What is the purpose? To give the bride built-in helpers for at least one afternoon or evening.

The Rehearsal Dinner

The rehearsal dinner is an occasion for attendants, guests, family, and perhaps out-of-town guests to get acquainted, reminisce, and wish you well. (If you prefer to keep the guest list intimate—e.g., immediate family and wedding party—be sure to schedule a *Welcome Tea* or *Welcome Cocktail Party* for all out-of-town guests at another location.) Perhaps your aunt or a family friend will offer to host the event in their home or in a restaurant. Send the invitations after receiving guests' R.s.v.p.'s. This event will make all arriving guests feel welcome, a part of the wedding excitement, and give them a chance to get acquainted with other guests. (See Chapter 10, "Special Weddings/New Ways to Wed.")

Who hosts? Though almost anyone can host the rehearsal dinner, the groom's parents traditionally do the honors. It's perfectly correct, however, for the bride's parents, grandparents, or another relative on either side of the family to host the dinner.

When is it held? The rehearsal and festivities that follow are usually held the night before the wedding. Participants go directly from the church sanctuary to the dinner site. However, you may want to schedule the rehearsal and rehearsal dinner two or three days before the wedding, especially if your ceremony is early in the day, to make sure attendants and guests are well rested.

Who's invited? The guest list usually includes attendants, immediate family members, spouses of married attendants, parents of children in the wedding (young children are optional), and the officiant and his/her spouse. You may also decide to invite grandparents, aunts and uncles, and out-of-town friends arriving for the wedding.

How to celebrate? Don't let the name fool you. A rehearsal "dinner" can also be a poolside barbecue, a potluck brunch or lunch buffet at home, or a seated meal in an elegant restaurant. It can be as formal or as informal as you like, as long as the gathering doesn't upstage the wedding itself.

What happens at a rehearsal dinner?

The rehearsal dinner is a celebration planned for the wedding participants. In this setting, toasts can be longer and more personal than those given on wedding day. Guests might want to include humorous vignettes or perform skits. You might also ask each guest to bring a favorite framed picture of you or your fiancé from throughout your lives; display them on a table near the entrance to the room where the dinner will take place. Your relatives may also compile and show slides of you both as infants and children.

The best man may offer a toast, followed by good wishes from the groom to you and your parents. Next, you might toast your fiancé and his parents: *To my future husband, and to his mother and father. They raised a man so special, I couldn't help but say yes.*

The best man might continue to act as a master of ceremonies, introducing other key guests who may rise to make toasts to you and your fiancé. (The rehearsal dinner, not the wedding reception, is the best setting for the couple, their friends, and parents to make humorous, more personal toasts.)

The best man may also introduce special entertainment, such as the slide show or a song from the groom's fraternity brothers, and call the guests' attention to the framed photos of the couple on display, and other meaningful symbols throughout the room. The groom should be prepared with a wrap-up thought that will bring the evening to a close and get everyone home early enough so that they will be well rested for the wedding the next day. Many couples pass out attendants' gifts at the rehearsal dinner. This is also the time to go over last-minute details: transportation to the reception, arrival time at the ceremony site for attendants, seating procedures for ushers, receiving-line instructions.

Any seating-plan ideas? If a large group is invited, use place cards at the table, arranged so that those who don't know one another will become acquainted before the wedding. Avoid a rush for seats. Many brides and grooms arrange to sit at a table alone with their parents; it may be the first time that they are all meeting, if they live at a distance from each other. A rehearsal-dinner seating plan is optional, though, and some couples may choose to sit with their wedding party or siblings.

The Wedding Breakfast

The wedding-day breakfast or brunch is a wonderful way to gather female guests who are especially close to the bride in an informal setting, and give them a chance to wish the bride well and distract her from any prewedding stress.

Who hosts? A friend, neighbor, or relative who has offered to host some form of prewedding party.

Who's invited? Out-of-town guests, anyone to whom you might want to give an extra-warm welcome. (The bride and groom and their families are not expected, but may wish to attend, as well.)

Can there be a postwedding brunch? Just because you and your groom have left for your honeymoon doesn't mean the celebrating has to stop! Families or friends might host an "epilogue" brunch, lunch, or pool party the next day for guests who have traveled far to attend. Many newlyweds go to this postwedding brunch—before leaving on their honeymoon. It's a relaxed way to visit with faraway family members, old friends, and to talk about wedding highlights. The wedding video may even be available for a first screening!

PLANNING YOUR WEDDING

4

The beautiful, formal weddings that most couples dream of can take over a year to plan in big cities—less time in rural areas. Even the simplest, most intimate ceremony and reception require two to three months of planning. Before you begin, though, you'll need to decide when, where, and how you'll marry.

When–Date and Time

The number of weddings planned during your chosen month will eliminate some dates at the start. June is still the most popular wedding month, followed by August, July, May, September, October, April, and December. Anticipate as many pros and cons as possible when you choose your date and time. Think about:

Time of day. A busy church or synagogue may have multiple weddings on weekends, so reserve a slot as soon as possible. The hour you choose may be influenced by the wedding style and dress that you envision. (For example, a *very formal wedding*, in which the groom and ushers wear white tie (full-dress tailcoat, matching trousers, white waistcoat, white bow tie, wing-collared shirt), is held in the evening, with the ceremony beginning after 6 p.m. (see "How—Style and Formality" section and Chapter 7, "Wedding Clothes.")

Your wedding time may also be influenced by where you live, and your religion. In the South, evening weddings are popular, while afternoon ceremonies are prevalent in the Southwest. For Protestant weddings, afternoon and evening nuptials are common, while Roman Catholic weddings traditionally begin at 11 a.m. or noon. If your heart is set on a Saturday wedding and you are Jewish, it will have to be after sundown, which marks the end of the Sabbath.

If there will be other weddings at your ceremony site that day, be sure there will be enough time for your wedding-service professionals to set up flowers,

wedding decisions

- religious vs. civil ceremony
- seated meal vs. buffet; or cocktails
- large guest list vs. reception with all the trimmings
- orchestra vs. soloists, combo
- evening vs. daytime
- weekend vs. weekday
- hometown vs. city of employment, honeymoon destination

cameras, food; to assemble your wedding party; and clear guests out leisurely when it's over. If another bride will marry shortly before or after you, consider sharing ceremony flowers, greenery, or decorations.

If the church or synagogue is available only in the morning, but you want an evening reception, do *not* leave your guests with a big block of unscheduled time in between. (If this is unavoidable, arrange for a hospitality suite with drinks and snacks at a local hotel.)

Religious Holidays. Consider season, holidays at that time of year, religious observances, and local customs. Some faiths do not allow formal weddings on certain days or during some hours. Ministers and priests may not be willing to perform ceremonies during the solemn days of Lent, for example. Rabbis cannot marry couples during high holy days, such as on Yom Kippur. Remember that some religious holidays fall on different days every year, so get out next year's calendar.

Secular holidays. The Fourth of July is a patriotic choice—just remember that the town parade, complete with high school band, may march past the church while you are saying your vows. Spring, summer, and fall festivals, with accompanying traffic and tourists, proliferate in smaller towns. Even in cities, ethnic-pride parades can shut down major roads for several hours. Check with the chamber of commerce for upcoming dates. Marrying on a holiday may also require more long-range planning. Your guests may have booked vacations around long

weekends, such as Labor Day, many months in advance. Whether to attend your wedding or go on a longed-for vacation may be a difficult choice.

Season. You may have a season in mind—Christmas, with the church bedecked in holly and pine and bridesmaids in plaid taffeta; or spring, when tulips bloom and pastel dresses are naturally appealing. Each season has virtues and drawbacks. Snowstorms can cause transportation nightmares not only at the wedding site, but for airline travelers. As you choose a summer date, remember that you'll be responsible for keeping two hundred guests cool in August. Is your house of worship air-conditioned? A honeymoon wedding on a Caribbean island might be better scheduled before or after hurricane season.

Allergies. Consider your and your guests' allergies when selecting a wedding site and season. Hay fever strikes in different seasons or year-round, depending on the region. (Who wants to say their vows in between sneezes?) (See "Allergy-Attack Tips" box.)

Romantic/symbolic days. Do you want to marry on the anniversary of the day you met? Perhaps you want to say your vows on your parents' or grandparents' wedding anniversary. Would you like to commemorate your mother's birthday by choosing that date? Mention the coincidence in your wedding program.

Logistics. Maybe you've dreamed of a Valentine's Day wedding, but it's on a Wednesday. If it's a small wedding with

---

allergy-attack tips

- Visit sites beforehand. Are they ventilated? Dust-free?

- Do you or someone in the wedding party suffer from hay fever? Choose an indoor, air-conditioned site.

- Schedule outdoor photos for late morning, mid-afternoon when pollen's less prevalent.

- Choose a gown in a breathable fabric.

- Stick to makeup and fragrance you've worn before.

- Try out over-the-counter antihistamines and decongestants that don't make you sleepy.

- See an allergist, who can find out what you're allergic to, teach you to reduce exposure, and prescribe medication. New prescription antihistamines don't cause drowsiness. Your doctor may also prescribe topical steroid nasal sprays. (These medications shouldn't interact with alcohol.) Ask about immunotherapy (allergy shots) to build up an immunity to allergens for over six to eighteen months.

few out-of-towners invited, you may choose a weekday. For a larger wedding, most couples choose the Saturday or Sunday closest to that holiday—to facilitate travel and prevent scheduling conflicts with guests' workday lives.

Cost. Some caterers may offer slightly better deals during less popular wedding months (January or March, for example) in order to stimulate business during slow times. Incidentally, the earlier you begin to plan, the more time you will have to compare services and choose ones best suited to your budget.

Protection. Consider taking out Weddingsurance, offered by Fireman's Fund Insurance Company (see Appendix, under Chapter 4, "Planning Your Wedding") to protect the investment you're making. For a reasonable amount, you can take out a standard package or arrange customized coverage, which will reimburse you for lost or damaged negatives or a photographer who fails to arrive; if wedding attire or gifts are damaged or stolen; if the wedding is canceled due to hurricane, fire, or crime damaging your site; if the bride, groom, or an immediate family member gets ill beforehand; if a non-family member is injured at the wedding or reception and the site does not have liability insurance; if the bride or groom is called away to civil or military duty.

Where–Choosing the Site

Sit down together and figure out priorities. You may feel that a church wedding is essential, your fiancé may want the ceremony and reception to take place under one roof so guests don't have to travel. When weighing locations, first consider the approximate number of guests, activities (dancing, eating—buffet, finger food, or seated meal?), budget limitations, proximity to your home or honeymoon site.

Traditionally, the bride and her parents chose the site, since they would be footing the bill. Today, however, many couples either pay for the entire wedding, or split the costs into thirds (among themselves and both sets of parents). Both bride and groom are the instrumental decision makers. Some couples choose to marry in the city where they are currently working; others travel to the home of the bride's parents for a family wedding, then attend postwedding receptions—a Progressive Wedding—in relatives' hometowns (see Chapter 10, "Special Weddings & New Ways to Wed").

Below are some reception-site options:

A small college chapel. Whether it is your alma mater or a nearby local university, many colleges have exquisite old buildings and halls that are unused for months at a time.

A vast cathedral with spires and stained glass. This may require more traveling for you and for guests, but the dramatic space may be your dream come true.

A stately and dignified judge's chambers. Interfaith couples sometimes

---

creative wedding sites

- yacht
- sports arena
- barn
- restaurant
- mansion
- private school
- carnival
- theater
- underwater
- fire station
- skydiving
- hot-air balloon
- ski slope
- mountain slope
- beach
- tennis court
- roller rink
- ice-skating rink

For more ideas, see Appendix, under Chapter 4, "Planning Your Wedding."

outdoor-site considerations

- accessibility
- parking space
- privacy
- presence of traffic
- permits, fees
- inclement weather (rent a tent, have an alternate site)

site decorations

- **Home wedding:** Choose a single color scheme for flowers, linens—to unify various objects, elements.

- **Country setting:** Dress up white linens with stripes, polka dots; go for splashes of table color—buckets of vivid wildflowers, fresh fruits; cover the ground with straw, bright quilts.

- **Outdoor lighting:** paper lanterns, a chandelier hung in a tree, hurricane candelabrum with tapers on each table.

- **Outdoor decoration:** a rainbow of ribbons, "curtains" of rice paper hanging from trees.

- **Victorian wedding:** Cluster collectibles on tables (porcelain figurines, silver frames, ribboned nosegays); dress tables with damask cloths, lace runners, doilies, brocade napkins.

- **Formal evening:** Go bold— red, burgundy, black overlays on gold-fringed tablecloths; rent statuary, leather screens, Doric columns topped with huge floral arrangements, topiaries to flank doorways.

- **Romance:** Tapers throughout the room, votive candles on each table, pastel shades (peach, pink, lavender, cream), centerpieces of roses in full bloom, rose petals scattered on tables.

- **Scent:** Fragrant flowers (e.g., roses, lilacs, gardenias), scented oil in votives.

- **Garlands:** Adorn with flowers, fruits, vines, ribbons. Drape across doorways, windows; swag around tables; intertwine among buffet dishes.

choose this intimate setting.

A glamorous old hotel ballroom. Plants and decorations can be used to separate the ceremony and reception areas. Or, a ceremony setting can simply be removed after the vows.

The home where you grew up. This sentimental choice may save on the cost of a hall, but rental costs of utensils, chairs, etc., add up quickly. (See "Reception Rental Tips" box and Chapter 10, "Special Weddings & New Ways to Wed.")

Your grandmother's/relative's garden. An outdoor ceremony amid blossoming flowers is charming—just make sure that guests have some shelter from the sun (hand out parasols), and have an alternate rain plan. Rent a tent, no matter what the weather forecast.

A public park. Many have pretty gazebos on small lakes or ponds, and well-landscaped gardens. Check with authorities in your city or town about permits and regulations.

Rooftops. Check out the tops of new high-rise condominiums or older buildings that have gardens. Views from these spots can be spectacular. Check on the number of people allowed by law, and whether heavy band equipment can be transported there easily.

How-Style and Formality

Will your wedding be religious or civil? One faith or interfaith? Traditional or non-traditional? Formal or informal? A traditional wedding reflects society's accepted patterns. What's traditional can change, depending on your age, region of the country, what's in fashion. Formality is the degree of decorum shown in your invitations, flowers, decorations, attire, mood of entertaining, and number of wedding guests.

When choosing your wedding style, zero in on the type of attire with which you and your families will be most comfortable (see Chapter 7, "Wedding Clothes"). Each of these degrees of formality is altered when the time of day is factored in (e.g., very formal evening dress calls for a bride in a traditional gown with a long train; a groom in white tie. Very formal daytime dress calls for a bride in a traditional gown—a shorter train is optional; a groom in a cutaway coat.)

You can plan a wedding in any of the four styles with a traditional (in a banquet hall or house of worship) or non-traditional (on a beach, in a sports arena) location.

Visiting Your Clergymember

Before making a final decision about a site, consult your clergymember about religious requirements. The Catholic Church, for example, prefers to celebrate nuptial masses in a church only. Some churches require that you join their congregation. Jewish couples may marry in a synagogue without being members of the congregation, although regular attendees may receive first choice of times and dates. Some houses of worship will rent all or part of their spaces. Check with clergy, however, about their religious requirements for interfaith marriages and remarriages (see Chapter 9, "Religious Rituals & Requirements" and Chapter 11, "Remarriage").

When approaching an unfamiliar house of worship, explain to the clergymember why a religious service is important to you—rather than why you want to borrow the setting for a few hours. Be prepared to field questions about your lack of involvement in the parish (if this applies to you), but remain open to the idea that a wedding can initiate religious affiliation.

If personalities clash, try another house of worship rather than abandoning a religious wedding.

Make an appointment to visit your officiant—minister, priest, rabbi, or judge—so that he or she can check his or her schedule. Call your local city hall or marriage license bureau for referrals for judges, justices of the peace (see the "Planning a Civil Ceremony" section and Appendix, under Chapter 4, "Planning Your Wedding").

Bring certificates of baptism and confirmation if you are not members of the same church. If either of you is divorced, bring a letter or decree attesting to your marital status. Different faiths? You may need to get special dispensation and arrange to have religious instruction before your wedding.

Complete or sign documents relating to marriage. Depending on your faith, you may be asked to fill out an "Application to Marry," sign a "Letter of Intention to Marry," or begin a "Preliminary Matrimonial Investigation." Usually, such forms state your willingness to participate in counseling together with your clergymember. These sessions can be opportunities to strengthen your religious understanding of marriage. Most clergymembers require at least one conference with you before performing your ceremony. Some religions require several meetings.

Realize that an officiant may bring up topics you'd rather not discuss. A previous marriage, for example, would probably be covered (what went wrong, how you tried to resolve matters). The clergymember is not being intrusive; he or she is required to see that you are marrying in good faith, after considering potential problems.

Consider attending Engaged Encounter or another premarital counseling group. It's worthwhile to pursue any worrisome issues that your clergymember brings up in your initial meeting (see Appendix, under Chapter 4, "Planning Your Wedding," for more information). Counseling groups help couples clarify their feelings about money, sex, children, religion, family relations, goals, how to handle conflicts, and other subjects

degrees of wedding formality

- very formal
- formal
- semiformal
- informal

ceremony and officiant fees

The best man will give the clergymember, organist, any ceremony assistants, an envelope with appropriate payment after the ceremony.

- There is a fee (approximately $15) for a civil wedding ceremony performed at city hall. Call for details.

- State law dictates whether judges can accept money (in some states, they can accept up to $50). Perhaps give an appropriate gift (e.g., theater tickets, a wallet, a key case, a pocket diary).

- Clergymembers usually receive a donation to the house of worship ($20 and up); ask the church secretary or sexton what is the suggested fee, gratuity, or donation made payable to the house of worship. A more generous fee is suitable for a large wedding for which the clergymember attends the rehearsal and reception and performs the ceremony; he or she may have also spent many hours counseling the couple prior to wedding day.

- If there are no payment guidelines, give the clergymember a gift (see gift suggestions for a judge, above).

- Ask if fees for altar servers, sextons, cantors, choir directors, organists, are included in the church or synagogue fee; an additional gift or money amount may be appropriate.

- Donate a hymnal, prayer book, memorial window, candelabrum, kneeling cushions, baskets, to the house of worship in honor of your marriage.

that often come up after marriage. You may discover some surprises about each other (e.g., he wishes he could work up the nerve to make a job change; you're envious of the time he spends with his friends) and come to an understanding that will create a stronger, healthier marriage.

Confirm your ceremony date. Have several choices in mind, since many churches and halls may be booked a year or more in advance. (Only when your house of worship, clergymember, and reception site are confirmed for your date is it safe to order invitations.)

Review ceremony details and make a second date to discuss specifics. For starters, ask about the seating capacity of the sanctuary and how large a wedding party will fit comfortably in front of the altar. How many can walk down the aisle abreast? Are there any church restrictions? Where is the best place for soloists to stand? If it will be an interfaith ceremony, what is the format? (See Chapter 8, "Your Wedding Ceremony" for questions to ask then.)

Are there restrictions on ceremony attire? Ask if men must wear *yarmulkes* in the synagogue sanctuary, if bride's and bridesmaids' shoulders must be covered, if the bride must wear a veil. Is there a changing room for the bride? How early can you have access on wedding day?

Will the clergymember perform a ceremony at a non-religious site, if this is your preference? If the ceremony will be in the house of worship, ask whether alcoholic toasts are permitted on the premises. Some congregations will permit a champagne toast but do not allow any other alcoholic drinks.

Will the clergymember marry you in his or her study or chambers? Some couples prefer an intimate ceremony. Is there a small chapel?

Speak to the sexton, verger, or church secretary. He or she can explain the fire laws governing evening candlelight ceremonies (see Chapter 10, "Special Weddings & New Ways to Wed") and tell you about aisle runners, prayer (kneeling) benches, canopies, candelabra, any special equipment needed. Ask whether rice or birdseed can be thrown, and where. Reserve time for your rehearsal, as well as parking spaces the day of the wedding. Is there adequate air-conditioning in summer, heat in winter? If the reception will be in the house of worship, are there any dietary restrictions (e.g., kosher)? Where can the receiving line be held? Ask about appropriate fees for the house of worship, clergymember, organist, and other staff members (see "Ceremony and Officiant Fees" box).

Meet with the organist. It is wise to discuss your musical program in advance. Get suggestions and make sure that he or she is availaible for your rehearsal *and* ceremony. If additional musicians or a soloist will perform, schedule extra rehearsals. (For musical selections, see Chapter 14, "Wedding Music.")

Planning an Interfaith Ceremony

You're Catholic, he's Jewish. He's an Episcopalian, you're Moslem. After crossing initial hurdles posed by different cultural backgrounds, there is one more challenge to face: Who will marry you—and how? An interfaith couple might consult an organization that is tolerant of two-religion marriages, such as a campus ministry group, a Unitarian Church, or an Ethical Culture Society for guidance (see Chapter 8, "Your Wedding Ceremony,"and Appendix, under Chapter 4, "Planning Your Wedding").

Here are several other options:

Combine both faiths in the service. Start searching for co-officiating clergymembers early. Contact each clergymember to find out if they are willing to participate. If they are reluctant, seek out college chaplains, more liberal-minded clergy in your area, and referrals from the college dean's office and friends (see Chapter 8, "Your Wedding Ceremony" and Appendix, under Chapter 4, "Planning Your Wedding").

Turn to a third religion that is supportive of interfaith couples. The Unitarian Universalist Society, for example, will perform interfaith marriages for couples who do not belong to its denomination (see Appendix, under Chapter 9, "Religious Rituals & Requirements"). Many Christian/Jewish couples choose this route because Unitarian Universalists encourage couples to participate in structuring a service that reflects both traditions. Societies and fellowships associated with the American Ethical Union and its New York City affiliate, the Ethical Culture Society, perform interfaith marriages. There are twenty-five such societies nationwide in this 113-year-old humanist group, which is dedicated to the ethical guidance of individuals without imposing strict religious dogma (see Appendix, under Chapter 4, "Planning Your Wedding").

Choose one religious ceremony over the other. This may be agreeable if one partner has maintained strong ties with a denomination and the other severed ties with his/her faith at a young age. This does not mean that you should exclude the religious heritage of the non-practicing mate. Invite the secondary cleric to offer a special prayer or blessing during the service or at the reception. Prepare family members in advance for the type of ceremony you will have.

Plan two ceremonies. When an agreement cannot be reached about combining two faiths, some couples simply marry twice. Only one date of marriage can appear on your marriage certificate, but each ceremony can satisfy the requirements of that religion. If you do not want to plan two weddings, some Protestant denominations have a "Blessing of the Marriage" service (the same day, or at a later date), which has similar wording to the real wedding ceremony, although no rings are exchanged.

Plan a civil ceremony. Just because you've ruled out a church or synagogue as a ceremony site doesn't mean the only option is a quick ceremony in a public office.

Planning a Civil Ceremony

A civil ceremony can be short and functional or as formal as you wish, followed by a reception with a luncheon, seated dinner, or simply champagne and cake. It can be held at your home or in a hotel, in a park or garden, or in the county clerk's office at city hall or the local Marriage License Bureau. You might invite just two friends or relatives to be your witnesses, immediate family, or 150 guests or more.

Who can perform the ceremony? Depending on where you live, justices of the peace, Superior Court clerks, county clerks, judges or magistrates, township-committee chairs, mayors, and governors can perform legally binding ceremonies. Since marriage laws vary by county, call your local Marriage License Bureau for details; also ask clergymembers, family, and friends for referrals. Remember that some public officiants are not willing to work outside of their offices or after normal business hours. If you've planned a large reception and the officiant has traveled to perform the ceremony, it is polite to invite him or her, with their spouse, to your reception.

Where can a civil ceremony be performed? Most take place in a courthouse, judge's chambers, or the county clerk's office during regular business hours, or in the home or office of a justice of the peace. A large civil ceremony may be performed at home or in a club or ballroom.

What official documents are needed? Obtaining a marriage license takes time. Check requirements with your local Marriage License Bureau (see "The Marriage License" section and Appendix, "Marriage Laws" chart). If the ceremony will be in a clerk's office, remember to invite at least two close friends or relatives along, since you may need two official witnesses. Their participation will be more meaningful than having two office employees sign your marriage license.

What should we wear? As the bride, you can wear anything from a traditional bridal gown to a suit or street-length dress; later change into a ball gown for a hotel reception. The groom can wear a dark suit to city hall, formalwear for the reception—based on formality and time of day. (See Chapter 7, "Wedding Clothes.")

civil-ceremony officiants

- county clerk
- mayor
- township committee chair
- governor
- clerk of Superior Court
- judge
- magistrate
- justice of the peace

Can we add personal touches? Of course. Mail out printed invitations, or send brief, personal notes if your guest list is small. If it is a second marriage, include your children as attendants; ask them to read Scripture or poems, hold your bouquet for the ring exchange. Give them a Family Medallion (see Chapter 11, "Remarriage"). Don't forget to carry a bouquet and pin a boutonniere on your groom. Photographs will also be cherished keepsakes; hire a photographer or invite a close friend who is an experienced photographer along to city hall. Have champagne on hand to toast your joy after the vows. Even if the ceremony is at city hall over your lunch break, plan a honeymoon, or at least a romantic wedding night in a hotel.

The Marriage License

Don't leave this until the last minute. Each state sets its own requirements regarding age of consent, blood tests, documents, time of validity; you shouldn't apply too early or too late! See "Marriage Laws" chart in Appendix and follow these steps:

Find out where to apply. Call city offices until you determine if you apply for a marriage license at city hall, your city or town clerk's office, or the Marriage License Bureau. Ask what hours the office is open. (If your wedding will be a civil ceremony in this same office, get precise directions, parking information, for yourselves, and any guests.)

Find out when to apply. While on the phone, ask when you should apply for a marriage license (usually two to three weeks before the ceremony). The license may be valid for sixty days, and there may be a "cooling-off" or waiting period (the license will not be valid until several days after you've applied for it).

Find out if you need blood tests. Also ask how long the results will be valid. (Many a couple have scrambled for new blood tests at the last minute!) Each state sets its own requirements for blood tests. If required in your state, go to your doc-tor or a clinic and ask for the standard prewedding blood test (this test for vene-real diseases may take several days for results). Results for an AIDS test may take six to eight weeks.

Bring the right documents. Find out the age of consent. You'll probably need to bring birth certificates for written proof of age; proof of citizenship if you were not born in the United States; identifica-tion; parental consent if you are under-age; and, in most states, blood test re-sults. If one of you is divorced or wid-owed, you will also need a divorce de-cree or death certificate.

Come prepared with the fee. Ask in ad-vance what this will be, so that you'll have a check or enough cash on hand.

Go for a quiet lunch afterward. Since you'll both need to be present to apply, take time out from wedding plans for a special date—to mark the occasion.

documents for marriage license

- birth certificate
- proof of citizenship
- identification
- parental consent if underage
- death certificate if widowed
- divorce decree if divorced
- blood test results if required

The Marriage Certificate

Before or after your wedding ceremony, two witnesses of your choice (often the best man and maid of honor), the officiant, and the bride and groom must all sign the civil certificate. Some couples include the signing in their ceremony (a Quaker custom; see Chapter 9, "Religious Rituals & Requirements," and Appendix, under Chapter 4, "Planning Your Wedding"). Your church or synagogue may also issue its own certificate—a page scribed in calligraphy, suitable for framing, or a lovely booklet (with the words of your ceremony) for participants and even guests to sign. The signing of the marriage certificate makes a great photograph, so alert your photographer.

Your clergymember will file your marriage certificate with the proper authorities; you'll receive a copy a few weeks later by mail.

The *Ketubah*. This traditional Jewish marriage contract is the agreement that specifies the groom's responsibilities toward his bride, including that he "honor and cherish" her. It is required for a valid Jewish marriage and is usually provided by the rabbi. Originally, the *ketubah* also provided a financial settlement for the wife in case of divorce or widowhood. Now some rabbis allow a more egalitarian version of the *ketubah*, which pledges equality in marriage. The *ketubah* is mandatory for Orthodox and Conservative Jews; Reform Jews should consult their rabbi for requirements. It's signed by two witnesses before the ceremony, and is handed to the bride by the groom afterward, for her safekeeping. After the wedding, the *ketubah* (which may be lavishly illustrated) may be framed and hung on the wall.

The Persian Wedding Covenant. This document is traditional, but does not make the marriage legal. It is a modern interpretation of a traditional Iranian wedding certificate. Decorated with birds, flowers, and Islamic symbols, the Persian document is signed by the couple and guests.

The Quaker Marriage Certificate. Colorfully bordered and written in calligraphy, this certificate records family histories, vows exchanged, and has room for guests' signatures.

Amish and Mennonite Wedding Certificates. These documents are illuminated in the *fraktur* folk-art style. Symbolic angels and birds surround the couple's names and wedding date. The crowned angel at the top represents the angel who watches over and blesses mankind; the birds pecking their chests denote sacrificial love.

Prenuptial Agreements

These documents are no longer requested only by wealthy individuals seeking to protect their estates. Nor are they strictly for second marriages, where one or both spouses hope to protect their children's inheritances. Today, both bride and groom are entering marriage with earned retirement benefits, IRAs, invested savings, property; they want to hold on to these hard-earned assets, in case the marriage doesn't last a lifetime. Besides protecting your legal rights, a prenuptial agreement is a useful tool for evaluating your financial situations before marriage, and your beliefs about your life together. Such an agreement should be well thought out, reviewed by two lawyers (one representing each of you), signed by you and your groom plus witnesses, and notarized. It's also wise to make it a *pre*nuptial, not a *post*nuptial agreement.

At what time should a prenuptial agreement be drawn up? Well in advance of the wedding, to allow time for both the bride's and the groom's lawyers to review the document, and to cut down on added prewedding stress. A prenuptial agreement often covers ownership of present property and future ownership of expected inheritances.

When is a prenuptial agreement especially important? If it's a second marriage for either or both of you have children and personal assets, your agreement should protect the rights of each of the children. If your parents are giving you the family's valuable antiques, your agreement might specify that these heirlooms would remain in your family should you divorce. If you have a family trust fund, or substantial property, you should also specify that these things will remain outside marital property.

Can lifestyle issues be specified? Yes. A contract may state whether or not you will have children; how you will handle savings and household tasks; whether or not you will keep your maiden name. Some even specify who will do household chores, feed the pet, and diaper babies.

Will a prenuptial agreement hold up in court? Prenuptial agreements have had mixed success when challenged in court. However, what will matter in determining financial distribution is that each of you had ample time to review the document with your own attorneys, prior to signing. Some couples have a videotape made of themselves signing the agreement, which may hold more credence when shown later in court. While lifestyle issues may not be legally enforceable, writing down your inner expectations about your life together can clarify important issues and help your marriage—whether you sign the agreement or not.

before
you wed

- Discuss whether or not you'll pool incomes or keep them separate; what the arrangement would be if one of you stopped working.

- Collect all financial statements from credit cards, banks, pension plans, student loans. Subtract debts from assets to determine net worths.

- Draw up a budget together. List all fixed expenses; allow for extras and emergencies.

- If you want a prenuptial agreement, you should each have your own lawyer. Meet separately to discuss issues of the agreement. Review every word before signing.

The Name Decision

After marriage, you will have the choice of keeping your maiden name, taking your husband's surname, or choosing an alternative option. Whatever your decision, it will have long-term implications for your career, family relationships, and financial future. Here are the possibilities:

name-change steps

If one or both of you will be changing your name after marriage, update your listing with and for:

- government agencies (e.g., Internal Revenue Service)
- social security card(s)
- driver's license(s)
- car registration(s)
- telephone company
- bank account(s)
- insurance policy(ies)
- lease(s)
- deed(s)
- property title(s)
- passport(s)
- voter-registration card(s)
- will(s)
- stock certificate(s)
- post-office listing(s)
- employee ID card(s)
- school ID card(s) and alumni/alumnae listing(s)
- magazine subscription(s)
- credit card(s)
- employer(s)

Keeping your own name. Many women have already established professional reputations in their careers, and like having a separate identity. This is the easiest option. If you decide to keep your maiden name, in forty-nine states you simply continue to use it consistently. *Note*: Residents of Hawaii must declare what their married name will be when signing their marriage certificate.

Keeping your own name selectively. It is possible to continue to use your own name professionally and legally, and use your husband's name for social purposes only (correspondence, for invitations, for things relating to your children). Or, you can change your surname to your husband's on all legal (and financial) documents, and use it everywhere *except* at work. Be consistent in the usage (see "Name-Change Steps" box).

Changing your name. If you decide to change your name, you should assume your new name right after the wedding by notifying various government agencies, so that your name can be changed on official documents and identification cards (see "Name-Change Steps" box). For instance, write and tell the Internal Revenue Service: *Please be advised that social security number ____, previously in the name of Jane Smith, should now read Jane Miller.* Ask that a separate credit history be maintained under *each* of your names—John Miller *and* Jane Miller, so you maintain a credit rating of your own. This can be helpful when applying for a bank loan or mortgage. (It's also wise to *keep* one or more credit cards in your own name—to maintain your credit rating should you be divorced or widowed). Below are the options:

Adopt your husband's surname. This is the most common and traditional change that women make.

Use your maiden name as your middle name. Some women drop their middle name and begin to use their maiden name in its place, before their married name. (*Peggy Lynn Smith* becomes *Peggy Smith Jones.*)

Hyphenate your maiden and married names. For example, *Peggy Smith* could become *Peggy Smith-Jones.* If your husband adopts this same hyphenated name as his surname, he must change his name legally, in court.

Create a new hybrid name that both you and your husband adopt. Some couples opt to choose an entirely new name that reflects their newly formed family unit. For example, *Sue Hanson* and *Doug Everly* might become *Sue and Doug Hanly.* Others have simply opened the phone book and chosen a name they particularly like. This name change for bride and groom must be done legally.

Letting everyone know. If you will be changing your name, tell your employer and friends. Send out printed name cards or combine the information with your new address on an at-home card (see Chapter 5, "Invitations & Announcements").

Tell parents and in-laws about your name decision before they hear it from others. If you will keep your own name, be sensitive to your in-laws' concerns. Explain that you've already established a career identity, and perhaps reassure them that your children will have your husband's name. Enlist your spouse's support in affirming your decision, especially if you two have *both* opted to change your names. Perhaps explain that it in no way reflects on your respect for your in-laws' name, but indicates the new commitment you have to each other.

Selecting Your Rings

Shopping together for engagement and wedding rings assures that you both will be pleased with the choices (see Appendix, under Chapter 8, "Your Wedding Ceremony").

Engagement rings vary widely in style and design; gemstones (e.g., sapphires, rubies, emeralds) vary in color and shape; rings vary in the use of gold or platinum; finishes are matte or polished—with surface texture (Florentine) or an etched design (diamond-cut). Diamonds are judged by strict standards (the four C's: color, cut, clarity, and carat; see "The Four C's" box).

Wedding bands may be chosen to match the engagement ring or to be worn alone. The bride's rings may or may not match the groom's. All rings should flatter the hand.

Engraving personalizes these keepsakes. Inscribe the couple's initials and their wedding date (*"R.G.S. from J.R.B. 8/22/94"*) or a phrase (*"I'll always love you"*).

Double-ring ceremonies are more popular today, since more men are choosing to wear wedding rings. Your honor attendant will hold the groom's ring and the best man will hold yours, until they are exhanged during the vows. (It's wise to have a faux ring attached to a ring bearer's pillow!)

Innovative wedding-rings are being chosen by some brides. Some options: *colored-diamonds* (e.g., pink, yellow, blue, purple, cognac); *rattle rings* (loose diamonds fill a hidden compartment in a rounded gold band); *tension rings* (a center diamond holds the band apart, so almost the entire stone is visible).

Sharing Expenses

Traditionally, the bride's family was responsible for the cost of the wedding; they were "marrying off" their daughter. Today, however, sharing expenses is much more the norm. Here are the options (also see "Who Pays for What?" chart):

a diamond's 4 C's

- **cut**—shape, cutting style, proportions, and finish.
- **clarity**—freedom from flaws (inner cracks, bubbles, specks); flawless is rated "F1"; "I3" is imperfect.
- **color**—rated on a letter scale, from D (absolutely colorless) to Z (yellow). Most contain yellow or brown traces; clear white is most costly. This rating is not to be confused with the costly, much-sought-after colored diamonds mentioned in the "Selecting Your Rings" section.
- **carat**—standard way of measuring the stone's weight; 100 points equals one carat.

stone shapes

- **marquise**—oblong with pointed ends
- **pear shaped**—round on one end, pointed on the other
- **heart shaped**—romantic variation
- **round/brilliant**—traditional cut (58 facets reflect the most light)
- **oval**—round adaptation (same carat weight as round stone, but appears larger)
- **emerald cut**—rectangular with "steps" on sides, corners

You and your groom may contribute to your parents' overall budget, or pay for the wedding yourselves. In this case, your parents may still issue the invitations, still be host and hostess, and your fiancé's parents may still be the honored guests. Decisions should be made with the feelings of both sets of parents in mind, no matter who pays the bills.

Your fiancé's family may offer to share the costs. They may suggest splitting the wedding expenses, contributing a set amount, or covering specific things, such as the flowers, music, and/or liquor. All bills would be sent directly to them, to avoid awkward requests for money. (It's best to have the groom discuss with them, in private, what they will contribute financially—to avoid tension between families.) There are no firm rules about wedding protocol when families are sharing expenses. Your mother would still head the receiving line, your father make a wedding toast. You would probably, however, want to highlight your groom's parents, too. Both sets of parents' names might appear on the wedding invitations (see Chapter 5, "Invitations & Announcements"); his father might be asked to say a blessing or give a toast, too.

Another alternative: One family might pay for (and plan) the ceremony; the other, the reception. In this case, the names of the groom's parents would appear on the invitation or reception card (see Chapter 5, "Invitations & Announcements"). Or, the groom's parents may finance the entire wedding. Although they will serve as host and hostess on wedding day, the bride's parents should still be honored in the traditional way.

You may split the wedding expenses (and guest list) in thirds—one third for each set of parents, one third for the couple. It is still the prerogative of the bride's parents to politely decline all offers of financial help, if they wish.

Hiring a Wedding Consultant

If you and/or your mother are busy with work responsibilities, a wedding consultant may be the answer to your wedding-planning needs. Also consider hiring one if you are planning a wedding in another state (see the "Planning Long-Distance" section) and cannot be on the scene; or for an at-home wedding and reception where there are innumerable details (you shouldn't be digging out necessary supplies, washing dishes, on your wedding day!), a wedding consultant is invaluable.

How do we find a wedding consultant? Ask friends for recommendations, and contact the Association of Bridal Consultants (see Appendix, under Chapter 4, "Planning Your Wedding") for a professional in your area. Bridal salons may also provide leads. Ask florists, caterers, photographers, and check the Yellow Pages under "Wedding Supplies and Services."

a wedding consultant's duties

The person you hire should:

- listen to your and your fiancé's ideas; make suggestions, research your options

- come up with an overall wedding plan that meets your tastes and budget

- make appointments with wedding-service providers

- visit the bridal salon and Wedding Gift Registry with you

- help handle the selection of bridesmaids' dresses, invitations, flowers, caterer

- make sure the plan is carried out smoothly by staying in touch with the businesses, vendors

- be on hand on your wedding day to see that all services and details proceed as planned (e.g., the tent is set up correctly, the cake is the one ordered, the flowers arrive, the service personnel know what is expected)

- deal with any emergencies that occur; an experienced consultant is well versed in wedding etiquette and has directed many weddings

Who Pays for What?

SERVICE	BRIDE AND/OR HER FAMILY	GROOM AND/OR HIS FAMILY	MAIDS/ USHERS	OPTIONS TO SHARE
RINGS	Groom's ring.	Bride's engagement and wedding rings.		Bride's or groom's family may offer heirloom rings.
PREWEDDING PARTIES	Bride's family may host the first engagement party to announce the news. Bride hosts bridesmaids' luncheon.	Groom's family may host engagement party (should follow any festivities hosted by bride's family). Groom and/or his family may host bachelor dinner, rehearsal dinner.	Maid of honor and/or bridesmaids host a shower; in some areas, a bridesmaids' party. Best man and/or ushers host a bachelor party. Friends may host an engagement party.	Bride's family may host the rehearsal dinner if groom's family is unable. Out-of-towners' brunch or pool party and barbecue may be co-hosted.
STATIONERY	Invitations, announcements, enclosures, personal stationery, thank-you notes, newsletters, wedding programs.	Groom's thank-you notes, personal stationery.	May help with assembling and addressing invitations.	Friends and/or attendants may do calligraphy for addresses, wedding programs, *ketubah* (Jewish wedding contract).
CLOTHES	Bride's dress, veil, accessories; her mother's dress, father's attire. Bride's trousseau (clothes, lingerie).	Groom's wedding outfit; his mother's dress, father's attire.	Maid of honor, bridesmaids pay for their dresses. Ushers pay for rental/purchase of their outfits.	Bride or her family may pay for maids' dresses, accessories. Groom or his family may pay for ushers' rentals, accessories.
FLOWERS	Arrangements for church, reception, *huppah*. Bouquets, corsages, for maids, flower girl.	Bride's bouquet and going-away corsage. Boutonnieres for men in wedding party. Corsages for mothers, grandmothers.		Bride's flowers may be purchased by bride's family. Bride may give corsages to mothers, grandmothers.
CEREMONY	Fee for church, synagogue, sexton, organist, soloist. Rental of aisle carpet, marquee, *huppah*.	Marriage license. Clergymember's or judge's fee.	May provide packets of rice, birdseed, potpourri, for guests to toss.	Couple may cover all ceremony costs.
PHOTOGRAPHY/ VIDEOGRAPHY	Engagement and wedding photos, video.		Attendants may supplement photographer by taking behind-the-scenes shots, candids.	One family may pay for photography, one for videography. Groom's parents, couple, may pay for additional prints not included in package.
TRANSPOR-TATION/ LODGING	Transportation of bridal party to ceremony, reception sites.		Attendants who live in wedding area may lodge out-of-town attendants.	Either family may arrange transportation, pay for fruit baskets, baby-sitters, welcome buffet for out-of-town guests, lodging for out-of-town attendants.
RECEPTION/ HONEYMOON	All professional services—food, drinks, decorations, music/entertainment, etc.	Limousine to airport. Complete honeymoon.		Groom's family may offer to share cost by covering specific services (e.g., hors d'oeuvres, liquor).
GIFTS	Bride buys wedding gift for groom, each of her attendants.	Groom buys wedding gift for bride, each of his attendants.		Couple may buy gifts to thank their parents, helpers.

How expensive will it be? Consultants may charge: a flat rate, a percentage of the total wedding budget, or by the hour. Be sure to sign, and have countersigned, a contract that specifies responsibilities and fees. (It is to the couple's advantage *not* to have the consultant's fee based on the wedding budget.)

I want this to be *my* wedding, reflecting my taste. Won't I have to agree to what she

Bride's Calendar

12 MONTHS BEFORE:

☐ Buy a wedding planner, memory album.
☐ Consult fiancé, all parents, about budget, style—from colors to cake.
☐ Select attendants.
☐ Decide on wedding and reception sites.
☐ Confirm ceremony date, time, and site with officiant.
☐ Plan reception, make reservations.
☐ Book consultant, caterer, photographer, videographer, florist, musicians, etc.

9 MONTHS BEFORE:

☐ With fiancé, see clergymember, judge.
☐ Choose and order dress, accessories.
☐ Register for china, linens, etc.
☐ Inquire about wedding insurance.
☐ Begin your guest lists.
☐ Consult travel agent about honeymoon.

6 MONTHS BEFORE:

☐ Plan wedding details with florist, etc.
☐ Shop for new home if you're moving.
☐ Book calligrapher, limousines for wedding party, portrait photographer.
☐ Order invitations and announcements; begin addressing them upon receipt.
☐ Complete honeymoon plans with groom.
☐ Order attendants' dresses.
☐ Discuss rehearsal dinner with groom.

3 MONTHS BEFORE:

☐ Finish guest lists.
☐ Shop for trousseau.

☐ Order wedding rings.
☐ Confirm delivery dates of all dresses.
☐ Make appointment with gynecologist.
☐ Hire stylists for wedding hair, makeup.

6–8 WEEKS BEFORE:

☐ Mail your invitations.
☐ Choose gifts for groom, attendants.
☐ Have final dress, headpiece fitting.
☐ Have wedding portrait taken.
☐ Pick up rings; check engraving.
☐ Plan your bridesmaids' party.
☐ Write thank-you notes for gifts.
☐ Send announcement to newspapers.
☐ Submit request lists to photographer, videographer, musicians.

2 WEEKS BEFORE:

☐ Go with fiancé for marriage license.
☐ Check honeymoon reservations.
☐ Finish addressing announcements to mail on wedding day.

1 WEEK BEFORE:

☐ Pack; get going-away outfit ready.
☐ Purchase traveler's checks.
☐ Give final guest count to caterer.
☐ Host and/or attend bridesmaids' party.
☐ Check final details with florist, etc.
☐ Arrange to move belongings to new home.
☐ Keep up with gift acknowledgments.
☐ Remind attendants of rehearsal dinner details; give them gifts that night.

or he recommends? Absolutely not. A wedding consultant is your researcher. She or he can scout out the best services and sites, narrowing down each wedding-service category, but you make the final selections. You should meet with the consultant regularly to approve details and assess progress. Hiring a wedding consultant does not mean that you give up control of your own wedding. Rather, you add a very competent facilitator to your wedding staff.

Groom's Calendar

12 MONTHS BEFORE:

- ☐ Pick out bride's engagement ring from jewelry store (if not yet selected).
- ☐ If you'll share wedding expenses, discuss with fiancée, all parents.
- ☐ Discuss with fiancée how many ushers you'll need (1 per 50 guests); select.

9 MONTHS BEFORE:

- ☐ Arrange a visit with clergymember, justice of the peace, to discuss ceremony.
- ☐ Visit bridal registry with fiancée.
- ☐ Start making out your guest list.
- ☐ Discuss honeymoon plans with fiancée; consult travel agent for ideas.
- ☐ If traveling abroad, update passports, arrange for visas, international driver's license; check inoculations.

6 MONTHS BEFORE:

- ☐ Arrange to pay for bride's bouquet; order boutonnieres, corsages.
- ☐ Complete honeymoon plans; buy tickets.
- ☐ Arrange transportation (limousines) for wedding party to ceremony, reception.
- ☐ Plan rehearsal dinner with parents.

3 MONTHS BEFORE:

- ☐ Complete guest list; give to fiancée.
- ☐ Consult with fiancée; order wedding attire for self, men in wedding party.
- ☐ Shop for honeymoon clothes.

- ☐ Order wedding rings.
- ☐ Consult with fiancée and arrange lodging for out-of-town relatives and attendants.

6–8 WEEKS BEFORE:

- ☐ Select gifts for bride, ushers.
- ☐ Check marriage-license requirements.
- ☐ See your doctor for checkup, blood test.
- ☐ Give or attend bachelor party.
- ☐ Pick up wedding rings, check engraving.
- ☐ Help fiancée with thank-you notes.

2 WEEKS BEFORE:

- ☐ Make a date with your fiancée to get the marriage license; have lunch afterwards.
- ☐ Arrange with best man for transportation from reception to airport, train.
- ☐ Double-check honeymoon reservations.

1 WEEK BEFORE:

- ☐ Explain special seating arrangements for family, guests, to head usher.
- ☐ Put officiant's fee in a sealed envelope and give to best man, who will deliver it after the ceremony.
- ☐ Purchase traveler's checks.
- ☐ Get your going-away clothes ready so you can change after the reception.
- ☐ Pack for your honeymoon.
- ☐ Arrange to move belongings to new home, if necessary.
- ☐ Remind groomsmen of rehearsal dinner details; give them gifts that night.

Planning Long-Distance

Few brides today work in their hometown, which means that often, a bride who will return home for the wedding is planning it long-distance. Here are some helpful tips:

Have a planning assistant in that town. Either hire a local wedding consultant (see "Hiring a Wedding Consultant" section) or ask a relative or friend in that town to gather information from various wedding professionals for you. You'll need brochures, instant photos of reception sites, cake and flower samples, musicians' audition tapes, etc. Also ask them to compile addresses for those on your guest list.

Find out what it will take to plan the reception style you want in this location. A medieval wedding with authentic costumes and food may be difficult to stage unless you find the right resources. Ease the strain of long-distance planning so you can sit back and enjoy the event.

Ask the phone company to send a copy of the Yellow Pages from that town or city. This will put the phone numbers of a variety of businesses at your fingertips, avoiding the costs of long-distance directory assistance. It will also reveal the services for which you'll have to search further (a nearby town).

Ask companies you call to send you information. They should be willing to mail brochures, price lists, services, as well as a contract.

Keep long-distance calls to a minimum. Use postcards, letters, and faxes to communicate with assistants. Keep a running list of things to be discussed, then call once a week, and later, once every two weeks.

Plan at least one visit to the wedding town. Tell your planning assistant or wedding consultant in advance when you will be arriving, and have appointments set up with all of the wedding-service professionals hired. Make final arrangements and payments in person. Check on hotel reservations for other long-distance travelers. Book a makeup person and hairstylist for the wedding day, if you want one. Thank assistants with a lunch, dinner, and/or gift.

If Someone's Disabled

When planning your ceremony and reception, take into account your needs and those of your groom, or any of your guests, if physical limitations are a factor. Whether your college roommate is temporarily on crutches from a ski accident, your grandmother has a walker, or the groom or your father is in a wheelchair, you will have to consider the accessibility of your sites. See the tips, below (and the Appendix, under Chapter 4, "Planning Your Wedding").

Transportation and parking. If your guest doesn't drive, and is coming alone, is there an accessible public transportation system? Perhaps invite your guest with a friend—to simplify logistics. If there are not "handicapped parking spaces," allocate a few near the entrance to the site.

Accessibility. There should be street-level ramps leading from your sites—for wheelchairs. If not, build or rent portable wooden ramps. Rest rooms should have accessible entranceways and one stall at least 32 inches across and complete with grab bars for those in wheelchairs. If bathrooms in the house of worship are not accessible, warn guest(s) in advance.

Low elevator controls are needed for guests in wheelchairs, and elevator buttons in Braille that emit a tone at each floor, for the blind. Elevator hallways and doorways should be wide enough for easy wheelchair passage.

Ask a disabled guest if they have any other special needs; if so, invite him or her with a guest. Describe physical layout to a blind guest in advance.

Seating. Tell ushers to reserve seats next to aisles for guests in wheelchairs or on crutches, but allow these guests to sit where they are most comfortable—with family and friends. Tell the banquet manager to set one less chair at a table where a guest in a wheelchair will sit. Try to leave room between tables for a wheelchair to negotiate, and fit comfortably for a meal. Seat guests who are deaf near a wooden dance floor; they'll feel the music's vibrations.

Ceremony. If you or your groom is in a wheelchair, arrange for the other partner to be seated, as well, at the altar. Will there be enough room for easy chair movement? Attach a bouquet with Velcro™ to a bride's wheelchair to leave hands free to maneuver; decorate wheel spokes with flowers and bows. Don't choose a gown or veil that is long enough to get caught in the wheels.

Dress any person assisting a disabled attendant in the same attire as the rest of the wedding party. If an attendant is on crutches, provide a seat for her or him. If the bride or groom is in a wheelchair, you might seat the entire wedding party.

Review the words and Scripture, and the way the clergymember or officiant plans to present them. Don't assume that he or she won't say the wrong, patronizing thing (e.g., *"Who would have thought that this would be possible?"*).

Seat hard-of-hearing guests near the front of your church or synagogue, where they can read lips or follow a certified sign-language interpreter. Many houses of worship have amplified earphones in the front pews; ask the sexton to be sure they are turned on. The printed word can help, with signs pointing to rest rooms and exits, and a program (with a Braille insert?) that includes the words to prayers and hymns—if several guests are blind.

If one of you is blind, rehearse at the

caterer's contract tips

- date, time, site, and room; adjustment policy if room is switched, party is canceled

- type of food service (e.g., buffet, seated meal, cocktails and hors d'oeuvres)

- menu and courses; food stations, hors d'oeuvres

- type of service (e.g., French; see the "Reception Glossary" section); whether first course will be preset

- staff-per-guest ratio (including waiters, bartenders, valets, coat-check, rest-room attendants)

- liquor arrangements (will you supply? bottles, brands, amounts; returns on unopened bottles; hours of open bar; whether wine or soft drinks will be served during meal); number of bars; policy for serving after-dinner drinks, liqueurs

- payment schedule (never pay *everything* in advance)

- sales tax, gratuities, bar fees, waiter fees

- whether musicians, photographer, wedding consultant will be fed

- food substitutions, quality (e.g., no prepackaged foods?)

- when final head count is due

- cancellation, overtime fees

- prices quoted for foods (set ninety days before wedding); services you might add, with a ceiling on menu increases (often 10 percent)

- names of banquet manager and staff members who will be present at your wedding

- insurance (liability) coverage

sites till you're completely familiar with them. Ask a blind guest if they'd like someone (their guest?) to sit next to them to quietly describe the ceremony.

Dining and dancing. Ask guests in advance if they have any special dietary restrictions—food allergies, diabetes, low-salt needs. Rather than alter your party menu, order specially prepared plates for these guests. Serve finger foods or those easy to cut if hand and arm motility, or coordination, is a concern for some guests.

Make sure the dance floor is not heavily waxed, which is hazardous for someone using crutches, a walker, or a wheelchair. Remember, people in wheelchairs will get out on the dance floor and dance.

Have a certified sign interpreter for deaf guests present at the reception to explain traditions, relay toasts, and other activities.

Hiring a Caterer

Through word of mouth, advice from recent brides, your wedding consultant, other wedding professionals, you will find a caterer (or a reception site with a banquet manager) with whom you feel comfortable planning your wedding. Book your caterer or banquet location twelve months before your wedding; the best will be engaged early. Review the tips below, and be sure to execute a signed and countersigned contract (see "Caterer's Contract Points" box).

Credentials. Hire only state-licensed caterers, ensuring that they have met the local health-department standards and carry the necessary liability insurance (see Appendix, under Chapter 4, "Planning Your Wedding," for information about insurance and caterer referrals). If the caterer is not insured, you could be sued if someone gets food poisoning, chokes, chips a tooth, or has an auto accident after drinking too much.

Shared halls. If other events will take place during your wedding, be sure there is an empty room or hallway in between parties (and bands!). Ask if guests will know which room is for your celebration; whether the entryway, valet-parking staff, is large enough for crowds from several parties; if there are separate coat checks for each event; whether your attendants have a private suite or if the rest room will be shared. If there is another party that coincides with your starting time, consider making your starting time earlier or later. Ask how much time there will be to set up.

Package deals. Get a detailed list of what is included (cost per person and extras); security deposit, sales tax, gratuities, and bar fees may hike the total over your budget (see "Wedding Tipping" chart). Ask about overtime fees. Are linen colors and floral arrangements flexible if you pay an additional fee?

Pacing. Review your vision of the reception timetable with the banquet manager. You can request that waiters slow service and let guests dance longer in between courses; you can serve dinner to soft music, then heighten the decibels for dancing after, or you can stick to a tight schedule and avoid overtime fees.

Hidden embarrassments. Check the policy on tipping for valet parking, coat-check attendant, rest-room attendant, and bartender. You can arrange to cover these fees so baskets soliciting tips will not be left out. (Signs can be displayed that say: *"Gratuities have been taken care of by your host."*)

Menu options. Make sure the chef or caterer is flexible and will accommodate your needs. Ask about house specialties; what are the crowd-pleasing entrées? (See "Reception Menu" section.) Your caterer should be willing to help you find a menu that pleases you and is within your budget.

Wedding cake. Don't settle for the "house" variety. Ask to speak to the baker about cake flavors and decorations

(see Chapter 13, "Your Reception," "The Wedding Cake" section). If you are not pleased, negotiate to hire your own baker. (Ask if you may bring in traditional family cookies, or pastries.)

Reception rooms. Look at the space where your reception will be—when it's empty and when it's set up for a wedding. Evaluate ambience, acoustics. Ask if you can pay more to add decorations (a draped ceiling), topiaries, potted plants, if needed (see "Site Decorations" box). Can lighting be adjusted? How will the head table and guest tables be arranged? Where is the dance floor positioned? The band's stage? Is there a sound system, microphone (rental fee?), a generator and backup generator? Is there a piano on the premises?

Who's in charge? Insist that someone in authority be present on your wedding day to ensure that all runs smoothly. Meet in advance; find out who will distribute favors, set out alphabetized place (escort) or table cards, hang the skirting on tables. Too often, these carefully planned extras get lost in the shuffle.

Reception Menu

When deciding what to serve your guests, there are certain things to consider.

Time of day. If your reception will be beginning at a time when most people normally eat a meal, it's courteous to serve them the amount of food they are expecting. For example, after a noon church ceremony, most guests will be hungry for lunch; if the ceremony ends at

6 p.m. or 7 p.m., they'll most likely be expecting dinner.

Cost. If you're trying to host a large party on a limited budget, simply serve champagne and cake after a 2 p.m. wedding. Or, schedule a morning wedding follow-

reception rental tips

- Select rentals and finalize three to six months before the wedding.

- Ask for referrals, check Yellow Pages under "Party Rentals" (see Appendix, under Chapter 4, "Planning Your Wedding").

- Visit showrooms; check variety, cleanliness, equipment condition.

- Visit the site with the rental agent. Evaluate lighting and sound needs, layout, decorations. Ask about extras (margarita machines, fountains, cake stands).

- Rent one-and-a-half times as many place settings as guests for a seated meal, twice as many for a buffet; twice as many napkins as guests; one-and-a-half to two times as many glasses as guests, depending on beverages served.

- Save: Rent high-quality disposable place settings, table covers, napkins.

- Outdoors: Rent weatherproof coverings (canopies to protect from sun, drizzle; tents in decorative shapes with sides, flooring). Control tent temperature with heaters, ceiling fan, air conditioner.

- Outdoors and at home: Rent portable latrines, coatracks.

- Sign and countersign an itemized contract. List equipment to be supplied, rental fees, delivery and setup charges, delivery date and location, waivers against damage to equipment, deposit paid (usually 25 percent), if deposit is refundable, and when balance is due.

creative menu tips

- help-yourself dishes of dried fruits and nuts

- mangoes, kiwis—unusual fruits, new flavors

- fresh tuna marinated with oils, garlic, herbs, then grilled; fresh sturgeon or swordfish—similar to meat, it's hearty

- rack of lamb, lighter than roast beef

- vegetables grown organically

- fresh vegetables tossed in cholesterol-free olive oil (instead of butter)

- steamed golden acorn or butternut squash

- sautéed wild mushrooms (chanterelle, shitake)

- make-your-own-salad bars; unusual lettuces and accompaniments

- risotto (Italian rice dish cooked with stock, seasonings)

- couscous (grainlike African pasta)

- Italian polenta (cornmeal baked into cakes)

- serve-your-own vinegars— clove vinegar on salmon, anise vinegar on salads or melons

ed by breakfast; a tea or cocktail reception, featuring light nibbles and hors d'oeuvres, following a ceremony between one and four.

Style. For a formal, evening wedding, a seated dinner—with several courses—or a lavish buffet is a common option. For large, less formal celebrations, many couples choose a sumptuous cocktail buffet. Food stations—individual buffet tables with a variety of foods (e.g.,sushi, enchiladas, tacos, stir-fry vegetables, sliced meats)—might also be positioned around the room.

Beverages. A reception should include a bubbly beverage to toast the future. Champagne, or a quality sparkling wine prepared by the *champagne methodoise* technique, is the traditional drink for wedding toasts and can be served at any time of day. Offer non-alcoholic beverages such as ginger ale, club soda, punch, or white grape juice for toasting, as well.

Consider your menu and time of day when deciding on beverages. Ice-cold punch (both non-alcoholic and with champagne) might be offered at morning tea receptions; mixed drinks, white wine, liqueurs, and champagne or sparkling wine for dinner receptions. If you wish to serve a sparkling beverage for the entire meal, serve something dry (brut) with the main course and switch to an extra-dry (somewhat sweeter than brut), a sec (sweet) or demi-sec (the sweetest) champagne or sparkling wine with the wedding cake and dessert. (A sweet champagne or sparkling wine will complement the sweetness of cake better

than a dry one.) Also consider a fruity champagne sangria, rum-based mixed drinks, or club soda splashed with vodka and scoops of sorbet.

Special dietary needs. Provide for any special requirements of your guests (i.e., vegetarian, kosher, low-cholesterol, low-sodium, diabetic). Many couples offer guests a choice of fish, chicken, or red meat, along with steamed vegetables. Do you prefer a few gourmet choices or a wider selection of food? Discuss all options.

Ethnic and regional flavor. Offer foods that have special meaning to you and your groom, such as the swordfish you ate on your first date or the Sacher torte that reflects your groom's Austrian heritage. Offerings can also reflect a wedding theme, such as barbecue-style food (fried chicken, corn bread, black-eyed peas, biscuits and honey) at a Southern-style wedding. If you're Middle Eastern, borrow from that cuisine (season foods with cinnamon, coriander, rosewater); French, design the menu accordingly.

Seasonal foods. Select produce grown in your area and take advantage of in-season prices. (For a reception in citrus season in California, serve orange tarts; in New England in apple-picking season, serve apple bread, cider.)

At-home receptions. Showcase family recipes, made in advance and frozen. Consider this option only if you have hired someone, or have a friend who has volunteered to be responsible for thawing, heating, and serving food.

Reception Glossary

Confused by the latest buzzwords? Here is a list of terms to refer to when selecting your reception-food style:

American Plate Service—Food is artfully arranged on plates in the kitchen, then presented to seated guests.

Cocktail Buffet—Guests sit informally around small tables and help themselves to hors d'oeuvres throughout the reception.

Dinner by the Bite—Mini-portions of various foods are served from different food stations positioned throughout the reception room so that guests can enjoy a balanced meal throughout the celebration.

Edible Flowers—Nasturtiums, roses, pansies, violets, add visual appeal and delicate flavor to salads and cakes.

English Service—Once a "groaning board" of food set out after a hunt, this is now a buffet from which guests may help themselves.

Ethnic Cuisine—Couples select the foods traditionally linked to their heritages (e.g., sushi and sake—Japanese; a fruitcake—English, Irish; a *croquembouche* ("crisp in the mouth"), a tall cone of caramel-coated cream puffs—French.

Food Stations—Individual buffet tables that offer everything from crepes and sushi to omelets, enchiladas, tacos, shellfish, fruit, vegetables, salads, shish kebabs.

French Service—Food is presented and then carved, boned, flambéed, or otherwise finished by waiters tableside.

Grazing—Guests nibble refreshments from food stations around the room. This activity starts during the receiving line and continues throughout the reception.

Nouvelle Cuisine—A form of French cuisine that uses little fat or flour and stresses light sauces and fresh seasonal produce.

Service *à la Russe*—Roasts are carved, food divided into portions and placed on platters; waiters serve from platters at the table.

Viennese Table—Sumptuous dessert buffet, including napoleons, mousses, petit fours, crème brulée, tarts, fruits, ice cream.

reception-meal options

- seated breakfast
- seated brunch
- seated luncheon
- buffet brunch, lunch, or dinner
- afternoon tea
- punch and cake
- cocktails and passed hors d'oeuvres
- cocktail buffet
- dinner by the bite
- seated dinner

Wedding Tipping

WHOM TO TIP	HOW MUCH TO TIP	WHEN, AND BY WHOM
Caterer, club manger, hotel banquet manager.	15–20% of bill if not covered by gratuities. Just 10% of bill if there is also a maître d' hôtel.	Reception host may be asked to pay bill in advance. If gratuities not covered, host or wedding consultant pays in envelope during reception.
Maître d' hôtel.	15–20% of bill or $1.50–$3.00 per guest.	Reception host or wedding consultant pays in envelope during reception.
Waiters, waitresses, table captains.	15–20% of bill given to captain or maître d' hôtel to be distributed to rest of staff, if not covered by gratuities.	Reception host may be asked to pay bill in advance. If gratuities not covered, host or wedding consultant pays in envelope during reception.
Bartenders.	Optional: 10% of total liquor bill, above gratuities.	Reception host or wedding consultant pays in envelope during reception.
Powder-room attendants, coat-room attendants in hotels or clubs.	$.50–$1.00 per guest, or arrange a gratuity with the hotel or club management.	Reception host may be asked to pay bill in advance. If gratuities not covered, pay in advance, so guests will not be asked to pay.
Parking attendants.	$.50–$1.00 per car, or arrange a gratuity with the hotel or club management.	Reception host may be asked to pay bill in advance. If gratuities not covered, pay in advance, so guests will not be asked to pay.
Limousine driver(s).	20% of total limousine bill.	Ceremony host or wedding consultant tips driver(s) at reception site.
Delivery-truck drivers for florist, baker, etc.	$5.00–$10.00 each.	Host or wedding consultant tips drivers at delivery site(s).
Musicians, disc jockey.	Optional: $20.00–$25.00 each.	Reception host or wedding consultant pays in envelopes at end of reception.

Tipping is a personal expression of gratitude for service given graciously and efficiently. The figures given above are only guidelines.

thoughtful gestures

Before your wedding day, make arrangements to remember those who will be unable to attend your wedding, as well as those less fortunate than you.

● *Recycle flowers.* Take or send the floral arrangements to an elderly married couple at a nearby home or hospital.

● *Share food.* Arrange to have leftover food, hors d'oeuvres, non-alcoholic punch, soft drinks, delivered to a soup kitchen or homeless shelter.

● *Make postwedding visits.* Share the wedding excitement with elderly or infirm friends and relatives who were unable to attend the wedding. In your wedding gown and formalwear, visit with a keepsake package of wedding cake, favors, flowers, instant photographs. Make a date to return with popcorn, sodas, and your wedding video—for a personal screening.

INVITATIONS & ANNOUNCEMENTS

The style of your wedding should determine the type of invitation you choose. For a very formal wedding, a classic white or ecru invitation engraved with black lettering is the traditional choice, although there are more decorative designs from which to choose. For less formal weddings, there are a large variety of invitations— including everything from pastel lettering to lace and beads from the bride's gown.

Compiling Your Guest List

Decide how many guests you'll be able to invite, after determining the budget with your families. Usually, each family invites half the guests, though sometimes one family will have a longer list (if, for instance, only the groom's immediate family will be traveling from a distance to the wedding). The guest list may also be split three ways: The bride's parents, the groom's parents, and the couple each invite one third of the guests.

Make a master wedding-invitation list. The bride usually compiles a list for her side of the family with her parents; the groom, with his parents. Also compile a "wish list"—to invite as guests refuse. (If one of you has divorced parents, rely primarily on the parent who raised you for help in drawing up your list.) Be sure all names (first, middle initial, and last) are spelled correctly; all titles (e.g., Dr., Ms., Sgt.) are correct, zip codes are included, and addresses are updated. (You may use index cards or a computer to alphabetize the lists easily and eliminate duplications.)

Make a master wedding-announcement list. Include all of your acquaintances not invited to the wedding with whom you wish to share the news of your marriage. (Refer to old address and telephone books, alumni directories, holiday-card lists, and club rosters to make sure no one is left out.) Announcements should be stamped, addressed, and ready to mail on your wedding day.

Remember, neither an invitation nor an announcement obligates the recipient to send a gift. If you won't be sending announcements, send invitations to all friends and relatives whom you would like to have with you, even if you don't think they'll be able to attend. (Anyone receiving an invitation may, however, decide to come—so allow for this possibility in your budget!)

You are not obligated to invite guests—or escorts—with your single friends. If you do decide to, however, find out beforehand whom they intend to bring and ask for their name and address; it is proper to send a separate invitation to that person. *Don't write "And Guest"* on the inner and outer envelope of your friend's invitation. If the couple live together, you may send one invitation to them both, just as you would to a married couple (their names would be listed alphabetically on the envelope).

Send invitations to the principals in the wedding. This includes your parents, the clergymember and his or her spouse, your fiancé's immediate family, the members of your wedding party (and their parents if you can), even though they've been invited informally. Some brides even mail an invitation to themselves—which lets them know which day their guests receive the invitation in the mail.

ordering invitations

Before you visit your stationer, you should know:

- if the groom's parents' names will be on the invitation.

- wedding day, date, time.

- name and address of ceremony and reception sites.

- how many invitations you'll need (count couples, not number of guests).

- whether all guests are invited to both ceremony and reception.

Printing Techniques

Invitations can be ordered from a printer, jeweler, stationer, or department store (a computerized printing and calligraphy service, and a computer software package, are also available; see Appendix, under Chapter 5, "Invitations & Announcements"). Below are some printing methods:

Engraving involves using a steel or copperplate die to "cut" letters into the paper (the die will be given to you as a keepsake). These letters look and feel raised from the surface of the paper, both front and back. The process may take up to eight weeks.

Thermography is a heat process that fuses ink and powder and closely resembles engraving, but is less expensive. The letters are raised on the front, but they cannot be felt on the back. Ther-

mography techniques can reproduce calligraphy and handlettered Hebrew or Chinese characters. Ask your stationer to show you samples.

Embossing raises dimensional lettering, borders, artwork, from the surface in relief without printing.

Offset printing uses a rubber cylinder to transfer inked letters onto paper. It is an excellent option for informal invitations, and when time and budget are limited.

Working with a Stationer

Like working with any wedding-service professional, you should be a wise consumer (see Appendix, under Chapter 5, "Invitations & Announcements").

Get referrals from friends and relatives. Keep a folder of wedding invitations that you've received and like. Once at the stationer's, review sample books. Ask for price estimates and have a ceiling price in mind.

Order invitations and announcements at least six months before the wedding. This will allow plenty of time for printing (which may take two–eight weeks—engraving takes the longest), proofreading, correction of errors, addressing (allow one–two weeks if using a calligrapher), and mailing (which may take longer near holidays). Have the envelopes sent to you in advance, and start addressing them at once; they can be addressed, stamped, and ready to mail when you receive the invitations.

Order extras. It's wise to order fifty extra invitations, perhaps one hundred extra envelopes (to allow for addressing mistakes and last-minute additions to your guest list). Your fiancé's mother and your mother should receive three or four unsealed invitations—wedding mementos—as soon as they are ready. These may be accompanied by a note from you telling them when the others will be mailed. Also remember to tuck a few invitations away for yourself.

Have a return address printed in the upper left corner of the envelopes for invitations and announcements to expedite mail handling. The post office encourages this practice, rather than having the hard-to-read, colorless, embossed return addresses once traditionally put on envelope flaps.

Proofread carefully. Ask the stationer to call you to come in and proofread the master invitation, envelope (if return address is printed), and enclosures before the final order is sent to the printer. This may save disappointment, time, and money. Proofread slowly and carefully (the eye often sees what it wants to see!). Double-check spelling of all names, addresses, sites, date, time, punctuation. Check type (placement, any broken letters?). If anything needs correcting, point it out.

Reread the invitations, envelopes, and enclosures when you pick up your order. If you find any errors, tell the stationer at once so he or she can rush corrections.

popular lettering styles

Royal Script

Palmer Script

Shaded Antique Roman

London Script

St. James

Flemish Script

Solid Antique Roman

Cathedral Text

Rook Script

Statesman

Invitation Styles

The invitation will set the tone for your wedding. It will cue in guests to the formality of your wedding, or the theme (e.g., ribbon-tied parchment for a medieval wedding; lacy, floral invitations for a Victorian wedding; patterned black-and-white for an Art Deco wedding).

stationery budget tips

Prices will vary greatly, based on the order you place. Note the following:

- Colored paper or parchment costs more than white or ivory paper.
- Sheets with printed or embossed designs are more costly than plain.
- Colored inks, a photograph or illustration, increase the bill.
- Enclosure cards will increase the printing-order cost *and* the postage for each invitation.

Formal invitations. For weddings with over fifty guests, it is traditional to have invitations engraved or printed by a stationer. Formal printing is done with black, brown, or gray ink. The invitation is engraved or printed on the top page of a folded sheet of white, rich ivory, or ecru paper. It is slipped inside an inner ungummed and unsealed envelope on which the guests' surnames are written—*Mr. and Mrs. Jones*; then slipped inside an outer envelope (which is addressed and stamped with full names—*Mr. and Mrs. John Jones*).

Creative, informal invitations. Handwritten invitations may be sent for a small wedding ceremony of fifty or fewer guests. If buying or ordering more personalized invitations, steer clear of invitations that will embarrass you later. An invitation shaped like a balloon or a baby-picture postcard may not be the best choice for a formal wedding. Even for an informal wedding, the invitation style is usually more sophisticated. Below are some ways to personalize your invitations:

Color—Order translucent or shiny paper, colored ink, a border or trim. Envelopes should be addressed in the same color ink as that on the invitations.

Shape—The invitation might be shaped like a piano or a top hat, embellished with pearls or feathers, rolled like a scroll, sent inside a bottle, or might even have a computer chip that will play a traditional wedding song when the invitation is opened. (See Appendix, under Chapter 5, "Invitations & Announcements," for sources for creative wedding invitations.)

Theme—Coordinate your invitation with the theme of your wedding. For example, simulate the white moiré tablecloths with a white moiré effect on the invitations. Planning a Victorian-style wedding? Send an invitation with Old English wording and envelopes lined in maroon velvet. If the color scheme includes black, silver, and gold, design the invitation in those three shades.

Tone—Set the mood of your wedding with the invitation. Planning a small, intimate celebration? Tuck handwritten notes into small fabric-lined baskets, and have them hand-delivered to guests. Or, have the invitation embroidered on white lace handkerchiefs.

Artwork—Some couples print a line drawing of their ceremony or reception site on the front of their invitations, or a meaningful photograph. Consult with your printer/stationer about what types of artwork will reproduce well, whether a photo can be reduced in size, and what negative quality is best with which to work. Allow an extra month for printing if your invitations will include intricate custom work such as this.

Wording Invitations

The typical formal wedding invitation gives the following information in this order:

The sponsors of the wedding—usually the bride's parents—issue the invitations and announcements, whether or not the bride still shares their home. (The sponsors do not necessarily pay for the wedding, so even if you and your fiancé are paying, the bride's parents may still be listed at the top of the invitation.)

If your parents are divorced, the person who raised you customarily issues the invitations and announcements.

If your parents are deceased, your guardian, closest relatives, or family friends may sponsor the wedding and issue the invitations and announcements.

Spell out words in full. This includes names (don't use nicknames) and numbers. Abbreviations are not used, with the exception of *Mr.* and *Mrs. Doctor* and *junior* can be spelled out if space permits, but are also commonly abbreviated. If *junior* is spelled out, it always has a lowercase *j* and a comma before it.

Use the wording ...*request the honour of your presence* for a religious service. Use ...*request the pleasure of your company* for a civil ceremony or for the reception. (*Honour* and *favour* ["the favour of a reply is requested"] are spelled with a *u*—the more formal British version.)

You may request a reply to the invitation with *R.s.v.p.*, *Please respond*, *Kindly respond*, or *The favour of a reply is requested*.

Traditionally, the bride's surname is not listed unless it is different from that of her parents. Be consistent with the use of titles (e.g., Mr., Miss, Ms., Dr.). If you wish to use one for the groom, then use one for the bride as well. Or, simply use first and middle names for both bride and groom.

Military titles are spelled out, with service designations on a separate line. Those with the rank captain and higher in the army, air force, and marines, and commander and higher in the navy, use their titles before their names, with their service designation listed on the next line. (The service designation line is omitted if the invitation is being *issued* by an officer and his wife.) Junior officers list their title on the line beneath their name, before their service designation. Non-commissioned officers list only their service designation, on the line under their name.

The wedding date is written, *Saturday, the sixth of July,* with the year spelled out on

the following line. (You may omit the year if you wish.)

Indicate the correct time of the ceremony. List it as *four o'clock*. (Some couples decide to list a time that is actually a half hour before the procession will start, to ensure that late-arriving guests will still be seated by ushers.) If the ceremony will start on the half hour, use the phrase *half after (four o'clock)*. The phrase *in the afternoon* or *in the evening* is optional.

Check the correct name of the ceremony site. If there are churches with similar names in the same city, and most guests will be unfamiliar with the location, indicate the street address beneath the site. Spell out *Saint* in church names, as well as numbers. List the city or town; the state is optional (depending on how familiar guests are with the area).

Below are examples of the various ways to word invitations:

When the bride's family hosts the wedding:

Mr. and Mrs. Charles Andrew Jones
request the honour of your presence
at the marriage of their daughter
Mary Lynn
to
Edward Paul Hill
Saturday, the sixth of May
at four o'clock
All Saints Church
Barton, Texas

When the invitation includes the bride's and groom's parents:

Mr. and Mrs. Charles Andrew Jones
request the honour of your company
at the marriage of their daughter
Mary Lynn
to
Edward Paul Hill
son of
Mr. and Mrs. Donald Lawrence Hill
Saturday, the sixth of May
etc.

Joint sponsorship by the bride's and groom's family: This wording does not clearly spell out the relationship of the sponsors to the bride and groom. Some couples may not be comfortable using the word *children*, while others feel it has a warm sound.

Mr. and Mrs. Charles Andrew Jones
and
Mr. and Mrs. Donald Lawrence Hill
request the pleasure of your company at
the wedding reception of their children
Mary Lynn
and
Edward Paul
Saturday, the sixth of May
etc.

When a widow who has not remarried hosts the wedding: Although a deceased parent is mentioned in a newspaper engagement or wedding announcement, he or she is not listed on the wedding invitation. This is because an invitation is issued to share an occasion together. And, a wedding is a happy occasion; mentioning the deceased parent's name would strike a note of sadness.

Mrs. Robert Kowolsky
requests the honour of your presence
at the marriage of her daughter
Theresa Louise
etc.

When a widower who has not remarried hosts the wedding:

Mr. Robert Harris Kowolsky
requests the honour of your presence
at the marriage of his daughter
Theresa Louise
etc.

When the bride's mother has remarried after being widowed or divorced:

Mr. and Mrs. Ricardo Rojas
request the honour of your presence
at the marriage of Mrs. Roja's daughter
[or, if the bride is close to her stepfather, *their daughter*]
Angela Madelena Mendoza
etc.

When the bride's father has remarried after being widowed or divorced:

Mr. and Mrs. Victor Mendoza
request the honour of your presence
at the marriage of Mr. Mendoza's daughter
[or, if the bride is close to her stepmother, *their daughter*]
Angela Madelena Mendoza
etc.

When the bride's parents are divorced, the invitation is issued by the parent who raised her.

When a divorced mother is not remarried: If issuing the invitations, she may use the traditional divorcée's combination of her maiden and married surnames (*Mrs. Collins Anderson*), or she may drop *Mrs.* and substitute her first name (*Sarah Collins Anderson*). It is also acceptable for her to use her first name, middle name, and married surname (*Mrs. Sarah Beth Anderson*). The rest of the invitation is worded as for a widowed parent.

Sarah Collins Anderson
requests the honour of your presence
at the marriage of her daughter
Abigail Blake
etc.

When a divorced father is not remarried: If he issues the invitation, it carries his full name and the phrase *his daughter*. The wording is the same for a widower who has not remarried (above).

When divorced parents send a joint invitation: This may be sent if parents are still very friendly. Avoid using *Mr. and Mrs.*, since that is no longer the case, and list their names on separate lines—remarried or not.

Sarah Collins Anderson
(or *Mrs. Peter Smith*, if remarried)
and
Steven Randolph Anderson
(or *Mr. Steven Randolph Anderson*)
request the honour of your presence
at the marriage of their daughter
Abigail Blake
to
Christopher Howard Geist
etc.

When divorced parents send two separate invitations: If divorced parents don't want their names to appear together, but the bride wants to acknowledge them equally, a solution is to have one parent issue the invitation to the ceremony and the other to the reception. These are assembled and mailed together like any other wedding invitation.

The ceremony invitation:

Sarah Collins Anderson
(or *Mrs. Peter Smith*, if remarried)
requests the honour of your presence
at the marriage of her daughter
Abigail Blake
to
Christopher Howard Geist
etc.

The reception invitation:

Steven Randolph Anderson
requests the pleasure of your company
Saturday, the sixth of May
at five o'clock
Glen Oaks Country Club
R.s.v.p.
Sixty-two Laurel Lane
Barton, Texas 12345

When the groom's parents are divorced and included on the invitation, adapt the previous examples or follow this:

Mr. and Mrs. Charles Andrew Jones
request the honour of your presence
at the marriage of their daughter
Mary Lynn Jones
to
Edward Paul Hill
son of
Mrs. Sheila Jane Smith
and
Mr. Donald Lawrence Hill
etc.

When a married mother of the bride or groom goes by her maiden name, the parents' names are listed on separate lines, similar to an invitation for divorced parents sending a joint invitation (see previous example).

When a single parent hosts the wedding with a live-in partner, grandmother, aunt, etc.: This form lists the sponsors separately and indicates which is the parent.

Mrs. Estelle Mahoney
and
Mr. Stephen J. Barkley
request the honour of your presence
at the marriage of Mrs. Mahoney's
daughter
Ellen Victoria
etc.

When related hosts, other than parents of the bride, host the wedding: The sponsor's relationship to the bride is spelled out with such words as *his sister*, *her sister*, or *their niece* substituted for *their daughter*.

If friends host the wedding: The invitation lists the bride's full name with *Miss* (or *Ms.*) before it:

Mr. and Mrs. George Anthony Donato
request the honour of your presence
at the marriage of
Miss (Ms.) Cheryl Diane Callas
to
Mr. Arnold Lee Gregory
etc.

The bride's surname appears on the invitations in these special circumstances:

The bride's mother has remarried and is sponsoring the wedding with her new husband (see previous example).

The bride has been previously married and has retained her ex-spouse's name:

Mr. and Mrs. George W. Harvey
request the honour of your presence at the
marriage of their daughter
Ms. Stephanie Harvey Milsap
to
Mr. G. Allen Montclair
etc.

When the couple host the wedding:

If the bride does not have a sponsor, or she and her fiancé wish to sponsor their own wedding, they may issue the invitations themselves.

The honour of your presence
is requested at the marriage of
Miss Margaret Jean Murphy
to
Mr. Leo Stanley Stark
Saturday, the fifth of November
at eleven o'clock
Saint Cecilia's Church
South Bay, California

Personalized printed invitations: Some couples and their parents word their own invitations as a personal expression or to share religious feelings with their guests. Adapt the traditional invitation any way you wish (don't feel you must spell out numbers—7 p.m., for instance), but be sure the necessary information (sponsors' names; ceremony site, date, time; reception site, date, time; address, if any, for replies) is included and is easy to follow. The invitation should be warm, concise, and fit the formality of the celebration:

Warner and Paula Simpson
and
William and Mary Marcus
invite you to share in the joy
of the marriage uniting our children
Nicole and Jerry
Saturday, August 30, 1993
at 4 p.m
at the First Baptist Church
607 Lincoln Avenue
New Petersburg
Worship with us, witness their vows
and join us afterward at
the Church Fellowship Hall.

If you are unable to attend, we ask your
presence in thought and prayer.

R.s.v.p.
(301) 223-1234

Double wedding: The brides are usually sisters, and a single invitation is issued.

Mr. and Mrs. Nicholas Pappas
request the honour of your presence
at the marriage of their daughters
Katherine Denise
to
Milton Zara
and
Christina Eugenia
to
Matthew Homer
Saturday, the first of August
at half after seven o'clock
Saint Barbara's Greek Orthodox Church
Inport, Connecticut

When the brides are not sisters, separate invitations may be sent by each family, or they may issue a joint invitation:

Mr. and Mrs. Samuel Catt Saulsberry

and

Mr. and Mrs. Gaylord Rogers

request the honour of your presence

at the marriage of their daughters

Susan Ann Saulsberry

to

Bruce Raymond Harnett

and

Brenda Lou Rogers

to

Randolph Sloan Lincoln

etc.

Professional Titles

Traditionally, only the groom's full name was used on a wedding invitation, preceded by a title (*Mr.* or *Doctor/Dr.*). The bride's professional title and last name, as well as the title of her mother, were omitted in favor of social titles—*Miss* and *Mrs.* Today, couples often want their names to be printed in the same form: Both either use or omit their titles, and both use their first and middle names. They're also choosing to include their mother's professional titles (if she is a doctor, clergymember, member of the armed services on active duty). Titles of senators and judges and other high officials may be used, but those of lesser officials are usually omitted.

When the bride has a professional title:

Mr. and Mrs. George W. Harvey

request the honour of your presence

at the marriage of

Dr. Stephanie R. Harvey

to

Mr. G. Allen Montclair

etc.

When the bride's father is a doctor: The name of a medical doctor and sometimes a person with a Ph.D. is preceded by *Doctor/Dr.* instead of *Mr.*

Dr. and Mrs. Charles Andrew Jones

request the honour of your presence

at the marriage of their daughter

Mary Lynn

to

Edward Paul Hill

etc.

When the bride's mother is a doctor: The names of the two parents appear on separate lines, in the format of divorced parents.

Mr. Charles Andrew Jones

and

Dr. Susan Jones

request the honour of your presence

at the marriage of their daughter

etc.

When the bride's mother is a judge:

Mr. John Smith

and

The Honorable Jane Smith

request the honour of your presence

at the marriage of their daughter

Jessica Ann

etc.

When the bride's father is a clergy-member: A clergymember's title (*The Reverend, The Reverend Doctor, Rabbi*) is spelled out in full before his or her name.

The Reverend and Mrs. Charles Andrew
Jones
request the honour of your presence
at the marriage of their daughter
Mary Lynn
etc.

When the bride's mother is a clergy-member: The parents' names would appear on separate lines, in the format of divorced parents.

Mr. Charles Andrew Jones
and
The Reverend Susan Jones
request the honour of your presence
at the marriage of their daughter
Mary Lynn
etc.

Military Titles

When used with social invitations, military titles are subject to changing regulations and should always be verified with the commanding officer. The titles *Mr., Mrs., Miss, or Ms.* should never precede a name that mentions a rank and branch of service. A bride or mother in the military may choose not to use her title in favor of the familiar first-name form; if she uses her title on the invitation, she would also use her last name, as she would with any title. Reserve officers do not use military titles unless they are on active duty.

When the bride's father is a military officer hosting the wedding with the bride's mother, his title is spelled out and precedes his name; the branch of service is not mentioned.

Captain and Mrs. Gregory Connor
request the honour of your presence
at the marriage of their daughter
Margaret Kelly
etc.

The groom's or bride's military title appears before his or her name only if he or she holds a rank equivalent to or higher than captain in the army or commander in the navy.

Mr. and Mrs. Michael Simmons
request the honour of your presence
at the marriage of their daughter

Commander Karen Ann Simmons
United States Navy
to
Captain Mark William Burns
United States Navy
etc.

If the bride or groom occupies a lesser rank, it may be listed on the invitation with the branch of service.

Mr. and Mrs. William MacGregor
request the honour of your presence
at the marriage of their daughter
Lisa Susanne
to
Jeffrey Ronald Sherman
Lieutenant, United States Army
etc.

assembling invitations

- Fold the traditional engraved double sheet like a book, with the type on top, the fold to the left.

- Enclosures are usually inserted inside the invitation (or announcement).

- Enclosures may also be placed directly on top of the invitation, before all are slipped inside inner envelope.

- Tissue paper—inserted by the printer to keep ink from smudging—is usually tossed away, but may be left in place.

- Insert invitation in inner envelope with the print facing up toward the back side of the envelope.

- The unsealed inner envelope is inserted into the outer envelope, so that handwritten guests' names are visible when the outer envelope is opened.

If the bride or groom is enlisted, the branch of service may be listed without the rank.

Mr. and Mrs. William MacGregor
request the honour of your presence
at the marriage of their daughter
Lisa Susanne
to
Jeffrey Ronald Sherman
United States Marine Corps
etc.

When the bride's father is a military officer hosting the wedding alone, the line after his name indicates his branch of service (include the word *Retired* if applicable).

Captain Gregory Connor
United States Navy, Retired
requests the honour of your presence
at the marriage of his daughter
Margaret Kelly
etc.

When the bride's parents are divorced and one is in the military, the civilian is listed first, the military person on a separate line, with branch of service on the next line:

Mrs. Jane Hanson
and
Admiral John Hanson
United States Navy
request the honour of your presence
at the marriage of their daughter
Joan Mary
etc.

When the bride's mother is a military officer, she has the option of following the same wording for a military officer issuing an invitation alone (see previous example). However, if issuing the invitation with her husband, the civilian is listed first, the military person on a separate line, with the branch of service on the next line (similar to when parents are divorced, and one is in the military; see previous example):

Mr. Gregory Connor
and
Captain Barbara Connor
United States Navy
request the honour of your presence
at the marriage of their daughter
Margaret Kelly
etc.

Addressing Envelopes

Address all invitations by hand. Use blue, blue-black, or black ink. Never use a typewriter, though you may consider some computers that are able to print envelopes in script type. Most couples address invitations together, often with their families' and wedding-party members' help (see Chapter 3, "Prewedding Parties").

Consider hiring a calligrapher or secretarial service to address invitations. Calligraphy is elegant handwriting done with pen and ink. If you don't know anyone who can execute this classic style, ask friends and family, your stationer, or wedding consultant for referrals. Your stationer will also be able to tell you about the new computerized calligraphy services (one, called The Social Secretary, is found in stationery stores; see Appendix, under Chapter 5, "Invitations & Announcements").

Don't abbreviate streets, cities, or states, and be sure to use zip codes. The only abbreviations used are *Mr., Mrs., Ms., Jr., Dr.,* and *Esq.,* which is abbreviated in social correspondence for an attorney. (Never use *Esquire* or its abbreviation on an invitation addressed to both a husband and wife.)

Note that the guests' full names and addresses (*Mr. and Mrs. James Wallace McDermott*) are written only on the outer envelope, which is stamped and sealed. First names and addresses are *not* written on the inner envelope (just titles and last names—*Mr. and Mrs. McDermott*—are written), which is ungummed and remains unsealed when it is slipped inside the outer envelope.

The proper way to address mail to your guests:

A divorcée is addressed by either the very traditional *Mrs. Phillips Ross* (a combination of maiden and married surnames) or *Mrs. Joan Ross.* She can also revert to her maiden name (*Mrs. Joan Phillips*).

A separated woman is addressed on an envelope as *Mrs. Joan Ross.*

A widow is addressed on an envelope as *Mrs. Earl Jones.*

A single woman, even a child, is addressed as *Miss (Ms.) Sandra Lightner.*

A boy under age 13 is addressed as *Master Jordan Sullivan.*

Follow these guidelines when sending invitations:

Children under 18 are not listed in the address on the outer envelope. Their names *should* be listed under their parents' names on the inner envelope.

    Mr. and Mrs. McDermott

    Kevin, Christopher, and Mary

Avoid using the phrase "*And Family*" so that everyone who is invited feels the invitation is especially for him or her.

A person over 18 years old should receive a separate wedding invitation, whether or not he or she is currently living with his or her parents.

If two siblings live together at another address, one invitation may be sent, with the brother's and sister's (or two brothers', two sisters') names listed alphabetically on the envelope:

Mr. Arther Reed

Ms. Kellie Reed

A married woman who uses a military title, and her husband:

Outer Envelope:

Captain Sheila Vincente

Mr. David Vincente

1010 Maplewood Road

Metropolis, Ohio 12345

Inner Envelope (on one line):

Captain Vincente and Mr. Vincente

another formal invitation option

Some formal invitations are folded twice—reminiscent of the time when envelopes were smaller than the invitations.

- Fold these formal invitations first in half, from left to right (forming a "book"), then again, from top to bottom. Printing may run across both sides of the second fold.

- Enclosures are inserted inside the second fold of the invitation.

- Insert invitation in inner envelope fold-side down.

- Unsealed inner envelope is inserted into the outer envelope (address side facing the back flap), so that handwritten guests' names are visible when the outer envelope is opened (see illustration, opposite bottom).

mailing invitations

- Weigh a sample assembled invitation to gauge correct postage. Enclosures may require extra postage. (The last problem you want: All invitations are missing, or returned, due to insufficient postage!)

- Mail invitations six weeks before the wedding (eight weeks before if the wedding falls on a holiday or long weekend, or if you're inviting many out-of-town guests).

- Expect regrets. On average, about 25 percent of those you invite will not be able to attend. These refusals will give you the opportunity to invite people who had to be eliminated from your guest list—now on a "wish list."

- It's acceptable for guests to receive invitations up to two weeks before the wedding. Your friends and relatives will enjoy the invitation whenever it arrives.

Married woman who uses a professional title, and her husband:

Outer Envelope:

Dr. Carol Kim

Mr. Keith Kim

Inner Envelope (on one line):

Dr. Kim and Mr. Kim

A married couple who are both doctors are addressed as follows:

Outer Envelope:

The Doctors Klein

Inner Envelope:

The Doctors Klein

A married couple with different last names or an **unmarried couple living together** receive one invitation with their names listed alphabetically.

Outer Envelope:

Mr. Joshua Adams

Ms. Jane Moore

393 Atlantic Boulevard

Metropolis, Ohio 12345

Inner Envelope:

Mr. Adams and Ms. Moore

Two unrelated friends who are roommates should be sent two invitations.

Quick Invitations

If you're getting married quickly—between one and six weeks from now—there will not be time to get invitations formally printed and mailed. (There are, however, formal preprinted invitations available with space to fill in names, date, and place, as well as computerized calligraphy services, available at stationery stores.)

If possible, guests should receive an invitation at least two weeks before the wedding. If time is tight, your parents may send handwritten notes or invite guests personally by telephone, telegram, or mailgram. Be sure that all information that would be included on a printed invitation—who's getting married, where, when, style of the service, location of the reception, R.s.v.p. address, and a return address (so that guests know where they may send gifts)—is passed along to guests, however you spread the word. If you are telephoning, indicate that your parents are the sponsors by saying *"Mom and Dad wanted you to be with us...."*

Handwritten quick invitation:

Dear Rose,

Judith and Michael are to be married at half past three on Sunday, the fifth of September, in the chapel of Temple Emanuel in Green Heights. It will be a small wedding with a reception afterward at our house. You know how much we all want you to be with us on that day.

Affectionately,

Ruth

Please respond to:

Mr. and Mrs. Andrew Hastings

Fifteen Stone Drive

Birmingham, Alabama 12345

Forms of Address

PERSONAGE	INVITATION: OUTER ENVELOPE	INVITATION: INNER ENVELOPE/ NAME CARD
Clergymember* Protestant (no degree)	The Reverend Paul Jones	The Reverend Jones
Clergymember Protestant (with degree)	The Reverend Doctor Paul Jones or The Reverend Paul Jones, Ph.D.	The Reverend Doctor Jones
Clergymember Roman Catholic	The Reverend Paul Jones	Father Jones
Eastern Orthodox Priest	The Reverend Father George Kontos	Father Kontos
Roman Catholic Bishop	The Most Reverend Daniel Bell, Bishop of Texas	Bishop Bell
Vicar	The Reverend Robert MacDonald	Monsignor MacDonald
Dean	The Reverend Samuel Brandon	The Reverend Brandon
Rabbi (no degree)	Rabbi Nathan Ziff	Rabbi Ziff
Rabbi (with degree)	Rabbi Nathan Ziff, D.D.	Dr. Ziff
Cantor	Cantor David Levy	Cantor Levy
Professor	Martin S. Severino, Ph.D. or Professor Martin Severino	Dr. Severino or Professor Severino
Judge	The Honorable Walter Reynolds	Judge Reynolds
Lawyer	Mr. Alfred Standish or Alfred Standish, Esq.	Mr. Standish
Mayor	The Honorable Patricia Kelly, Mayor of Middletown	Mayor Kelly or Ms. Kelly
Army Officer	Captain Lee Wainwright, U.S. Army	Captain Wainwright
Navy Officer	Lieutenant William G. Smith, U.S. Navy	Lieutenant Smith
Physician	Marcella D. Hopkins, M.D.	Dr. Hopkins

*Check with your clergymember's office to confirm his/her title, as there are many variations.

Enclosures

These small, printed cards are enclosed with the invitation and match the invitation in style and paper quality.

Reception Cards

The formal reception card:
> Mr. and Mrs. Charles Andrew Jones
> request the pleasure of your company
> Saturday, the sixth of May
> at five o'clock
> Glen Oaks Country Club
> Barton, Texas

R.s.v.p.
Sixty-two Laurel Lane
Barton, Texas 12345

The simplified reception card:
> Reception
> immediately following the ceremony
> Glen Oaks Country Club

Kindly respond
Sixty-two Laurel Lane
Barton, Texas 12345

A combined ceremony-and-reception invitation without enclosure cards: This popular invitation is often sent when all guests are invited to both ceremony and reception. (If you are having both the ceremony and reception at home, there is no need to mention the reception, since it will be assumed that one will follow and all guests will be included.)

> Mr. and Mrs. Charles Andrew Jones
> request the honour of your presence
> at the marriage of their daughter
> Mary Lynn
> to
> Edward Paul Hill

> Saturday, the sixth of May
> at four o'clock
> All Saints Church
> Barton, Texas
> and afterward at
> Glen Oaks Country Club

Please respond
Sixty-two Laurel Lane
Barton, Texas 12345

When parents are divorced and one hosts the reception:
> Mr. James Gilrod
> requests the pleasure of your company
> at the wedding reception of his daughter
> Sarah Jessica
> Saturday, the fifteenth of June
> at six o'clock
> Maple Hill Inn
> Little Rock, Arkansas
> etc.

When the couple host the reception, they may enclose this reception card (or a *simplified reception card*—see earlier example):
> The pleasure of your company is
> requested
> Saturday, the fifth of November
> at half after eleven o'clock
> The Waterside
> South Bay, California

R.s.v.p.
1600 Ocean Parkway, Apartment 12L
South Bay, California 12345

Ceremony Cards: If you will invite people to the reception who will not be included at the ceremony, send invitations to the reception and enclose ceremony cards (or informal notes) for a select few.

Reception invitation:

Mr. and Mrs. Charles Andrew Jones
request the pleasure of your company
at the wedding reception of their
daughter
Mary Lynn
and
Edward Paul Hill
Saturday, the sixth of May
at five o'clock
Glen Oaks Country Club
Barton, Texas

R.s.v.p.
Sixty-two Laurel Lane
Barton, Texas 12345

The separate ceremony card:

Mr. and Mrs. Charles Andrew Jones
request the honour of your presence
Saturday, the sixth of May
at four o'clock
All Saints Church
Barton, Texas

A simplified ceremony card: If very few people are invited to the ceremony, the ceremony invitations may be printed or handwritten on informal note cards.

Ceremony
at four o'clock
All Saints Church

Ceremony-admittance cards: These small cards are printed when there is a chance that an uninvited person may try

to attend the ceremony, or when the wedding is held in a public place (e.g., a museum, mansion, yacht). Ceremony cards are enclosed with the invitation; guests present the cards to ushers for admittance, upon arrival:

Please present this card
The First Congregational Church
Saturday, the twelfth of March

At-home cards: These small cards may be enclosed with formal invitations, but are more often included with announcements (see "Announcements" section). They announce your new address and the date that it is effective. You may either print your names on the cards or not, and mail them with your invitations and announcements.

Traditional at-home card:

At home
after the twenty-sixth of August
1413 Fountain Avenue
Atlanta, Georgia 12345

At-home card with names:

Mr. and Mrs. John Simon Eagle
after the tenth of April
1035 Fifth Avenue, Apartment 9B
New York, New York 12345

If the bride is keeping her name, or decides to hyphenate it with her husband's surname, she may announce it on the at-home card:

Dr. Mary Ann Janacek
(or Dr. Mary Ann Janacek-Eagle)
Mr. John Simon Eagle
after the tenth of April
123 Robin Lane
Phoenix, Arizona 24689

Name cards: If you wish, you may send separate name cards in invitations or announcements, or alone, after the honeymoon. These cards will inform professional colleagues of the decision to change or hyphenate your name.

Kirsten Andrews
will be changing her name to
Kirsten Andrews Sullivan
following her marriage
June 16, 1994

When a couple adopt a new surname together:

Kirsten Andrews and Roger Sullivan
will be adopting the surname
Andrews-Sullivan
following their marriage
June 16, 1994

Pew cards: These small cards are used to assign special seating to very close friends and relatives at the ceremony. They may be sent with the invitation—or better still, after the acceptance has been received. Pew cards may be handwritten notes from the bride's parents or printed cards.

Please present this card
The First Congregational Church
Saturday, the twelfth of March

Pew number 9

Within-the-ribbons cards: For large formal weddings, small printed cards may be sent with the phrase *within the ribbons* in the lower left corner, where the pew number is usually listed. This phrase will indicate to ushers that guests should be seated in a special reserved section; the *last* row is decorated with festive bows or ribbons.

Please present this card
The First Congregational Church
Saturday, the twelfth of March

Within the ribbons

Reception response cards: Traditionally, response cards were avoided for formal weddings, as they implied that the person invited would not know that proper etiquette required them to respond with a handwritten note. (See Chapter 18, "Wedding Guests," for how to word handwritten responses.) Today, however, for convenience and immediacy, they are almost always sent with wedding invitations. (Guests can also enclose a personal note with the response card, expressing their best wishes.)

Check post-office regulations regarding size of cards and envelopes and placement of the return address. Return envelopes should be stamped and have printed addresses.

Some response cards are blank, with an *R.s.v.p.* date (usually three weeks before the wedding) printed in the bottom left corner. They allow guests to write a personal note on the card; these cards become keepsakes for the bride, and might be saved in a scrapbook.

Blank response cards:

The favour of a reply is requested
by the fifteenth of September
or
Kindly respond
by September 15

Fill-in response cards: Other response cards allow guests to fill in their name and circle or check appropriate wording; add the word *not* next to *attend* if they will not accept the invitation.

_____

accepts

regrets

Saturday, July second

Court Hotel

Charlottesville

    or:

_____*will___attend*

Rain cards: If an outdoor wedding is planned, enclose rain cards with an alternate location, just in case.

In case of rain

the wedding and reception

will be held in

Myers Park Methodist Church

424 River Road

one o'clock in the afternoon

Travel cards: Enclose travel cards to let guests know that you've chartered a bus or ferry to get them to a distant or out-of-the-way site.

Special-transportation cards:

A special bus will leave

Saint Mary's Parish Hall

at three o'clock in the afternoon

and arrive back in Washington

at eight o'clock in the evening.

Please present this card to the driver.

Travel cards are also used to inform guests that you've arranged for them to park at a nearby garage. The card can serve as an admission pass if you've arranged to pick up the cost and gratuity.

Parking-arrangements card:

Parking provided

McKenzie Parking Garage

2018 Main Street

Gratuities included. Please present this card to the parking attendant.

Direction Cards/Maps: These directions to the ceremony site should be enclosed with the invitation and printed in a manner as beautiful and professional as the invitation itself. Check that they are accurate, and have extras available at the ceremony site. After the ceremony, the ushers see that guests have directions and transportation to the reception.

Accommodation cards: These cards are sent to out-of-town guests who will need hotel reservations. The cards, which may be printed by the hotel or reprinted by you in a style that matches your invitation, let guests know that a block of rooms has been reserved, and list the hotel's phone number. Guests can then call and make their own reservations.

Long Weekend Wedding response cards: A weekend wedding filled with festivities calls for several invitations (see "Long Weekend Wedding Invitations" section). Along with the wedding invitation, enclose an itinerary of Long Weekend Wedding events, and one longer R.s.v.p. card with boxes to check off for each event. Or, enclose small printed R.s.v.p. cards for each additional party. Print addresses on each stamped response envelope, since each might have a different host. (Hosts of each weekend party may instead opt to send separate invitations and response cards.)

long weekend wedding response cards

Have response cards printed for these or other similar festivities, and enclose them with the invitation:

- **welcome cocktail party**
- **rehearsal dinner**
- **museum tour**
- **bride's team vs. groom's team softball game**
- **pool party and picnic**
- **wedding-day breakfast**
- **postwedding brunch**

Progressive Wedding Invitations

When the relatives of either the bride or the groom live in another city than that where the wedding is held, someone (a parent, grandparent, the couple) may host one or more postwedding parties. Then friends and relatives in those towns and cities can meet and celebrate with the newlyweds (see Chapter 10, "Special Weddings & New Ways to Wed"). These second or third receptions need not be gift-giving occasions, but are often formal events with receiving lines, and require invitations that are equally formal.

Formal Progressive Wedding invitations or handwritten notes are appropriate.

Progressive Wedding invitation:

Mr. and Mrs. Albert Hughs Hudson
request the pleasure of your company
at a reception in honour of
Mr. and Mrs. Theodore Russell Hudson
Sunday, the fourteenth of January
at four o'clock
Castle Mountain Inn
Woodtown, Vermont

R.s.v.p.
263 Spruce Road
Woodtown, Vermont 12345

Progressive Wedding reception cards:

If you are sending announcements after the wedding, you can tuck in the appropriate second or third reception card (use the wording for reception cards in previous examples) to invite those who weren't at the wedding to the follow-up celebration(s). It is not unusual to have different guest lists for each Progressive Wedding reception—depending on the city where each celebration takes place.

Long Weekend Wedding Invitations

If several wedding celebrations are planned during your wedding weekend, send wedding guests a packet or invitational brochure detailing all of the festivities. Perhaps print a sketch of the wedding site on the brochure's cover; place the wedding invitation inside. Additional pages might include a map outlining the wedding route, invitations to the rehearsal dinner, brunch, and other events. Also enclose a chronological list of events, with suggested clothing (e.g., *bathing suits and shorts for the Saturday afternoon barbecue*). Long-distance guests may be more likely to make the trip if they know there will be many opportunities for them to visit with other friends and relatives.

Keeping Track of Responses

Once invitations arrive, you will receive formal written acceptances or regrets, informal notes, response cards, even phone calls! Set up a system to record who's coming, who's not. Also track the gifts sent (include each guest's complete name, address, gift, when thank-you note is sent). Finally, note their table number once the seating plan is complete.

No response. If your R.s.v.p. date arrives and you still haven't heard from some guests, call them and ask if they received the invitation. Your caterer or banquet manager will need a final head count, and you will have to finish your seating plan.

Recalling Invitations

If a formal wedding must be canceled or postponed after the invitations have gone out, guests should be notified as soon as possible. It is best to do this with printed cards rush ordered from a stationer.

If there has been a death in the family:

Mrs. Gerald Timothy Allen
regrets that the death of
Mr. Allen
obliges her to recall the invitations
to the wedding of her daughter
Sarah Louise
Saturday, the third of February

has been postponed from
Saturday, the fourth of June
until
Saturday, the eighteenth of October
at four o'clock
Grace Episcopal Church
Wilfordshire, CT

The above wording indicates that the wedding will not take place *as planned.* A death or serious illness in the family means that a large wedding would be inappropriate, but the marriage may still take place as a small family ceremony. The couple may dress in their formal wedding attire, but the only attendants to participate are the honor attendants.

If the wedding is canceled, invitations are recalled with engraved or printed cards if there is time. If time is short, however, invitations may be recalled with personal notes, telegrams, or by phone. Calls are made in the name of the bride's parents. Reasons other than a death or illness in the family need not be mentioned.

If the wedding is postponed and a new date has been set:

Mr. and Mrs. Stuart Dean Jefferson
announce that the marriage of their
daughter
Virginia Ann
to
Frank Martin Gallagher

If the wedding is canceled:

Mr. and Mrs. Warren Troy Peterson
announce that the marriage of
their daughter
Ellen Marie
to
Henry Carl Smith
will not take place

invitation-response tips

Here are ways to keep track of R.s.v.p.'s:

● *Index cards.* Create an alphabetical file with each couple's/family's information on 3x5-inch cards. Later, you can reorganize and group cards by tables.

● *Notebooks.* Reserve a page for each couple's/family's information.

● *Ledgers/Planners.* Many wedding planners, such as BRIDE'S Wedding Planner, have pages set aside for guest responses.

● *Computer.* Programs are now available to keep track of all planning information—from florists and bakers to guests.

Announcements

Wedding announcements may be sent after a family ceremony or an elopement, or to those cut from the guest list or on your "wish list." They are usually not mailed to anyone who received an invitation, and do not obligate the receiver to send a gift; they simply spread the happy news.

who gets announcements?

- business associates
- guests invited by phone
- friends, relatives, not receiving invitations

Include the date, year, and city in which the marriage took place. It is optional to mention the actual ceremony site.

Printing, paper, style, and addressing should match invitations. Order announcements when you order invitations and enclosures. Ask bridesmaids to help address announcements and invitations at a wedding work party (see Chapter 3, "Prewedding Parties"). Or, bring announcement and invitation envelopes to the same calligrapher.

Enclose at-home cards and name cards, if you'll send them, with your announcements (or with your wedding invitations).

Mail announcements immediately after the ceremony. You (or a bridesmaid) can drop them in the mail as you leave the wedding reception.

Traditional announcement wording:
Mr. and Mrs. Peter Young Chow
have the honour of announcing
the marriage of their daughter
Annette Elizabeth
and
Leonard Park Ling
on Friday, the tenth of July
One thousand nine hundred and
ninety-three
Our Redeemer Lutheran Church
Seattle, Washington

Other announcement wording:
Mr. and Mrs Peter Young Chow
have the honour to announce
the marriage of their daughter
etc.

Mr. and Mrs. Peter Young Chow
announce the marriage of their daughter
etc.

When the bride or her parents are divorced or widowed, wording is varied as in printed invitations. For example:
Sarah Collins Anderson
and
Steven Randolph Anderson
have the honour of announcing
the marriage of their daughter
etc.

When the bride and groom issue the announcement: This is an option if you have no parents or close relatives to send announcements, have been previously married, or have been on your own and want to announce your own wedding.
Deborah Suzanne Schwartz,
[Dr. Deborah Schwartz, etc.]
and
[Mr.] Eric Davis Fisher
announce their marriage
Friday, the twenty-seventh of November
One thousand nine hundred and
ninety-four
Chicago, Illinois

Other Printing Needs

It will save time if you order all of your stationery needs when you order your invitations. Then, all printed material will be compatible and will be on hand when needed, throughout your engagement months.

Thank-you notes: It is best for the bride and groom to each choose formal notes, since each will be writing thank-you notes before the wedding. The couple's name (*Mr. and Mrs. Jon Word*) or a joint monogram can be printed on the stationery they will use after their wedding. You should never use stationery printed with your married name or initials until after the wedding. (See Chapter 17, "Wedding Gifts.") Be sure to check post-office regulations regarding size of cards and envelopes and placement of the return address before you order.

Gift-received cards: If you're planning a long honeymoon or a large wedding and know that you won't be able to send thank-you notes as promptly as you should (see Chapter 17, "Wedding Gifts"), order printed gift-received cards. These acknowledge your receipt of the gift and promise that a personal thank-you will follow.

Ann Marie Brown
[or *Steven Ray Jones*, if a second set is ordered]
acknowledges with thanks
the receipt of your wedding gift
and will take pleasure in writing a
personal note
at an early date.

Notepaper can be engraved with your new address only, so you can both use it after the wedding (or before, if you live together). City and street names are printed in full, not abbreviated. Numerals may be spelled out if you prefer.

Wedding programs are extremely helpful in guiding your guests through the ceremony, and they are special mementos. They include the date, time, and place of the ceremony, as well as a listing of the participants (the couple, parents, wedding party, officiant, organist, soloist, choir members). Programs are very useful for translating prayers and explaining customs at an interfaith or intercultural wedding that may be unfamiliar to some guests. You can also preserve original vows, a special greeting you have written, a tribute to a deceased relative or friend. Your program can be elaborate or simple. Some couples prepare a booklet that matches their wedding colors and has a cover sketch; a preprinted wedding bulletin (from religious supply houses) with your wedding service photocopied inside; or a calligraphy-inscribed scroll (see Appendix, under Chapter 4, "Planning Your Wedding").

Reaffirmation of Vows

Whether they have eloped, married in city hall, or come to the point of celebrating a very special wedding anniversary, many couples decide to have a reaffirmation ceremony, during which they repeat their marriage vows to each other. The officiant often designs the service, which may take place at a house of worship or at home (see Chapter 20, "Reaffirmation").

Reaffirmation-invitation wording:

The honour of your presence
is requested at the reaffirmation
of the wedding vows of
Mr. and Mrs. Walter May
Saturday, the eighth of June
at three o'clock
Christian Reformed Church
Amsterdam, Michigan
and afterward at a reception in
the church parlour

Wedding Anniversary Invitations

You may issue a formal invitation to a formal celebration with fifty or more guests. Often, the couple's children and their spouses are the hosts for this event.

Wedding anniversary-invitation wording:

Mr. and Mrs. Joshua Spiegel
request the pleasure of your company
at a reception to honour the thirtieth
wedding anniversary
of Mrs. Spiegel's parents
Mr. and Mrs. Morris Weidman
the evening of Wednesday, the second of
August
half after eight o'clock
1614 Greatfalls Avenue
Minneapolis, Minnesota 12345

Kindly reply

THE WEDDING PARTY

A wedding celebrates family and friends as well as the bride and groom. Although the marriage can be legally performed with only five people present—the couple, two witnesses, and an officiant, most couples want those who are important in their lives to be part of the wedding party. The traditional roles of best man, maid of honor, bridesmaids, ushers, and child attendants have changed dramatically over the years, due to the changes in society at large. Couples are marrying at a later age, and the nuclear family has often been replaced by the blended family, which includes stepparents and stepsiblings. The bride's honor attendant may be a man; the groom's best man may be his father. The logistics of organizing the wedding party may also be more complex, since friends often live long-distance. (The earlier they are asked to be in the wedding party, the sooner they can make travel and vacation plans.) Below are the members of the wedding party and their responsibilities.

The Bride's Role

Traditionally, the bride (and often her mother) has been largely responsible for coordinating the wedding and ensuring the comfort and enjoyment of all the guests. Today, however, the bride and groom may plan—and pay for—all or part of the wedding, and share in all of the planning decisions. Since most engaged couples are two-career couples, the bride may also hire a wedding consultant—a wedding-planning professional who will do the shopping legwork for her, interview wedding-service professionals and present her with options, and coordinate the details of the prewedding parties and of the wedding day itself.

THE BRIDE:

Discusses budget with groom, her family and the groom's family (if appropriate). This is the first step in planning.

Chooses the wedding date, style, and site. In most major cities, weddings should be planned one year—sometimes two years—in advance, in order to book the sites and wedding-service professionals of preference.

Visits the ceremony officiant with her fiancé to discuss procedures and any special requests. Signs up for premarital counseling, (see Chapter 4, "Planning Your Wedding").

Chooses the honor attendant and bridesmaids. Shortly after telling them of the engagement, she invites each in a personal way, expressing what the individual's participation would mean to her, being forthright about expenses involved. (While it's not customary to pay for maids' dresses, hotel accommodations, or travel, the bride may make that her thank-you gift to her attendants. If so, she should tell them this when she invites them to be in the wedding party.)

Seeks recommendations for photographers, florists, stationers, other wedding-service professionals from family and friends. (See Chapter 4, "Planning Your Wedding.")

Shops for bridesmaids' dresses. Considers attendants' budgets, prospects for wearing the dress again, body shapes, and tastes. Tries to let bridesmaids make the final selection from the three styles she likes the most (see Chapter 7, "Wedding Clothes").

Delegates duties among attendants. Tries not to overload her bridesmaids with requests to shop for dresses, bands, or for help in addressing invitations, making favors, sampling menus. Doesn't expect any one person to share every planning trauma or delight.

Gives each attendant a small thank-you gift (e.g., a pendant or silver picture frame, perhaps engraved with attendant's initials and wedding date). This may be presented at the rehearsal dinner, or perhaps the bridesmaids' luncheon or tea, if she is hosting it (see Chapter 17, "Wedding Gifts").

Plans a bridesmaids' luncheon or tea. Getting the bridesmaids together is a fun way for them to get acquainted (if they don't already know each other).

Arranges lodging for any long-distance bridesmaids, if needed. (The bride may choose to pay for this cost, as her thank-you gift to them.)

Shops with groom for wedding rings, and has them engraved. More grooms than ever before are choosing to wear wedding rings, and most ceremonies are double-ring ceremonies. Traditionally, the bride pays for the groom's wedding ring; the groom, for the bride's. The groom may have strong opinions about the style and should be consulted. Many couples choose matching bands.

Shops for a wedding gift for the groom.

This is an optional but meaningful gesture. Gifts may range from the traditional, such as gold cuff links to wear down the aisle, to the more creative—a scrapbook filled with courtship mementos (see Chapter 17, "Wedding Gifts").

Stands in the receiving line with the groom. The receiving line is optional, but more couples are realizing that guests want to share the joy of the marriage with them immediately after the ceremony ends. Mothers and attendants also stand in the line, but today, attendants, as well as fathers, may circulate among guests.

May be introduced by the bandleader—with groom (after the wedding party)—to all reception guests.

Dances a first dance to a preselected song with the groom. She may also dance during the same song with both fathers and the best man (see Chapter 13, "Your Reception." Later, she may dance again with her father to a preselected, sentimental song just for father and daughter (see Chapter 14, "Wedding Music"). She may also dance with her brothers, the ushers, and special guests at the reception.

Takes time before leaving the reception to spend a few moments alone with her parents. Also sends them thank-you flowers from the honeymoon destination.

Sends thank-you notes. With her fiancé, the bride acknowledges every gift in a personal note to the sender (see Chapter 17, "Wedding Gifts").

The Groom's Role

As mentioned earlier, grooms today play an active role in wedding planning—sharing the finances and decisions. Often, the negotiating skills developed during the engagement months set a precedent for the way the couple will work as a team throughout their marriage. Together, the bride and groom should decide early on what responsibilities and areas of wedding planning he is interested in—and best able to handle.

THE GROOM:
Discusses budget with the bride, his family, and the bride's family (if appropriate).

Makes sure that his family's guest list is compiled early. Ensures that titles (e.g., Miss/Ms., Sgt.), first and last names, middle initials (for formal invitations), are filled in, as well as cities and states, street numbers, zip codes, and phone numbers. Keeps list to the number he and his fiancée have agreed upon.

Helps fiancée research and compare the services of wedding professionals. Helps compile a list of the caterers, photographers, videographers, florists, musicians, and other individuals they want the wedding consultant to interview. Or, if couple will not be hiring a wedding consultant, the groom divides up the list so that he and his fiancée *each* visit a few. Reviews the information gathered with fiancée before making decisions.

Visits the ceremony officiant with fiancée to discuss procedures, music, and special requests.

Chooses the best man and ushers. Asks them to stand up for him shortly after he tells them the news of his engagement. Tells them about the wedding attire that will be required, and the expected rental fee (unless he will cover this, as his gift to them).

Reminds his parents of their role in planning the rehearsal dinner. Traditionally, this prewedding party is hosted by the groom's parents (see Chapter 3, "Prewedding Parties"). The groom may take responsibility for it, especially if he is financing it. That evening, he presents his ushers with thank-you gifts that show his appreciation, such as cuff links, initialed key rings (see Chapter 17, "Wedding Gifts").

Pays for the flowers for the bride (her bouquet and going-away corsage), mothers, any women of honor (e.g., grandmothers, aunts, friends). Although the bride will most likely choose the floral arrangements, it is traditional for the groom to make the romantic gesture of picking up this tab.

Shops with bride for wedding rings and has them engraved. The groom should ask her if she prefers a plain gold band, one with gemstones or diamonds, or one that matches her engagement ring. Many couples choose matching bands.

Shops for a gift for the bride (optional). He might send her a strand of pearls to wear with her gown (the traditional gift), or a gold locket with a favorite picture of them together (see Chapter 17, "Wedding Gifts").

Sets up the day and time for getting the marriage license and any other necessary documents (see Chapter 4, "Planning Your Wedding"). Afterward, he might take his fiancée to lunch or tea to celebrate the occasion.

Makes all reservations and arrangements for the honeymoon. Usually, the bride and groom will both decide where they want to go, but traditionally, the groom surprises the bride with some of the details, and pays the tab. Two-career couples may share the expense.

Reserves a block of rooms in a local hotel for out-of-town wedding guests. The groom is also responsible for arranging lodging for any long-distance ushers, if needed. (He may choose to pay for this cost, as his gift to them.)

Researches, hires, and oversees contract details for one or more specific areas of the wedding—unless involved in everything. Many couples target key areas, such as music, liquor, photography, as the groom's responsibility.

Stands in the receiving line (if there is one) with bride.

May be announced by bandleader—

with bride (after the wedding party)—to all reception guests.

Dances a first dance to a preselected song with the bride. May also dance during the same song with both mothers, the honor attendant (see Chapter 13, "Your Reception"). Later in the reception, he may dance again with his mother. Just as the bride dances with her father, the groom should share this sentimental moment dancing with his mother, to a preselected song (see Chapter 14, "Wedding Music").

Responds to the best man's toast at the reception. The groom should rise to thank the best man for his good wishes, then toast his bride and thank her parents for hosting the celebration.

Takes time before leaving the reception to spend a few moments alone with his parents. Sends them thank-you flowers from the honeymoon destination.

Sends thank-you notes, together with his bride, to acknowledge each gift (see Chapter 17, "Wedding Gifts").

The Honor Attendant's Role

The role can be filled by anyone who is very close to the bride—single or married, young or old, usually female. The matron of honor is a married woman, the maid of honor is a single woman, and the maiden of honor is a young girl or child. A male honor attendant might be called a person of honor (see "New Attendants' Roles" section). You may choose your sister, a longtime friend, favorite cousin, or roommate. Some brides have asked their mother or grandmother, or a favorite aunt, to fill this role. *Note*: You needn't ask your fiancé's sister to be your honor attendant unless she also happens to be a close friend. If you have two sisters, or two best friends, ask both to be honor attendants, and divide the duties between them.

THE HONOR ATTENDANT:

Assists the bride with prewedding tasks whenever possible. There are no responsibilities that necessarily set an honor attendant apart from the bridesmaids during the engagement months. She might help address invitations, take charge of recording and displaying wedding gifts. Since she is especially close to the bride, she will probably share confidences and offer moral support.

Arranges a date to have all bridesmaids' gowns fitted. A lot of logistics are involved in coordinating the schedules of several bridesmaids for fittings and prewedding festivities. It helps if the honor attendant conveys scheduling information. She might even send out a "wedding newsletter" to all attendants—to communicate information about clothing, travel plans, prewedding parties (see Appendix, under Chapter 4, "Planning Your Wedding"). On wedding day, the honor attendant checks that each bridesmaid is properly dressed (e.g., flowers on the same side of each maid's hair, pearl necklaces in place), and on

a pregnant attendant

Today, pregnancy does not rule out an attendant's participation in the wedding ceremony, as long as both the bride and the mother-to-be feel comfortable with the role. Below, some questions to discuss and consider.

● How pregnant will the attendant be by the wedding date? Might she give birth near the wedding date?

● Will the attendant be uncomfortable standing at the altar for a long period of time? Arrange to have chairs set up for the entire wedding party.

● What style of dress might she wear to match what the other bridesmaids will wear? What will her dress size be at the time of the wedding? Can you order extra material to enlarge her dress, just in case it doesn't fit?

● What other positions of honor might she fill, if she chooses not to walk down the aisle? Perhaps she might read a poem or Scripture, sit near the guest-book table, carry a bouquet, and be seated in a pew of honor before the first attendant walks down the aisle.

time for the ceremony.

Pays for her entire wedding outfit, except the flowers. The bride may offer to help out with, or completely cover these expenses, as her thank-you gift.

Attends all prewedding parties and may host one with the other attendants. Along with the other bridesmaids, she may co-host a shower, a bridesmaids' luncheon or tea for the bride, or a wedding breakfast the morning of the wedding for the bride and her close female relatives and friends.

Greets the ceremony officiant and shows him or her where to change clothes, if it's a home wedding. The bride and her immediate family will be too busy to deal with these details.

Precedes the bride and her father down the aisle. Two honor attendants might walk side-by-side in the procession and recession.

Arranges the bride's train and veil, holds the bride's bouquet as she stands next to her during the ceremony. Two honor attendants divide the responsibilities for veil, train, bouquet, ring.

Holds the groom's ring during the ceremony, till it is needed. The honor attendant might slip it onto her middle finger or her thumb, or carry it in a hidden pocket or small satin bag (held with her bouquet) for safekeeping.

May sign the marriage certificate as one of the two witnesses required by law. The witness, who must be at least 18 in order to sign a legal document, and the maid or matron of honor do not have to be the same person. For example, if the bride's best friend breaks her leg and can't walk down the aisle, she could still be designated as the witness and sign the certificate. A second-time bride might choose to have her young daughter as the honor attendant, then designate someone of legal age to be the legal witness.

Stands next to the groom in the receiving line and sits on his left at the head table if it's a seated reception. Once the receiving line disperses, she's free to enjoy the reception as an honored guest.

May be announced—with the best man—to all reception guests immediately before the newlyweds.

May dance with the best man during the newlyweds' first dance. May dance with the ushers throughout the wedding.

May take time out to help the bride bustle her train, remove her headpiece, change for the honeymoon. She should be alert to the bride's needs throughout the wedding, and be available to run short errands, and retrieve accessories from the changing room. She may also take charge of bringing the bride's gown home or to a dry cleaner, and with the best man, may deposit any gifts of checks or money in the bank while the couple are on their honeymoon (first listing the guests' names and the amount of each gift). She may also be asked to move gifts from the wedding site to the newlyweds' home.

The Best Man's Role

This indispensable role is usually filled by the groom's most trustworthy friend or relative. His brother, cousin, best friend, father, even a close female friend—or "best woman (see the "New Attendants' Roles" section) are all appropriate choices. The best man's duties are many and varied. He usually organizes the bachelor party, is chief of staff at the wedding, toastmaster at the reception, and personal aide and adviser to the groom. Although any of his tasks may be assigned to one of the ushers, the best man is expected to hold the bride's ring during the ceremony, offer the first toast, and lighten the groom's load.

THE BEST MAN:

Checks on such wedding details as bills for the flowers (the groom's responsibility) and accommodations for out-of-town ushers.

Sees that the groom is properly outfitted and at the church or synagogue on time for the ceremony. The best man is the groom's personal bodyguard/valet for the hours leading up to the wedding.

Hands the ceremony officiant a sealed envelope with his fee (from the groom) immediately after the ceremony. He will also make sure any altar servers are remembered with a gift, envelope, or whatever is recommended.

May sign the marriage license as a witness. The officiant will file the license at the municipal hall after the wedding, and may give the couple a copy on wedding day. It is the best man's job to make sure the groom knows where this copy is at the end of the wedding.

Carries the bride's wedding ring down the aisle. (He may keep it in a pocket.) At the appropriate moment in the ceremony, he hands it to the officiant.

Oversees the ushers, making sure that all are uniformly dressed (e.g., cummerbunds are pleat-side up), thoroughly briefed, and at the ceremony site at the appointed hour. Someone will have to remind ushers how to properly seat guests (see "The Bridesmaids' and Ushers' Roles" section).

May stand in the receiving line or circulate among guests. Attendants' participation in this tradition is optional (the bride's decision).

May be announced—with the honor attendant—to all reception guests, immediately before the newlyweds.

May dance with the honor attendant, then the bride, during the newlyweds' first dance. Later, at the reception, he should dance with any single attendants or guests. The best man should also encourage the ushers to do the same.

Sits to the right of the bride, if it's a seated reception, and proposes the first toast to the new couple. The best man should rise, raise his glass, mention the couple by name and his relationship to

---

why you should have a wedding party

- You'll have people to share in the excitement and planning.
- You'll have help when shopping, addressing invitations, etc.
- You'll have help on the wedding day with errands, changing, bustling your gown, and dealing with the caterer.
- Close friends, relatives, might be hurt if they're left out.

them. It is also traditional to offer a wish for health, happiness, and prosperity (see Chapter 13, "Your Reception").

Collects any congratulatory telegrams or faxes and reads them aloud if the couple wish, after the toasts. He makes sure these documents get back to the couple's home after the wedding. He may also introduce other guests.

Ensures that the reception goes as planned, and that no unpleasant practical jokes are played on the bride and groom. In particular, he is the guardian of the couple's luggage until they leave the reception, and makes sure it does not disappear and is not tampered with (it should be locked in the car's trunk).

He makes sure that the windshield of the honeymoon car isn't overdecorated. For safety, the driver's view should be unobstructed. Also, he should make sure that only removable materials are used to decorate the car (no paint).

Helps the groom change into his going-away clothes. He might also assist with any last-minute packing.

Escorts the bride and groom to the limousine or car, or may drive the couple to their station, airport, or hotel. As they leave, he hands over the keys, tickets, and baggage checks given to him for safekeeping.

Sees to it that all the men's rental clothes are returned to the formalwear store the first business day after the wedding.

With the honor attendant, he may make sure that any gifts of money received at the wedding are deposited in the bank (after making a list of guests and amount of each gift). The honor attendant may take the checks, the best man the cash, or vice versa.

New Attendants' Roles

Some brides choose a *man of honor* (as their honor attendant) or a *bridesman* (instead of bridesmaid) when they want to include a close male friend in the bridal party. The groom may choose a *best woman* to fill many of the traditional roles of the best man, or a *female usher*. These new roles can be incorporated into the most traditional wedding if done tastefully. Inform wedding professionals, such as photographers, in advance that you have non-traditional attendants, to ensure that they are not left out of photos, or inserted by the photographer into traditional portrait positions (e.g., the bridesman with the ushers, the best woman with the bridesmaids).

THE MAN OF HONOR/BRIDESMAN/BEST WOMAN/FEMALE USHER:

Helps run errands, address invitation envelopes. Assists in many of the ways that other attendants might be helpful.

Should not have to perform awkward duties usually reserved for an individual the same sex as the bride or groom.

A bride should not ask a man to attend all-female showers (it would be awkward) or ask him to help shop for a gown or help bustle her gown at the reception (her bridesmaids, who will be permitted into restrooms and fitting rooms, can assist). Similarly, a groom should not expect a best woman or female usher to try on tuxedos with him, or attend the bachelor party (unless it is co-ed).

Usually wears the same attire as the other attendants of his/her sex in the wedding party. A man of honor or bridesman can be given some distinction with a unique boutonniere, cummerbund, or bow tie.

A bridesman walks down the aisle with the bridesmaids and stands with them during the ceremony. If the bridesmaids are being escorted by ushers during the recession, the best woman can escort an elderly or unaccompanied female family member, such as the bride's grandmother. Another option: Each attendant can walk back up the aisle alone.

The best woman walks in the procession and recession. The best man might walk in between her and the maid/matron of honor, or she might walk alone. Or, the three attendants can walk down and up the aisle together.

May be announced—with the best man and honor attendant—before the wedding party and before the newlyweds, to all reception guests.

May dance with other attendants during the newlyweds' first dance.

The Bridesmaids' and Ushers' Roles

The number of bridesmaids and ushers in your ceremony will depend on its size and style. At a small, informal wedding, you may have just one maid or matron of honor, and a best man. At a large, formal wedding, you may have twelve or more. (You will need at least one usher to seat every fifty guests, to avoid seating delays.) Don't worry about having an equal number of male and female attendants; the clergymember will arrange the aesthetics of the procession and altar lineup. And remember, attendants do not have to walk up and down the aisle in pairs (some of the ushers can escort a maid on each arm).

It is the bride's and groom's prerogative to choose attendants from among their close friends and relatives. Although it's not necessary, it is thoughtful to invite at least one of the groom's sisters to be a bridesmaid, and one of the bride's brothers to be an usher. If one of your attendants is married, it is *not* necessary to invite his or her spouse to be in the wedding party. If you and your fiancé *do* ask a couple to be in the wedding, they need not be paired in the recession (e.g., an usher can escort a bridesmaid, even if his wife is the matron of honor). And, if an attendant's spouse, girlfriend, or boyfriend is not in the wedding party, you need not seat them together at the reception (see Chapter 13, "Your Reception").

If a bridesmaid or usher drops out at the last minute because of illness, remember that you do not need balanced pairs for the procession and recession. (Besides, it is impolite to ask someone else to stand in at such a late date.) Send flowers and wedding keepsakes (place card, table favor) to the indisposed attendant; be sure to invite him or her to look through the wedding album or for a screening of the wedding video.

Custom dictates that bridesmaids and ushers are close to the bride's age. If you have sisters or cousins between the ages of nine and fourteen, however, you may ask them to participate as junior bridesmaids (see "Child Attendants' Roles" section, and Chapter 7, "Wedding Clothes").

THE BRIDESMAIDS:

Offer to run errands, address invitation envelopes, and help the bride in any way they can. They may scout out bridesmaids' dresses, research hotels, write place cards, assemble favors.

Are invited to all prewedding parties and may co-host a bridesmaids' luncheon or bachelorette party. Consideration should be given to out-of-town attendants when planning events for which they may have to travel. If most maids are long-distance, showers can be planned for the week of the wedding, when everyone will be in one location (see Chapter 3, "Prewedding Parties").

Usually pay for their own wedding outfit, chosen by the bride. As a gift to her attendants, the bride may assume the entire clothing expense for her maids, or present them with an accessory to be worn that day, as a thank-you gift. (Junior maids' dresses are usually paid for by their parents.)

Pick up their bouquets at the bride's home an hour or so before the ceremony, unless all the flowers are being delivered directly to the ceremony site. It is customary for the maids to also partic-ipate in the prewedding photograph session at the bride's house, or in the dressing room at the ceremony site.

Walk first in the procession and, if they are junior maids, need no partners in the recession. Junior bridesmaids precede the maid of honor in the procession. Bridesmaids usually stand at the bride's side during the ceremony. Younger attendants have no other specific responsibilities, although they stand next to the bridesmaids.

May walk back up the aisle alone or escorted by groomsmen.

May greet guests in the receiving line. Some brides and grooms prefer to have their attendants circulate among guests.

May be announced—with the wedding party—to all reception guests, before the newlyweds.

May dance with the ushers during the newlyweds' first dance.

Sit alternately with the ushers at the head table, if there is one.

**Single attendants are often called onto

the dance floor or into a hallway to catch the bride's bouquet.

If there is no honor attendant, one maid, designated by the bride, may take responsibility for the wedding gown if the bride changes at the reception. After the couple depart for their honeymoon, this bridesmaid may carefully hang or pack the gown to take to the bride's home or to a dry cleaner to be professionally cleaned and preserved.

THE USHERS:
Attend all prewedding parties the groom goes to and may host a bachelor party.

Provide their own wedding clothes, renting the appropriate formal attire if they don't own it. The groom supplies the boutonnieres, neckwear, and gloves when these are not included in the rental package. He may also offer, as a gift, a shirt, cuff links, or other accessories.

May pick up ceremony flowers, aisle runner, from the florist. This is usually done the day of the wedding.

Seat the guests at the wedding ceremony. Ushers should arrive at the ceremony site forty-five minutes to an hour before the ceremony begins. They assemble near the entrance and review any special seating requests.

Step forward and offer right arm to each woman, as guests arrive. When a couple enter, traditionally the woman takes the usher's arm, and the man follows them down the aisle. Ushers make

quiet, polite conversation as they walk unhurriedly down the aisle with guests. New trend at informal ceremonies: Ushers just lead people to their seats. As they greet each guest, they might simply say, "Please follow me."

Seat the oldest woman first if several guests arrive together. Unless a man is elderly and needs assistance, he may simply be accompanied to his seat.

Ask if the guest is a friend of the bride or the groom if he or she does not have a pew card and is unknown to the usher. The bride's guests are seated on the left (facing the altar); the groom's guests, on the right. The opposite is true for Jewish ceremonies.

If one side has many more guests than the other, explain that everyone will be sitting together. This will give all guests the best view.

Unroll the aisle runner and tie pew ribbons (if used). Usually, the groom appoints two ushers to handle the aisle runner and pew ribbons.

Participate in both the procession and the recession. Ushers return after the recession to escort mothers, as well as elderly or disabled guests, from the church or synagogue first.

Loosen pew ribbons after the recession. Two ushers usually return after the recession to loosen the ribbons at the end of each pew, then pause at the side of each, signaling guests to file out row by row, from front to back.

the head usher

- The groom designates one groomsman as head usher to supervise special seating arrangements.
- If the bride or groom has divorced parents (see Chapter 8, "Your Wedding Ceremony"), one parent may be seated in the first row, one in the third row.
- If there are elderly guests, they'll be seated up front.
- If there are guests in wheelchairs or on crutches, they'll be seated at the front or end of pews, near family and friends.
- If the bride and groom do not each have brothers in the wedding party to seat their respective mothers, the head usher will seat them.

Are prepared to direct guests to parking and restroom facilities, and to the reception site. They also make sure all guests have rides.

Escort guests to their cars with umbrellas if it rains. Guests will appreciate this thoughtful gesture.

Make certain the ceremony site is cleared of the wedding party's belongings before leaving. Avoid unnecessary trips back later in the day.

Sit at the head table, if there is one, but do not stand in the receiving line, if there is one. Ushers circulate among guests at the reception and make sure that everyone has a wonderful time. They also dance with the bridesmaids and single female guests.

May be announced—with the wedding party—to all reception guests, before the newlyweds.

May dance with the bridesmaids during the newlyweds' first dance. Should also invite single attendants and guests to dance throughout the reception.

Are alert to potential problems. Ushers (as well as bridesmaids) should keep their ears and eyes tuned to any difficulties that might interrupt the smooth flow of the reception. They may help to resolve problems or questions that the caterer, photographer, or other wedding-service professionals have.

Propose toasts to the bride and groom. After the best man makes the first toast, and the groom thanks him (perhaps followed by the bride), the ushers may keep the festive comments going.

Decorate the couple's going-away car. The ushers may drape the car with flower garlands, streamers, balloons, and signs that won't be hazardous on the road. The windshield is left clear.

The Child Attendants' Roles

Having young children in the wedding party is a popular European custom that can delight guests and add charm to the ceremony—especially if they're supervised and well behaved. When the children are from a previous marriage, including them in the festivities is a must so they won't feel left out of their parents' lives (see Chapter 11, "Remarriage"). A young son may even escort his mother, the bride, down the aisle. If no children are to be part of the ceremony, you may want to have them pass out programs in the sanctuary, oversee the guest book, or serve punch at the reception.

Very young children who are not often dressed up, or are never in a crowd, may behave unpredictably. Thus, you may want to have only one or two child attendants, between the ages of four and eight, as *pages*, *ring bearer(s)* or *flower girl(s)*—the most often included child attendant. *Junior bridesmaids*, *junior ushers*, and *candlelighters* (for safety's sake) are between the ages of nine and fourteen. Although traditionally a boy, today the *ring bearer* may be a girl. *Candle lighters*, common in some regions, are often two boys from either (or both) family(ies) who light the ceremony candles.

THE FLOWER GIRL:

May walk alone, with the ring bearer, or with another flower girl about the same height. The flower girl immediately precedes the bride down the aisle in the procession. (See Appendix, under-Chapter 6, "The Wedding Party".)

Dresses in a more youthful version of the bridesmaids' outfits. Usually, this is a tiny, floral print accented with a silk sash (no low back or neck). Another option: a white pinafore over a velvet dress, with ballet slippers or black or white patent-leather shoes.

Traditionally carries a basket of rose petals to scatter in the bride's path. Due to the very real possibility of someone slipping on dropped petals, flower girls now often carry a basket of posies or a tiny nosegay. The flower girl's flower arrangement should be the same front and back—so blossoms will look pretty no matter how they are held.

THE RING BEARER

Immediately precedes the flower girl (if there is one) or the bride down the aisle. The ring bearer may also be paired with the flower girl or another ring bearer.

Balances a white lace or satin pillow with a faux bride's ring tied to the center with ribbons, or stitched down lightly with satin thread. (A second ring bearer might carry a pillow with a groom's ring attached.) The real rings are safe with the honor attendants. After the ceremony, turn the cushion upside down to hide the dummy ring.

If a boy, the ring bearer wears a satin or velvet suit (perhaps a dark-blue Eton suit, or white shorts, a navy blazer, and white or blue knee socks). If a girl, a pretty dress, similar to what a flower girl wears, is appropriate. Other young attendants dress similarly, in colors coordinating with bridesmaids' gowns.

THE PAGES/TRAIN BEARERS:

Follow the bride down the aisle and carry her train. Pages are very common in English weddings.

Always walk down and up the aisle in pairs and are about the same height. Generally, they are little boys, but girls may also carry the bride's train. (Pages are needed only when the wedding gown has a very long train.)

THE CANDLE LIGHTERS:

Wear dress clothes similar to junior ushers and junior bridesmaids. Dress styles should be complementary, but not identical to bridesmaids' gowns—if necklines or backs are low.

Step forward to light the candles just before the mother of the bride is seated. Ceremony musicians may begin a new prelude selection as the candle lighters step forward.

Snuff the candles after the recession, as guests are filing out of the sanctuary. The ceremony musicians may continue to play selections in a postlude.

child attendants' dos & don'ts

DO include child attendants in the rehearsal so they can practice their parts and become familiar with the site.

DON'T invite children to attend an evening rehearsal dinner or other prewedding parties.

DO invite child attendants to the reception, along with their parents.

DO seat the parents of child attendants on the aisle, in one of the front pews. Parents are familiar faces, and can offer encouragement to their children as they walk past. Children may also sit with them after going down the aisle. This eliminates the risk of young attendants fidgeting while standing at the altar and distracting everyone's attention from the ceremony.

DO assign a relative (or hire a baby-sitter) to supervise young attendants at the reception. A teen-age guest might set up a play area with activites and snacks. Or, include a children's table in your seating plan. (Arrange for an adult or teen to supervise; provide coloring books and crayons.)

DO choose outfits in which young attendants will be comfortable, and which are appropriate for their age (i.e., nothing too low-cut).

DON'T insist on a cummerbund, bow tie, or other accessory if a child resists wearing it.

DO thank the children for their participation with a gift (e.g., a teddy bear dressed as a bride or groom). Thank their parents, as well, perhaps with a nicely framed photograph of their child walking down the aisle.

The Mother of the Bride's Role

Your mother is the official hostess of your wedding, unless you are serving in that capacity yourself, or some other close relative or friend is filling this role. Her duties will vary, depending on whether you're planning an out-of-town wedding *and* on the amount of free time the bride and her mother have.

divorced parents

Below are etiquette tips to follow if your parents are divorced and you have a stepfather you hope to include on wedding day.

- Your father may still escort you down the aisle and give you his blessing (give you away) at the altar.

- Your father sits in the third pew on the bride's side of the aisle. (The parent who raised you sits in the front row.) (See Chapter 8, "Your Wedding Ceremony.")

- Perhaps share the father's duties between your father and stepfather. *Both* may escort you down the aisle, if they are comfortable with the idea. Or, have one do the honor during the ceremony, and the other dance with you at the reception (see Chapter 13, "Your Reception").

- Be certain each parent has a partner if invited onto the dance floor during the first dance.

- Do not position your parents together in the receiving line. Even if they're on friendly terms, guests may misunderstand their relationship.

- Seat divorced parents at different reception tables (see Chapter 13, "Your Reception").

THE MOTHER OF THE BRIDE:

Helps bride compile the guest list. She, or the bride, should tell the groom's parents how many people may be included on their guest list.

Helps arrange the details of the ceremony and reception. She may be the main contact between the bride and all wedding-service professionals (unless a wedding consultant is hired).

May assist with selecting the bride's wedding outfit and trousseau. It is the bride's choice whether she comes to shop for the wedding dress and honeymoon outfits.

Is invited to most prewedding parties. The mother of the bride attends (but never hosts) all showers. She also attends the prewedding breakfast (if there is one). She is probably not invited to the bridesmaids' tea or bachelorette party (see Chapter 3, "Prewedding Parties").

Keeps track of wedding gifts. She sees that they are displayed attractively in a safe place. She may also be invited to go along on visits to the Wedding Gift Registry, to advise the couple.

May scout out reception sites, photographers, florists, caterers, and other wedding-service professionals—espe- cially if the bride lives out of town. She may purchase two identical wedding planners (one for herself and one for the bride), and schedule regular long-distance calls if the bride lives far away—to communicate information.

Chooses her dress first, then informs the groom's mother of her selection. The wedding attire of the two mothers should be the same length, similar in style (formality), complementary colors.

Keeps the bride's father and the parents of the groom posted on the progress of the wedding plans. The groom's parents will want to feel included in the planning process.

Runs errands as the need arises. These might include mailing and following up on invitations, addressing and mailing announcements and change-of-address cards the day of the wedding (see Chapter 5, "Invitations & Announcements").

Provides family recipes, menu ideas, to caterer. She may also give the bride family heirlooms to wear on wedding day (e.g., the pearls *she* wore, a grandmother's lace handkerchief, a blue garter, a family sixpence to tuck in her shoe).

May accompany the bride down the aisle. This traditional Jewish wedding-ceremony custom, in which the mother *and* father of the bride flank the bride and link arms (or hold hands), as they all walk down the aisle, is being adopted by many couples in all religions.

Is seated in the first pew on the bride's side of the aisle. If walking the bride down the aisle with the bride's father, she will slip into the front row with him after leaving the bride at the altar (if not standing under the *huppah* at a Jewish ceremony). If not walking the bride down the aisle, the mother of the bride is the last to be seated before the procession begins. If her son is an usher, he escorts his mother to her seat. Otherwise, the head usher does the honor.

Is the first guest to be ushered out, with her husband or escort, after the recession is over. Two ushers unhook pew ribbons and stand at each row, motioning guests to file out in order.

Serves as official hostess. The mother of the bride greets guests at the head of the receiving line, sits in a place of honor at the parents' table, makes sure everyone has a good time, and stays until the reception's end to say good-bye to guests.

Joins the newlyweds on the dance floor with the father of the bride during the first dance. May dance with her son-in-law at some time during this dance.

Is on hand to keep the bride calm, smooth out last-minute crises, and offer moral support throughout the wedding.

The Father of the Bride's Role

As the official host of the reception, the father of the bride often plays a prominent role in prewedding decisions and organization on the day of the wedding. Although today expenses are split among the couple and the groom's family (see Chapter 4, "Planning Your Wedding"), the father of the bride still plays a major role in wedding finances.

THE FATHER OF THE BRIDE:

May share in scouting out wedding sites and assorted wedding services. How much the father of the bride involves himself in wedding plans varies with family situation and interest.

May set up travel arrangements for all out-of-town guests. Many fathers pick up arriving relatives and friends at the station or airport, and arrange for rides to and from prewedding parties and the wedding.

May draw map of sites with directions. These may be printed and sent to guests as invitation enclosures (see Chapter 5, "Invitations & Announcements").

May attend the bachelor party. (See Chapter 3, "Prewedding Parties.")

Gets fitted for formalwear which blends with that of the groom and other men in the wedding party. He should inform the father of the groom if he must be fitted for matching formalwear. (Tradi-

special members of the wedding

- Ask young girls or boys to distribute Mass books, *yarmulkes*, or wedding programs, or serve as acolytes during the ceremony.

- Ask an uncle to read a Scripture or poem at the ceremony.

- Ask family members to join in "sentence prayers"—each adding a line to continue the prayer.

- Seat grandparents in the front row as honored guests, or include them in the procession (traditionally a Jewish custom).

- Give your grandmother a corsage or nosegay; your grandfather, a boutonniere.

- Ask children to take charge of the guest book, pass out groom's cake or packets of birdseed, or help with refreshments.

- Designate friends and relatives as "persons of honor." Ask them to greet guests at the door, direct them to restrooms, help seat guests, carry the guest book at the cocktail hour, or hand out programs. They need not walk down the aisle or wear a tuxedo or a bridesmaid's gown. Still, you might order a small bouquet, corsage, or a boutonniere to honor them; ask them to wear the same color dress, suit.

- Include well-behaved dogs as flower dogs, who may be walked down the aisle. Slip a flower collar around the pet's neck, perhaps attach the wedding rings (or replicas).

tionally, all men walking down the aisle wear matching formalwear.)

Rides to the ceremony with the bride in the limousine and escorts her into the ceremony site. Prior to the procession, he waits in the vestibule with her.

Walks the bride down the aisle (perhaps with her mother on the bride's other arm). If the bride's father is deceased, her brother, uncle, or other male relative; a close family friend; or an usher may escort her down the aisle, then serve as her mother's escort for the reception festivities. The bride's mother may instead walk her down the aisle if she feels closer to her than to any male relative or friend. The bride may also choose to walk alone.

At the altar, offers his support or blessing (what has traditionally been called "giving away the bride"). Many clergymembers will offer the traditional or updated wording for this part of the wedding ceremony.

Joins the bride's mother in the first pew. If divorced, he sits in the third pew (see Chapter 8, "Your Wedding Ceremony").

May mingle with guests, instead of standing in the receiving line. If the

bride prefers, her father may stand in the receiving line, to the left of her mother (unless they're divorced) (see Chapter 13, "Your Reception").

Keeps an eye on the bar and champagne supply, alerts banquet manager if more is needed. Also is alert to any other problems that may arise and may speak with the banquet manager, wedding consultant, or bandleader, to resolve them.

Joins the newlyweds on the dance floor—with the mother of the bride—during the first dance. Later in the reception, he dances with the bride to a preselected, sentimental song appropriate for a dance with his daughter.

May make a short toast or welcoming speech. At Jewish weddings, the father of the bride traditionally offers blessings over the wine and bread before the reception meal begins. At all weddings, he may make a toast after the best man gives the first toast, and the groom (and perhaps the bride) have responded.

Leaves the reception last, after bidding all guests good-bye. He may also settle outstanding bills at this time with caterer, bandleader, coat-check, rest-room, and parking attendants.

The Parents of the Groom's Roles

Although their roles are smaller than those of the bride's parents, they are considered co-hosts of the wedding, regardless of whether or not they've contributed financially. It is a gracious gesture to include their names on the wedding invitation (see Chapter 5, "Invitations & Announcements").

THE PARENTS OF THE GROOM:

Contact the bride's parents by phone or letter. They should let them know they're pleased about the upcoming marriage. They should also arrange a prewedding meeting with the bride's parents—at their home or in a restaurant (see Chapter 1, "Your Engagement").

May host an engagement party (after the bride's family first hosts one), tea party, or luncheon to introduce the bride to their friends see Chapter 3, "Prewedding Parties").

Provide a list of an agreed-upon number of guests. Included are full names, middle initials, titles, zip codes.

Let bride know about family traditions (e.g., ethnic dances or festive dishes) to include in the celebration. A wedding is a merging of both families.

Consult with the bride's parents on the proper wedding attire. The dress of the groom's mother should be the same length as that of the mother of the bride, in a shade that complements the wedding color scheme. The father of the groom should wear an appropriate suit or jacket—if a tuxedo is not required (this is particularly necessary if he is walking down the aisle.) (See Chapter 7, "Wedding Clothes.")

Traditionally, they do pay for some wedding expenses. These may include the engagement and wedding rings, marriage license, clergy fees, corsages, boutonnieres, bride's bouquet, ushers' gifts, honeymoon, liquor, and music.

May give the couple a special gift. Possibilities include a family heirloom, a home appliance, an entertainment center, a storage unit, a convertible sofa, or perhaps a monetary gift toward a car or the honeymoon.

Are invited to all prewedding parties. The mother of the groom attends (but never hosts) all showers. She also attends the prewedding breakfast, if there is one (see Chapter 3, "Prewedding Parties"). The father of the groom may be invited to the groom's bachelor party.

Attend the rehearsal and practice any special duties (e.g., lighting the Unity Candle, reading a Scripture).

Traditionally host the rehearsal dinner. If the parents of the groom are from out of town, the bride's mother may suggest a site or caterer. (The groom's parents are invited to the rehearsal dinner if not hosting it.)

Arrive fifteen minutes before the ceremony's scheduled starting time. The mother of the groom is escorted to her seat by the head usher (unless her son is in the wedding party), followed by the father of the groom, just before the mother of the bride. As honored guests, the groom's parents are seated in the first row on the groom's side of the aisle (unless they will stand under the *huppah* at a Jewish ceremony).

Escort the groom (one on each side) down the aisle, if the couple choose to include this traditional Jewish wedding-ceremony custom.

The groom's mother stands second in the receiving line, after the bride's mother and before the bride. The groom's father usually mingles with guests; otherwise, he stands to the left of his wife in line, before the mother of the groom.

Sit at the parents' table with the bride's parents. The wedding day is the perfect time to establish warm relations for future holidays to come.

Dance with the newlyweds. During the first dance, they may be invited onto the dance floor together, or to dance with the newlyweds. Later in the reception, after the bride's special dance with her father, the groom should ask the band to play a meaningful song to which he'll dance with his mother. The father of the groom may also ask the bride to dance sometime during the reception.

May be served the fifth and sixth pieces of wedding cake (after the newlyweds each cut pieces to feed each other, and after the bride's parents are served). This is a lovely gesture of respect.

Play a more visible role if they are solely sponsoring the wedding. The father of the groom then oversees the wedding-reception personnel. The mother of the groom presides as hostess and first greeter in the receiving line. Both parents stand near the door for good-byes.

WEDDING CLOTHES 7

Your gown will set the style for the entire wedding. Before you shop, have fun exploring your fantasies—look through the pages of BRIDE'S and other magazines with friends, mark the pages of anything that captures your dream, whether it's a particular fabric, setting, dress feature, or an entire gown that appeals to you. You may fall in love with a particular dress, then plan your wedding around it. Or, you may determine the day, time, and formality of your reception, then shop for the most beautiful and appropriate look (see the "Guide to Wedding Clothes" chart for the appropriate style of dress for each style of wedding, daytime and evening).

Once you've found your dream dress, select bridesmaids' and ushers' attire that is complementary in formality and style. Mothers' dresses should also complement the wedding color scheme.

Shopping for Your Gown

Choosing a wedding gown is a unique experience, one you might want to share with a close friend or your mother, lest you become overwhelmed by all the decisions. As you familiarize yourself with what styles are available, you'll begin to narrow down your preferences (see Appendix, under Chapter 7, "Wedding Clothes").

Finding a gown that suits your personality, flatters your figure, *and* meets your budget may seem like a daunting task, but you can shop smart without compromising on style. To get the best service and quality for your money, don't leave home without these savvy shopping secrets:

Start shopping at least nine months before the wedding. You'll be able to shop for good prices rather than settle on a dress because time is running out. Order your gown at least six months before the wedding. This allows three to four months for the dress to be made and delivered to the store, another two months for fittings and portraits.

Make an appointment. Bridal shops are busy places. The most popular wedding months are May through October; brides will be shopping nine months before their wedding date, and having final gown fittings the month before their wedding date. For the most relaxed, attentive service, avoid Saturdays and evenings.

gown-shopping list

Here are what to wear, bring, when shopping for your gown:

- strapless bra or bustier—to give you the versatility to try on all gown styles (you may buy a specific nude or white bra or bustier, a petticoat, after selecting your gown)

- white control-top panty hose or regular white panty hose

- white slip (petticoat should be bought with dress—a special one may be made for the dress)

- shoes the same heel height you'll wear on wedding day (buy wedding shoes to match dress style, before the first fitting)

- hairstyle planned for wedding day (certain headpieces are better for hair worn up or down)

Take advantage of the bridal-shop consultant's expertise. He or she can recommend cleaning or heirlooming services (see Appendix, under Chapter 7, "Wedding Clothes"), photographers, caterers, and offer advice on what formalwear looks are appropriate for the time and style of your wedding.

Tell salespeople your price ceiling. They'll save you time by showing you only gowns that are within your price range.

If you fall in love with a gown that's out of your budget, explore possibilities. Ask if the salon owner or bridal consultant can find you a similar dress that is priced more moderately, perhaps in poly-shantung instead of silk shantung, or with laces and beading that are applied by machine rather than by hand.

Ask about quality. Are the seed pearls sewed on, sequins sewed or glued on? Can the gown be dry-cleaned? Ask, in advance, about on-the-spot cleaning advice for spills on the particular fabric of your gown.

Take advantage of discontinued samples or stock dresses. These gowns are usually reduced, and will look like new once they are dry-cleaned. Also consider out-of-season gowns, bridesmaids' dresses in white or ivory (for an informal wedding).

Inquire about special payment and layaway plans. Some shops offer minimal interest that isn't charged until the dress arrives.

Get a price quote for alterations before buying your dress. Try to avoid major changes to the dress structure, such as the neckline or waist height, which are costly.

Consult bridal stores about embellishing an heirloom veil. If you have your heart set on wearing a veil and headpiece worn by your mother and grandmother, but fear it looks faded, dated, find out how you can make it look more contemporary (see "Wearing an Heirloom Gown" section).

Ask for a description of the dress in writing (including fabric and lace types, neck-

line, sleeves). This description will come in handy for newspaper announcements, and when others ask you to tell them about your gown.

Put all points of the sale in a signed and countersigned contract or bill of sale. The best protection for you—and for the bridal salon—is to clearly list the specifications of the gown you have ordered and the terms of the sale. (See "Wedding-Dress Contract Tips" box.)

Your Fashion Dilemmas

There will be many questions that come to mind while you are finalizing your wedding-fashion decisions. Here are some answers:

Which gown fabrics would be most comfortable on a hot summer day? *Chiffon*—a fluid, slightly sheer fabric woven of silk or rayon; *linen*—a stiffer, lightweight fabric that is best for structured couture dresses in simple designs (note: it wrinkles easily); *organza*—crisp, light, and diaphanous, it is excellent for a classic ball-gown skirt; *light lace*—romantic, sometimes worn over a pale-colored satin, good for a country wedding; *voile*—a sheer, fine fabric of cotton, silk, or rayon, which drapes easily.

Which gown fabrics are best for a fall wedding? Choose year-round fabrics with a light, lush feel—*shantung, brocade, tulle, taffeta, textured cotton.* Perhaps wear a gown with a full taffeta skirt, long sleeves of medium-weight lace. Other great fall features: high collars or illusion necklines. If you prefer a low-cut or strapless gown, cover up for the ceremony in a matching jacket or lace jacket, silk shawl, and long kid gloves. Expecting an early chill? Snuggle in a fur muff, satin car coat, low boots with a Louis heel.

What is a snowball wedding? A snowball wedding means that the female members of the wedding party all wear white. The key to a great look is having the shades of white *match.* Match a blue-white bridal gown to blue-white bridesmaids' gowns (*not* with ivory, which would look "dirty" in comparison). Your mothers should also wear the same shade of white. (Carry vibrant flowers to keep the whites from looking flat.)

The men in the wedding party should wear black tuxedos or full-dress white tie (see the "Groom's Formalwear Glossary" section). They might also wear white dinner jackets with black trousers (see "Guide to Wedding Clothes" chart for the appropriate style of dinner jackets).

How can I choose a hat to wear with my gown? Your hat choice is based on your height, proportions, face, hairstyle, and dress style. Proportions must be balanced; a large dress calls for a large hat. Wear a large picture hat for a dress with a ball-gown

---

*wedding-
dress
contract
tips*

Specify these points in a signed and countersigned contract or bill of sale:

● dress manufacturer and style number, size, color (white, eggshell, ecru?)

● embellishments (hand-embroidered Alençon lace, sequins, pearls)

● special-order requests and costs (e.g., raise the back three inches, taper dolman sleeves)

● delivery date

● price and payment schedule, deposit paid, fitting and pressing costs

● store's policy on refunds (should be 100 percent if garment is never delivered), cancellations

● store policy for gown storage, pickup (can gown be borrowed for a prewedding photo session and returned?)

skirt or off-the-shoulder neckline. Choose a smaller hat for a short dress. Work with a milliner to find the right hat for your personality and dress, incorporating your dress fabric, adding tulle veiling, perhaps an organza brim, and matching beading and lace. Also consider the style and site of the reception. An oversized hat and ball-gown skirt will be overpowering in a small restaurant, but not in a hotel ballroom; a straw hat with flowers on the crown and brim is perfect for a garden wedding.

What shoe styles are best for a wedding gown? For bridal footwear, select evening shoes in white or cream. Consider innovative styles: modern or medieval pumps, slippers with sling backs, leather lace-up boots for Victorian wedding gowns. Select luxurious fabrics: brocade, linen, silk, quilted satin. The mood of the shoe should match the mood of the gown. Wearing a Renaissance gown? Select a baroque, court-heeled shoe. Also echo your dress's trim or appliqués in your shoe details: rosettes, pearls, rhinestones, bows.

Does my hosiery really matter? It won't really show, anyway. A peek of ankle and calf may indeed show as you waltz around the dance floor, are swept up on a chair during the traditional *horah*, or when your groom removes your garter to toss it at the reception. Beautiful hose will make you feel luxurious, regal. Your hosiery should complement, not overpower, your gown. Consider ultra-sheer, shimmery hose in white, pearl, or pale pink. Look for delicate appliqués—pearls along the back seam, or bows with pearls, bridal bells at the ankles. Wearing a simple gown? Choose an all-over fun print, such as confetti or Swiss dots! (Bridesmaids might wear a pastel shade—from seashell to celadon—to complement dress hue.)

Is it proper for guests to wear white or black to the wedding? In general, women guests should *not* wear white dresses (or off-white, ivory), or multicolored dresses in which white is the dominant color. This is because white is the color reserved for the bride, and any guest wearing it is considered to be competing with her. (At an informal wedding, a guest in a white suit might even be mistaken for the bride!) Black, however, can be an appropriate color for a formal evening wedding with colored or metallic accessories— shoes, belt, jewelry, purse. Avoid all black, black veils, anything funereal.

Is there a way to bustle my gown for reception dancing? Most trains today are designed to "bustle" for the reception and dancing. If yours isn't, have your salon arrange for the alteration department to sew in snaps, hooks, or other methods of securing the train into a bustle. Many manufacturers and bridal shops automatically sew in special fasteners to draw the fabric up to floor-length in back (ask if this is the case). Bring your honor attendant along for the final dress fitting so she can learn how to bustle the train for you.

Today, many long and short dresses are made with detachable trains (unfasten the

Velcro™, hooks, buttons, or snaps). Sweep trains are short enough to maneuver without bustling. Or, have a loop attached to the train, to hold while dancing.

What fashion accents can I add to a Christmas wedding? Choose colors and details that evoke the spirit of the season. Select jewel-tone bridesmaids' gowns—in ruby red, amethyst, or emerald green. Consider velvet or silk ottoman dresses with fur collars, cuffs, heavy metallic brocades. Trim dresses in gold lace; order metallic trim on gowns and headpieces. Choose gold or silver shoes and purses. (See Chapter 10, "Special Weddings & New Ways to Wed.")

My fiancé and I, and our attendants, are all in the military. What should we wear? Men and women in a military wedding may wear the full ceremonial dress uniform of the appropriate service and rank—precedent is usually set by the groom. (Ushers not in the military may wear formalwear appropriate to the time and style of the wedding.) Brides almost always choose to wear a traditional wedding gown (bridesmaids may also wear traditional maids' dresses). A bride in uniform can carry a bouquet; military decorations (if the men have any)—never boutonnieres—are worn by a groom and ushers in uniform. Whether the uniforms worn are dress blues or dress whites is determined by season and regional regulations. States with warm weather may require summer dress longer than states with a cool season. (See Chapter 10, "Special Weddings & New Ways to Wed," and Appendix, under Chapter 10.)

Sizing Your Gown

Your salesperson should measure your bust, waist, hips, and length—from shoulder or nape of neck to the floor. (Dress sizes usually differ by one inch.)

When deciding on the size of your gown, choose the size that matches the largest part of the gown. (If your bust is 36 inches and your waist is 23 inches, order the size gown that fits a 36-inch bust; take in the waist.)

Order the size you are *that day.* If your weight tends to fluctuate or you plan to lose some pounds before the wedding, schedule fittings six weeks to a month before the wedding day, with the final fitting within ten days of the wedding (timing will depend on the workload of the seamstress). If you do lose weight, the gown can always be taken in. A too-small gown, however, cannot be made more than one size larger.

Fitting Your Gown

Since most gowns are made to order, you're not likely to find a shop that has samples

---

*dress
features
for each
body type*

- **Hourglass shape**—off-the-shoulder portrait neckline flatters large chest; V-shaped basque waist and full skirt slim waist and hips.

- **Short waist**—princess shape creates long, slim silhouette; high-low waist lengthens torso.

- **Thick waist**—Empire line with skirt flowing from below the bust minimizes waist, creates a long, lean silhouette.

- **Boyish figure**—ornamentation at neckline enhances bust; wide band of pleating at waist adds dimension to lanky upper body.

- **Full figure**—tapering leg-of-mutton sleeves flatter full arms; V-neck and dropped, V-waist de-emphasize bust, hips.

- **Small bust**—flowers around strapless bodice balance pear-shaped figure; bows on off-the-shoulder neckline add shape to slim torso.

- **Petite**—simple gown flatters a tiny figure; sheath elongates look; subtle shoulder detail keeps focus up and adds height.

- **Great legs**—above-the-knee sheath with detachable overskirt or simple mini-dress plays up perfect legs.

Guide to Wedding Clothes

	VERY FORMAL EVENING 200 GUESTS OR MORE; AFTER 6:00	VERY FORMAL DAYTIME 200 GUESTS OR MORE; NOON, AFTERNOON	FORMAL EVENING 100 GUESTS OR MORE; AFTER 6:00	
BRIDE	Dress with a long train. Veil (often same length as train) to complement dress. Long sleeves or gloves to cover arms. Shoes to match dress. Full bouquet or flower-trimmed prayer book.	Same as very formal evening, but shorter train is also appropriate.	Long dress with a chapel, sweep, or detachable train. Veil of a length to complement dress. Accessories the same as those for a very formal wedding.	
GROOM AND MEN OF THE WEDDING PARTY	Full-dress tailcoats with matching trousers, white waistcoats, white bow ties, wing-collared shirts. (Optional: Black top hats, white gloves.)	Cutaway coats, gray striped trousers, gray waistcoats, wing-collared shirts, and ascots or striped ties. (Optional: Top hats, spats, gray gloves.)	Black tuxedos with matching trousers, dress shirts, bow ties, and vests or cummerbunds. (Optional: White or ivory dinner jackets.)	
BRIDESMAIDS AND WOMEN OF THE WEDDING PARTY	Between 4 and 12 attendants, including honor attendant. Long dresses, gloves to complement sleeve length. Any style bouquet, shoes to match color scheme. Hair ornaments or flowers.	Between 4 and 12 attendants, including honor attendant. Same overall style as very formal evening, but dresses are often less elaborate.	Between 2 and 6 attendants, including honor attendant. Similar to very formal, but dresses are sometimes short. Gloves are optional.	
MOTHERS OR HOSTESSES (COLOR COORDINATES WITH BRIDESMAIDS' DRESSES)	Long or short evening dresses. Small hats or veils. Shoes, gloves, and flowers to match color scheme.	Long or short dresses, not as formal as those for evening. Shoes, gloves, and flowers match color scheme. Hats optional.	Long or short dresses, or evening suits. Shoes, gloves, and flowers.	
GUESTS	Women: Long or short evening dresses. Men: Black tie (tuxedos) or white tie (tails).	Women: Elegant short dresses or suits. Men: Suits.	Women: Elegant long or short evening dresses, or suits. Men: Black tie (tuxedos).	

FORMAL DAYTIME	SEMI-FORMAL EVENING	SEMI-FORMAL DAYTIME	INFORMAL
100 GUESTS OR MORE; BEFORE 6:00	100 GUESTS OR LESS; HOME, CHAPEL	100 GUESTS OR LESS; OFTEN HOME	SECOND WEDDING; DAYTIME (PICNIC, BEACH, OR OTHER THEME WEDDING)
Same as formal evening or a shorter dress that can have a detachable train. Hat or veil of a length to complement dress.	Long or shorter dress, white or pastel. Train is optional. Veil from floor-length to flyaway. Same accessories as for a formal wedding, but simpler bouquet is used.	Stylish dress, white or pastel color, short veil. Small bouquet or flower-trimmed prayer book.	Suit or stylish dress (white is optional). Veil or hat, gloves, shoes, and bag. Small bouquet.
Gray strollers, waistcoats, striped trousers, shirts, striped ties. (Optional: Homburgs, gloves.) Or, groom may choose formal suits in white or light colors for summer, darker shades for fall; dress shirts, bow ties, vests or cummerbunds.	Tuxedos or dinner jackets, dress shirts, bow ties, and vests or cummerbunds.	Suit; white or striped shirts; four-in-hand ties.	Suits or classic blazers with coordinating trousers.
Between 2 and 6 attendants, including honor attendant. Dresses either long or shorter, but not too elaborate. Matching or color-coordinated accessories, including bouquets.	Seldom more than one bridesmaid, plus an honor attendant. Elaborate evening dresses. Small bouquets.	Seldom more than an honor attendant. Suit or dress, less elaborate than semiformal evening. Small bouquet.	Honor attendant only. Suit or stylish dress. Small bouquets.
Elegant dresses or suits. Other accessories to match. Flowers to wear. Hats optional.	Elaborate stylish evening dresses or dinner suits with appropriate accessories. Flowers to wear.	Daytime luncheon suits or dresses, somewhat less elaborate than semiformal evening. Flowers to wear.	Stylish dresses or suits. Flowers to wear.
Women: Elegant daytime dresses or luncheon suits. Men: Suits.	Women: Stylish evening dresses or dinner suits. Men: Black tie (optional) or suits.	Women: Stylish dresses or luncheon suits. Men: Suits.	Women: Stylish dresses or suits. Men: Suits.

how to walk in a gown

Here are tips for walking gracefully, without tripping, in a floor-length gown, with or without a train:

- Scuff new bridal shoes in advance.
- Practice walking at home in your gown and shoes.
- Keep head erect, shoulders back, so gown hangs properly on your body.
- Hold gown from the sides and slide it smoothly upward a few inches when ascending and descending stairs.

of every dress in every size. To get a sense of how a gown will look, a consultant will pin the gown to fit or have you try on a similar dress that fits. The gown you choose will be ordered in your size, then altered to fit perfectly. For the best results:

Inquire in advance about the fee for alterations. Costs for alterations are not usually included in the price of the gown. Some shops charge a flat fee, others bill according to the work required, which can range from taking in the waist, shortening sleeves and hems, to adding appliqués or beadwork. If there is hem detail (such as lace), order the gown in the length you need, so the hem will not have to be altered. (Expect to pay ten to fifteen percent extra for a customized hem.)

Expect to return to the shop for at least two fittings. Three or four are sometimes necessary. Make and write the appointments in your calendar shortly after ordering your gown, so that the time is reserved on your busy schedule.

Be sure that your gown is short enough. Too many brides spend the day tripping over their skirts, from their first step out of the limousine, while walking down the aisle, and while dancing at the reception. *The bottom line*: The hem of the gown should gently skim the front of the shoe's toe area. If the gown is too long, the front of the skirt will skim the floor, causing the gown to wrinkle and the bride to step on it.

Wedding Dress Glossary

SILHOUETTES

Ball gown—fitted waist and bodice, full skirt.

Basque—natural waist with V-front.

Empire—small, scooped bodice, gathers at high waist; a slender, yet elegant and graceful skirt.

Princess/A-line—slim-fitting; vertical seams flow from shoulders to hem. There is no seam on the waist.

Sheath—narrow, body-conscious style indented at the waist or sculpted, following the bust, waist, and hips.

LENGTHS AND TRAINS

Short—above-the-knee length.

Knee-length—hem just covers knees.

High-low—hem falls from slightly below the knee to ankle length in front; ankle to train-length in back.

Mid-calf/Ballet-length—hem reaches to center of the calf to ankle length.

Floor-length—hem fully skims the floor.

Sweep Train—shortest train; extends back eight to twelve inches after touching floor.

Chapel Train—trails three-and-one-half to four-and-one-half feet from waist.

Semicathedral Train—extends four-and-one-half to five-and-one-half feet from waist.

Cathedral—flows six-and-one-half to seven-and-one-half feet from waist.

Extended-Cathedral/Monarch Train—cascades twelve feet from waist.

FABRICS

Brocade—Jacquard-woven fabric with raised designs.

Charmeuse—lightweight, smooth, semi-lustrous satiny fabric.

Chiffon—delicately sheer, a thin, transparent fabric of silk or rayon with a soft finish.

Crepe—silk or rayon fabric made with crepe yarn, with a slight pebbly texture.

Eyelet—open-weave embroidery; may be allover or decorative.

Linen—cloth made of flax, noted for its strength, coolness, luster.

Moiré—silk taffeta; wave-patterned to glisten like water when illuminated; dramatic.

Organdy—sheer, transparent, crisp silk or rayon fabric; is sometimes printed or embroidered.

Organza—sheer, crisp fabric like chiffon, but with a stiff finish.

Silk Gazar—a four-ply silk organza with a box weave.

Silk-faced Satin—smooth, lustrous silk fabric woven with a glossy face and dull back.

Shantung—plain-weave silk or man-made fiber fabric; rough texture, like slubs.

Taffeta—crisp, smooth fabric with a small, crosswise rib.

Tulle—fine, sheer, open-weave net in silk, nylon, or rayon; for skirts, veils.

Voile—fine, soft, sheer fabric; more like linen than cotton.

LACES

There are many kinds of laces; below are today's most popular:

Alençon—needlepoint lace with designs in deep relief on sheer net; originated in Alençon, France; can be re-embroidered.

Battenberg—made by applying a coarse linen Battenberg tape to the design and connecting tape with a decorative linen stitch by hand or machine; coarser than Renaissance lace.

Belgian—pillow laces made with machine-made grounds from Belgium.

Bobbin—category of handmade lace made with small bobbins holding each yarn attached to a small pillow; paper design is placed on pillow, pins inserted, and yarns interlaced around pins to form pattern.

Chantilly—scrolls and floral designs on fine mesh, often with scalloped edges; from Chantilly, France.

Duchesse—bobbin lace with floral designs and a tape effect made with fine thread and much raised work; allover effect with irregularly shaped spaces between designs.

French—machine-made lace fabrics made in imitation of handmade French lace.

Guipure—heavy lace with large patterns in needlepoint or bobbin over a course mesh ground.

Honiton—bobbin lace similar to duchesse, made in England; made first and then appliquéd to machine-made net ground or lace with round heavy motifs made of fine braid joined together like guipure lace.

Renaissance—heavy, flat lace made with tape laid out in pattern and joined together with various stitches.

Rose-point—Venetian needlepoint similar to Venetian point, but finer and with smaller motifs of flowers, foliage, and scrolls; buttonhole edges and a heavy cordonnet.

Schiffli—machine-made with delicate floral embroidery.

Venise—heavy needlepoint lace with floral sprays, foliage, or geometric designs; first made in Venice, Italy.

Spanish—lace with a flat design of roses on a net background; used for mantillas.

Venetian point—heavy needlepoint lace with floral sprays or foliage, or geometrical designs, made in high relief by buttonhole stitches; usually made in Venice.

NECKLINES

High—high band collar; fits close to the neck.

Sabrina—gently follows curve of the collarbone, almost to the tip of the shoulders—same across the back.

Off-the-Shoulder—below the shoulders, with sleeves.

Portrait—off-the-shoulder; extra fabric framing neckline.

Jewel—round neckline at base of throat.

Queen Anne—rises high at the back of the neck; sculpts low to outline a bare yoke.

Scoop—square with rounded edges.

Sweetheart—shaped like the top half of a heart.

SLEEVES

Balloon—very large puff sleeve extending to elbow, set into a regular armhole, frequently made of organdy.

Bell—sleeve narrow at the top and set into regular armhole; bell flare at lower edge.

Bishop—fuller in the lower forearm, then gathered at wrist into a wide cuff.

Butterfly—wide flaring sleeve; set in smoothly at armhole; extending to elbow or wrist, giving a cape-like effect.

Cap—short and fitted sleeve.

Dolman—extending from an armhole so large that it creates a cape-like effect; often fitted at wrist.

Double-puffed—full sleeve with band around arm that divides it into two puffs.

Fitted—narrow sleeve set into small armhole; fitted all the way to wrist.

Juliet—long, fitted sleeve with puff at the top.

Leg-of-mutton (or Gigot)—sleeve with gathered, full top; tapers to snug fit at wrist.

Poet—extravagantly rounded from shoulder to wrist.

Puff—short sleeve gathered into gentle, rounded shape.

Short—sleeve loosely fitted, ending above the elbow.

Three-quarter—sleeve ending between elbow and wrist.

HEADPIECES

Bow—positioned at back of head; usually of lace or satin, often flower-trimmed.

Floral wreath—circlet of flowers that can nestle on top of the head or at mid-forehead.

Garden Hat—crownless hat, usually of horsehair, trimmed with flowers and ribbons.

Headband—raised hairband, decorated and ornamented.

Juliet Cap—ornate cap; hugs crown and/or back of the head.

Mantilla—fine-lace veil, usually secured to an elegant comb; gently frames the face.

Picture Hat—ornamented hat with a very large brim; can be wrapped in tulle.

Pillbox—small, rounded hat worn on front of head.

Profile—silk flowers with pearl sprays and crystals secured on a comb; worn asymmetrically on one side of head.

Tiara—ornate crown resting high atop the head.

VEILS

Blusher—loose veil worn forward over face, and after the ceremony, turned back, over the headpiece; often attached to longer, three-tiered veil, or attached to hat.

Fly-away—multiple layers that brush the shoulders; usually worn with informal, ankle-length dress or a style with details in back.

Fingertip—several layers of veiling that touch the fingertips.

Ballet-length/Waltz-length—falls to the ankles.

Chapel-length—cascades two and one-third yards from headpiece.

Cathedral-length—cascades at least three and one-half yards from headpiece, usually worn with a cathedral train.

Wearing an Heirloom Gown

Do you dream of walking down the aisle in the gown your mother—or her mother—once wore? Here are suggestions on how to update and restore a family treasure.

Contact an experienced dressmaker or wedding-gown designer who specializes in antique gowns and lace. He or she can assess what alterations and adjustments are possible and recommend a good dry-cleaner (see Appendix, under Chapter 7).

If parts of the dress are stained or torn, you can mix new lace with old. Consider replacing the sleeves or bodice fabric. You might also update the look with new accessories, such as a headpiece and veil.

If the gown is deteriorating or is too small for you, you might remove the lace and have it added to the bodice or skirt of a new gown. Heirloom lace can also be used to create your headpiece or mantilla. Also consider transferring buttons, beads, and other detailing, from a family gown to personalize a new dress.

Preserving Your Gown

If you want your dress to last until *your* daughter grows up or to remain in perfect condition for sentimental reasons, take these protective measures:

Have your dress and veil cared for by a professional dry cleaner immediately after the wedding. Point out where any beverages (champagne, etc.) spilled on the dress—they may be invisible at first, but can stain later.

Ask the dry cleaner to test the beads and trim with solvent before cleaning. Some dresses can't be dry-cleaned if beads are glued (not sewed) on; the glue may dissolve during the cleaning process, and you could lose all of your beads and pearls!

Remove protective shields and bra inserts. They may cause staining over time.

Have the dress packed in an acid-free storage box with acid-free tissue paper. Use tissue paper to protect against creases and to puff up sleeves and bodice. Avoid "vacuum-packed" boxes (there is no such thing!); cellophane windows keep air from circulating and can discolor fabric.

Alternative idea: Wrap the gown in a white muslin sheet. Hang it on a well-padded hanger in a closet.

Store the gown at room temperature. Never leave it in an attic (too hot) or basement (too damp). Make sure the room is dark—sunlight causes decomposition of fibers.

Never store a wedding gown in mothballs. Fumes can damage some textiles.

Don't smoke, drink, eat, in storage area. Cigarette butts, crumbs, sweet residues may attract silverfish, mice—all a threat to your fabric.

Check gown yearly. If slow-to-emerge stains have appeared, bring dress back to your dry cleaner. Rewrap it just as carefully as before.

Accessories

Whether you want to create a romantic Victorian mood or evoke the refined, elegant look of today, accessories can help carry out the theme of your wedding. The perfect finishing touches:

Jewelry. Brides often wear a sentimental gift—an heirloom in their family or a gift from their groom. All wedding-day jewelry should be in keeping with the elaborateness of your wedding gown; the more heavily beaded or ornate the gown, the simpler the jewelry.

If you choose, move your engagement ring to your right hand until after the ceremony, when you'll return it to your left hand. Avoid wearing any ring on your right hand for the receiving line; it may be painful when shaking hands.

Lingerie. Fine lingerie will enhance the overall line of your wedding dress and give you that inner confidence that's so important for public occasions. When you are buying your wedding dress, the bridal-shop consultant will tell you what sort of slip your dress requires. A petticoat made of firm fabric (nylon taffeta, for instance) adds body to a full skirt; a soft, body-hugging liner smooths the lines of a sheath silhouette. Below are some shopping tips:

Buy all lingerie before the first fitting. Undergarments should be chosen with a critical eye—a sheer bodice may call for a lacy camisole; a clinging fabric may need control-top panty hose and a fitted slip to preserve the look's formality.

Choose the right petticoat: white to wear under any shade of white gown (if you want a uniform look); a nude petticoat to wear under a pastel gown. Some brides, however, choose to make a theatrical statement by wearing a brilliantly colored petticoat that flashes all day.

Make sure your petticoat is short enough. It's wise to wear a petticoat two to three inches shorter than your dress—so it doesn't show while you dance (unless you want it to show, in which case,

ask the bridal consultant for advice).

Have your brassiere fitted professionally. You want to be comfortable. Bras should be well-made, fit correctly. Check that the cup is the right size, that the bra isn't too tight. Secure bra straps in place at the shoulders with lingerie straps. Or, wear a strapless bra and check that the shape conforms to your dress. Cups, or a complete bra, can be sewn into a low-cut dress to avoid the chance of any undergarment showing. Full-busted and full-figured women should shop for a strapless bra with underwire—to offer the best support and enhance their figure. Or, they might opt for a long-line bra with vertical boning (to prevent rolling)—for waist control and to smooth back bulges.

Hosiery. Stockings can be plain, patterned, or embroidered. Choose a shade that's harmonious with the color of your gown or any color accents, such as white, ivory, or the lightest pastel. Follow these shopping tips:

Shop at legwear stores and bridal shops. You'll find an assortment of stockings and bride's garters in various

colors, styles. The garter, an optional accessory, is worn just below the knee. Some garter options: Wear your moth-

*wedding-
day
jewelry
ideas*

- tasteful earrings—of diamonds, gemstones, gold, or pearls
- a strand (or strands) of pearls
- a classic gold chain (with pendant)
- a diamond-drop necklace
- ribbon with cameo or locket
- pearls or gemstones twisted around upswept hair
- jewelry for going-away outfit

er's; make one yourself with lace, satin, or a sentimental ribbon (perhaps a piece of blue ribbon that your groom's mother saved from his baby sweater). (See Chapter 2, "Wedding Customs," for more on the bride's garter.)

Buy an extra set of hosiery for yourself and for each bridesmaid. Be prepared on wedding day for runs!

Wedding Shoes. White is the most popular shade for the bride's shoes, but be sure these are the same shade of white as your wedding gown. Materials range from lace-covered fabric to beaded satin. Follow these guidelines:

additional bridal accessories

- bridal handbag
- soft, lacy money bag
- embroidered parasol
- lace fan
- prayer book and flower
- heirloom handkerchief (your "something old")

Shoes may be dyed to match bridesmaids' gowns. Or, they may be silver or gold, or harmonizing metallic shades.

Choose a medium heel for maximum comfort. You'll be on your feet all day. You'll want shoes that will walk you steadily down the aisle, let you stand through a long receiving line, and dance for hours. Flat-heeled shoes may be classic, but some heel height is more elegant with a long dress. Ballet slippers look pretty when laced with satin ribbon. Avoid open-toe shoes; exposed toes walking down the aisle look too informal, and the style may be uncomfortable—after a few hours.

Shop for shoes late in the day. This is when feet are most tired, swollen (as yours will be on wedding day).

Scuff the soles of new shoes to avoid slipping on polished floors and carpets.

Gloves. Gloves should reflect the formality of your wedding, the season, and the style of your gown. Follow these guidelines:

Choose the right fabric for the season. For a summer wedding, wear crocheted, satin, cotton, or stretch-lace gloves. For a winter wedding, select satin or white kid gloves.

Choose the right color and accents. White or ivory is the best choice. Search for custom touches—lace, beading, or other designs, such as rosettes, that echo the embellishments on your gown. Reminder: When gloves become less than spotless, remove them.

Select the right length for your gown. Cover bare arms for modesty when in a house of worship. If you'll wear a sleeveless gown, wear lace gauntlets or opera-length gloves. Wrist-length gloves are appropriate for longer sleeves and for puffed sleeves during summer months, at an outdoor wedding.

Prepare in advance what you will do with your glove during the ring exchange. If you wear short gloves, simply remove the left glove and hand it to your honor attendant once you reach the altar. Or, beforehand, unstitch or slit the underseam of the left glove's ring finger lengthwise, so that you can slip your finger out. (Gloves can be restitched later.)

Gauntlets, which leave fingers exposed, may remain in place.

Remove your gloves during the receiving line. These days, women remove their gloves to shake hands with their wedding guests as a friendly gesture. Also remove your gloves during dinner and any other time you're eating, smoking, or drinking that day.

Groom, Attendants, Fathers

Clothes for the groom and other men in the wedding party are governed by tradition, style and time of day of the wedding—with the exception of outfits that reflect heritage (e.g., a Scottish kilt) or military service (see "Your Formalwear Dilemmas" section).

The groom and his attendants wear the same formalwear; accessories distinguish the groom and best man—they wear matching ties and cummerbunds that differ from those worn by the other ushers.

Fathers may walk down the aisle, stand in the receiving line (if they choose), and pose in wedding portraits; their attire should coordinate with that of the other members of the wedding party.

Although you can buy a tuxedo, most grooms and ushers decide to rent. The groom should try on the suit style and color that match the formality, color, and theme of the wedding (see "Groom's Formalwear Glossary" section). Formalwear should be ordered at least three months before the wedding, and tried on by each attendant as soon as it is picked up, to be sure the outfit with accessories fits correctly, and is complete.

You and your groom may also find a range of formalwear styles with a contemporary twist. New hues, fabrics, and accessories are creative, witty, and appropriate, as long as they complement your dress and the time and style of the wedding. (See "Guide to Wedding Clothes" chart for the appropriate formalwear for each style of wedding, daytime and evening.)

Your Formalwear Dilemmas

Your groom and his ushers will have many questions when they are ordering and being measured for their formalwear.

Can the men in our wedding wear dress oxfords with their tuxedos? A heavy everyday business shoe clashes with the elegant style of a tuxedo. Formal shoes are sleeker, lighter; the most traditional formal shoe (perfect with a full-dress tuxedo or white tie) is a black tuxedo pump—a plain slip-on shoe in silk, velvet, or patent leather, often with a grosgrain bow; or a suede or quilted slipper. Other formal options: black slip-ons, lace-ups made of fine leather with a soft matte finish (for a morning suit—or cutaway, stroller, or tuxedo). Or, add pizzazz with a black silk

*formalwear
contract
tips*

Specify these points in a signed and countersigned contract or bill or sale:

- size, style, and color of outfits; number of suits ordered

- specific accessories covered in suit-rental fees (e.g., gold studs, striped ascots, etc.)

- additional accessories (e.g., black matte-leather lace-up shoes)

- date outfits will be ready for pickup

- total cost; deposit paid, payment schedule

- additional charges (e.g., fitting, cleaning, late-return fees)

- what store will do if formalwear is fit incorrectly, soiled, ripped when tried on after pickup

- refund and cancellation policies

handwoven slip-on (rented at most most men's formalwear stores).

If the ceremony begins before six, the reception after, what is the appropriate formalwear? Formalwear style used to be determined by the time of the ceremony. This is no longer the case, however. If the ceremony is scheduled for four o'clock or five o'clock in the afternoon, and a very dressed-up dinner will follow at six or seven o'clock, men still might wear black tie or white tie. If a simpler event is planned, men can dress less formally.

My ushers live in different cities. How can I be sure their formalwear matches? The only guarantee is to order everyone's complete ensemble in one store. The groom can choose a formalwear store convenient to the wedding site. After choosing his formalwear style, the store gives the groom measurement forms to mail to his ushers. They then visit a formalwear store in their own area to try on a jacket and be measured (most stores will do this as a courtesy and is a precaution against ending up with incorrectly fitted formalwear). It's not enough to measure chests; some men have well-developed biceps and triceps.

The groom may be able to secure the entire order with his credit card; later, as each usher comes in for a final fitting, he can pay for his own outfit. Even if an usher will wear his own tuxedo, the shirts and accessories should all be rented, since colors, styles, ties, studs, and cuff links may vary.

Can my groom's outfit distinguish him from his ushers? Everyone, including your fathers, wears the same formalwear. What can vary are the accessories. Creative ways to set the groom (and perhaps the best man) apart:

Texture. If the ushers are wearing black cummerbunds and bow ties, perhaps vests, have your groom's (and perhaps the best man's) accessories be of woven or jacquard fabric. Or, if the male attendants are all wearing color accents, the groom can wear black accessories.

Colors. Ushers might wear paisley bow ties and cummerbunds in soft pastels. Order solid accessories for your groom (and best man), or vice versa.

Patterns. If wearing ascots, the groom's and best man's might be in a different pattern than the ushers'.

Bridal echoes. The groom's cummerbund might echo the same trim on the bride's gown, especially if it has rich embroidery.

Boutonnieres. The best man and ushers wear identical flowers in their left lapels. The flowers worn in the groom's left lapel may be a different variety and color to indicate his position of honor.

Accessories. The groom may also distinguish himself by being the only one to wear a top hat (with tails), a cummerbund (instead of a vest), or gemstone studs (a gift from his bride).

What accents can we add to the formalwear for a Christmas wedding? Choose bow ties and cummerbunds with metallic accents or holiday colors or tartan plaids to coordinate with bridesmaids. Rent or buy vests with flecks of gold or silver. Instead of cummerbunds, personalize outfits with festive suspenders (or braces).

Can my groom wear a national costume? Yes, in the most formal version. A groom of Scottish descent may wear his own clan tartan kilt with either a daytime or evening jacket. As with a military wedding (see "Your Fashion Dilemmas" section), only those men eligible to wear a specialized formal outfit do so; other attendants wear traditional formalwear appropriate to the time of day and style of the wedding.

Anatomy of a Tuxedo

Today, there are many creative options in formalwear which can reflect the personalities of those wearing it. Before your groom and his attendants begin to shop for their wedding-day outfits, they should consider these basic points. (For more information on formalwear, see the "Guide to Wedding Clothes" chart and the "Appendix, under Chapter 7, "Wedding Clothes.")

The jacket. Tuxedo jackets may have notched or peak lapels, or shawl collars. Single-breasted or double-breasted styles are equally appropriate.

The pants. Trousers should break about five inches above the ankle. Bottoms are hemmed, never cuffed.

The shirt. Traditionally, a pleated shirt is worn with a tuxedo. The proper closures: studs in black, white, or gold, or enhanced with precious stones.

The shirt sleeve. Allow one to one-and-a half inches of shirt sleeve to show beneath the sleeve of the jacket.

The cuff links. These may match the shirt studs or, for a dash of wit and whimsy, can be hearts, checkerboards, *Phantom of the Opera* masks, or other designs. Try to suit the wearer's personality.

The collar and tie. These options exist: the wing collar, the turn-down collar, and the stand-up collar. All are paired with a bow tie for formal evening dress. (Bow ties rest in front of the wings.)

The cummerbund. Always wear a cummerbund with pleats facing upward. Cummerbunds were once laughingly referred to as *crumb catchers* because they caught the crumbs when a gentleman ate! The pleats held theater tickets, keys, or money, so that bulging pockets wouldn't ruin a tuxedo's slim line. (Many cummerbunds from England still have hidden cummerbund pockets!) Colorful patterned suspenders (braces) may be substituted for the cummerbund; they hook onto the waistband of the pants, look stylish when jackets come off.

tying a bow tie

It's as simple as tying a shoelace:

- **Place tie around your neck, with ends hanging down.**
- **Tie a bow.**
- **Don't look in mirror or look down; it will confuse you.**
- **Once tied, use a mirror to straighten bow.**
- **Practice making a bow around your knee, before tying around your neck.**

pocket squares

Instead of a boutonniere, some men prefer to tuck a pocket square in their jacket's left breast pocket. There are four proper handkerchief folds:

1. *The multipronged*—elegant fold, best with linen or cotton. Resembles four overlapping mountain peaks.

2. *The pouf*—informal fold, best in silk. Handkerchief is softly stuffed into pocket, with ends fluffed out.

3. *The square-ended*—the most common fold, best in linen or cotton. Handkerchief is folded into a square; top strip shows outside of pocket.

4. *The triangle*—debonair fold, best in linen or cotton. Small triangle peaks from top of breast pocket.

The vest. Instead of a cummerbund, a colorful solid or patterned vest can add personality to the most conservative tuxedo! Vests also look sharp when jackets come off! (Buy them as ushers' gifts; they can be worn again and again….)

The boutonniere. The boutonniere is always worn on the left lapel, but never with a pocket square (see "Pocket Squares" box). A vibrantly colored flower is a dramatic accent for black-and-white formalwear.

The shoes, hose. Black patent oxfords or pumps are the best shoe choices. Men should wear hose that match the color of their trousers.

Formalwear Sizing

Here are key points to consider when ordering the formalwear for the groom, fathers, and ushers.

Ask if the store has a tailor on the premises. If pant legs are too long or too short (the most common fitting error), they can be hemmed in ten minutes.

If not, ask if the store has an affiliation with a tailor. Can he or she do small alterations—turning up sleeves, sewing on buttons?

Have each attendant come into the store to check the fit of his formalwear and all accessories.

Shirts should hug the neck; if too tight, ask for a collar extender (an elastic hoop or button).

Pants should touch the top of shoes.

Waistbands are often adjustable—check for side buckles.

Jackets should fit snugly, yet comfortably, around shoulders—no arm bulges—with some room at the waist.

The *collar* should hug the neck, the lapels shouldn't buckle.

"Vents," or panels, found on the side or in the back of the coat, should lay smoothly, following body lines.

Jacket sleeves should end at the wrist bone, each with the same number of sleeve buttons.

Also: Ask ushers to check their formalwear for any stains, fabric snags, or cigarette burns before leaving the store. They should also be sure they have all accessories that go with their outfit.

Appoint an attendant to return all formalwear to store on time. Late fees may be five to ten dollars per day, per outfit. Food and beverage stains can usually be dry-cleaned out. If there are more serious stains (e.g., grease, blood), expect to be asked to pay the cost of replacing the clothing.

Groom's Formalwear Glossary

THE COAT

Shoulders—can be natural or padded.

Lapels—the pieces of fabric that extend from the collar and lay folded back on the chest.

Peaked—a cut in the lapel points upward, adds to a broad, V-line look.

Notched—a triangular piece in the lapel is cut at the collar line and points outward.

Shawl—there is no cut in the lapel, creating a rounded effect.

Pockets—may be flapped or may have a decorative border at the top.

Besom—inset pockets with a narrow trim (often satin) across the top.

Single-Breasted—coat with one vertical row of buttons to close the front.

Double-Breasted—coat with two rows of vertical buttons; one to close the coat front, the other for decoration.

CLASSIC FORMALWEAR

Tails—a formal coat that is short in front and extends to two "tails" in back; a stiff-front white piqué vest, a white shirt, and black shoes complement tails.

White or gray full dress—tailcoat, trousers, and accessories are all white or gray.

Black full dress—tailcoat and trousers are black; accessories, white.

White tie—tailcoat, trousers, and shoes are black; accessories are white.

The Tuxedo—the most popular formalwear, available in a variety of fabrics and colors; it can be single- or double-breasted (see above definitions).

Black tie—tuxedo, trousers, bow tie, vest or cummerbund, are black or charcoal gray.

Cutaway Coat/Morning Coat—a long coat that tapers from the waistline button to one broad tail in the back, with a vent.

Stroller Coat—a semiformal suit jacket cut like a tuxedo; worn in daytime.

Spencer Coat—an open coat without buttons, cut right at the waistline.

Dinner Jacket—tuxedo-cut jacket in white, ivory, or novelty fabrics; worn with black, satin-striped trousers.

THE SHIRT

Traditional Formal Shirt—is white; some shirts have buttons, others may need pearl, onyx, gold, or diamond studs as closures.

Shirt with French Cuffs—calls for elegant cuff links.

Pleated Shirt—the front panels on either side of the buttons are pleated.

Wing collar—the collar has downward points; looks great with an ascot or bow tie.

Spread or Turned-down collar—similar to a business-shirt collar.

THE TROUSERS

Most are adjustable at the waist. Variations include:

Double-pleated—a double pleat in the front of trousers.

Striped—a satin or silk stripe down the outside of each leg.

ACCESSORIES

Neckwear—selected to match the coat, vest, or cummerbund; the various options include the following:

Bow tie—a short tie resembling a small bow; can be worn with any collar.

Four-in-hand tie—a knotted tie that hangs vertically, like a business-suit tie; can be fastened with a tie tack and should be worn with a spread collar.

Ascot—a broad neck scarf looped under the chin; fastened with a tie tack or stick pin, worn with a wing-collar.

Cummerbund—pleated sash made of brocade, silk, or satin; worn instead of a vest or suspenders to cover the trouser waistline. The pleat width, either horizontal or slanted to the right, varies; pleats are worn facing up.

Vest/Waistcoat—worn instead of a cummerbund or suspenders under the coat; adjustable behind neck and waist.

Other options—tie tacks, stick pins, cuff links, studs, pocket squares, suspenders (braces), canes, top hats, shoes, and scarves; all can be rented from formalwear shops. Personalize the formalwear with creative accessories.

shopping for maids' gowns

- Shop with honor attendant; choose her dress first.
- Narrow the choices for the maids' dresses to three styles.
- Let maids make the final decision since they are, most likely, buying their own dresses.

Bridesmaids and Honor Attendants

Proper dress varies with the hour and the season, but your wedding party will look most striking coming down the aisle and standing in the receiving line if their dresses are similar, if not the same.

Bridesmaids and honor attendants should wear dresses that complement the style and formality of your gown. Attendants may wear short dresses, even if the bride wears a floor-length gown, but *never* a long dress if the bride is in a short gown.

If you don't want all bridesmaids to dress alike, ask each to select her own style of dress in the same color family.

You may wish to distinguish your honor attendant. Order her a dress in a shade different than the other bridesmaids' dresses—in a contrasting color (deep rose instead of pink), or with contrasting trim or accessories.

If there is just one honor attendant, she should dress in a style similar to that of the bride.

Order similar headpieces and bouquets for attendants. Select floral wreaths or combs, or ribbon headbands that match or harmonize with the dresses. Bouquets should resemble the style of the bride's bouquet and have similar colors (unless it is all white).

Shoes should be similar. They should match the mood and color of bridesmaids' dresses and be the same heel height. They may be white or black, or dyed to match gowns; perhaps metallic, in silver, gold, or pewter.

Jewelry should be similar and simple. Ask maids to wear a single strand of pearls, a gold chain, or a locket (perhaps a thank-you gift from you!).

Mothers of the Bride and Groom

The dresses of the mothers of the bride and groom should be dignified, yet stylish; flattering to figure and personality; and complement each other's dress and those of other bridesmaids in the wedding party.

Traditionally, the mother of the bride selects her outfit first. She then describes it to the mother of the groom, allowing her enough time to shop. The mothers will most likely talk about the wedding style and agree on complementary colors before either shops, however. Style and length should be appropriate to the style and time of the wedding (see "Guide to Wedding Clothes" chart). The color should blend with (rather than match) the color worn by the wedding party. Mothers should avoid all black or all white—black is too somber and white is reserved for the bride. (The exceptions are a *snowball wedding*, where the entire wedding party wears white, and an *Art Deco wedding*, where the entire wedding party wears black and white.)

Both mothers may wear the same color, but not the *same* dress, although they should be the same degree of formality, and, preferably, the same length.

Mothers' dresses will set the style for your wedding guests. Keep in mind what guests will feel comfortable in for the occasion.

Order flowers for both mothers: a nosegay, handtied bouquet, one striking bloom, a wrist corsage or floral bracelet, a pocket posy (for a suit). If walking down the aisle, mothers should leave handbags and wraps with seated family members, and carry only flowers.

Child Attendants

Children will perform better if they're happy and comfortable with the way they look (see Chapter 6, "The Wedding Party").

Junior bridesmaids' dresses should be styled for their age (no low-cut necklines). They might wear the same color and fabric as the bridesmaids, and the same wreath or hair flower; bouquets should also match (see Chapter 15, "Wedding Flowers").

Flower girls' dresses may echo the bride's gown. For example, shop for a dress with the same leg-of-mutton sleeves, but in a floral print, with a silk sash to match the bouquets. Other style options: white organza pinafores over forest-green velvet dresses; miniature flowers and pastel hair ribbons; ballet slippers or flat black (or white) patent leather pumps trimmed with bows, flowers, or buckles.

Ring bearers or pages (if males) might wear traditional satin-and-velvet suits.

Other style options: dark-blue Eton suits, white shorts, and white or blue knee socks. For a summer wedding: white linen suits with white knee socks and white shoes. For a semiformal or an informal weddings: matching suits or matching long pants and jackets, boutonnieres to match those of the ushers.

Children in a semiformal or informal remarriage ceremony wear "special occasion" outfits. Boys might wear matching neckties; girls, lacy tights and identical bouquets (see Chapter 15, "Wedding Flowers").

Familiarize your child attendants with the outfits they'll wear. Together, look, at pictures in storybooks about weddings, perhaps page through bridal magazines. Rent videos of films that have child attendants in them. Point out the flower girl's and ring bearer's clothing. Draw pictures of wedding clothes with the children, and perhaps display their efforts at the rehearsal or rehearsal dinner. Play "dress up" with the children, draping the girls in lace curtains (for the gowns), and tying old bow ties on the little boys. Let them look in the mirror.

Shop together for the flower girl and ring bearer outfits. Let your child attendants feel part of the wedding excitement. Spend time with them (and their mothers) trying on the clothes in the dressing room.

Try to have your child attendants' outfits fitted at the same time that the ushers' and bridesmaids' outfits are fitted. This will make your child attendants feel special, part of the wedding party, and very grown up.

Encourage your child attendants to try on their outfits briefly at home. This will get them accustomed to wearing and walking in the clothes in advance.

Encourage the mothers of your child attendants to not dress them hours in advance of the cermony on wedding day. They may get fidgety, and may soil, or tear their outfits before it's time for them to walk down the aisle.

YOUR WEDDING CEREMONY

All wedding planning culminates in the moment you two turn to each other and begin to say your vows. Whether your wedding ceremony is steeped in tradition or was written by you a few weeks ago, it will seal your status as a married couple. The ceremony, more than any other part of the day, will have to convey the importance of getting married, as well as express your own personalities through unique personal touches.

Questions for Clergy

By this time, you have already settled general logistics with your clergymember such as date, time, size, religious requirements, and general style of the wedding. (If you haven't, turn back to Chapter 4, "Planning Your Wedding," and contact your officiant as soon as possible!) Perhaps you have scheduled counseling sessions—required by your religion. Wedding-ceremony details are usually covered during one of these conversations. To make sure, take along this checklist and ask your officiant about the points that apply to your situation.

☐ When do we give our marriage license to you? How many witnesses do we need? When is the document signed?

☐ May our photographer use a flash during the ceremony? How close to the altar may he or she stand?

☐ Are wedding guests allowed to throw rice or flower petals within the building or on the steps?

☐ When can we gain entry into the church, synagogue, on wedding day?

☐ What area is recommended for setting up the receiving line?

☐ Do you have samples of wedding programs? When are they passed out?

☐ Which accessories are provided (*huppah*, candelabra, aisle runner)?

getting guests involved

- If marrying in a house of worship, reverse positions with officiant so bride and groom face guests.

- Move *huppah* or portable altar closer to pews to increase the feeling of community.

- At a small wedding, have guests stand around altar in a semicircle.

- Stand outside the house of worship to greet arriving guests—an Oriental custom.

- Welcome guests with bagpipers, saxophonists, classical guitarists, outside ceremony site; a flutist or harpist indoors.

- Divide a prayer for attendants or guests to say in unison.

- After sealing your vows with a kiss, ask the clergymember to pass the Kiss of Peace—once a kiss, but now most often a handshake passed from clergymember to you, to attendants, to all guests.

- Ask ushers to distribute candles to each guest as he or she is seated. After lighting the Unity Candle, the bride and groom walk to the first pew on their sides of the church. With their own candles they each light the candle of the guest in the first seat of the first pew, who lights the candle of the person next to him or her, till all of these Candles of Peace are lit, throughout the room.

- To brisk recessional music (a trumpet fanfare, a serenade of French horns?), stop at each pew to greet guests as you walk up the aisle.

☐ Can we include a wine ceremony, communion, ethnic traditions?

☐ How long will the ceremony last? Will you be delivering a homily or speech? Can we preview it to prevent surprises on wedding day?

☐ Can we write our vows, personalize our ceremony? Can we read wording of the service and make outdated phrases more contemporary?

☐ Must all readings be religious? When will they be performed?

☐ Will you explain the symbolism of the ceremony to guests who may not be familiar with the rituals?

☐ Is a kiss permitted at the end of the marriage ceremony?

☐ Is it possible to reserve seats for family members?

☐ Can you suggest roles for children from previous marriages? May children of another religion serve as altar servers, candle lighters?

☐ When is the rehearsal held? Will you coordinate the procession, recession?

☐ Will you and your spouse be attending the rehearsal dinner, reception? Will you bless the meal?

☐ Can you arbitrate between divorced parents or feuding in-laws?

Planning the Ceremony

Ask your priest, minister, or rabbi to review the ceremony with you step by step. You may have some options: the number of readings, if communion is celebrated, if you include poetry, prose, favorite song lyrics, or write your own vows. A common misconception is that a wedding without witnesses or the exchange of vows is illegal. Matrimonial laws vary by state; some require witnesses, others specify just that the couple and the officiant be present. A ceremony may not be required to legally join a couple in wedlock. However, most states require that the bride and groom assure the officiant they are entering into marriage of their own free will. Most religious ceremonies include the following elements, which may be personalized.

The Greeting/Call to Worship. These first words will welcome the guests and set the tone. For example, the traditional, well-recognized greeting from *The Book of Common Prayer* of The Episcopal Church is:

"Dearly beloved: We have come together in the presence of God to witness and bless the joining together of this man and this woman in Holy Matrimony…"

At this part of the ceremony, you might include an anecdote about how you met, a favorite poem or quotation, a wish for your family, a reading from a friend about love and friendship. Your clergymember might also express your personal philosophy about marriage.

"Jane and Kevin feel that their lifelong companion should be…"

The Charge to the Couple. This is the part of the ceremony that determines that the bride and groom have come together to marry of their own free will. For example, the well-recognized questions from the Protestant ceremony:

"Will you have this man/woman to be your wedded (husband/wife) to live together in holy matrimony...?"

The Presentation/Giving Away. Traditionally, at a point in the ceremony, the clergymember asks:

"Who gives this woman to be married to this man?" (Episcopal)

The bride's father, who has escorted her down the aisle, replies, *"I do."*

The "giving away" dates back to the time when patriarchal ownership of a daughter was transferred to a husband in marriage. Today, many couples choose to vary these traditional words. For example, the minister might ask, *"Who blesses/supports this marriage?"* Both your parents and your groom's parents might respond, *"We, their parents, do."* The entire wedding party and congregation might also respond, *"We do."*

At this point, the couple and their attendants ascend to the altar from the head of the aisle to say their vows.

The Vows. These public promises join you together emotionally and proclaim your intentions to love, trust, and honor each other. In traditional Christian weddings, the couple promise *"to have and to hold...for better or for worse."* Most couples today choose to substitute the word *"cherish"* in the woman's traditional pledge for the words *"to obey."*

The Exchange of Rings. Traditionally, the bride and groom place a wedding ring on each other's finger, stating, *"With this ring, I thee wed."* You may, however, want to also state what the rings mean to you as a couple.

The Pronouncement. At the end of the ceremony, the officiant will declare to those assembled that you are legally wed. The words traditionally heard:

"I now pronounce you man and wife. Those whom God has joined together, let no man put asunder."

Today, most clergymembers have changed the pronouncement to the more egalitarian words, *"I now pronounce you husband and wife."* He or she might also personalize the pronouncement.

Remember, it is wise to keep your kiss at the altar in good taste. There will be scores of eyes focused on you.

Ceremony Readings

Whether you and your groom compose your own poem or prayer to accompany your vows or choose a verse from another source, a brief reading is a lovely way to express any special thoughts you may have. You might also include beloved friends or siblings by asking them to recite the reading for you. The best time for readings to be offered is before the vows and after the exchange of rings. Guests may enjoy following along with their own copy of the reading, perhaps included in a wedding program. Be sure to consult with your clergymember for approval, as well as other suggestions.

creative ceremony touches

- Have children pass out *yarmulkes* (skullcaps) for a Jewish ceremony, candles, flowers.

- Print greetings, poetry, tributes, in wedding programs (see "The Wedding Program" section).

- Hang a floral wreath on the door of the house of worship, announcing "wedding in progress."

- Bride and groom walk down the aisle escorted by both parents—a Jewish tradition.

- As bride is escorted to the altar, she might pause at the first pew to give her mother a flower and a kiss; do the same for her mother-in-law as she leaves the altar with her groom.

- Sip from two goblets of wine—a Jewish tradition—to symbolize the joy and sorrow of life.

- Seal your vows with nine sips of sake (three sips from three cups)—as the Japanese do.

- Have attendants release helium balloons, brightly colored butterflies, as you emerge from the house of worship.

- Travel to the reception in creative transportation—a horse and buggy, an antique car (see Chapter 19, "Going Away").

to find Scripture

If you remember several words or phrases from a particular passage, but don't know how to find it:

- Look in a religious *concordance*, a reference book in libraries, bookstores, which lists key words ("love," "marriage") alphabetically; under each word is listed every verse and phrase where that word appears, and the citation where it can be found in the Bible.

- Compare translations in the King James version and Today's English version of the Bible, to select the version you prefer.

- Check a Bible dictionary, which is filled with entries about phrases and words from the Bible. If you turn to "children," "family," "marriage," or "love," you may pick up other references to Scripture.

Sacred Scripture

Read many translations before you choose your Scripture selections. Wording may vary and one might seem more meaningful, but remember that not all versions are acceptable in every church. Below are sections from both the Old Testament (the Jewish Scripture), appropriate for a Jewish or Christian wedding, and the New Testament, appropriate for a Christian wedding. Check Today's English Version of the Bible (see Appendix, under Chapter 8, "Your Wedding Ceremony," for source).

On husbands and wives:
- Proverbs 17; 20; 25–29, 31:10–13
- Hosea 2:21–22
- Ephesians 5:28–33
- Ruth 1:16
- Genesis 2:18–24
- Song of Solomon 4:1–3; 5:10–14; 7; 16
- Isaiah 61:10—62:5

On marriage:
- Hebrews 13:4
- Ecclesiastes 4:9–12
- Matthew 19:4–6
- Mark 10:6–9
- John 2:1–11

On home and family:
- Matthew 7:21, 24–27
- Ephesians 3:14–19
- Proverbs 24:3–6

On praise and joy:
- Psalms 23; 33; 34; 63; 90; 100; 103; 139; 145; 150
- Isaiah 61:10–11
- Jeremiah 33:10–11
- Ecclesiastes 9:7–9
- John 15:9–17

On love:
- I John 3:16; 3:18–24; 4:7–19
- John 15:9–17
- I Corinthians 13:1–13
- Song of Solomon 7:11–12; 8:6b–7
- Ephesians 4:1–4; 5:1–2
- Isaiah 43:1–5; 54:10; 60:19–22
- Matthew 22:35–40
- Romans 12:1–2, 9–18
- Colossians 3:12–13
- Proverbs 3:3–6
- 1 Peter 3:7

Secular readings

Visit your local library to research inspirational prose and poetry that express your convictions. Here are four types of readings:

Authors such as Rollo May, R.D. Laing, Paul Tournier, Denis de Rougemont, and David Viscott, Alice Walker, D.H. Lawrence, Emily and Charlotte Brontë.

Poetry from the works of e.e. cummings, Robert Frost, Rainer Maria Rilke, Sara Teasdale, Percy Shelley, Elizabeth Barret Browning, John Keats, Shakespeare. Also consider the work of Rod McKuen, Kahlil Gibran (*The Prophet*).

Novels and plays from such writers as John Updike, Thornton Wilder, Neil Simon, and Anne Morrow Lindbergh (*Gift from the Sea*).

Song lyrics from show tunes or current love songs (see Chapter 14, "Wedding Music," for suggestions).

Unity Symbols

Many couples choose to incorporate symbols of unity into their wedding ceremony to demonstrate that two families are becoming one through marriage.

The Unity Candle. The bride's parents and the groom's each light a candle on their respective sides of the altar, which remain burning throughout the ceremony. A taller candle remains unlit in the center, till the officiant pronounces the couple husband and wife. Then bride and groom each carry their respective candles to the center, to jointly light the Unity Candle, then return their candles to the sides of the altar. The lighting of the Unity Candle symbolizes the joining of their families, the merging of two individuals into one married couple (the light of their love burns jointly, as their inner candles continue to burn separately), the blending of two religions or heritages, or the creation of a new blended family (if it is a remarriage with children.) (See Chapter 2, "Wedding Customs," and Chapter 11, "Remarriage.")

The Unity Cup. Each family fills goblets from separate decanters. The bride and groom each pour half of the wine into a separate cup, from which each sips. The half-filled goblets are a reminder of your individuality; the single cup marks your new life together.

The Marriage Vessel and the Rose, is a ceremony created by The Reverend Roger Coleman (see Appendix, under Chapter 8, "Your Wedding Ceremony"). After the officiant pronounces the bride and groom husband and wife, the officiant picks up an earthenware vase and a fresh or silk rose (perhaps brought forward by a family member). He or she explains that the vessel is a symbol of love's strength and endurance, and that *"The Lord formed the human from the clay of the ground"* (Genesis: 2:7). *"The miracle of the vessel is that it not only protects but is enriched by that which it holds, The Rose."* The rose is a symbol of the *"potential and beauty contained in love's promises."*

The groom presents the rose to the bride: *"Jane, may this gift represent my Gratitude/for the person you are/ And the person I am becoming."*

The bride presents the vessel to the groom: *"Paul, may this gift represent my Gratitude/for all you have given me/And all we share together."*

The bride places the rose in the vessel; they hold it together and repeat after the officiant: *"As our gifts bring beauty And purpose to each other,/May our lives continue/To enrich and strengthen one another."*

The officiant takes the vessel and rose and says: *"Jane and Paul, as you share each passing day and as your days become years, may you remember this tradition you have created."*

On each anniversary, the couple is urged to add an additional rose to the marriage vessel, a symbol of their ever-growing love for each other. (Some couples may add a silk flower each year, or order a fresh bouquet of flowers with a symbolic number of blossoms.)

honoring deceased relatives

- Include a period of silence to honor a deceased relative.

- Lay a bouquet on an empty seat in the first pew in a missing parent's honor. Make note of the symbolism in the wedding program.

- Print a tribute or dedication in the wedding program.

- Carry or wear a memento from a deceased relative (a favorite flower, a handkerchief, a strand of pearls).

- Select the person's favorite song as your processional, or have a soloist sing it during the ceremony.

- Ask the clergymember or officiant to mention him or her during the ceremony.

- Light a symbolic candle during the ceremony, and announce its significance to those assembled.

- Visit the relative's grave site after the ceremony and leave your bouquet.

- Make a donation to a favorite charity in their name, on the occasion of your marriage.

Writing Your Own Vows

A popular way to personalize your ceremony is to write vows that express your own beliefs and feelings (see Appendix, under Chapter 8, "Your Wedding Ceremony"). Working on the ceremony together will also bring you closer together. Here are tips for pledging your love:

Tell your officiant your plans. If you are having a religious wedding, he or she must make sure that your wording does not go against the beliefs of your house of worship. Also, the clergymember may have other original ceremonies for you to examine. Don't wait until the last minute. If there is a disagreement, it's much easier to find out early on, when you can find another officiant if necessary.

Incorporate old and new if you wish. It can be satisfying to use old, well-loved phrases and vows amid your own words. Some couples are fond of the traditional Protestant query, *"...will you love her/him, comfort her/him, honor, and keep her/him...as long as you both shall live?"* so they use it with their own sentiments.

Be personal. This is a perfect time to address your unique situation. If this is a second wedding (see Chapter 11, "Remarriage"), talk about your faith in marriage and the miracle of new love. If you have children, evoke your commitment to creating a new family. If you have different backgrounds, promise to respect and honor both heritages while creating your own traditions.

Ask yourselves questions. "What does marriage mean to me?" "Which promises are the most important to us?" "What can I promise to provide my fiancé?" "What do I need from him?" Contemplate what the words *love, trust, honesty, compassion, friendship, forgiveness, fidelity, faith, honor,* and *respect* mean to you.

Remember the solemnity of the occasion. Avoid overly cute pledges (e.g., *"the bride will never leave her stockings to dry in the bathroom"*). And address child-rearing and financial issues privately. It's also best to avoid very intimate thoughts and controversial political statements, which might upset other guests.

Don't make your vows too long. Your spoken vows should be limited to one to three minutes. You need not deliver a sermon to the assembled guests on your views of marriage. Rather, let some of your views and beliefs be expressed through readings, songs, and prayers read by family and friends.

Read your vows aloud in advance. Sometimes a sentence that looks fine on paper is difficult to understand when spoken. Change anything that trips your tongue or sounds awkward.

interfaith-ceremony tips

- The clergymember at the house of worship where the ceremony takes place is the host. He or she is in charge of arrangements, has final service approval, and officially invites the other clergymember. You can pave the way by finding out if both are willing to participate (see Chapter 4, "Planning Your Wedding").

- Bride and groom should each feel their religion is respected equally. Intertwine symbols on wedding invitation and program.

- Emphasize shared symbols—candles, wine, bread.

- Add prayers and music from each religion, praying and singing in unison.

- Select words and Scripture that emphasize what you both have in common. Have your sister read a Scripture from your fiancé's religion, while his brother reads a passage from yours.

- Have clergymembers alternate religious rituals (see Chapter 9, "Religious Rituals & Requirements").

- Ask clergymembers to explain religious traditions to guests. Explain traditions in program.

- Involve members of each family meaningfully in the ceremony (reading poems, Scripture, lighting candles).

- Compromise on traditions. Plan a garden wedding where your minister and his rabbi co-officiate under a floral *huppah* (see Chapter 9, "Religious Rituals & Requirements").

Make clear, legible copies of your vows and carry them on wedding day. No matter how comfortable you feel with the words, nervousness can wipe phrases from your memory. At least you'll be able to read the vows if you forget. Give a copy to the clergymember as well. He or she can read the words, and you can repeat them. Or, carry a copy down the aisle inside a prayer book decorated with flowers.

Your Rehearsal

You, your groom, your clergyperson, and all members of the wedding, including ushers, readers, and musicians will gather at the ceremony site (usually the night before or a few days before the wedding) to go through the basics and answer last-minute questions. After the rehearsal, the groom's parents traditionally host a rehearsal dinner (see Chapter 3, "Prewedding Parties"). The entire wedding party, immediate families, and clergymember are invited. Out-of-town guests may be included in some cases. Some couples hold the rehearsal and rehearsal dinner two nights before the wedding so the party can go on as long as guests wish, without worrying about rushing home for a good night's rest. If this is not possible, make sure that you and your fiancé leave at a reasonable hour.

If your ceremony is simple and involves very few people or will be held in a public place such as a hotel, your clergymember may not schedule a rehearsal. Instead, brief instructions would be given to those involved before the ceremony begins.

Although superstition once held that the bride had a stand-in for the rehearsal, today she is urged to participate so she'll feel confident on wedding day.

Remember these rehearsal basics:

Let your officiant take charge. He or she has handled many ceremonies and can tell everyone exactly where to stand, walk, sit.

Resist making major changes or introducing new ideas. Time is short, everyone is excited, and a rehearsal is meant to calm and clarify, not confuse. Discuss ceremony ideas during your premarriage conference with your clergymember. Go over plans with bridesmaids, ushers, and honor attendants before the rehearsal to avoid upsets about assigned responsibilities at the altar (who stands next to each of you, who holds your bouquet, arranges your train, holds the bride's and groom's rings).

Review any special variations you've planned in the service. Although the entire marriage service will not be read, special variations will be reviewed, key phrases that will act as cues for the honor attendant and best man will be noted.

Rehearse the roles of those assigned a special task. Anyone who will light a candle, read a lesson, sing a solo, should run through his or her part. Go over whether or not

civil-ceremony tips

- The usual civil ceremony is an adaptation from the *Book of Common Prayer*, modernized at many city halls. It lasts not much more than a minute. (See Chapter 4, "Planning Your Wedding," for more on civil ceremonies.)

- Ask your judge or justice of the peace if you can add to the ceremony. Many officiants will add to the ceremony themselves!

- Feel free to read passages from your favorite poetry, music, song lyrics, books. Or, write personal vows (see "Writing Your Own Vows" section and Appendix, under Chapter 8, "Your Wedding Ceremony").

night-before-the-ceremony tips

DO get enough sleep. You'll be on your feet through most of your exciting and demanding day, greeting more people than you've seen in years—plus dancing!

DO take time to visualize each step of the day beforehand. This will calm you and give you a chance to anticipate any hitches.

DO leave enough time to bathe, dress, and reminisce with family. Take time to talk privately with your parents and tell them that you appreciate all that they've done for you.

DON'T bring along too many personal items to the ceremony; you'll just worry about them.

DO have a small meal or a snack of cheese or fruit before you leave for the ceremony. Don't risk feeling faint at the altar!

DO snap a few photos of the last hours at home.

DON'T panic if you fall behind schedule. The ceremony will wait for you. Remain flexible and calm. Guests want to see you smile. Looking and feeling your best is more important than starting on the dot.

the reading will be waiting on the lectern or carried by the reader on wedding day, how to turn on the lectern light, adjust the microphone.

The clergymember or wedding consultant will brief ushers on protocol. They'll review the procedure for seating guests, including the bride's and groom's mothers, and assign special tasks, such as spreading the aisle runner or unrolling pew ribbons. Ushers should learn the answers to typical questions (e.g., "Where is the restroom?" or "Where can we get a drink of water?").

Take along dummy bouquets (a clutch of gift-ribbon bows from your shower). Then you and your honor attendant can practice passing your flowers. Also practice the necessary turns at the altar.

The officiant may review with your mother phrases that will lead to guest participation. Since her actions will cue everyone else, she will want to know at what points the clergyperson will say things such as, "All rise."

Seating Guests

During the rehearsal, you should explain the seating positions to your ushers, who will be escorting the guests to their seats (see Chapter 6, "The Wedding Party").

In a Christian wedding, the bride's family and friends are seated on the left side (referred to as the Gospel side) of the church as you face the altar. (This will be the side of the church that the bride will be standing on as she faces the altar.) The right side of the church is reserved for the groom's family and friends. If the church has two center aisles, the bride's contingent sits on both sides of the left aisle, the groom's on both sides of the right aisle. The parents sit in the center section; the bride's on the left, the groom's on the right.

In a Jewish wedding, the bride's guests sit on the right side. (This will be the side of the synagogue that the bride will be standing on as she faces the rabbi.) The left side of the synagogue is reserved for the groom's family and friends. All parents remain standing under the *huppah* throughout the ceremony.

If one family will have many more guests than the other, everyone may sit together. This will fill up the empty seats on one side and serve to introduce everyone earlier in the celebration.

Certain pew rows will be reserved for family members, special guests. Parents of both the bride and groom sit in the first pews on their respective sides, grandparents

CHRISTIAN CEREMONY SEATING:

The bride's family is seated on the left, the groom's family on the right, as you face the altar.

1. Bride's mother
2. Bride's father
3. Bride's siblings
4. Bride's grandparents
5. Bride's special guests (aunt, godmother, elderly relatives, parents of flower girl)
6. Bride's father and spouse (if divorced from bride's mother). Or, bride's mother and spouse; if father is custodial parent, *he* sits in front row.
7. (Optional) Close relatives and friends, elderly guests of the bride
8. Groom's father
9. Groom's mother
10. Groom's grandparents
11. Groom's siblings
12. Groom's father and spouse (if divorced from groom's mother). Or, groom's mother and spouse; if father is custodial parent, *he* sits in front row.
13. Groom's special guests (aunt, godmother, elderly relatives, parents of ring bearer)
14. (Optional) Close relatives and friends, elderly guests of the groom

in the second pews (along the aisle) to ensure that they'll get the best view, alongside siblings of the bride and groom. You may reserve additional pews on each side for other honored guests, parents of the flower girl and ring bearer—their children may join them during the ceremony. If you have a blended family with stepsiblings, you may reserve additional pews. (Mark these pews with flower garlands or ribbons.) Pew cards or "within the ribbons" cards may be sent to those guests you wish to honor with special seats (see Chapter 5, "Invitations & Announcements").

If your parents are divorced, your family situation determines the seating. For example, if neither has remarried and they are on friendly terms, they may sit side by side in the front pew. If this is not possible, the custodial parent takes the front pew and the other parent should sit in the third pew with his or her spouse if he or she has remarried. (In a Jewish ceremony, the parents stand under the *huppah*; their spouses sit in the second and third pews.)

Seat all other guests from front to back as they enter the church. Late arrivals should slip into back rows, since no one should be seated by ushers after the bride's mother.

Ceremony Countdown

In some regions of the country, the groom's parents will stand in front of the house of worship to greet guests. Especially if it is a small, informal ceremony held at a non-religious site, the couple, as well as both sets of parents, may mingle with guests before the start of the ceremony. If this is the case, draw up your own timetable.

JEWISH CEREMONY SEATING:

The sides assigned for a Christian ceremony are reversed. Instead, the bride's family is seated on the right, the groom's family on the left, as you face the altar. All parents remain standing under the *huppah* throughout the ceremony. (If divorced, parents' partners will be seated in the second and third pews.)

1. Bride's grandparents
2. Bride's siblings
3. Spouse or companion of bride's mother (if mother is divorced from bride's father)
4. Bride's special guests (aunt, godmother, elderly relatives, parents of flower girl)
5. Spouse or companion of bride's father (if father is divorced from bride's mother)
6. Close relatives and friends, elderly relatives of the bride
7. Groom's siblings
8. Groom's grandparents
9. Groom's special guests (aunt, godmother, elderly relatives, parents of ring bearer)
10. Spouse or companion of groom's mother (if mother is divorced from groom's father)
11. Close relatives and friends, elderly relatives of the groom
12. Spouse or companion of groom's father (if father is divorced from groom's mother)

The sample timetable below is based on a large, formal wedding that will take place about fifteen minutes from the bride's house. Adapt it to your own situation, allowing plenty of time—in traffic—to arrive at the ceremony site relaxed.

Two hours before the ceremony: You, your mother, and your attendants begin dressing. If you're getting ready at the ceremony site, arrive there at least an hour and a half before the service.

One hour before the ceremony: Any bridesmaids who have dressed elsewhere gather at your house to pick up their flowers and pose for photographs.

Forty-five minutes before the ceremony: Ushers arrive at the ceremony site and pin on their boutonnieres. They distribute Mass books and wedding programs, pick up seating plans from the head usher, then gather at the entrance to wait for the first guests to arrive.

Thirty minutes before the ceremony: The organist starts the prelude, while ushers escort guests to their seats. Your mother and attendants leave for the ceremony site.

Twenty minutes before the ceremony: The groom and his best man arrive. Your clergymember makes certain that the marriage license is in order, and gives any last-minute instructions. Meanwhile, you and your father (or whoever will escort you down the aisle) leave for the ceremony site.

Ten minutes before the ceremony: Your attendants arrive, followed by your mother, the groom's parents, and other close members of your families. The bridal party and the parents wait in the vestibule (or hallway) while the other relatives are seated.

Five minutes before the ceremony: The groom's mother is escorted to her seat (unless it is a Jewish ceremony). The groom's father follows a few feet behind the usher, then takes his seat beside his wife, on the aisle. You and your father arrive and, if possible, park at a back entrance where you won't be seen by late-arriving guests. As your mother (the last person to be seated by an usher) starts down the aisle, you and your father join the wedding party in the vestibule (or hallway).

One minute before the ceremony: Two ushers walk in step to the front of the aisle to unroll the pew ribbons and lay the aisle runner, if they are used.

The pew ribbons are wound or folded and waiting in the second or third pew on each side of the sanctuary. Ushers pick them up and walk toward the back, stretching them across each aisle post and tying them on the last ones. (The ribbons remind guests to remain in their seats; ushers remove them after the recession.)

The aisle runner (on a spool or in pleats at the steps to the chancel) is unrolled next. One usher holds each corner of the aisle runner, and they both walk in step down the aisle, smoothing the white canvas in place behind them. The ushers then return to the vestibule and take their places in the procession. (The aisle runner, which protects the bride's gown, remains till all guests have left the sanctuary. After the ceremony is over and guests have departed, the church sexton or the maintenance crew of the synagogue, hotel, or banquet hall will remove it.)

Ceremony time: The minister, priest, or rabbi takes his or her place, followed by the groom and his best man. (In a Christian wedding, the groom and best man enter from the chancel door and stand facing the congregation—at an angle—with the groom next to the officiant, the best man one step behind the groom. In a Jewish wedding, the groom and best man are part of the procession.) As the procession begins, guests rise and turn to watch the bride enter.

The Procession

Some churches have two center aisles. In such cases, use the left aisle for the procession and the right aisle for the recession, or close off the second aisle entirely. Houses of worship with one center aisle are more common, however, and this aisle is used for both the procession and the recession.

The Protestant Procession

The ushers enter first from the back of the church, in pairs, by height—from shortest (first) to tallest. If there is an extra usher, the shortest leads, alone.

ceremony tips

- The congregation should be able to hear your voices. Anyone speaking should turn at a slight angle toward the congregation. Ask your clergymember if the house of worship has a sound system. If not, ask if you can rent one for the day.

- Members of the wedding party, even those of different faiths, should realize that accepting the invitation to be an attendant means they will fully participate in the religious rituals: kneeling (in a Catholic ceremony), praying aloud, singing hymns, wearing a *yarmulke* in a Jewish ceremony. Anyone who feels uncomfortable should excuse themselves when first asked.

- If you are required to kneel or climb steps during the ceremony, your groom should plan to take your arm to help you up and down.

- The best man and honor attendants should have your rings handy (on her thumb, in his pocket), so that they can quickly give them to the officiant when asked, for the exchange of rings.

- After you two say your vows and the officiant has congratulated you, your groom should be prepared to lift your veil for the kiss.

- Afterward, your honor attendant should give your bouquet back (she has held it during your vows) and arrange your train as you turn to face the guests for the recession.

CHRISTIAN PROCESSION:

1. Clergymember
2. Groom
3. Best man
4. Ushers
5. Bridesmaids
6. Honor attendant(s)
7. Ring bearer
8. Flower girl
9. Bride
10. Father of the bride

Ushers walk slowly, in step, leaving three to four pews between each pair.

The bridesmaids walk down the aisle next, four to five pews behind the ushers. They walk alone if there are fewer than four; otherwise, they are paired according to height. If there is not an even number of bridesmaids, the shortest person leads, alone.

The junior bridesmaid precedes the honor attendant; if there are two junior bridesmaids, they may walk together.

The maid of honor or matron of honor precedes the child attendants (if there are any), or the bride (if there aren't). If there is both a maid of honor and matron of honor, they may either walk together or separately. Whoever has the most duties walks last, directly before the bride.

The ring bearer walks alone or may be paired with the flower girl.

The flower girl precedes the bride (traditionally strewing rose petals in her path; today, practicality often rules that she simply carry a basket of flowers).

The bride and her father enter next, the bride on her father's left arm.

The pages (if there are any) end the procession, carrying the bride's train.

The Catholic Procession

The same order is followed, although the ushers may forgo the walk down the aisle and be met at the chancel door by the priest, the groom, and the best man.

The Jewish Procession

Orthodox, Conservative, and Reform Jewish processions vary according to local custom and the family's preferences.

In the most formal procession, the rabbi

140

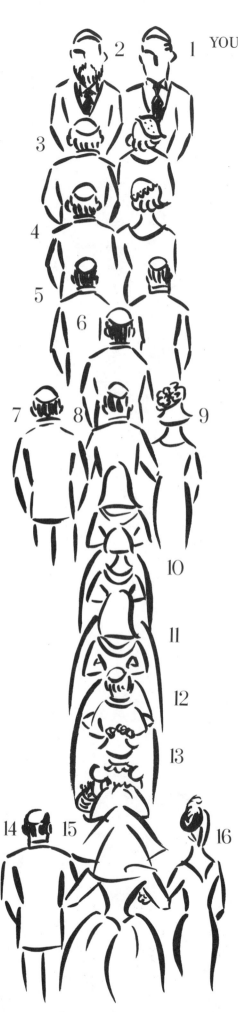

and cantor (walking on the rabbi's right) walk down the aisle first, followed by:

the bride's grandparents

the groom's grandparents

the ushers in pairs, by height; from shortest to tallest (last)

the best man

the groom on his father's right, his mother's left

the bridesmaids, individually by height (shortest first); if there are more than four, they may walk in pairs. If there is not an even number of bridesmaids, the shortest walks alone, first.

the honor attendant(s); the one with the most duties precedes the bride

the ring bearer

the flower girl

the bride on her father's right arm, her mother's left

In the most simple Jewish procession, the ushers walk down the aisle first in pairs, by height, followed by the bridesmaids in pairs, the best man, the groom, the honor attendant, the flower girl, the bride on her father's right arm. It's optional for the groom's parents and the bride's mother to join the procession.

The Informal Procession:

At very small weddings, such as simple civil ceremonies, the bride is preceded by one attendant and escorted into the room by her father. Or, there may not be a procession. The bride and groom might stand before the minister, with guests standing in a circle around them.

For a large civil ceremony in a ballroom or other formal setting, choose the procession that suits the site.

JEWISH PROCESSION:

1. Cantor
2. Rabbi
3. Bride's grandparents
4. Groom's grandparents
5. Ushers
6. Best man
7. Groom's father
8. Groom
9. Groom's mother
10. Bridesmaids
11. Honor attendant
12. Ring bearer
13. Flower girl
14. Bride's father
15. Bride
16. Bride's mother

Your Ceremony Escort

Traditionally, the bride is escorted down the aisle on her wedding day by her father. Many couples are following the Jewish tradition of having both parents escort the bride and groom down the aisle, no matter what their religion. There may be several nontraditional family situations, however:

If your father has died, you may choose to walk alone. Or, consider asking your mother, stepfather, brother, uncle, another relative, or a close family friend to escort you. Whoever takes the place of your absent father will sit in the front pew after the procession.

Your special escort may also respond when your clergymember asks, *"Who gives/supports this woman in marriage?"* If your mother has not walked you down the aisle, she may still nod or respond *"I do,"* or *"I, her mother, do,"* from her place in the first pew, or she can be escorted to your side at the appropriate time by the best man.

If your father is a widower, and you have asked an aunt or your grandmother to take your mother's place during the wedding, she should sit in the front pew with your father.

If your parents are divorced and mother is remarried, you will be faced with a dilemma: Should your father or your stepfather walk you down the aisle? There is no single answer to this choice. Each family situation is different.

If you've remained close to your father, you may want him to fulfill his traditional role. There is no need for your stepfa-

CHRISTIAN CEREMONY POSITIONS:

1. Bride
2. Groom
3. Honor attendant
4. Best man
5. Officiant
6. Flower girl
7. Ring bearer
8. Bridesmaids
9. Ushers

ther to be completely left out, though. He can do a reading during the ceremony, propose a special toast at the reception, or dance the first dance with you.

If your father and stepfather are on good terms, you may ask both men to walk you down the aisle (one on each arm). Together, they respond *"We do,"* when the clergymember asks, *"Who gives/supports this woman in marriage?"*

Or, your stepfather might walk you halfway down the aisle and then sit down in a front pew as you take your father's arm to the altar.

In a Jewish procession, many divorced parents still escort their son or daughter down the aisle together, on either side of him or her. They stand together under the *huppah*; their partners sit in the second and third pews.

When there is rancor over this issue, some brides simply choose to walk down the aisle alone, or with their grooms.

Altar Procedures

Once attendants pass the first row of seats, they form one of these arrangements:

Diagonal lines. Each individual usher turns to the right to create a diagonal line behind the groom and best man, while each individual bridesmaid assembles in a similar line on the other side.

Single row or two rows. Each pair of attendants goes to an alternate side of the bride and groom. The pairs stand side by side or the bridesmaids stand one step ahead of the ushers.

A semicircle. Bridesmaids and ushers gather in a semicircle around the bride and groom, facing the congregation. (In some churches with a freestanding altar, the minister stands with his back to the guests, while the wedding party faces the congregation.)

Children. The ring bearer and flower girl may stand at the altar throughout the ceremony (the flower girl directly in front of the bridesmaids, the ring bearer in front of the ushers), if you think they are old enough to stay still that long. Young children are usually happier if they are directed to slip into the second or third pew and sit with their parents for the rest of the ceremony.

A Protestant service. As the bride and her father reach the head of the aisle, the bride is on the left of the altar. Her father may remain standing between his daughter and her groom until the part of the ceremony where the minister asks, *"Who gives/supports this woman to be married?"* He replies, *"I do"* or *"Her mother and I do,"* then takes his seat next to her mother in the first pew (or third pew, if he is divorced from the bride's mother—where he'll join his new wife or partner, or his relatives or friends).

Or, the bride's father may kiss his daughter, take one step back, place his

remarriage ceremony escorts

- If this is a remarriage, there are several options for your walk down the aisle.

- Walk down the aisle with your groom, with your children preceding you down the aisle together. The inclusion of children is a clear statement that "we are making this important step together."

- Walk down the aisle with one or all of your children (if there are more than two, have two escort you on each arm, any other walk before you, singly or in pairs). This is a meaningful, sentimental statement that shows how important your children are to you.

- Be escorted again by your father. There is no reason why your father cannot "give you away" or "bless you in your marriage" more than once. After all, he has stood by you through a first marriage and divorce and is now supporting your decision to marry again.

- Walk down the aisle alone. This is an acceptable alternative. (When a marriage takes place during a worship service, such as during a Quaker meeting, the bride and groom are usually seated at the front of the sanctuary and simply step forward at the proper time.)

daughter's hand in her groom's, then take his seat. The honor attendant and best man take their positions on either side of the bride and groom, while the other attendants turn toward the altar. From his seat, the bride's father can respond to the minister's question at the appropriate time.

A Catholic service. The procedures are nearly the same as above. Most often, the bride's father simply places her hand in the groom's, pauses to give her a kiss (lifting her veil and putting it back down, if necessary) before joining her mother, as the couple ascend to the altar.

A Jewish service. The entire wedding party and the parents of the bride and groom stand under the *huppah* throughout the ceremony. The *huppah* may be made of greenery and flowers, and may stand on its own. If it is a sheath of silk, satin, brocade, or velvet, or a prayer shawl spread across the top of four slender poles, these poles are held aloft throughout the ceremony by honored friends or relatives, often the ushers. (This is a strenuous task; assign it accordingly.) If the wedding is in a synagogue, the *huppah* is positioned on the pulpit.

The bride stands on the right side, facing the rabbi and cantor, who is on the rabbi's left; the groom stands on the left side. The honor attendant and best man stand one step diagonally behind the bride and groom, respectively; the parents of the bride and groom stand one step back diagonally behind the honor attendants. The bridesmaids and ushers form a diagonal line next to the parents, on either side of the couple. If the flower girl and ring bearer remain standing under the *huppah* (instead of joining their parents in a front pew), the ring bearer should stand to the right of the ushers; the flower girl, to the left of the bridesmaids. (For more information on Jewish-wedding ceremony procedures, see Chapter 9, "Religious Rituals & Requirements.")

what's in a program?

tell your guests what to expect. Include:

- reception site
- date, time, place of wedding
- names of bride, groom
- names of attendants, officiants
- names of soloists, musicians, pieces performed
- parents' names
- tributes to deceased parents, relatives, friends
- words to readings, songs, prayers, blessings (include sources)
- foreign-language translations
- explanations of religious or ethnic rituals, customs; military traditions
- thank-yous to parents
- new name, address, phone number; date in effect

The Wedding Program

A wedding program will help your guests follow your ceremony with ease, especially appreciated if it will be an interfaith or intercultural marriage, or if you are writing your own vows. If the words of prayers or hymns are also included, this will assist guests in participating if acoustics there are inadequate.

Printing styles. The program can be a single photocopied sheet or a professionally printed booklet in a style that complements your invitations. (See Chapter 5, "Invitations & Announcements," and Appendix, under Chapter 4, "Planning Your Wedding," for program source.)

Consider programs personalized to coordinate with your wedding style (e.g., programs rolled up as scrolls and tied with ribbons in your wedding colors; a photograph of you two or a pen-and-ink sketch or original watercolor of your ceremony site on the front of each).

Program information. Use your program to explain ceremony traditions to your guests and introduce the participants. (Listing the names of your wedding party, officiants, and musicians is a way to say thank-you to them.) Printing the titles and words of readings, songs, or prayers, and the explanation of any religious or ethnic customs, will also make guests feel more a part of the ceremony. (See "What's in a Program?" box.)

Distribution. On wedding day, leave wedding programs on each pew, or have your ushers, a special friend, or a teenager pass them out to each guest at the door—from a rustic basket. If you are planning a Long Weekend Wedding, include the dates, times, locations, and themes of all festivities in your wedding programs; send the programs to guests or leave them in the hotel rooms of all out-of-town guests.

JEWISH CEREMONY POSITIONS:

1. **Bride**
2. **Groom**
3. **Honor attendant**
4. **Best man**
5. **Cantor**
6. **Rabbi**
7. **Flower girl**
8. **Ring bearer**
9. **Bride's parents**
10. **Groom's parents**
11. **Bridesmaids**
12. **Ushers**

The Recession

When the organist sounds the triumphant chords of the recessional, the bride in a Christian ceremony turns around in place and takes her groom's right arm (centuries ago, once the marriage was official, it was deemed less likely that the groom would have to use his sword to keep his bride from being kidnapped!). In a Jewish ceremony, the bride turns and takes her groom's left arm. Then, the newlyweds walk back up the aisle together, leading the recession of the wedding party, in their first walk as husband and wife.

CHRISTIAN RECESSION:

1. Bride
2. Groom
3. Flower girl
4. Ring bearer
5. Honor attendant
6. Best man
7. Bridesmaids
8. Ushers

In a Christian recession, you will be followed up the aisle by the flower girl walking on the ring bearer's right. Each of your bridesmaids will line up with an usher as they file down the aisle: the honor attendant on the right arm of the best man, each bridesmaid on the right arm of an usher. (One usher may escort two bridesmaids if there is not an even number.) An extra usher walks alone; two extra ushers walk side by side.

When you reach the vestibule, ushers designated in advance return to unhook pew ribbons and to escort the mothers of the couple and any other honored guests from the house of worship.

Then you, your groom, and both honor attendants will probably join your clergy-person in his or her chambers. There, you'll sign the marriage license, although this may be incorporated into your ceremony (as it is in a Quaker wedding, for example). To facilitate this legality amid all the excitement, the marriage certificate may be set on a table off to the side at the altar or at the back of the church. Just before the close of the service or immediately after the recession, the bride, groom, witnesses, and clergymember step over to sign their names. This is when the best man will also hand the officiant a sealed envelope with his or her fee. (See Chapter 4, "Planning Your Wedding," under the "Ceremony and Officiant Fees" box).

The wedding party may return with you to the church or synagogue for more photos. Guests will wait in front for you to appear and receive their hugs and applause, and run through a shower of bird-seed passed out by attendants.

Form a receiving line in the church vestibule or on the steps. This is a natural time and place for this tradition, if you, the groom, and your honor attendants already signed the marriage license (perhaps at the rehearsal or before the ceremony). Then your officiant will just have to add his or her signature. (For large weddings, it might be sensible to form the receiving line at the reception.)

The ushers will clear the church of personal items, direct guests to the reception. It is important that no guests be left stranded without rides to the reception site. Ushers might also distribute copies of directions to the reception.

The bride, groom, and bridesmaids dash into waiting cars to travel to the reception site. There, you'll be able to freshen your makeup, pose for pictures, bustle your train, perhaps form the receiving line before guests arrive.

In a Jewish recession, you and your groom will be followed up the aisle first by your parents (your mother on your father's left arm), the groom's parents (his mother on his father's left arm), the flower girl walking next to the ring bearer (on his left), your honor attendant on the best man's left arm, and the bridesmaids on the ushers' left arms. The cantor walks at the end of the procession, on the rabbi's left.

The yichud *traditionally follows the recession.* The bride and groom disappear for

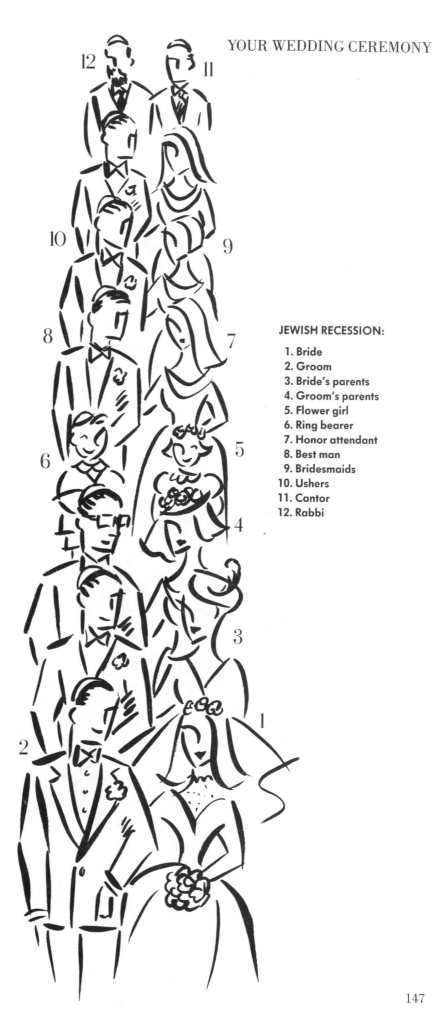

JEWISH RECESSION:

1. Bride
2. Groom
3. Bride's parents
4. Groom's parents
5. Flower girl
6. Ring bearer
7. Honor attendant
8. Best man
9. Bridesmaids
10. Ushers
11. Cantor
12. Rabbi

a private time alone (fifteen minutes), symbolic of when the groom brought his bride to his tent to consummate the marriage and share their first meal together—breaking their fast (see Chapter 9, "Religious Rituals & Requirements"). Today, the *yichud* is a time to let the reality of the marriage sink in. Two witnesses stand outside the door, specifically appointed for this task; when the couple emerge, the witnesses proclaim them husband and wife. They may be greeted by a toast or a shower of birdseed, even singing and dancing!

In the meantime, the ushers will direct guests to the reception site. Once the couple emerge, the wedding party may pose for photos, travel to the reception site with the newlyweds, and form the receiving line.

RELIGIOUS RITUALS & REQUIREMENTS

Today, wedding ceremonies are more attuned to the equality of marriage partners, the importance of family support, the existence of interfaith marriages, and the recognition that some couples may choose to have a childless marriage. Since much of the rigidity in form and liturgy is gone, couples now have the opportunity to arrange a wedding service that expresses their own hopes and beliefs. Each religion has traditions associated with its liturgy. You can add significance to an interfaith ceremony by learning about the customs of each faith and incorporating something meaningful into your wedding service.

In reviewing this chapter, you'll notice that there are many similarities in the marriage ceremonies of religions practiced in the United States. At the same time, you may discover that within the same faith, local customs may influence the style of the wedding service. Discuss ceremony details with church or synagogue officials early in your engagement (see Chapter 4, "Planning Your Wedding," and Chapter 11, "Remarriage," for positions on religious remarriage for major U.S. denominations, and the Appendix, under Chapter 9, "Religious Rituals & Requirements").

Religious Marriage Requirements

Below is a summary of the doctrines, marriage rituals, and marriage requirements of the major religious denominations in this country.

Baha'i

Baha'i is an independent world religion started in 1844 by the prophet Baha'u'llah, whose primary mission was to unite the world. Bahaists believe that there are three basic unities: 1) There is only one God, though we may call Him by many names. 2) There is only one religion and all major religions are divine in origin. 3) There is only one human race.

Parental Consent. Marriage in the Baha'i faith begins with the understanding that individuals are free to choose their own mates. In keeping with the primary teaching of unity in all realms, however, they must get the consent of all living parents. By seeking this unity within the immediate and extended family, the couple assure support for their marriage. The parental consents, presented in writing to the local spiritual assembly (nine elected individuals), state simply, *"I, John Smith, give approval for my daughter, Mary Smith, to marry John Doe."* The consents may also be presented as a more elaborate, personal letter.

Public Statement. All that's required for a Baha'i marriage is a simple public statement in the presence of two witnesses. The two individuals must say to each other, *"We will all verily abide by the will of God."* The witnesses will be chosen by the spiritual assembly unless the couple designate special persons. The marriage ceremony can be shared with family and friends anywhere, or with as few as two attendants (witnesses).

Ceremony Additions. A traditional wedding ceremony is also possible, as long as this public statement is included. There is no prescribed worship ritual in the Baha'i faith. If a couple choose to have a lengthier service, they devise it.

Since so much personal thought goes into the ceremony, there is usually an explanation provided for guests in the form of a wedding program or verbal commentary from one of the witnesses. Ceremonies might include readings from Baha'i Scripture and those of other faiths, since this religion accepts the teachings of all prophets. Other important elements: music, singing, secular readings including poetry, flowers, the recitation of the vow, and signing of the marriage certificate.

Attire. Wedding attire is up to the couple; many brides wear a traditional white wedding gown.

Buddhist

The wedding ceremony is set for an auspicious time, which is determined by an astrologer, based on the bride's and groom's horoscopes. Be aware that different sects of Buddhism have different customs. Not all Buddhist wedding ceremonies follow the rituals mentioned below.

The *Poruwa*. A Buddhist ceremony takes place in a special structure known as a *poruwa*, symbolizing the establishment of the couple's new domicile. This platform has pots of flowers at the corners and a canopy of white flowers or white silk overhead.

Betel Leaves. After religious chanting by the officiant (an elder *or* a Buddhist priest), the couple share betel leaves (used in many festivals to show respect and thought to be a stimulant) with each other and with their parents.

Ceremony Customs. The couple then exchange rings and gifts. Finally, the officiant pours water over their fingers, which are bound with gold thread. There are closing chants and songs of blessing.

Eastern Orthodox

Eastern Orthodox Christendom, including Greek, Syrian, Armenian, and Russian Orthodox, is not Roman Catholic, but the liturgical services do share similarities with those of the Roman Catholic church. Interdenominational marriages are accepted when the non-Orthodox party is a baptized Christian. Banns of marriage may be proclaimed in accordance with the practice of the local diocese.

Timing. Eastern Orthodox weddings usually take place in the afternoon or early evening and may not be solemnized in church during Lent, on the eve of certain holy days, during the week after Easter, or in the two weeks prior to Christmas.

Ceremony Content. The Eastern Orthodox Marital Rite is rarely celebrated in conjunction with the Divine Liturgy. Due to the length of the ceremony, rich with symbolism and spirituality, it is expected that the couple shall have attended liturgy and received Holy Communion just prior to the wedding. Traditionally, the music of the Orthodox Church is that of a choir or the singing of ancient Byzantine and Russian chants.

Attire. Traditionally, a Greek Orthodox bride wears a face veil; a Russian Orthodox bride does not.

Wedding Party and Guests. Personal taste and local custom determine the size and arrangement of the wedding party. At some Russian Orthodox churches, guests remain standing during the ceremony, but in most Orthodox churches in the United States, they may sit.

Giving Away the Bride. The standard wedding procession in which the bride's father "gives her away" is customary in most Greek Orthodox ceremonies. In the Russian Orthodox ceremony, however, the clergymember meets the wedding party at the vestibule door and the bride is "given away" prior to the procession.

The Betrothal Ritual. An Eastern Orthodox wedding begins with a betrothal ritual, usually at the front or center of the church. This includes the blessing of the rings by the priest and the exchange of the rings, three times, between bride and groom to signify that the bethrothal is taking place among God: the Father, Son, and Holy Spirit. Wedding rings are worn by both bride and groom on their right hands, fourth fingers.

The Order of Marriage. After the close of the betrothal ritual, the celebration of the sacrament of marriage begins. Two crowns are placed on the heads of the bride and groom and exchanged between them three times. In the Russian variation of the ceremony, the honor attendant and the best man hold the crowns above the couple's heads. The crowning of the wedding couple—the bridegroom first, followed by the bride—signifies their coronation into a new family realm; both are rulers, together, of their house.

The Dance of Isaiah. After the Gospel is read, the bride and groom partake three times from a common cup of wine, sym-

bolizing the joys and the sorrows they will share together in marriage.

The *koumbaros*, or sponsor (traditionally the groom's godfather, but can be any person who will continue to have a significant relationship with the couple), then accompanies the bride and groom three times around a ceremonial table set with with sugarcoated almonds (symbolizing the bitter and sweet in life), candles, and icons. (The circling is a reminder that marriage is never-ending.) At the close of the ceremony, the congregation joins in singing—or wishing that—*"God Grant Them Many Years."*

Favors. In some Orthodox churches, after the recession, friends of the family may stand on the church steps and distribute festive packets of candy, sugarcoated almonds, or rice to guests. This custom has the same significance as the shower of rice tradition originated among the Chinese: *"May you always enjoy a life of plenty."*

Hindu

Before a Hindu wedding ceremony begins, a holy fire is lit to the fire god, Agni, who traditionally will bear witness to the wedding. The fire burns to symbolize purity and the eternal flame of love. A tree is planted (it was an ancient belief that plants and animals were representations of the gods, and this ensured their presence!). Although marriages traditionally were arranged by the couple's parents, this is no longer a requirement. Neither bride nor groom need be Hindu, but one should be a member of the temple.

Attire. The bride often wears a sari; the special colors of marriage are red and, depending on the region in India, yellow. She may wear a red veil; at the end of the ceremony, the groom might see the

bride's face for the first time, reflected in a mirror which she sits before. The bride's and groom's faces may be covered with red paint; their hands and feet may also be decorated the night before with elaborate red swirled designs of vermilion henna. In certain regions, the bride's hair is parted and marked with red (vermilion), symbolic of the original blood convenant by which she was introduced into her husband's sect.

Giving Away the Bride. Customs during the service are both religious and cultural. The bride's father gives her hand to the groom, then sprinkles her with holy water to indicate his ties with her are washed away. Garlands are exchanged between the couple and hung around their shoulders. A consecrated cord is wound around their necks, uniting them, accompanied by prayers.

The Bride's Jewelry. A *thali*, a gold ornament threaded on a gold string, is tied on the bride's neck by her mother (who has been collecting gold jewelry for her since her birth) and the groom's sisters. The bride will wear the *thali* throughout her married life, its three knots reminding her of her duty to serve her parents, husband, and sons. During the wedding ceremony, the bride receives a nose ring, a symbol of married life, removed only if she becomes a widow.

Circling the Flame. The ceremony concludes when the couple circle the holy fire seven times, throwing offerings of rice and flowers into the air.

Islamic (Muslim)

A Muslim man may marry a non-Muslim woman, providing she is Christian or Jewish (people of the Book or Bible), but a Muslim woman may not marry out of the faith. The two witnesses, including the bride's counsel—a close friend or relative—may be of any faith.

The Betrothal. In traditional arranged marriages, the Muslim groom would not cast his eyes on his bride until the wedding. This is not usually the case in today's Islamic marriages. The bride's consent to the union is required, however, before the wedding can take place.

Two witnesses and the bride's counsel ask for her consent, then communicate it to the groom, who is waiting in a separate public place or registry. The representatives say to him: *"Assalam o alaikum warehmatullah"* or *"God's peace and blessings be upon you."*

There is no formal clergy in Islam, so any religious leader, registrar, or person may be authorized to conduct a wedding. The registrar asks the groom if he is prepared to accept the bride, then has him present his *dower* to his fiancée. The *dower*, similar to a bride's dowry, may be given immediately or deferred, and is in any amount agreed to between future husband and wife. The largely symbolic exchange allows the woman to maintain her economic independence when she comes to her new home, and serves to boost her self-esteem. Although the couple are now legally married, Islamic marriages can't be conducted in secrecy, and a public announcment or wedding must follow.

Ceremony Site. The ceremony is held in a magistrate's office in an Islamic country, but may be conducted in a mosque or any public place in the United States. Men and women, including the bride and groom, are seated separately.

Ceremony Customs. An old custom—not often practiced today—is to henna the hands of the bride and groom (paint them in an elaborate pattern of swirls, with a vermilion dye) at festive gatherings the night before the wedding.

At the wedding, the couple join hands under a white cloth, while an officiant may lead them in reciting their vows. The officiant gives an address or *khutba*, noting that both husband and wife should treat each other with respect and compassion. Then he offers *dua*, a prayer to God to bless the bride and groom and the wedding, and the couple vow to live and die as Muslims.

The bride and groom may be enthroned for the reception, although many Muslims emphasize simple weddings with no music or dancing. At least one day after the marriage is consummated, the groom throws a feast, called *walima*, for family and friends.

Jewish

No single set of rules applies to all Jewish weddings, for there are differences among the Orthodox, Conservative, and Reform branches of the faith. Individual rabbis and synagogues are likely to have their own interpretations of the marriage ceremony, so verify all procedures with the officiating rabbi before plans are finalized (see Appendix, under Chapter 9, "Religious Rituals & Requirements"). As a rule, Orthodox and Conservative rabbis will not perform interfaith marriages. Some, but not all, Reform clergy will participate in interfaith ceremonies (see "The Intefaith Wedding" section).

Timing. According to Orthodox law, Jewish weddings may take place at any time except on the Sabbath (from sundown on Friday to sundown on Saturday), on Holy Days, during a three-week period in mid-summer, and during almost all of the time between Passover and *Shavuot*. Most weddings are on Saturday evening after sundown or on Sunday.

Ceremony Site. Jewish weddings may occur almost anywhere, and many are not performed in synagogues or temples. It is more usual in some locales for the ceremony to take place at a club, hotel, or catering hall where the centuries-old splendor of the wedding feast and dancing may follow.

Attire. Conventional wedding attire, including a face veil for the bride if she is Orthodox, is generally worn. In a prewedding Orthodox ritual, the bride is "veiled" by the groom as a sign that she is, indeed, his betrothed. In Conservative and Orthodox ceremonies, all the men are required to cover their heads with either *yarmulkes* or silk top hats; the women, with hats or kerchiefs. If planning a Reform ceremony, ask the rabbi if there are any head-covering requirements.

Prewedding Traditions. The bride and groom may not see each other before the "veiling" (if there is one), which occurs just before the ceremony. The bride and her attendants may wait, in wedding attire, in a separate room, where they receive guests beforehand. In some places, there may be a brief cocktail-and—hors d'oeuvre reception preceding the ceremony, while the prewedding rituals are carried out.

Seating. At the appropriate time, the bride's family will be seated on the right side of the hall or temple, the groom's family on the left, before any other guests are ushered to their places.

The Procession. The order of the procession and positions during the ceremony are set by local custom, with Orthodox and Conservative processions usually including the groom, the bride, both sets of parents (who walk them down the aisle), both sets of grandparents, bridesmaids, ushers, and child attendants (see Chapter 8, "Your Wedding Ceremony").

The *Huppah*. Jewish marriages are traditionally performed under a *huppah*, a heavily ornamented canopy symbolizing the ancient bridal chamber of consummation; shelter from the open sky in nomadic times; and the home the couple will share together. The *huppah* may also be embellished with—or woven entirely of—fresh flowers. It is usually placed in front of an attractive background at one end of the room, or in front of the Ark in a temple. Each person in the procession takes a prearranged position under or near the *huppah* (see Chapter 8, "Your Wedding Ceremony").

Under the *huppah*, the rabbi and cantor stand next to a small table covered in white, set with one or two goblets for ritual wine.

The Ceremony. As the bride arrives under the *huppah*, she may walk three (the Bible mentions betrothal three times; a husband has three obligations to his wife—food, clothing, conjugal relations) or seven (the number of completion—the number of days it took God to create the universe) times around the groom in an Orthodox ceremony. The circles perhaps symbolize that the woman is a "protective wall" for her husband; that by drawing invisible walls with her body and then stepping inside, the couple have a new status, or family circle, separated from society, that no one can interfere with; that the love that makes life beautiful spreads to society's larger circles.

The service begins with a betrothal ceremony, followed by an introductory blessing. Next, the groom sips from a goblet of wine and passes it to the bride. After the couple have spoken their vows, the groom recites a marriage proposal in English and in Hebrew and places a plain gold band on the bride's right index finger in the Conservative and Orthodox ceremonies; on her left ring finger in the Reform ceremony. Conservative, Orthodox, and some Reform rabbis read aloud the *ketubah*, or traditional marriage contract, detailing what the groom promises to provide for the bride. The *ketubah* is then given to the bride, who hangs it in their new home.

The ceremony ends with the traditional reciting of the Seven (the number of completion) Blessings by the rabbi, or others given the honor. The blessings cover the creation of the world and humanity, the survival of the Jewish people and of Israel, the marriage, the couple's happiness, and the raising of the family. They are a reminder that life's goals are not selfish, but designed for the betterment of the world, the glory of God.

Breaking the Glass. At the close of the ceremony, a wine glass is wrapped in a cloth napkin or handkerchief and placed on the ground. The groom stamps down, smashing it not for good luck or to display machismo, nor for the symbolic loss of the bride's virginity (as is commonly believed), but as a reminder of the destruction of the Holy Temple in Jerusalem, and of other calamities that befell the Jewish people that should not be for-gotten, even during this most joyous occasion. Amid joy, there is sorrow. The breaking of the glass generally signifies the close of the marriage ceremony and may be greeted with shouts of "*Mazel Tov!*" or "Good Luck!" from guests.

The *Yichud*. Traditionally, the bride and groom spend fifteen minutes alone together in *yichud*—seclusion. This is symbolic of ancient days, when a groom brought his bride to his tent to consummate the marriage. This has not been the literal custom for centuries. These private moments, however, are a symbolic consummation, a demonstration of the couple's right to privacy.

The Wedding Feast. The reception feast is traditionally begun with a blessing (by the fathers, the rabbi, or the couple) over a *challah* (a braided loaf of egg-rich bread). It then is cut and distributed to each table for good luck.

Protestant

There are a wide number of denominations within the Protestant church. One may be liturgical, another Pentecostal in spirit. The Protestant wedding is a worship service and guests are both participants and witnesses; there may be standing, singing, and praying aloud. A homily or sermon by the officiant is common.

Almost all Protestant churches use a variation of the standard ("*Dearly Beloved...*") wedding service, and most request that the congregation stand during part of the ceremony. Many Protestant clergy are reluctant to perform wedding ceremonies on Sundays and religious holidays, but this is dictated by preference rather than canon law. (There *is* a growing trend among some congregationally governed churches toward Sunday weddings. In these cases, if the wedding follows the Sunday-morning service, an open invitation is often issued to members.)

Rules about music vary; it's wise to get prior approval from a church authority for the use of secular music, especially any modern popular songs. There may be guidelines, rather than rules, about decorations and attire for the sanctuary. It's possible that bare-backed or strapless gowns will require a jacket or wrap until the reception. (Many dresses for brides, bridesmaids, and mothers come with coverups for this very reason.) Discuss any questions about the appropriateness of the bride's and bridesmaids' gowns with the clergymember.

The following variations can be found among some of the Protestant faiths:

Amish

The Amish service is quite simple. There is no instrumental music, nor does the couple enter to a wedding march. Weddings take place after the harvest is completed, on Tuesdays or Thursdays. The choice of day assures that the whole community will have time to prepare, participate, and clean up, leaving the weekend free for church activities.

Assemblies of God

The minister counsels the couple and must be convinced of their "forethought, wisdom, and sobriety" in seeking marriage. While the church leaves the decision to marry interfaith couples to each individual minister, it is preferred that both partners be committed, born-again Christians.

Baptist

In Southern Baptist and American Baptist congregations, the local church sets the policy—from marrying only members of the church, to marrying people of any religion. Consult your local clergymember.

Christian Scientist

The Church of Christ, Scientist, is a church of lay members and has no ordained clergy. When members marry, they are free to choose a minister ordained in another denomination or a proper legal authority to perform the ceremony. The ceremony's format is determined by the bride and groom in collaboration with the officiant.

Episcopal

At least one partner must be a baptized Christian to be married in the Episcopal church. A couple must give thirty days' notice of their plans to marry and sign a declaration of intention for a lifelong union. The priest is required to conduct premarital counseling and be sure that there is a serious commitment to marriage. Clergymembers of other faiths sometimes co-officiate.

A Nuptial Mass may be included in the service. The church usually discourages formal weddings during Lent.

Lutheran, Methodist, Presbyterian

Weddings are performed at the discretion of the clergymember after counseling the partners to determine their commitment. Each faith has a service book, worship guides, and other resources for planning weddings.

Mormon

The Church of Jesus Christ of Latter-Day Saints recognizes two kinds of marriage.

The first is for the faithful found worthy (by the head of the local congregation) of marriage in one of the church's holy temples—of which there are forty-five. Such couples are wed in a *sealing ordinance* "for time and eternity" (instead of "until death do you part"), with both man and woman wearing white to symbolize purity. Their children are believed to potentially belong to them for all eternity as well—contingent on worthiness (how the couple live their lives according to the saviors).

The second is a civil ceremony performed by bishops of the church or other legal authorities. These couples are sometimes re-wed in a temple at a later date, "sealing" their marriage for eternity. A Mormon and a non-Mormon may be wed in such a civil ceremony.

Quaker

A Quaker wedding requires prior approval (which may take up to three months) from the monthly meeting of the Society of Friends.

Traditional: The marriage itself takes place during a meeting for worship, where those in attendance meditate quietly. The bridal couple enter the meeting together and join the circle of Friends already seated. (A traditional procession, comprised of the couple, their parents, honor attendants, and the committee members, is another option). There is usually no music. The bridal party takes seats on benches facing the entire meeting.

In the midst of the traditional Quaker silence, the bride and groom rise, join hands, and say their vows. The groom speaks his promises first, then the bride. The bride is not given away, nor does a third person pronounce the couple married, for the Friends believe that only God can create such a union.

The marriage certificate is then brought to the couple to sign, after which it is read aloud by a member of the meeting. The gathering may continue until the bride and groom feel ready to leave. All guests sign the marriage certificate before departing, a custom which couples marrying in other faiths may choose to incorporate. Further details of the Quaker wedding are usually worked out in advance between the couple and an appointed group of meeting members. It is this group that oversees the wedding.

Contemporary: Today, a Quaker couple may design a highly personalized service with attendants, flowers, musical solos, or readings. The wedding still remains a simple one—very much in the Quaker tradition. Although neither a bridal party nor the exchange of rings is necessary, both are commonly seen. It is the custom for bridesmaids to dress quite simply. In some areas of the country, the meeting will have a pastor, who naturally would take part in the ceremony and in the prewedding discussion.

Unitarian-Universalist Society

This religion incorporates tenets from all faiths into its worship, and wedding ceremonies are no exception. There is no set liturgy. The minister and couple work together to fashion a service that fits the beliefs and ideals of this unique marriage. There may be Christian or Jewish symbols or readings, but the interpretation is as likely to be humanistic as religious. This pluralistic religion is a comfortable meeting ground for couples of different faiths and beliefs, where a thoughtful, reverent service can be worked out.

United Church of Christ

Although not a requirement for marriage, couples are expected to participate in two to three sessions of premarital counseling with a pastor. The bride and groom are often encouraged to compile their own wedding service from a menu of prayers, Scripture, readings, and hymns (with the pastor performing the service), so that they invest something of themselves into the ceremony. Increasingly, today, either one or both of the prospective spouses is expected to be a member of or a participant in the congregation where the wedding ceremony is held.

Roman Catholic

The easiest marriage to arrange in the Roman Catholic church is one between two never-married adults who grew up as Catholics in the same parish. Every other scenario requires extensive paperwork. (See Appendix, under Chapter 9, "Religious Rituals & Requirements," and Chapter 11, "Remarriage.")

The Banns. Before a couple wed, it's customary for the banns (intentions to marry) to be published in the parish churches of both the bride and groom (some parishes, however, may waive this practice). These announcements may be made from the pulpit at the principal Mass on three consecutive Sundays before the wedding, or published in the church calendar or bulletin. (The banns originated as a way for the church to make sure that each party was free to marry.) The banns are not usually proclaimed for an interfaith marriage, nor for the marriage of an older couple (it is assumed that any encumbrances to the marriage will already be known by the couple's priest).

Permissions. A Catholic wedding ceremony can take place in the parish of the bride or groom. If another parish is chosen, permission is necessary. The officiating priest will need proof of baptism for baptized persons (a baptismal certificate) and evidence of freedom to marry (divorce and nullity decree, as well as the sworn declaration of witnesses; death certificate).

Co-officiating. Catholic weddings are rarely conducted outside a church building, although inter-denominational marriages are sometimes performed in the church of the non-Catholic. In such cases, a Roman Catholic priest may pronounce a prayer or blessing over the couple. (If the ceremony is an interfaith one, it is more common for it to be performed in a secular place, such as a hotel ballroom.) When someone other than a priest (or bishop or deacon) is to officiate at a wedding, a dispensation from canonical form is requested. The Catholic party must make this request through his or her parish priest.

An interfaith or interdenominational wedding with two clergymembers participating may also be held in a Roman Catholic parish, in which case a Roman

Catholic priest will officiate (including the exchange of vows) while the non-Catholic minister may address and bless the couple. The host clergymember is always the principal.

The non-Catholic bride or groom in a mixed marriage need not be baptized, but must be free to marry in a Catholic church. The Catholic party will first have to obtain a dispensation from the bishop of the diocese. It is easy to secure if you've never been married before; the priest who will marry you will most likely handle the procedure. The Roman Catholic partner must promise to baptize and raise as Catholics any children of the marriage.

Additionally, both the bride and groom, even if they are both Catholic, must be free to marry in the church. This means that they cannot have been previously married, unless widowed. If either was married before, they must receive a tribunal's decree of nullity.

Prewedding Counseling. Couples planning to marry in the Catholic church attend a series of prewedding sessions with the priest, an Engaged Encounter weekend, or some other marriage-preparation weekend or sessions (see Appendix, under Chapter 4, "Planning Your Wedding") before they wed. The couple may be asked to bring practical issues (such as money management) to the surface, as well as spiritual issues.

The Procession. In a Catholic wedding, the bride may be escorted down the aisle, but is not "given away." There are many options open to the couple in the new marriage rites. Each couple may

discuss these with the priest before the wedding.

Option 1: The bride's father, another person she chooses, or her father *and* mother, escort(s) her to the steps of the altar, where the groom and the priest are waiting. Many couples at this point exchange a greeting with the priest and with the bride's father, mother (or whomever escorted her down the aisle). Then, in a gesture of recognizing the groom, the person escorting the bride places the bride's hand in the groom's hand. He or she may lift the bride's veil and kiss her before taking a seat.

Option 2: Some couples choose to be greeted at the vestibule door by the priest, then be led by him to the altar.

Music. Certain popular music may not be allowed in some Catholic dioceses, as it is not seen as appropriate for worship. (See Chapter 14, "Wedding Music," and consult the priest.)

Timing. During Advent, Catholic marriages may be performed and Nuptial Masses celebrated; they may also be performed during Lent, but some parishes may discourage it. Most churches have no flowers during Lent, but if they allow weddings, they will not legislate the color of the blooms you provide.

Nuptial Mass. A Nuptial Mass may be arranged for almost any Catholic wedding, with the brief wedding ceremony being incorporated into the Mass, after the homily. Non-Catholics at a Nuptial Mass (including the bride or groom, if it is a mixed marriage) do not take Communion. Many churches have hymnals and worship books so guests may follow the ritual of the Mass. Non-Catholic guests needn't give the responses or kneel, but should sit quietly while others kneel. All guests should stand at the proper times in the ceremony.

During a Nuptial Mass, the entire wedding party is usually seated at the front of the church and stands for the exchange of vows. Because a non-Catholic partner and guests will not be able to receive Holy Communion, some Roman Catholics choose to attend a Mass earlier in the day with family, rather than exclude others from participation.

Ceremony Participation. There are many opportunities to include friends and relatives in the service—readings, presenting the elements for the Eucharist, attending the priest at the altar. Remember to give altar servers a gift—the best man can pass it along (see Chapter 17, "Wedding Gifts").

Flowers for the Virgin Mary. During or following the marriage ceremony, a Catholic bride may leave her flowers before a statue of Mary, the Blessed Mother, who is the patron saint of family life, with a prayer for her own new family.

Shinto

With its strong cultural roots, the ancient Shinto religion practiced by many Japanese seems to be more a matter of custom than the manifestation of deeply held religious beliefs. There is little conflict between the religous doctrines of Shinto and other sects, allowing them to coexist with Christian beliefs. Marriage is the main occasion at which a Shinto ceremony is performed and for which a priest is summoned.

Ceremony site. The ceremony may be held before a Shinto shrine, in the innermost shrine building (or, outside of Japan, in a Christian chapel).

Attire. The bride and groom may wear traditional, colorful, ceremonial kimonos, but either one or both may change later to Western-style wedding attire. During the reception, the bride exits and reappears up to three times in different outfits. Kimonos may be rented for the occasion, at great expense.

Ceremony Rites. Ancestors are honored in the ritual through the bowing and offerings of food before family ancestral shrines, and the ringing of bells. Prayers are recited by the officiating Shinto priest, and, traditionally, only close relatives are invited. There are no vows, but the couple exchange rings and share nine sips of sake, the *sansan kudo* (three sips from three cups of sake—a rice wine)—the essence of the ceremony. Later, sips of sake are exchanged with the couple's parents, both to honor them and to mark their formal acceptance of the marriage.

A Western-style reception, often held in a hall adjoining the shrine or a hotel, follows the religious ceremony. The wedding guests make speeches, and the wedding cake is cut and served.

The Interfaith Wedding

When the bride and groom are of different faiths, it is possible for them to be married in a ceremony that combines the rituals of both religions. The content of your interfaith wedding, sometimes known as the ecumenical service among Christian groups, will depend on your own wishes and those of the clergymembers involved. The ceremony can be performed almost entirely by an officiant of one faith, with the other one giving a short blessing at the end. For example, the couple might be married by a Catholic priest according to the ritual of the Mass, and have a rabbi present to offer the Hebrew Seven Blessings after the vows are exchanged.

Or, the service can be divided equally between the two faiths, with a minister and priest perhaps alternating religious readings, then joining together for the exchange of vows and the ring ceremony.

Emphasize what you have in common. At a Jewish/Protestant wedding, you might use only Scripture from the Old Testament. To demonstrate your respect for each other's faith, have your sister read a Scripture from his faith; his brother, a passage from yours. (See Chapter 4, "Planning Your Wedding," and Chapter 8, "Your Wedding Ceremony," for more on finding officiants for and planning an interfaith wedding, and the Appendix, under Chapter 4, for sources).

Religious Wedding Variations

Almost all religions allow certain variations in their ceremonies; many even have several services from which you might choose. You and your fiancé should discuss the standard vows with your clergymember. Is this what you want your wedding to express? If you desire changes—and they can be accomplished with dignity—alterations in the wedding service can greatly enrich this day in your memory. (For more on personalizing your ceremony and writing your own vows, see Chapter 8, "Your Wedding Ceremony," and the Appendix, under Chapter 8.)

SPECIAL WEDDINGS & NEW WAYS TO WED

Weddings today re-create rituals that make personal statements about the couple—their careers and interests, their ethnicity and backgrounds, their relationship. Floral arrangements may highlight the bride's Texas roots with bluebonnets, the state flower. Or the cake may be topped with seashells, instead of bridal figurines, symbolizing the couple's first meeting on the beach (see Appendix, under Chapter 10, "Special Weddings & New Ways to Wed").

Nineties celebrations also reflect new situations facing couples and their families. Men and women are marrying older. They may have grown up with different cultures. Friends and relatives are often scattered throughout the country, even the world. And few people marry the neighbor next door or live in their hometowns. Today's etiquette balances their needs and wants with tradition, consideration for others, and good taste.

The Long Weekend Wedding

You might have grown up in Chicago, your groom may be from San Francisco, and you may have met in Boston. Thus, your friends and relatives will be converging for the wedding from at least three different cities. The solution? A Long Weekend Wedding packed with activities and parties that will add incentives for guests who must travel a long distance to attend. The three to five days of parties and special events allow everyone to spend more time enjoying each other's company and having fun.

Friends and relatives on both sides of the family may host parties and get-togethers in your honor—an open-house breakfast, a backyard barbecue, an ice-skating party—with the wedding and reception as the central event of the weekend. This

long weekend wedding tips

- Sketch out a plan of the weekend—events, guests, ages, and interests. Offer activities for all age groups.

- Find out who can put people up in their homes, and who wants to host parties.

- Send out a newsletter or announcement of events. When invitations go out, include a tentative schedule, suggested attire, and separate R.s.v.p. cards for each event (unless party hosts prefer to send their own separate invitations).

- Reserve blocks of rooms and research airfares.

- Have guests met at the airport or station by attendants. Set up transportation to each event.

- Give phone numbers of hosts or friends whom guests can call for more information.

- Provide welcoming touches— a list of all long-distance guests and where they're staying, hosts' phone numbers; guest baskets with fruit, candy, and homemade cookies. Also, contact the local convention and visitors bureau for free maps, guides to local attractions, postcards.

- Suggest foods that complement the wedding-day fare, but that don't duplicate the foods at other parties.

- Attend every event, although you needn't stay from beginning to end. Greet all guests and thank party hosts.

- Give thank-you gifts to all who host parties (see Chapter 17, "Wedding Gifts").

approach need not cost more than a traditional one-day wedding. Guests usually pay for their own travel and lodging, and hosts (parents of the bride and groom, grandparents, friends, and other relatives) pick up the tab for the event they plan. Some activities, such as swimming at the beach or a volleyball game at the park, may be free or cost very little. Here are more ideas:

Get-Acquainted Tea/Cocktail Party. Friday afternoon or evening, once long-distance guests arrive in town, invite them to your house or a neighbor's for an informal gathering. A buffet dinner with a local theme, such as Cajun food and music for a New Orleans wedding, can help break the ice and get everyone to know each other before the wedding.

Saturday Bus Tour/Museum Visit. Hire a bus (an English double-decker?) to introduce visitors to the wedding town. Include tours of museums—appropriate to each age group. Historic sites might appeal to older guests; hands-on science exhibits will interest children.

Barbecue/Pool Party. A country club or neighbor's backyard could accommodate this gathering, suitable for all ages. Set up lounge chairs around the pool, a band on the deck, or a tent on the lawn with a buffet to bring guests together. Play pool volleyball or lawn crouquet.

Softball Game. Bride's Team vs. the Groom's Team at a local park or sports field encourages mingling and camaraderie. Touch football, volleyball, basketball, or a tennis or golf tournament are other possibilities. Consider using name tags or printing up team T-shirts or baseball caps to help introduce guests to each other before the wedding to build up team spirit.

Rehearsal Dinner/Dinner for Out-of-Towners. Be sure guests who aren't included in the rehearsal dinner aren't left stranded in an unfamiliar city: Arrange for a friend or relative to host an event for them during that time. Or consider having the rehearsal dinner on Thursday—there's no rule that says it must be the night before the wedding—so you can have a party for all long-distance guests on Friday night.

Wedding-Day Breakfast. A casual breakfast buffet at the bride's home, or at the home of a close relative, provides a place for out-of-towners to gather, savor private moments, and finalize plans for the main event. Plan a simple menu of coffee, tea, juice, muffins, eggs, and fruit, accented with arrangements of flowers cut from the garden. Feel free to excuse yourself at any time.

Day-After-Wedding Brunch. A late-morning or noontime picnic in a neighbor's yard, or a hotel buffet is a final get-together for the newlyweds, their families, and friends. Casual finger foods, such as barbecued ribs, corn on the cob, and sandwiches help guests relax after the long weekend. Also set up badminton or croquet. Guests have a chance to take last-minute photographs, reflect on the weekend events, and say their good-byes to each other and the honeymoon-bound couple.

The Progressive Wedding

When guests can't all travel to one location to celebrate, the bridal couple can bring the wedding to them! The bride and groom and their close relatives and friends take the celebration on the road, traveling to predetermined spots, such as his and her hometowns—for receptions and parties hosted in the newlyweds' honor. This works for couples with large groups of friends and family scattered in different locations or with divorced parents who are not able to attend the wedding. Here's how to schedule a Progressive Wedding.

Wed in the town you live in now. Planning the actual ceremony from your current residence makes the details, such as obtaining the marriage license and finding an officiant, much easier. Local friends and those relatives who can travel will be there to share the celebration.

Travel to your parents' hometown. Your parents may host the next wedding celebration by having a formal, seated dinner/wedding reception, following your arrival from the out-of-town ceremony. A receiving line, champagne, and cake are served. You may choose to wear your wedding dress; your groom, his formalwear.

Progress to your groom's hometown. The party at this stop—a day or two later—may be hosted by his parents. It may be as formal as the first wedding reception, or a casual open house for well-wishers. You may wear your gown again and at subsequent formal celebrations, but most brides choose an elegant cocktail dress instead.

Move to other relatives' towns and/or friends' towns. These next events may be smaller and less formal—such as cocktail parties or buffets—and may be held at individual homes.

Move on to your private honeymoon. You deserve the time alone—to relax, unwind, and simply be newlyweds.

Consider hosting a casual party for hometown friends once you return from your honeymoon. You'll have an opportunity to share the wedding photos and video, honeymoon adventures, and photographs.

The Sentimental Journey

This new way to wed is similar in style to the Long Weekend Wedding, except that it takes place at a spot with special meaning and memories for the couple (e.g., your college town, the seaside resort town where you first met). The Sentimental Journey is

progressive wedding tips

- Choose cities and towns closest to where most of your guests live.

- Appoint someone at each site to make arrangements with vendors—caterers, florists—for you.

- Send out invitations to guests in each city for each party (you can include more than one event on an invitation to inform guests of all your plans). Enclose the correct number of reply cards—one for each get-together.

- Work with a travel agent; he or she may be able to organize a free layover city for one stop, or special airfares.

- Have receiving lines at each party to enable guests to meet you and thank the hosts.

- Box pieces of the original wedding cake to bring to each host on the trip. You may wish to serve bottles of the champagne you poured at the wedding reception.

- Provide souvenirs from the city where the wedding was held as favors for follow-up parties (e.g., small pieces of pottery from Albuquerque, New Mexico).

- Show a videotape of the out-of-town ceremony at subsequent parties and receptions. (One couple had their marriage broadcast by satellite into the living room of the groom's parents, thousands of miles away, where a reception was being held in the newlyweds' honor. The couple traveled on to see the groom's family a few days later.)

also a nostalgic alternative for couples who may prefer not to marry in the bride's hometown. Although no one in either family may live at the site, it should have enough of an attraction that a substantial number of your wedding guests will want to make the journey. Below are a selection of Sentimental Journey locations:

A college campus. Return to your alma mater to relive good times. Perhaps plan the wedding celebration around your class reunion and include already-scheduled events so college mates, who are guests, could enjoy their own Sentimental Journey. Rent out one wing or dorm so everyone can stay together, but consider getting a special hotel suite for yourself to prepare for the ceremony. Hire the school's chamber quartet to play during the ceremony; a dance band to accompany you, the bridal party, and guests from the chapel to the reception.

A summer home or family vacation spot. Journey back to the beaches of Cape Cod, Massachusetts; or Monterey, California, where both families summered while the couple, as children, were growing up. Plan a rerun of past pleasures—clambakes, volleyball games, sand-castle and fishing competitions—as well as nostalgic visits to childhood haunts (e.g., an amusement park or zoo).

Summer camp. Rent cabins for the returning and visiting campers, and arrange to cater meals in the dining hall. Invite friends to sing old camp songs—provide the words and sheet music for all—and stage a canoe race reminiscent of your camp escapades. Don't forget a midnight swim on the beach for old times' sake!

sentimental journey tips

- Consider how many people will be able to fit at your Sentimental Journey site. If the area can't accommodate more than your immediate family, research nearby lodges, inns, for adequate space.

- Assemble a slide show of past events you fondly remember: shots from your college days or summers at the rustic camp you attended as a child. Enlist the help of friends and relatives.

- Assemble old friends to share their musical and theatrical talents with a short performance, song, or funny skit based on the memories you all share.

- Organize a tag-football game and give each player a scarf or bandanna with school or camp colors, or a college T-shirt in two team colors. Include activities for those guests not inclined or able to participate in group sports.

The Honeymoon Wedding

Couples can combine a romantic wedding ceremony with a fantasy vacation by transporting the whole celebration directly to the honeymoon site—be it a tropical island or a state park.

This new way to wed is especially well suited to couples with children from prior marriages; it allows the two merging families to spend time together just prior to and after the wedding. Guests may find this the perfect way to combine the vacation they need with the family reunion they've anticipated.

After the festivities, the newlyweds should go off on their own—perhaps to another part of the island or park—for some private time. Guests have the option of staying on and continuing their vacation at their leisure. The Honeymoon Wedding, which can combine the features of a Long Weekend Wedding, are often smaller, more intimate celebrations for immediate family and close friends. Although most guests will be responsible for their own airfare and hotel costs, you and your family may want to pay for younger siblings or elderly grandparents who wouldn't be able to afford the trip otherwise. More planning tips follow:

Select the site. Choose a location the same way you would a honeymoon spot. Contact tourist boards and travel agents, research travel magazines, and ask friends for recommendations. Find out about typical weather for the season you plan to go—Bermuda is coldest in December and Madrid is hottest in August. You can also make this a Sentimental Journey and return to a vacation area you've enjoyed previously as a couple. If you both met while interning one summer at Disney World, a wedding there will be great incentive for all of your guests to join you while visiting the theme park with their families.

Check legalities. Contact the consulate or tourist board where you plan to marry to learn about local rules and residency requirements. For example, France has a forty-day residency requirement prior to the wedding. Also write to the appropriate U.S. Embassy if it's a foreign site, or call the local Marriage License Bureau for a stateside event. Allow plenty of time—at least three months—to comply with rules and compile proper documents, once you know what's needed.

Check customs regulations. Many countries require that you declare any prescription medications or other pharmaceuticals upon entering. Alert guests that they should bring along all prescriptions and keep drugs in the bottles in which they were sold. Having to make a court appearance in a foreign country will put a damper on your celebration.

Hire an on-site consultant. Ask your hotel or the tourist board for names of local wedding planners to help organize and oversee your celebration. Some hotels offer wedding packages: Find out what they include and what fits your plans.

Send invitations to all. Although some may not be able to afford the extra time and expense involved, all will appreciate your thinking of them with an invitation. Some may surprise you by jumping at the chance to "jet set" off to an exotic site for your wedding. *Verbally*, let guests know that their presence alone will be a great wedding gift.

Choose an appropriate officiant. Do your research so there are no eleventh-hour surprises. Make sure your officiant is licensed to perform a wedding ceremony at your location. (A ship's captain, for example, cannot legally marry you on a cruise unless he or she is also a minister or judge. You *can* be married by a clergymember while on board ship. Check with the cruise line to learn if one may be coming aboard.)

Dress to suit the site. Consider the climate and ambience of the site when choosing wedding attire. A formal high neck and long sleeves are out for a tropical celebration; breezy, looser fabrics, such as chiffon and organza, are better choices. Many fabrics pack and travel well, but others—linen and silk taffeta—wrinkle easily and will require ironing.

Don't forget to pack wedding essentials. Many tropical islands will not have the wedding accessories you envision, so assemble your groom's and ushers' formalwear, your garter, and so on.

honeymoon wedding tips

- If foreign regulations and paperwork are too complex, wed legally at home, then travel to your honeymoon spot for a festive reception or reaffirmation.

- Host a second reception closer to home— to celebrate with those who can't make the honeymoon wedding.

- Check with guests you want at your wedding *before* finalizing plans.

- Keep guests' budgets in mind when choosing hotels—look into group rates or suggest hotels for all budgets.

- Arrive a few days early to finalize paperwork and details, and meet with the officiant, caterer, florist, and wedding planner.

- Encourage guests to mail gifts to your home or to your parents' home.

- Ask the bridal store to pack your dress in its own box; check it as fragile luggage. Other options: Bring the dress box on the plane or carry the gown in a garment bag. Let the stewardess know what your cargo is, so it can be stowed carefully or hung.

- Take advantage of local customs, food, music, and style (e.g., include ukulele players at a Hawaiian party). Wear the traditional attire.

- Favor guests with take-home gifts native to the wedding locale—calypso tapes, cookbooks of regional cuisine, or paintings or crafts by artisans from the area.

The Rush Wedding

Working couples cope with a quickly changing world that can affect even wedding plans. The Rush Wedding—with less than two months to plan—may come about because situations demand the couple marry sooner rather than later. A lovely wedding needn't be sacrificed to a deadline. Less elaborate options, however, may be more realistic, given the time frame. Reasons for a quick marriage:

Illness. A health problem, such as an impending operation, may dictate moving up the date, whether it involves a relative, bridal-party member, or the bride or groom.

Pregnancy. Depending on how the couple handle this issue, a small, quick wedding may be the most comfortable approach for everyone.

Job transfer. You or your fiancé may be scheduled to move cross-country to start a new job, away from family and friends. Instead of leaving your hometown and returning for a wedding, complete plans quickly, marry now, and leave together.

School. One of you may be moving to start graduate school; a quick celebration locally may be easier to plan.

Military service. A sudden call into combat or a change in job assignment may spur a couple to hastily arrange a marriage prior to departure. They may decide to marry prior to long-term, foreign duty for military or other career purposes, rather than wait for a partner's return. If the prospective spouse chooses to go along, married status may be required for the pair to live together, especially for overseas assignments.

Insurance benefits. If your fiancé has better health coverage than you, you may move up the wedding date to avoid any anticipated, major health expenses.

rush wedding tips

- Set priorities and make some compromises to come as close as possible to your dream wedding, given the short notice. You may have to settle for your second-choice reception site to get the earlier date you prefer.

- Delegate wedding tasks and research to friends and family; you'll be amazed at how fast wedding and reception plans come together.

- Consider having a civil ceremony, which can be arranged in most states in a matter of days (see Chapter 4, "Planning Your Wedding").

- If you elope, make it festive by wearing a wedding dress and carrying flowers. Toast each other then, and again at a reception when you return home.

- Take pictures at the ceremony and on your honeymoon to share with friends and family at a party later on.

The Military Wedding

A dramatic way to salute your military status, a Military Wedding is dictated more by tradition than strict laws. The military considers weddings to be "unofficial," social occasions. Both bride and groom, if each is in the military, have the option of wearing a military uniform or traditional wedding attire. Many choose to wed in uniform with formal flourishes, such as the arch of sabers or swords. Below are more tips:

Site. Choose your own church or synagogue or use the chapel at your military base. You can also wed at a military academy if you are a graduate (active or retired), a child of a graduate, or a member of the faculty or staff.

Attire. The full ceremonial dress uniform of the service and rank is often worn—blue in winter, white in summer—including white gloves and swords (for the navy, coast guard) or sabers (for the army, marines). Military decorations replace boutonnieres on men's uniforms, although a bride in uniform can carry a bouquet. Most servicewomen prefer to wear a traditional wedding gown. Non-military ushers dress in formalwear.

Invitations. Gold-braided edges or an ink drawing of crossed swords add a military flourish. The wording differs only in that the groom's and/or bride's rank and service are indicated (see Chapter 5, "Invitations & Announcements").

Protocol. When rank is captain or higher in the army, or lieutenant senior grade or higher in the navy, a guest's, bride's, or groom's title appears *before* the name. A lower rank would be listed *after* the name: *Max White, Ensign, United States Navy* (see Chapter 5, "Invitations & Announcements"). *Mr.* is never used to refer to an officer on active duty. Contact the protocol officer at the nearest base or a military chaplain for more information (see Appendix, under Chapter 10, "Special Weddings & New Ways to Wed").

Decorations. It's common to display the American flag and/or the standards of the couple's military units during the ceremony, in addition to flowers.

Procession/Recession. The military procession follows standard procedure, but the recession is dramatized by the traditional arch of steel—swords or sabers. The arch is formed by an honor guard, and symbolizes a safe passage into marriage. The arch may be formed outside the church or synagogue, in front of the chapel, or both, depending on church rules, branch of service, and personal preference. On command, swords or sabers are raised with cutting edges facing up. The couple enter the arch, kiss, then pass through. The newlywed(s) in uniform salute(s) the honor guard. Officers then sheath the swords or sabers and return them to the carry position.

Reception. You might feature regimental decorations and music, including miniature flags and the theme song of the groom's and/or bride's branch of service. At a seated reception, military guests are shown to their places in order of rank. The highlight of the celebration comes when the bride and groom cut the cake using a sword or saber.

military wedding tips

- Verify your plans well in advance with the proper military authorities. Get permission for flowers, music, and photography from the chaplain as each academy and military base has its own guidelines.

- If members of the honor guard are also wedding attendants, they must wear military dress. No one out of full-dress uniform can carry a sword or saber.

- For an overseas wedding on- or off-base, determine what papers are required before a spouse-to-be leaves the U.S.

- Contact the chaplain early if you wish to marry at a military academy chapel. Since undergraduates may not marry, back-to-back wedding ceremonies may be the norm following graduation.

- If the bride will not be in uniform, she should complement the very formal style of the military uniforms by wearing a long, elegant dress with a flowing train and veil (for a second wedding, omit the train and veil; see Chapter 11, "Remarriage"). Bridesmaids and honor attendant wear equally formal long dresses.

Wedding of a Clergymember

Today, either the bride or the groom may be a member of the clergy. The couple's wedding ceremony, reception, and rituals are largely the same as for non-clerics, with a few additional traditions expressly for clergymembers.

Site. When the groom is a clergymember, the ceremony still usually takes place in the bride's church or synagogue, unless the bride is a parishioner of the groom's. When the bride is the clergymember, the ceremony is held at her place of worship.

Attire. A cleric, whether the bride or groom, has the choice of wearing clerical garb or traditional formal attire. The groom also has the option of dressing in formalwear with a clerical collar. The customs of the couple's denomination and the formality of the wedding will determine specific details, such as the style of the wedding gown.

Officiant. The clergymember at the bride's house of worship officiates when the groom is a clergymember. If the bride is the groom's parishioner, then her fiancé's superior, or another member of the clergy of equal rank, might perform the ceremony, frequently with the entire congregation involved. The bride chooses the officiant when she is the clergymember.

Parent as Officiant. If one of the couple's parents is a clergymember, he or she may officiate at the ceremony. If it's the bride's father, another male relative may escort her down the aisle and her mother may step forward to give her away or "support her" in marriage.

wedding tips for clerics

- Choose a style of gown that suits the formality of the wedding and fits the customs of your religious denomination. Low-cut necklines or backs, or short-sleeved dresses may not be acceptable nor appropriate.
- Discuss choice of music, decor, and order of events with church or synagogue officials before finalizing plans. Clergymembers may be expected to adhere to traditions specific to their place of worship, if that's where the ceremony is held.
- Consider adding special blessings to address congregants and guests, and thank them for sharing the occasion with you.

The Double Wedding

Sisters, close relatives, or good friends may wish to express their mutual fondness for each other by sharing their wedding day and planning a Double Wedding. A Double Wedding, in the long run, is a savings. At the time, however, a Double Wedding can be quite an extravaganza to plan and coordinate, with twice the number of attendants and guests and a lavish outpouring of food and drink. A joint reception always follows a double wedding.

Site. Select a facility large enough to accommodate a joint reception and possibly a joint bridal-party table.

Attire. Brides wear differently styled wedding dresses with trains and veils of about the same length. Attendants of both brides dress with the same degree of formality, and in the same color or complementary shades (e.g., deep plum and pale lavender for bridesmaids). Ushers all wear traditional black-and-white formalwear (with different bow ties and cummerbunds for the grooms and bestmen) or, for a summer ceremony, formalwear in pale gray and rich beige.

Invitations. The two brides may wish to issue a joint invitation, particularly if they are sisters or very close friends (see Chapter 5, "Invitations & Annoucements, the "Wording Invitations" section.) List the elder bride's name first on an invitation for a double wedding. (If the brides are twins, list their names alphabetically.) It is also appropriate to send separate invitations if the two brides are not sisters.

Procession. If the church or synagogue has two aisles, the processions may take place simultaneously—one on each side, with each set of parents in the first pew on either side of their couple's aisle. With a single aisle, one couple may lead the procession and the other the recession. If the brides are sisters, the elder one usually leads with her set of attendants. Both grooms walk in together, behind the clergymember, and take their places side by side. The fiancé of the first bride stands nearer to the aisle.

Procession Order. Both sets of ushers, paired by height, lead the procession. The bridesmaids, honor attendant, and flower girl of the first bride come next, followed by the bride on her father's arm. The second set of attendants and second bride follow in similar fashion. Or, the attendants might walk two by two, one sister's maid of honor paired with the other's honor attendant, and so forth. At the head of the aisle, attendants usually separate so those of the first bride are on the left, those of the second bride are on the right.

The Brides' Escorts. If a father walks one sister down the aisle, a brother or other male relative may escort the second bride. Or, the father may walk his elder daughter down the aisle, then return to escort his younger daughter. Other options: The mother escorts the younger daughter or the father walks down the aisle with one bride on each arm, space permitting. That might be possible at an outdoor wedding or banquet site where aisle widths can be adjusted.

Altar Proceedings. The two couples stand side by side in front of the wedding officiant, the first bride on the left. The father of two sisters stands behind the elder bride until he gives her away, then moves over to give his younger daughter away before he takes his seat.

Ceremony. The ceremony may be divided into sections, with each couple completing each part in turn: First one couple speak their vows, then the other. However, the final blessing may be given to both at the same time. Then each pair kiss and turn to face their guests.

The Recession. The recession is led by the two newlywed couples, one preceding the other, followed by the two sets of honor attendants, then the bridesmaids and ushers in pairs. When the brides serve as each other's honor attendants, the best men escort the bridesmaids up the aisle, and the extra ushers bring up the rear.

The Receiving Line. Sisters receive guests in the same line, with the elder bride and her husband preceding the younger. Honor attendants may participate in the receiving line, but bridesmaids and ushers should circulate—to keep the line to a manageable length. When the brides are not sisters, each family may form a separate receiving line, including maids, if they wish.

The Reception. Available space and size of the bridal party will determine whether to have a joint table or two separate head tables. Each bride may wish to have her own cake, to be cut at the same time. Other traditions, such as tossing the bouquet, may be carried out simultaneously or one after the other, depending on the brides' preferences.

double wedding tips

- Discuss each couple's ideas for the celebration—style, formality, menu, decor, and entertainment—before planning a double wedding. The pairs' tastes and visions should be similar enough to allow compromise.

- Keep communication open among members of the bridal parties by meeting or phoning on a regular basis, or using computers and newsletters to update each other about plans (see Appendix, under Chapter 4, "Planning Your Wedding)."

- Consider the size of the guest list if four sets of relatives are involved. You may want to invite fewer guests than you normally would for a "single" wedding to make the event more manageable.

- Issue invitations jointly with both sets of hosts and couples noted. If the brides are sisters, the elder bride and her groom are usually mentioned first. Separate invitations may be sent if the brides are not sisters.

- Order napkins and imprinted favors with the names of both couples and the date. (These may also be ordered separately.

- Order two guest books, two journals to record gifts, two cake-cutting knives, and two ceremonial wine goblets, so each couple will have keepsakes. You may wish to hire two photographers—to assure no special moments are missed, especially with all the activities and guests at the joint celebration.

home or outdoor wedding site tips

- **Consult the local chamber of commerce, museums, historical associations, and travel guides—to find suitable outdoor locations in your area, if your own garden or lawn space is limited.**

- **Ask all attendants and immediate family members if they have any allergies relating to the outdoors, and the season. Select a site accordingly.**

- **Arrange for necessary permits. Sign contracts.**

- **Check out parking availability. Notify local police about traffic increase, need for public parking. Arrange for transportation by bus or "shuttle cars" from the nearest large parking area.**

- **Plan home renovations and major landscaping far in advance of the wedding.**

The Home or Outdoor Wedding

Marrying at your own home or that of a close friend or relative adds a warm, personal touch to the celebration. It may also be the most appropriate and affordable way for a couple to host their own event. Home weddings may be inside or outside, perhaps under a rented tent. Like any outdoor wedding, the degree of formality is determined by the site, choice of attire, time of day, and type of menu.

Ceremony site. At home, an attractive fireplace or a large, floral screen provides an appropriate backdrop for an indoor religious ceremony. An altar table and kneeling bench or a *huppah* or floral canopy can be brought in if needed. In your own backyard, pick the prettiest garden spot for the ceremony: before a trellis of fragrant roses, in a latticed summerhouse by a garden path, under a gazebo, perhaps beside a pool. Also consider a large, outdoor garden, a state park or meadow, a beach or public forest. Consider your needs for handling food, restroom facilities, and the ceremony itself. You may have to arrange spraying for insects and clearing away of debris just before the wedding.

Weather. If the ceremony and/or reception is planned for outdoors, prepare for inclement weather by renting a large tent or having an alternate indoor site (if the wedding is not at your home). You might even enclose a small card with the invitation with the following information: *"In the event of rain, the wedding will be held at Somerset Town Hall [or a private residence or other location]."* Scorching sun can also be a problem, so many outdoor weddings include a tent, rain or shine.

Tents. As a safety precaution, arrange for a tent to be set up the night before the wedding (before the ground can be wet by a rainstorm). Reserve your tent early; tents are in high demand during peak wedding months—May through October. Raise a canopy or awning over serving tables to protect food.

Wedding Consultant. Consider hiring a wedding consultant to handle arrangements for flowers, caterer, etc., and also to put the finishing touches on everything—making sure guest towels and tissues are available and any wedding gifts are stored safely. Having a large wedding in your home or outdoors is entertaining on a grand scale. You and your family should be free to enjoy the day.

Permits. Check to see if a permit is required for your chosen site, and if you must reserve the area with the local parks and recreation department. Also ask if you need a permit for the increased noise level a band or disc jockey will create. And find out whether you need permission to have cooking fires if you're planning to prepare or heat food there. You may be asked to leave a deposit to guarantee cleanup.

Contracts. Sign and countersign a contract that specifies what time your caterer, florist, and band can arrive to set up. Also note the length of time that your party can go on, whether or not you are allowed to serve food and alcoholic beverages (liquor use may be restricted in public parks), who's responsible for setting up and cleaning up, and precise fees and payment timing.

Food. For any outdoor reception, place food—especially the cake—in a shaded area that allows an easy flow of traffic. Waiters might circulate with trays of hors d'oeuvres and/or you can set up a buffet meal. Finger foods work best if guests are standing—plates, forks, and glasses are hard to handle all at once.

Furniture. Rental agencies can provide everything from chairs, tableware, and table linens to sound equipment (see Chapter 4, "Planning Your Wedding"). (Many also offer planning services to help organize the event.) Make sure you have enough chairs for everyone to sit down. Move some furniture out of your home for the day—to provide more space for guests to circulate.

Parking, Restrooms. Make sure you can accommodate whatever number of guests you invite with the necessary facilities. Hire a valet or ask a friend to help direct guests to parking areas. This lowers the risk of accidents and damage to your property. Warn the local police department about the increased traffic and parking in the area that day. Rent portable latrines, if necessary.

Music. Ask the bandleader to visit the site to make sure the proper acoustics and sound system will be on hand. Arrange for an extra generator to be there

the day of the party—just in case one doesn't work.

Lighting. Arrange for your photographer and videographer to visit the site in advance of wedding day—to test the natural lighting before and after dark. Be sure that you arrange for adequate outdoor lighting (e.g., Japanese lanterns, candles) if your celebration will continue after sundown. Nothing will make guests think of leaving faster than a sudden realization that they can no longer see the face of the person with whom they are speaking.

Greetings. Ask your mother or a close friend to greet guests at the door or entrance of your site and direct them to the wedding area and restrooms. Your honor attendant (or your wedding consultant) may be responsible for greeting the wedding officiant and showing him or her where to change.

Ceremony. The procession is a modified form of the traditional one, with the bridesmaids, honor attendant, and bride and her father making their entrance from an adjoining room, down a staircase, or across a lawn. The bride also may enter alone with her father meeting her at the foot of the stairs or at the entrance to the ceremony room; he would then escort his daughter to her groom's side. You may do without the recession and, instead, you and the groom can turn to form a receiving line to greet guests immediately after the kiss (perhaps near a row of trees or amid the garden). Ushers can lead the way to the reception and refreshments.

home or outdoor wedding planning tips

- Start planning early: Delegate responsibilities to friends and family; hire a wedding consultant.

- Stick to a detailed, realistic timetable to eliminate added prewedding stress.

- Invite neighbors, since there will be increased noise and congestion.

- Set up several bars outside and inside. Hire enough bartenders, waiters, and waitresses.

- Create an aisle trimmed with garlands of greens. Consult your florist for more ideas. If your dress has a train, spread out a canvas to protect it.

- Arrange for other rentals (see Chapter 4, "Planning Your Wedding," under the "Reception Rentals" box).

- Send a map with your invitations if you think guests may have difficulty locating the outdoor site.

The Candlelight Wedding

Marrying by candlelight can add a beauty and drama unmatched by any other decorative effects. A late afternoon or evening ceremony or a winter wedding after sunset is an ideal setting. Candles also may take on symbolic meaning at the ceremony if, for example, the couple carry separate candles to light one Unity Candle after the clergy pronounces them husband and wife. This graphic joining of families is especially touching for an interfaith wedding or in the creation of a new, blended family of two previously married parents (see Chapter 11, "Remarriage").

candlelight ceremony tips

- Decorate the candle stands or pedestals at each pew with a seasonal theme—green boughs and red ribbon at Christmas—or with classic white flowers and satin bows. Majestic silver candelabra add an elegant accent, and can be rented in sufficient number to use in the church.

- Consider carefully the building's structure before you set out candles. You'll want to keep them out of drafts caused by air-conditioning or heating, and natural breezes.

- Arrange to spotlight the altar if electric lighting is dimmed, so the clergymember can see to perform the ceremony.

- Save the Unity Candle to rekindle the flame on each anniversary.

- Thank acolytes with a tip or gift.

- Make sure fire-safety equipment, such as fire extinguishers and sprinklers, are in working order. Ask a caretaker for the church to check for you.

Regulations. Local fire ordinances may dictate the number and placement of candles; check with a church authority and local building or fire-safety inspector for details.

Placement. Candles can be situated to shine throughout the church. Large candles on stands, perhaps decorated by the florist, may be placed at the end of each pew. Another group of candles can define the area where the bridal couple will exchange vows. Candles may also outline the steps of the church or synagogue and create a romantic mood, lining the walk from ceremony site to reception.

Candle Lighting. Acolytes, a pair of boys or girls who are either special friends, relatives, or regular assistants at the church, might proceed slowly up the aisle, lighting the pew candles before the procession is to begin. They usually wear white vestments and take their instructions from the officiating clergymember or his or her designate. (Thank them for their help with small gifts; see Chapter 17, "Wedding Gifts.") A less ceremonial but practical approach is for the best man or head usher to light the candles as guests arrive.

Candle Bearers. Attendants can carry lighted candles, perhaps with sprigs of flowers at the base, as they make their way down the aisle to a very slow wedding march. The florist can provide holders that are easy to grip. A charming and safer option for maids is to carry hurricane lamps or lanterns with a soft glow.

Close of Ceremony. Once the recession has occurred and before ushers direct guests to depart, the acolytes may slowly make their way back to the altar, snuffing the candles row by row. This creates a meditative close to the ceremony, enhanced by soft postlude music. Or, the church lights may be raised gently before guests file out or people may walk out quietly under the candles' glow.

The Unity Candle. Two lighted candles, one each on the bride's and groom's sides, represent the pair's two separate lives and families. After the clergy's pronouncement of their union, the bride and groom carry their respective candles to kindle the taller, unlit Unity Candle, which symbolizes that their two lives are now becoming one (see Chapter 2, "Wedding Customs,' and Chapter 8, "Your Wedding Ceremony").

Candles of Peace. Ask ushers to distribute candles to each guest as he or she is seated. After lighting the Unity Candle, the bride and groom walk to the first pew on their respective sides of the church or synagogue; with their individual candles, they each light the candle of the person seated in the first seat of the first pew. Each guest, in turn, lights the candle of the person sitting next to him or her, until all of these Candles of Peace are lit, throughout the room. The officiant may acknowledge the symbolic flame of love and peace that all share, then ask guests to extinguish their flames (see Chapter 8, "Your Wedding Ceremony").

Reception. Candles at the reception are usually used to impart a mood or style to the celebration. Votive candles in sand-filled terra-cotta holders create a South-Western ambience. Candles for both the reception and ceremony may be all white or match your wedding colors.

More Ways to Wed

In addition to these new ways to celebrate your marriage, you can also create *Theme Weddings*, *Seasonal Weddings*, or *Period Weddings*, asking guests to wear outfits to match, such as Renaissance or medieval gowns, "Gone With the Wind" or Civil War–era gowns, or Halloween masks and costumes. *Surprise Weddings*, in which guests are invited to a party but aren't informed it's a wedding, can relieve the pressure of gift giving, particularly for second marriages or when the couple have already formed a household. *All-Night Weddings* are non-stop parties for diehard night owls.

Theme Weddings

Diverse lifestyles, interests, careers, favorite periods in history, and the season in which the wedding takes place can influence the theme that you choose for your celebration. The dress, flowers, decorations, and entertainment are limited only by your creativity! (Rent videos of classic movies—*Oklahoma* for a Western wedding, *Romeo and Juliet* for a Renaissance wedding, *The Bride of Frankenstein* for a monster wedding—for dress and formalwear ideas.)

Sports-Theme Wedding
- tennis-racquet–shaped invitations
- ceremony on basketball court; guests in bleachers
- reception on soccer field
- bride and bridesmaids in short white dresses; groom and ushers in suspenders with a tennis-racquet pattern
- favors: whistles with tags saying, "It's official! Bob and Sue, June 15, 1994"; baseball cards with newlyweds' pictures and vital statistics
- gifts: tickets to baseball game

Country Wedding
- floral invitations

surprise wedding tips

- Invite guests to a cocktail or costume party.
- Once guests have assembled, announce the surprise: That evening, a wedding will take place—yours!
- Announce that in lieu of a wedding gift, guests might make a contribution to their (or your) favorite charity.

all-night wedding tips

- Invite guests for 9:30 p.m.
- Begin the ceremony at 10 p.m.
- Follow it with cocktails and hors d'oeuvres, dinner and dancing.
- Create an atmosphere similar to Carnival in Brazil: Dress bridesmaids in festive, colorful gowns with bright petticoats.
- Hire two bands, so that the music continues till dawn.
- Serve a breakfast buffet.
- Give guests a morning newspaper as they leave.

- ceremony in a gazebo, by a goldfish pond, on a farm
- brides in light, airy fabrics; bridesmaids in soft floral prints
- bouquets of handtied wildflowers, sheaves of wheat, nosegays of herbs
- tables covered with white eyelet and checked gingham; white wicker chairs
- hearty food: potluck suppers; freshly baked breads, muffins; fried chicken, garden-ripe vegetables, fresh corn, carrot wedding cake with a fresh flower topper, or marzipan butterflies
- entertainment: hayrides, fiddlers, bluegrass band
- exit in a getaway tractor, covered wagon, or surrey with fringe on top!

Day-on-the-Water Wedding
- nautical invitations
- ceremony on board a yacht at sunset
- seafood buffet
- bride in white cotton gown; groom in navy blazer with gold buttons
- maids and child attendants in sailor-style clothing
- waiters in crisp nautical uniforms
- favors: silver whistles; candy-coated almonds wrapped in tulle
- cake topper: lobsters; seashells
- reception tables with ship names (sloop, dinghy)—not numbers
- groom's cake: shaped like a fish
- centerpieces: flowers inside wooden lobster traps

Southern Wedding
- magnolia blossom invitations
- site: antebellum mansion
- outfits: gowns with hoopskirts, parasols; grooms and ushers in military uniforms or in suits with white ruffled shirts and narrow string ties
- centerpieces: gardenias
- cake: replica of Southern plantation
- exit: in horse-drawn carriage

Renaissance/Medieval Wedding
- bride and bridesmaids in velvet or brocade gowns
- invitations: on rolled parchment
- music: mandolins, lyres, harpsichord
- entertainment: jousting, toasting, feasting, archery
- food: hearty stews, roasts served on trenchers (mats made of bread, to soak up juices), and spiced wines

Victorian Wedding
- invitations decorated with hearts, lace, roses, cupids
- style: bustled, high-necked, ivory lace; high-buttoned boots
- foods: claret, turn-of-the-century recipes, rosewater
- cake: gazebo cake
- favors: romantic fans
- place cards: valentines
- bouquets: nosegays, tussie mussies
- music: string quartet, barbershop quartet

Art Deco Wedding
- invitations: gold, black, and white
- bride's gown: knee-length silk chemise with silver and crystal beading, plunging back
- music: pianist playing 1920s tunes
- dances: the Charleston

Valentine's Day Wedding
- heart-shaped invitations; escort cards for guests on Victorian-style valentines with hearts and cupids

- bride's gown: blush-colored silk sheath overlaid with white lace; subtle pink or red accents
- petticoat: bright red
- bridesmaids' gowns: ruby velvet, rose chiffon, or pink satin
- bouquets, centerpieces: red, white, and pink blooms—sweetheart roses, ranunculus, calla lilies, stephanotis, gardenias, orchids, cyclamen, stock, peppermint-striped parrot tulips
- have your maid of honor deliver an original love poem to your groom before the ceremony
- favors: heart-shaped chocolates or long-stemmed red roses at each place
- heart-shaped groom's cake topped with a cupid
- have a singing cupid dressed in a red leotard stroll through guests and sing love songs during the cocktail hour
- bridesmaids' gifts: heart-shaped lockets or earrings
- ushers' gifts: heart-shaped cuff links; red cummerbunds and bow ties

Fourth of July Wedding

- site: historic site connected to the Revolutionary War
- music: fifes and drums
- bride's gown: 18th-century style
- bridesmaids' gowns and accessories: red, white, and blue
- food: all-American barbecue
- dessert: ice cream served with sparklers on top
- linens: red, white, and blue

Christmas Wedding

- bride's attire: white velvet gown, red cape, white fur muff
- bridesmaids, child attendants: dressed in red or green velvet
- favors: tree ornaments with your names and wedding date at each place setting
- music: festive holiday songs played during the cocktail hour; children pass out song sheets and carol at the reception; trim a tree
- flowers: holly and pomegranates painted gold for the bride; holly wreaths with tiny silver bells for the bridesmaids; table centerpieces of poinsettias and pinecones

Halloween Wedding

- bride and groom dress as a famous horror-film couple: Frankenstein and his bride, The Phantom of the Opera and his love, King Kong and his love
- wedding party in costumes
- orange-and-black linens
- favors: masks at each place setting
- recessional: "The Monster Mash"
- tarot-card reader available for guests during cocktail hour
- favors: cookies shaped like cats, witches, and pumpkins set at each guest's place
- pumpkin pie served along with the wedding cake
- centerpieces: carved pumpkins filled with candles
- special effects: strobe lights; clips of famous horror films projected on the wall during the reception

Thanksgiving Wedding

- bridesmaids: white aprons over long gowns; simple bonnets
- bouquets: autumn hues mixed with sheaves of wheat
- centerpieces: cornucopias filled with

ethnic wedding planning tips

- **Wear wedding attire that reflects traditional dress in your country of origin.**
- **Select traditional foods, drinks, and desserts.**
- **Ask the band to play traditional ethnic music.**
- **Plan your wedding color scheme around the colors in the national flag of your country of origin.**
- **Design centerpieces with your florist that include mini–national flags, flowers from those countries (e.g., tulips if you're from Holland).**
- **Choose favors to reflect your heritage (e.g., cowrie shells from Africa, mini-perfume flasks from France, or chocolates from Switzerland).**
- **Include traditional wedding customs from your country of origin (e.g., present guests with colorful handkerchiefs if you're from Belgium; tree saplings if you're from Bermuda; set aside time for "The Dollar Dance" if you're from Poland; jump the broom if you're African-American).**

- fresh fruit and gourds
- seasonal ceremony hymns, such as "We Gather Together to Ask the Lord's Blessing"
- bountiful buffet, including traditional foods: turkey, stuffing, sweet potatoes, pumpkin pie

St. Patrick's Day Wedding

- bride's gown: shamrock embroidery on bodice, sleeves
- green linens, green maids' gowns
- ushers wear green cummerbunds and bow ties, boutonnieres
- bouquets and boutonnieres: heather and greenery
- musicians: bagpipers and traditional Irish band
- music: "Oh, Danny Boy" during ceremony; Irish jigs at reception
- buffet with traditional foods: Irish

stew, corned beef and cabbage
- favors: cookies shaped like shamrocks, with date and couple's names, set at each guest's place
- cake: topped with leprechaun

Easter Wedding

- bride's gown: pink or blue pastel silk sheath overlaid with white lace
- bridesmaids: in various pastel hues or floral prints
- entertainment: crouquet, Easter egg hunt for children
- favors: handpainted wooden eggs, chocolate bunnies at each place
- centerpieces: Easter baskets filled with spring flowers
- throw a floral-trimmed Easter bonnet, not your bouquet!
- cake: topped with bunnies
- groom's cake: shaped like rabbit

Ethnic Weddings

Ethnic touches, which celebrate the couple's various cultures and traditions, add another important dimension for wedding celebrations today. Plan a wedding that includes traditions, food, music, perhaps clothing from both of your heritages. (See Chapter 2, "Wedding Customs," for more specific ideas.)

REMARRIAGE

With each passing year, a larger percentage of marriages are re-marriages. No longer an unusual happening, a second marriage is viewed by the couple and families as a happy new beginning. Many of the traditions that are part of a bride's first marriage can be celebrated again. Yes, you can wear white. Yes, you can make this wedding everything you've always wanted a wedding to be…and more! You have the freedom to be as creative as you please and to embrace timeless traditions. What's important is not your age, or what has happened before—it's the unique and personal way you celebrate the love you share. This chapter is designed to help you and your fiancé consider your options and choose just the right ceremony and reception for your style, your families, and friends.

Announcing Your Engagement

There are a lot of people in both your lives who will be affected by the news of your impending marriage (see Chapter 1, "Your Engagement"). When announcing your engagement, follow this list and advice.

Children from previous marriages. Tell them the news that you will remarry first. Consider their ages and their relationship with your fiancé. Speak with them privately, then arrange some time together to discuss the future of the new family. Every child will have unique questions and concerns about how the marriage will change his or her life.

Your parents and his. Give them the news once your children know. Speak with them as a couple, so that you can answer any questions they may have.

- **Great Outdoors Shower.** Gifts: (his and hers) gardening tools, deck chairs, or a gas grill.

- **Night-on-the-Town Shower.** Gifts: tickets to the theater or symphony, or dinner at an elegant restaurant.

- **Wine-Cellar Shower.** Gifts: corkscrew, ice bucket, wine rack, wineglasses, or an assortment of wines.

- **Self-Improvement Shower.** Gifts: lessons for ballroom dancing, cooking, furniture refinishing, scuba diving, cross-country skiing; memberships to a health club, book-of-the-month club, museum; ticket series for art-history lectures, the opera, the ballet; or gift certificates for a spa, or health-food restaurant.

Your former spouse(s) and his/her parents (if you had children together). They can be notified once your children and parents know of your engagement. If you feel uncomfortable phoning, write notes.

Friends and relatives. Wait until you are ready to go public with the announcement. Once just a few friends and relatives know, the news will travel fast. Don't hesitate to show them your engagement ring (the only ring you wear on your left hand during the engagement) and tell them how much you're looking forward to the upcoming marriage. Or, call close friends and relatives; tell others your news as you see them.

The outside world. If you are recently divorced or widowed, it is traditional to wait and announce just the wedding. Otherwise, feel free to announce the engagement in your hometown newspaper(s). (Check with the lifestyle editor(s) about format and deadlines.) Your parents may officially make the announcement—whether this is your first marriage and your fiancé's second, or even if this is your second marriage. It's also acceptable to announce your engagement yourselves (see Chapter 1, "Your Engagement").

Prewedding Parties

A second-time bride doesn't usually receive quite as lavish a round of parties as she did before her first marriage. However, you may wish to consider a dinner in your honor, hosted by your parents or other close relatives, or special family get-togethers where you all get better acquainted.

If you want to have a shower, hosted by your family or friends, help the hostess think up a party theme; clue her (or them) in on the style of your wedding; discuss whether a large traditional shower would make you uncomfortable. (It is appropriate to have a large traditional shower or a small couples' party.) Be sure to send flowers to each hostess before the party, and a written thank-you note afterward. For more ideas, see Chapter 3, "Prewedding Parties.")

- a mansion
- a loft
- a museum
- a ballroom
- a boat
- a garden

Planning Your Ceremony

Plan a celebration that reflects your personal style. Think back on the last wedding you planned and how you want this one to be different or similar. Ask yourself:

Do I want to do everything in a new way? If you eloped the first time, you may want the church or synagogue wedding you missed, complete with attendants and a floor-length white dress. (If you are worried that any of your more conservative relatives might find this inappropriate, alert them to your plans in advance and fill them in on the current remarriage etiquette.)

Did someone else run the show the last time around? This is your chance to get the wedding *you* want. Talk through each aspect with your fiancé—Scripture, vows, menus, music—and decide what you want.

Did I feel overwhelmed by the size of my last wedding? This time, consider an intimate ceremony—just family and a few close friends at the wedding followed by a reception that's as large as you'd like. You might plan a small religious ceremony at a chapel, rabbi's study, or friend's home.

Did the style of my first wedding reflect my tastes, regardless of its outcome? If so, feel free to celebrate in a similar way. Do not, however, return to the same reception site or repeat any unusual personal touches from your first wedding. This is a time for looking forward, not back.

Do I want to invite fifty or more guests to the ceremony? If so, you should choose attendants and ushers (at least one usher to seat every fifty guests). You can marry in a church, synagogue, large hall, restaurant, mansion, or club.

Do I want to find a special role for my children? If either of you have children, including them in the ceremony will make them feel part of the celebration. Teens can be junior bridesmaids or junior ushers. Young girls can be flower girls; little boys can be ring bearers or pages. If you are planning a very small ceremony, you might simply have them walk you down the aisle, stand with you at the altar, or read a special poem. If your children express a preference not to participate, it is, of course, best to respect their wishes. (It may also be a good idea to let your ex-spouse know of plans involving any children whose custody you share.)

Am I still close to my in-laws, my ex-spouse? If you are, you may wish to invite them, though you are not obligated to do so, nor are they expected to attend. An ex-spouse would rarely be invited—consider the feelings of other relatives, your children, and your fiancé. If you do invite an ex-spouse, you leave him or her the choice of refusing the invitation, and perhaps *looking* bad, or accepting the invitation, and perhaps *feeling* bad. It may be wiser to invite your ex-spouse to dinner with your family, so you all can get acquainted, after the honeymoon.

Would I feel more comfortable with a civil ceremony? You can be married (just the two of you and some attendants) at city hall, in a judge's chambers or at your own or parents' home. (See Chapter 4, "Planning Your Wedding," for more on civil ceremonies.) Remember, just because you have a small wedding ceremony doesn't mean that you can't have a large celebration! Many couples plan a hotel reception later that evening, or a large, informal party several weeks after their honeymoon, when they will be able to fully enjoy the festiviities along with their guests.

who pays for what

If this is a second marriage for both you and your groom, you'll probably handle wedding expenses yourselves. You may divide the costs, based on the financial status of each partner. Options:

- Assign expenses in advance— you pay for your dress, the flowers, and the cake. He'll pay for the church, the reception site, and the champagne.

- One person pays for the ceremony expenses; the other, the reception expenses.

- One person pays for the ceremony and reception; the other for the honeymoon.

- Both pay bills as they come up and total the receipts after the wedding. If one partner paid more, he or she pays less of the household expenses till the difference is evened out.

- Open a joint bank account for wedding expenses.

- The groom gives the wedding to his bride as a gift.

- The bride's parents pay for the wedding if she is a very young widow or divorcée, or if this is her first marriage.

- Both sets of parents pay for the wedding if the couple are not in a financial position to pay for it themselves.

Visiting Your Officiant

As soon as you've decided on the size and type of ceremony you'd like, make an appointment for you and your fiancé to visit your minister, rabbi, priest, or other ceremony official. This is the time to discuss:

Your chosen date and time for the wedding. Also bring up your wishes concerning the music, flowers, attendants, and so on. Some houses of worship have very specific rules about secular vs. religious music, or the use of an aisle runner, candles, etc.

Your ceremony officiant's suggestions and concerns. He or she may suggest the use of the chapel rather than the main church, for example. As discussions go on, you may find that your clergymember has problems performing the ceremony of your choice. It's best to find this out early, while you still have time to seek another officiant. You may choose to look for another church. Call local churches, talk with college chaplains, or call the church headquarters in your state for ideas (see Appendix, under Chapter 9, "Religious Rituals & Requirements"). Or, you may choose to marry in a civil ceremony (see Chapter 4, "Planning Your Wedding").

Your faith's view of your previous marriage. If you belong to a faith with its own divorce laws (Jewish or Roman Catholic, for example), you may have problems remarrying within the house of worship, even though you have obtained a legal civil divorce. Expect the clergymember to bring up your first marriage during your conference. While many restrictions in the remarriage of divorced persons may have eased in recent years, you may still need not only your own clergymember's permission but, in some cases, permission from higher religious authorities, as well. (See Appendix, under Chapter 9, "Religious Rituals & Requirements," for phone numbers of national offices of major religions. Some will recommend contacting a local clergymember.) In almost all denominations, the ceremony officiant will want to meet with you for premarital counseling (see Appendix, under Chapter 4, "Planning Your Wedding").

Below are the basic positions on religious remarriage for some of the largest U.S. denominations:

Amish

The wedding vow *"Til death do you part"* is taken very literally by the Amish; divorce is not recognized and remarriage in an Amish church is not possible unless the spouse dies. The person leaving the marriage is excommunicated; if the partner left behind remarries, he or she is excommunicated.

Assemblies of God

Two acceptable reasons for divorce and remarriage are recognized by the church's general constitution and by-laws: infidelity by a partner and divorce of the Christian partner by an unbelieving partner. A local minister may agree to remarry a divorced person under these "exceptional" circumstances, after counseling with the engaged couple.

Baha'i

The Baha'i religion recognizes civil divorce and does not require couples to obtain any special annulments, dispensations, or other church procedures before remarrying. The religion does, however, strongly discourage divorce, and, in fact, requires that a couple wishing one first undergo a year's separation (to attempt to work out the problems) before legally dissolving the marriage. After that time, the person is free to divorce and remarry.

Baptist

There is no churchwide policy; Southern and American Baptist congregations have local autonomy. Some ministers permit no second marriages; others recognize valid reasons for divorce.

Buddhist

A couple may remarry in the Buddhist religion after one or both partners have been divorced. The Buddhist priest may wish to meet the couple prior to the wedding to get a sense of their commitment. If the divorce is final and legal, and if the priest has no reservations about marrying the couple, the wedding can be performed.

Christian Scientist

There are no specific guidelines limiting or governing remarriage.

Eastern Orthodox

Civil divorce is not recognized, due to the sacramental nature of marriage that places it under the jurisdiction of Divine Law. If reconciliation attempts fail, a spiritual court must be convened to consider the granting of a church divorce, after which the bishop must write a letter of special dispensation sanctioning the second marriage. The marriage partner of the petitioner must be a Christian baptized in the Holy Trinity.

Episcopal

There is no churchwide policy on remarriage after divorce. Rectors review each case on its own merits (they ask the divorced person to discuss their previous marriage to determine if both parties are marrying freely and if there are issues lingering from the first marriage that may spill over into the second). Dispensations may be needed; rectors make recommendations to their bishop, who makes the final determination. The process takes one to two months. There is some variation on what bishops recognize as grounds for valid divorce; call your local church rector.

Hindu

Remarriage is recognized and accepted, but Hindu Scripture describe required codes of conduct to be followed, and community leaders must approve both divorce and remarriage. A person cannot dissolve a marriage against their spouse's will. The divorce is completed and remarriage possible only after the ex-husband returns to his former wife all property that was given to him by her. The ex-wife must cut off all claims to her former spouse's property.

Islamic (Muslim)

Remarriage is permitted in the Koran

(the Holy Book), but is not desirable. After the divorce is completed and the required time to wait has expired—three menstrual cycles (to be certain the divorced woman is not with child)—a Muslim may marry again, but not to the same partner. The person who was married before must have evidence (legal documents) to support the claim the divorce is final.

Jewish

Reform Jews require only a civil divorce. Orthodox and Conservative Jews must obtain a *get* (a Jewish divorce decree) from a rabbinical court before they can remarry. Customarily, women delay remarriage for at least three months after receiving a *get*.

Lutheran, Methodist, Presbyterian

A single, lifelong marriage is stressed, but the validity of divorce is recognized when marriage fails. The local minister counsels the engaged couple, and may marry them without seeking permission from any denominational office.

Mormon

The Church of Jesus Christ of Latter-Day Saints recognizes the validity of legal divorce. Couples who were married in a Mormon temple, however, were believed to marry for eternity. Such a sealing must be canceled before a second temple marriage can take place.

Quaker

Quakers do recognize civil divorces, and there are no special church-directed requirements that must be fulfilled by those remarrying. However, the couple (like any couple marrying for the first time) must get approval to marry in the church from the church's monthly meeting of the Society of Friends. In the case of a remarriage, the "committee" would, for example, judge whether you are deemed to be free of entanglements (i.e., the divorce is legal and final).

Roman Catholic

The belief is that a marriage can be dissolved only by death. You can, however, be free to remarry if you receive a decree of nullity (a judgment that the marriage was never valid in the eyes of the church). The petitioner must submit questionnaires and statements from witnesses to a diocesan tribunal, which will determine if the first marriage was entered into by two adults capable of lifelong commitment. Decisions take eight to twelve months. Call your local parish priest for more information.

Shinto

Remarriages for those who believe in Shinto (the "Way of the Gods") are permitted at Shinto shrines. All Shinto weddings take place in the innermost shrine building.

Unitarian Universalist Society

Local ministers set their own criteria; most will perform a second marriage if a couple demonstrate a readiness for long term commitment.

United Church of Christ

Remarriage is not prohibited by the church, but the decision to grant a second marriage is at the discretion of the church's pastor.

Invitations and Announcements

When it's time to invite or announce, follow these dos and don'ts:

DO make a careful and thoughtful guest list. Older couples—especially those paying for the wedding—may wish to invite more of *their* friends than their parents' friends. Professional colleagues may be among your closest friends. If you need to limit the guest list, you might invite only colleagues with whom you socialize, or only co-workers from your own department. You may also decide that you want to invite ex-in-laws and friends from a first marriage. This is fine if everyone feels comfortable with this decision.

DON'T forget to ask both sets of parents for names of close friends they'd like to invite, even though you may be paying for the wedding yourselves.

DO feel free to personalize your invitations and announcements. They may have a traditional look or a unique design. Some couples and their children jointly issue the invitation or "announce the formation of a new family," complete with a photo of bride, groom, and their offspring.

DON'T feel that formal invitations are necessary for a small, informal wedding. A brief note or phone call can take the place of a printed invitation when fewer than fifty guests are invited.

DO mail printed invitations for more than fifty guests (see Chapter 5, "Invitations & Announcements").

Typical remarriage invitation wording:

The honour of your presence
is requested at the marriage of
Marcia Maureen Craig
to
Nathan Randolph Carter
Saturday, the fourth of May
at four o'clock
Hotel Mark Hopkins
San Francisco

R.s.v.p.
1053 Foster Lane
Oakland, California 12345

DON'T shy away from more traditional wording on the invitation if this is what you feel most comfortable with. The bride's name can be written *Mrs. Marcia Maureen Craig*, or, in the case of widowhood, *Mrs. Albert Brendon Craig*. (If your parents or both sets of parents are issuing the invitation, use the appropriate wording found in Chapter 5, "Invitations & Announcements.") The invitation may be issued in the names of the parents whether or not they make a financial contribution to the cost of the wedding.

DO send formal reception invitations to guests if you are inviting a large number of people to the reception but only a few to the ceremony. Insert handwritten ceremony cards for those who are invited to both the reception and the ceremony.

DON'T neglect to announce your wedding to those who were not invited to the

introduction etiquette

Remarriages merge new family relationships with old. Here are suggestions for how to gracefully introduce your guests to each other and to members of your new family:

- Introduce a former in-law as a "friend" rather than as an ex-sister-in-law.

- Introduce your ex-mother-in-law as "Cindy's grandmother."

- Let guests know how you met other guests. Present your "neighbor from back home," your "co-worker."

- If your new husband's children refer to you as their stepmother, introduce them the same way: "This is my stepson, Rob."

- Introduce your new husband's son or daughter as your child's stepbrothers or stepsister, so that the children will understand what they are to each other. Introduce your husband's parents as their stepgrandparents. Remember that you are now one large blended family.

- Establish now what your ex-husband will call your new husband. Since they will both be partners in raising your children, the relationship between them should be polite and firmly established early.

wedding. Formal announcements sent after the ceremony frequently provide an excellent way to notify friends of your marriage. Your parents may have "the honour" of announcing your marriage, or you may send your own announcements:

Marcia Maureen Craig

and

Nathan Randolph Carter

announce their marriage

Saturday, the fourth of May

One thousand, nine hundred and

ninety-four

San Francisco

DO let newspapers know of your marriage. Check with the lifestyle editor for announcement requirements (see Chap-

ter 16, "Photography, Videography, & Publicity"). Such an announcement might read:

Marcia Maureen Craig and Nathan Randolph Carter, both of Oakland, were married Saturday, May fourth, at the Hotel Mark Hopkins in San Francisco by Justice James Howard of the California Supreme Court. The bride is the daughter of Mr. and Mrs. Daniel Ackerman of Los Angeles. She is employed by the University of California. Mr. Carter is the son of Mrs. Leon Ball Carter and the late Mr. Carter of San Francisco. He is an accountant with the firm of Richardson and Level. Mrs. Craig's previous marriage ended in divorce. The couple will reside in Berkeley.

your name change

To let your friends and colleagues know your preference:

- Enclose a name card with your announcement: *Barbara White Redford will be changing her name to Barbara Redford Smith following her marriage June 18, 1994*

- Announce it on an at-home card: *Barbara Redford-Smith Malcolm Ross Smith After the fourth of July* (See Chapter 5, "Invitations & Announcements.")

- Add a line to your newspaper announcement: *"The bride will retain the name Barbara Lynn White after her marriage."*

The Question of Names

Once you remarry, there are many options and alternatives available to you regarding your name. Review your options, below.

1. Barbara Lynn White

Your first, middle, and maiden names only. You've decided to keep the name you returned to after your divorce.

2. Barbara Lynn Redford

Your first and middle names and former married surname only. If you have already established a professional reputation, or have the same last name as your children, you may not want to add on to or change to your new married name (e.g., *Smith*). Some women use both names, for different aspects of their lives. For example, you could remain *Barbara Lynn Redford* for business, but use *Barbara Lynn Smith* socially.

3. Barbara Lynn Smith

Your first, middle, and new married names. You've decided to drop your former husband's surname in favor of your new husband's surname.

4. Barbara White Redford

Your first name, maiden name, and former married surname. Similar to Number 2, above, you already may have an established identity with this name professionally, and as the mother of your children.

5. Barbara Redford Smith

Your first name and former married surname, followed by your new married name. Some women drop their middle name and retain their first married name with their new married name, to help identification (if there are children).

6. Barbara White Smith

A combination of your first name, maiden name, and new married surname. You've decided to add your new husband's surname onto the name you returned to after your divorce, or never changed when you married the first time.

7. Barbara White-Smith or Barbara Redford-Smith.

You decide to use a hyphen between your maiden name and new married name, or your former husband's name and new husband's name. The latter choice will help identification (particularly if there are children).

Your Remarriage Wedding Dress

Romantically lacy, long and white, or traditionally elegant, street-length and pastel or ecru—the remarrying bride has many choices in a wedding dress today. On her wedding day, every bride should feel absolutely beautiful. Shop until you find a dress you love. Mothers and attendants should be guided by your choices of dress; men and children should wear traditional formal clothes appropriate for the wedding style and time of day (see Chapter 7, "Wedding Clothes"). Take this true/false quiz to separate the truth from the myths surrounding wedding dresses for the second-time bride.

Bridal white is for virgins.

FALSE: Bridal white is now recognized as a symbol of joy and celebration, not just virginity. If white is important to you for a second-time wedding, wear it. Pastels remain popular, too; consider mint-green, apricot, silvery gray, café au lait.

Bridal shops are for first-time brides.

FALSE: Bridal shops cater to the special needs of the remarrying bride. They will have many dresses just right for a second wedding, from a tea-length body-skimming chemise to a white moiré-taffeta suit.

A long train and veil are for the first-time bride.

TRUE: The long train and veil are symbols of virginity. The train, which creates a larger-than-life aura, is generally considered the prerogative of the first-time bride only. Complete your outfit with a dramatic picture hat wrapped in tulle or delicate flowers in your hair. Consider a turban or the surprise of a strand of faux diamonds or pearls laced through your hair.

The second-time bride should wear a short dress.

FALSE: You can wear any length you desire, depending on the formality of the ceremony and the time of day (see Chapter 7, "Wedding Clothes"). You can choose

ceremony roles for children

- Ask each to escort you or participate in the ceremony—as a flower girl, ring bearer, bridesmaid, usher, or honor attendant.

- Assign them a special seat and have them escorted there just before the seating of the bride's mother.

- Order special flowers for them to wear—a wrist corsage or boutonniere.

- Mention their names in a special prayer.

- Have their names printed in a ceremony program.

- Ask them to pass out hymnals or programs before the ceremony begins.

- Ask your teenager for a list of songs for the band.

- Give each child a gift to commemorate the day—an engraved locket, a camera, a special date with the two of you at the circus.

- With your officiant's help, write appropriate vows for your new spouse and your son or daughter to exchange (e.g., "I, John Smith, take you, Sara Jones, to be my new daughter. I promise to....")

- After you have exchanged rings, have the children join you at the altar for an affirmation of the family unit. Some couples present each of their children with a *Family Medallion* (see Appendix, under Chapter 11, "Remarriage")—three interlocking circles on a chain—and a pledge to love and care for them. Many children subsequently refer to the wedding date as "the day we all got married."

anything from a graceful, floor-length ball gown in white or your favorite color, to a short and sexy skirt. For a nighttime wedding, wear a cocktail-length or floor-length dress; for daytime, select a dress that is any length, from long or high-low to ballet-length or short. Be guided by the circumstances, your groom's wishes, the feelings of the families and your clergymember. (Remember: The degree of orthodoxy determines what you wear or do in any religion.)

A bridal dress must be traditional to be tasteful.
FALSE: Rather than traditional lace, taffeta, and satin, you can opt for jersey, chiffon, charmeuse, or silk. You needn't wear a voluminous dress, either. Sleek, body-hugging sheaths or gently flared skirts create a slender silhouette. Many second-time brides also prefer sophisticated beading and pearl embroidery to traditional ruffles or lace.

The Ceremony

You'll want the wedding ceremony to be an appropriate expression of the way you and your groom feel about one another. As the two of you talk about what this upcoming wedding means to you, you will find ways to express your ideas through both the ceremony and reception. There are many topics which you, your officiant, and your families should discuss:

Being "given away." Your father may "give you away" again, or he can escort you to the altar and when asked by the officiant, *"Who supports this couple in marriage?"* he can say, *"Her mother and I support and bless this union."* If you have older children from a previous marriage, you can walk up the aisle with them at your side. At the altar, your children might respond to the officiant with, *"We support and love Mom, and know she'll be happy with Jim."* Or, perhaps you and your groom will choose to walk down the aisle together.

The procession and recession. Discuss the procession and recession with your officiant. At a small wedding (perhaps with your family only), you may wish to skip the procession down the aisle and enter through a side or vestry door in the house of worship to meet your groom and best man, already waiting at the altar. After the ceremony, you might simply turn to greet your few guests.

At a civil ceremony—in a judge's chambers, perhaps—there will be no formal procession or recession. The bride and her attendant should enter the room to find the groom and his best man waiting for them.

Honor attendants. It is appropriate for a remarrying bride to have attendants who can serve as legal witnesses. Being surrounded by people who love you and support your new marriage is very important. Some brides and grooms ask the ushers and brides-maids who supported them at their first marriage to fill the same role, again.

Exchanging rings. Will this be a two-ring ceremony, or will you be the only one to receive a ring? The double-ring ceremony is considered to be symbolic of a marriage that will be based on equality.

The role of your children. Your children may escort you down the aisle, act as attendants, as mentioned above, altar servers (See Chapter 6, "The Wedding Party"), or readers. When children are a part of your life together, they should participate in the wedding, as well. Your vows to each other might be followed by a family prayer, with each person in the family adding a phrase. Light a Unity Candle, a touching symbolic ritual for families (see Chapter 10, "Special Weddings & New Ways to Wed"). To make your children feel like they are changing their status, too, you might present each of them a Family Medallion at the altar (see the "Ceremony Roles for Children" box). (For more ideas, see the "Helping Your Children Adjust" section.)

Vows. To express your feelings on embarking on this new marriage, you may choose to write your own wedding vows (see Chapter 8, "Your Wedding Ceremony").

Readings and responses. You might prefer an alternate Scripture reading, prayer, or response. Your clergymember can explain the options to you (see Chapter 8, "Your Wedding Ceremony).

Decorations. Express yourself with music, flowers, and decorations—within the acceptable bounds of the ceremony site. A Victorian mansion may restrict the use of candles as a fire hazard, for example. If you feel too youthful carrying a nosegay, carry an arm bouquet of spring flowers. Let the florist know this is a second wedding so he or she can create an arrangement with which you're comfortable.

Helping Your Children Adjust

As the wedding day grows nearer, your children may be hit with a wave of insecurity. A parent should take time to offer extra emotional support in the days preceding the wedding (see Appendix, under Chapter 11, "Remarriage"). Answer honestly any questions your children have about living space, lifestyle, or visits with their father. On your wedding day, plan to have a grandmother or aunt nearby for hugs and reassurance during the ceremony. Young children also need physical supervision; on wedding day, put someone in charge of this duty so you won't be distracted or worried about your children's whereabouts or safety. Below are ways to make your children feel they are an invaluable participant in your remarriage:

reception roles for children

Make a special effort to include your children and the children of your groom in the reception fun:

- Schedule an afternoon wedding, so they'll be awake.

- Offer them special seats of honor at the bride's table.

- Make sure the photographer takes lots of family candids.

- Take family portraits: your groom with his children, you with your children, the whole new family together.

*the if-
you-have-
children
honeymoon*

- **Plan a two-part honeymoon. Make arrangements for a family trip following your private honeymoon. With their sights set on "their honeymoon" (a trip to Disneyworld, white-water rafting), the kids will likely be content to stay behind while you and your groom first go off by yourselves.**

- **Go over the itinerary with your children, explaining where you'll go and who will take care of them while you're away.**

- **Send postcards.**

- **Call several times.**

- **Bring back souvenirs and photos to share.**

The Reception

Your reception can include the same formalities and traditions as a first-time wedding, including receiving lines, dancing, a traditional wedding cake, a groom's cake, and champagne. You and your groom may head up the receiving line yourselves while your parents circulate among the guests. You might—but need not—omit such first-wedding customs as tossing the bride's bouquet and removing and tossing the bride's garter, as well as exiting through a shower of rice. Your reception may follow all the first-time wedding—customs, including the first dance, the ceremonial cutting of the cake, and rounds of toasts from your parents, honor attendants, children, and friends. Don't expect gifts at a second wedding—especially from those who attended your or your partner's first wedding (many *will* send gifts, though, to mark your new beginning!). (For more on gift etiquette, see Chapter 17, "Wedding Gifts.")

The Second Honeymoon

Don't make the mistake of believing that a honeymoon isn't necessary "this time around." Make sure you get away—even if it's just for a few days. You'll need some rest and relaxation after the exciting but nonetheless exhausting events surrounding your wedding. And surely some time spent together—just the two of you, away from family and friends and responsibilities—is a perfect way to begin a new marriage.

For your honeymoon destination, choose any location *except* where you went last time. With so many wonderful vacation places to choose from, you should have no trouble picking a lovely spot that will be new to both of you.

UNEXPECTED SITUATIONS

12

Despite months of planning, chances are that something will go wrong on your wedding day. A sense of humor is essential to getting along in life—and a wedding is no exception.

When the unexpected happens, try not to panic. Assess your options and choose an alternative plan quickly. How you handle each dilemma will determine how serious it becomes. Remember, friends and relatives can help. For example, send a cousin to pick up the organist whose car broke down. Ask all of your guests to send you photographs as a backup if the photographer who arrives to cover the wedding is *not* the one whose work you've previously seen. Forget the vows you wrote? Your clergymember will help you through the ceremony.

Of course, the best way to protect yourself financially is to specify all terms in a signed and countersigned contract with each wedding professional hired. Below, a range of situations that could happen to you....

Wedding Dilemmas

My father is not in good health. What should I do if he is too sick to attend my wedding? When a parent is too ill to come, there are several options. Hook up a special telephone line to let your parent listen from a hospital bed. Otherwise, ask a close relative to stand in for your parent during the service. Be sure you pay tribute to the absent person during the ceremony (the officiant or person reading a Scripture might dedicate it to your parent and ask for everyone's prayers). Capture your wedding moments on video; at a later date, you'll be able to play back the video and share wedding photos with your father.

One of my bridesmaids will be seven months pregnant on my wedding day. What will I do if she is not able to attend? The show must still go on. It is really not polite to ask someone else to stand in at the last minute. Remember, it is not essential that you have an even number of ushers and bridesmaids. Maids can walk down the aisle in pairs or alone; one usher can escort a maid on each arm during the recession. Share the video and photos with your absent bridesmaid after the wedding.

My fiancé's brother, who was to be his best man, was recently killed in a car accident. He and his parents are completely devastated. Should we postpone the wedding? The decision is up to you and your fiancé. If a sibling or parent should pass away immediately before the wedding, you might decide to proceed with the wedding and reception, as that individual would have wanted you to do. As a gesture of respect, however, you might cancel the band or orchestra. Close family members and friends, who may be traveling long-distance to pay their respects to the deceased, may also want to help mark the start of your new life together. This new beginning that you make together can be a statement of faith and hope for the future.

At the reception, guests might make toasts that bridge the gap between the two events (*"Jim would want life to go on. We feel his presence with us today."*) Your clergymember will be particularly helpful with such situations and sentiments.

What if someone faints at the altar? If tears, heightened emotion, or a fainting spell threaten to upset any member of the wedding party or immediate family, offer your sympathy with a hug, touch, or sympathetic words. Ask a bridesmaid to carry an emergency kit for crises (see "Wedding-Day Emergency Kit" box) or tuck it under the front pew, ahead of time. Anyone who feels faint should sit down immediately and put his or her head between the knees until the feeling passes. The ceremony should continue unless there is a serious medical emergency.

My uncle has very high blood pressure and has had two heart attacks. How can we prepare in case he feels ill at our wedding? If someone becomes ill during the ceremony or reception, the normal activities should be interrupted until medical assistance arrives. The guest should be removed only by medical personnel. Consider hiring a nurse for the day, or having a doctor on premises with medical equipment nearby. Make sure that a family member has a cellular phone (in a purse) in case it is necessary to call 911.

If there is a medical emergency during your ceremony, remember that if you have already said your vows, you are already legally married, whether or not the entire ceremony is completed. If you have not yet said your vows when the illness occurs, continue with the service after medical personnel leave.

We live in an area of the country that has unpredictable winter weather. What can we do if there's a blizzard? If a snowstorm threatens the festivities, make arrangements with a snowplow operator to clear out the church or synagogue parking lot and your own driveway. You might also rent four-wheel–drive vehicles to ensure you'll have reliable transportation and be able to pick up guests at the airport.

Since no one can guarantee cloudless blue skies or moderate temperatures, have a backup location for anything planned outside. A ceremony in the garden of a museum might move to a room inside. A relative's car might substitute for a horse-and-carriage getaway. Torrential rain? Have oversized umbrellas on hand for ushers (and hired teens?) to use when escorting guests from the house of worship to their cars.

We live in Arizona. What can we do if there is a particularly brutal heat wave? Provide extra water for the flowers and the guests and have lots of non-alcoholic drinks on hand. If the electricity at the ceremony and reception sites can handle the extra strain, borrow small air conditioners or electric fans. (Otherwise, buy inexpensive handheld fans of paper or bamboo and place them in each pew.) Be sure that the site has a backup generator, or arrange for one to be there.

What if the organ breaks before the wedding? Other instruments (e.g., trumpet, flute, strings) can also provide beautiful wedding music. If you have some notice, locate an instrumentalist through city orchestras, the local musicians' union, or a college music department. A piano or portable organ can be rented or even moved from your home. Really desperate? Ask a talented friend or relative to bring a guitar.

If you find you are without an organist at the last minute, try to hire someone from another church or synagogue to play at your ceremony. Or, check with the house of worship to see if a qualified relative or friend would be permitted to play the in-house organ. The best solution may be recorded music. Records or tapes of wedding music should be available in most music stores (see Appendix, under Chapter 14, "Wedding Music"). Ask a church member who is familiar with the church's sound equipment to control the sound and the length of play.

What if my wedding gown is soiled or damaged on the wedding day? Anything can go wrong with clothes—zippers stick, trains get stepped on, hats blow away, dresses get spotted and shrink mysteriously. Follow these tips:

Ask your bridal salon in advance for emergency cleaning tips. The consultant there should be able to give you suggestions for your particular fabric when you buy the gown.

Be ready for emergency repairs. Bring along safety pins, needle, thread, tape, glue (see "Wedding-Day Emergency Kit" box) for last-minute repairs. Perhaps hold the bridal bouquet in a position that hides the spot or tear.

Try on your wedding clothes one week

wedding-day emergency kit

- smelling salts
- aspirin, Midol
- antihistamines
- needle and thread
- safety pins
- hairpins
- white masking tape
- Crazy Glue, rubber cement
- tampons
- tissues
- makeup
- comb and brush
- change for pay phone
- scissors
- nail file
- portable iron
- hair dryer

before the wedding. Try standing and sitting. If prewedding parties have added unwelcome pounds, return for a final fitting. (A steady exercise regimen will help you look better and feel calmer.)

Practice walking, sitting, rising, in your gown at home. Most women aren't used to walking in a long dress, or negotiating a long train and veil. Show your honor attendant how to arrange your train (so that it is not wrinkled as you stand at the altar, and so that your father or groom won't trip over it and rip it). Also be sure she knows how to bustle your train, so it won't get stepped on when you dance.

What if something happens to the ring? Follow these precautions:

wedding-contract musts

All contracts should list:

• dates

• times

• locations

• prices, including taxes and gratuities

• refund policies

• names of professionals hired

• expected attire of professionals hired

Sew a faux ring onto the ring bearer's pillow. Give the real one to the best man.

Ask the best man to keep the bride's ring in his pocket (check first for holes!). It's best for him not to slip it onto his finger; it might slip off or get stuck.

Suggest that your honor attendant wear the groom's ring on her thumb, which she should keep securely bent around her bouquet.

The bride and groom should rub their ring fingers with baby powder or a dab of petroleum jelly before the ceremony. Warm weather and tension make hands swell. The rings may not go on!

If your ring gets lost or is forgotten at home, borrow one from a parent or attendant. In a pinch, turn your engagement ring so the stone faces the inside of your hand. Later, your clergymember can bless the real wedding ring.

I'm concerned that an unwelcome guest might show up at our wedding and cause a scene. What can I do? Most reasonable adults know that an invitation is a prerequisite to attending a wedding. If your ex-mother-in-law or your ex-spouse does come and sits unobtrusively in the rear of the house of worship, their motivation might simply be to share your happiness. Greet them cordially at the end of the ceremony if you come face to face. Warn ushers beforehand if you are concerned that an uninvited guest might attend and create a disruption. Show them the person's photograph; they will then be prepared to turn this person away at the door. If safety is an overwhelming concern, hire a professional security guard (who should dress for the occasion).

If an unexpected cat or dog wanders into the house of worship, just let it sit and watch. If its behavior is potentially disruptive, an usher or family member might lead it quietly out of the building.

What if the band that shows up isn't the one I hired? Popular bandleaders may have several groups playing under their name. Read your contract carefully. Does it say that you have booked the company or a particular band? If you want the exact musicians you auditioned, you must list their specific names and their group name in your contract, along with wedding date, exact times, length of breaks or continuous music, overtime rates, total price and payment schedule, and any other special arrangements you have already made verbally.

My reception is at an out-of-the-way place. How can I make sure the florist, caterer, and other service providers find it on my wedding day? Some of the most romantic weddings take place at old mansions tucked into the countryside or in private gardens. The danger of getting lost on unfamiliar roads is very real. Even if your wedding is in a well-known spot, follow these steps:

Give professionals written directions and a map. Also give them phone numbers for your home, the reception site, the wedding consultant or banquet manager, another family member or friend who will be reachable if they get lost.

Confirm all plans by telephone one week before the wedding and the day before the wedding. If you are too busy, ask a friend or attendant to make these calls for you; ask someone to be on hand to check on and receive deliveries. Any mistakes in orders should be caught and rectified immediately, not hours later—when it may be too late!

My caterer seems overwhelmed by many events. What if my order gets mixed up with another? Keep checking with the caterer throughout your planning months, calling at least once a week the month before the wedding. Verify your order, date, time, and site. The arrival time of your guests cannot be postponed on wedding day— neither can the arrival of your food. If liquor or food goes astray, or the wrong order is delivered (e.g., sandwiches for fifty instead of hors d'oeuvres for two hundred), call the store or caterer at once. If the mix-up cannot be rectified quickly, send ushers or family members to delicatessens, bakeries, liquor stores. Once you have made additional purchases, do *not* accept a late delivery from your caterer. In this case, as in all cases of diminished services, a protective clause in your contract is essential. Never pay one hundred percent of the cost of a service until it has been delivered.

For information about what to do when unexpected situations occur on your honeymoon, see Chapter 19, "Going Away."

How to Prevent Problems

Ask for referrals from friends and family members. Talk to recent brides who have used the service you are considering. Ask for their pros and cons. Interview at least three different firms before committing. Don't accept a banquet hall's recommendation without checking out the firm. Don't accept an absolute (e.g., *"On tables, we always put carnations in bud vases."*). Insist on reviewing sample books of florists' and photographers' work.

Hire a company with a successful track record. A firm that has been in business for many years has proven itself worthy to hundreds of customers. Although this is not a guarantee (management can change), it is a positive sign.

Check with the Better Business Bureau in the city where the business is located or with your state's Department of Consumer Affairs (see Appendix, under Chapter 12, "Unexpected Situations"). Ask if there are complaints filed against the company. If a complaint was resolved successfully, it is not necessarily a bad sign. A series of unresolved problems, however, is a red flag. *Warning*: Some disreputable firms skirt around the records kept by the Better Business Bureau by changing their names after complaints have been filed. (Old complaints may not appear under a new name.) If the company's history is unavailable, be wary.

Trust your feelings. A wedding-service professional who seems haughty, patronizing, overly rushed, or resistant to your suggestion in an initial interview is unlikely to change over the next several months. If simple conversation is uncomfortable, go elsewhere. Avoid anyone who asks for an initial deposit that is more than fifty percent of the total price of the service. Withholding full payment is your only leverage if the service is not provided or if it is substandard.

Be suspicious of any professional who refuses to sign a contract. Anything that has been promised verbally should be spelled out in writing. If a company says they do not have standard contracts, ask for, or provide, a letter of agreement. Both you and the service provider must sign any document to make it legally binding.

Write in all services you have agreed upon (see specific chapters for points to be included in contracts with each wedding-service professional). Verbal agreements are often unenforceable in court (it's your word against theirs), and even honest people can forget things they've said. Specify in writing that you want white roses; list a backup color. If you want candid photos instead of posed shots, type that in.

Never be pushed into signing anything. Give yourself time to fully understand the document. Ask as many questions as you must. An ethical professional whose services are in demand should courteously answer all questions, never pressure you for a quick decision or deposit. For example, never cave in to pressure to put a deposit down on a gown before the store closes that day. If this means that you must return another day to finalize the deal, do that. If you were made to feel uncomfortable about delaying your decision, rethink hiring the firm or buying.

Keep tabs on the professionals once you've put down a deposit. Bands, in particular, may break up or re-form during your engagement months. Market changes may make it impossible for your florist to deliver a particular flower. Communicate.

if you've been ripped off

If you don't receive the services for which you've contracted:

- Withhold final payment.

- Write a letter to the company explaining your position, asking for a return of your deposit.

- Take the company to small-claims court (if the disputed deposit doesn't exceed the maximum—$2,000 in some states; check in yours).

- File a complaint with the Better Business Bureau (see Appendix, under Chapter 12, "Unexpected Situations") and let them contact the company. (Results rest with the firm's willingness to cooperate. Your letter will remain on file to warn future brides who check on the provider.)

- Report the case to your state's Department of Consumer Affairs. (If they receive similar complaints, they may investigate.)

- Hire a lawyer and sue to recover your deposit. (Your contract should stipulate a full refund for non-delivery of services.)

YOUR RECEPTION 13

A reception can include a sumptuous seated dinner and dessert buffet with a ten-piece band or just you two, your parents, and a few close friends around a big table at your favorite inn. As long as the celebration affords those who love you an opportunity to wish you happiness, a reception can be either of the above—or anything in between. All you really need is the opportunity and the space to gather everyone together, serve a sparkling beverage for toasting, and cake. (For more information on selecting a site and a caterer, see Chapter 4, "Planning Your Wedding.")

Reception Timetable

This is a schedule for a three-hour reception. (If your celebration will be longer, allow more time between events, or keep to this timetable and enjoy the dancing *after* dinner.) After you fill in time estimates for your reception, give this timetable to an organized member of your wedding party or a wedding consultant and ask her or him to make sure the caterer, florist, musicians (or disc jockey), and photographer are on track during the reception. The caterer should be told to discuss any scheduling problems with this person. Thank your (amateur) helper after the wedding with a note and token of appreciation.

The reception begins:
You, the groom, and the wedding party arrive at the reception site.

The first half-hour:
If the receiving line did not form at the ceremony site, it may assemble here to greet guests as they arrive. Photographs of you and your groom—alone and with the bridal party—may also be taken during this time—if the receiving line was held at the ceremony site.

receiving- line etiquette

- A day or two before the wedding, go over the guest list with your groom and parents so names are fresh in your mind.

- Remind receiving-line participants beforehand to keep comments brief.

- Position the line in a convenient spot near the entrance or exit, where guests can move down it easily, directly into the refreshment area (if receiving line is at the reception site).

- Ask waiters to pass food and drinks to those in line; keep chairs accessible for those who might need them.

- Provide musical entertainment, a photo display of old family wedding pictures, or snapshots of the bride and groom growing up, near the receiving line.

- If you don't know a guest, simply introduce yourself—he or she will no doubt offer his or her name in return.

- Women may wear hats and gloves, although it's friendlier to remove gloves for handshaking.

- Bride and bridesmaids should hold bouquets in left hands, or set them aside.

The second half-hour:
Musicians play, drinks are poured, hors d'oeuvres are served, guests mingle and pick up escort cards.

After one hour:
Dinner is announced. The wedding party is seated. Blessings may be said by clergymembers, fathers, and other guests.

Guests line up for the buffet or sit for table service. Wedding party is served.

Best man toasts the bride and groom, and the groom and bride may follow with their own thoughts and thanks. Music and dancing continue.

After one-and-a-half hours:
The first course is cleared from the head table, then from the guests' tables. The couple dance their first dance as husband and wife, followed by other traditional dances. Everyone then sits down for the main course.

After two hours:
Tables are cleared. Musicians signal time for the cake-cutting ceremony. Attendants and guests gather around to watch as the couple cut the cake and share a taste of the first slice. Dancing resumes. Caterer or banquet manager cuts and serves cake and any other dessert to guests.

Last half-hour:
The single women cluster together and the bride tosses her bouquet to them. The bride's garter may also be thrown by the groom to a group of bachelors.

Bride and groom slip away to change, say good-bye to their parents (if they will make an exit from the reception).

Bride and groom run out to their car in a shower of rose petals, confetti, etc.

Musicians stop playing, bar closes. Parents say farewell to guests.

The Receiving Line

After the ceremony, your guests will be eager to hug you and congratulate you. A receiving line is an efficient way for you and your parents to receive these good wishes and give a warm welcome to friends and family who have come to share this special day. At large weddings, it may be the only chance you get to speak to each guest.

When does a receiving line take place? The receiving line should form after the ceremony, but before the reception. If you aren't going directly to the reception site (because you'll be taking pictures, for example), set up the line at the church or synagogue. If you'll take bridal-party pictures at the ceremony site, form a receiving line at the reception site.

Who stands in the line? The wedding hosts head the line. If your parents are hosting, your mother would greet guests first, followed by your father, to her left; the groom's

RECEIVING LINE ORDER

1. **Mother of the bride**
2. **Father of the bride**
   (optional)
3. **Mother of the groom**
4. **Father of the groom**
   (optional)
5. **Bride**
6. **Groom**
7. **Bride's honor attendant**
   (optional)
8. **Bridesmaids (optional)**

mother, then his father to her left; the bride; the groom; the maid of honor; and the bridesmaids. (It is optional for fathers and attendants to stand in the line; you may prefer that they circulate among guests.)

If you do not have a mother or stepmother to receive your guests, your grandmother, a sister, or an aunt might head the line with your father. If the reception is hosted by persons other than your parents, they are the first in line to greet guests. If you and the groom are the wedding hosts, you would head the line.

What about divorced parents? If your parents or your groom's parents are divorced, it's often easiest to have fathers circulate among the guests rather than stand in the line. Even if divorced parents are friendly, having them stand together might be confusing to guests who might then assume they are married.

   If your parents are divorced and your father is hosting the party, you may want him to head the line anyway—just don't position him next to your mother. If you are close to your stepmother, you might want her to stand in line, too. In this case, position your mother at the head of the line, followed by your groom's parents, the bride and groom; your stepmother and father might stand to the left of the groom.

What should you say? Thank guests for coming, tell them how happy you are to see them, and introduce them to your groom or other members of the wedding party they may not know. When introducing them, try to give a small fact that will help them remember each other—*"Mary was Tina's college roommate,"* for example. If your groom or another receiving-line participant knows them, on the other hand, he or she can introduce them to you. Keep comments brief; otherwise the line may become too lengthy (you can chat later, during table visits).

guest-book tips

- Set your guest book on an attractive table in a prominent place at the reception site—at the end of the receiving line or near the reception-hall entrance.

- Provide several ballpoint pens (avoid felt-tip pens, which may run if the book accidentally gets wet).

- Ask the last person in the receiving line to point guests in the direction of the book.

- Later, ask your bandleader to remind guests to sign—or have an usher or another friend or relative circulate with the book.

reception seating tips

- **Start as soon as your R.s.v.p. cards are in. Determine number of tables, location, seats at each.**

- **Make up a chart outlining table positions; fill in guests' names. Don't seat older guests near the band, kitchen; it may be hard for them to hear.**

- **Consider interests and personalities. Seat friends who share hobbies or occupations together, as well as single guests, teens. Mix shy personalities with outgoing ones. Arrange a children's table with books, favors, chaperones.**

- **Seat divorced parents separately, each hosting their own table of family and friends. Or seat the parent who raised you with the groom's parents, the other with the officiant.**

- **Include spouses, girlfriends, boyfriends of attendants at the head table—if the bridal party is small. Or, seat attendants at the head table; partners separately.**

- **If there is no head table for the wedding party, seat the bridal couple alone or with parents, siblings.**

- **If not at the head table, seat parents, grandparents, aunts, uncles, with the clergymember.**

THE PARENTS' TABLE:

1. Mother of the bride
2. Father of the bride
3. Father of the groom
4. Wedding officiant
5. Mother of the groom
6. Wedding officiant's spouse or assistant, or another honored female guest

The Guest Book

A wedding guest book (often called "The Bride's Book") is a keepsake that preserves the names of friends and relatives who were present at your wedding. You can buy one at most stationery stores or choose an elegant leather album; or, make your own, which you can decorate with pictures from your childhood or courtship (make sure to leave space for congratulatory comments and addresses). Leave space for each guest to write personal remarks and good wishes.

Reception Seating

When planning reception seating, consider the style of food service. Cocktails and finger foods don't require formal seating—buffets (since they are full meals) do. All seated meals should have a seating plan; guests will appreciate the fact that you have thought of each one of them and specified a place.

If you're designating seating at the reception, write out table (or escort) cards with guests' names and table numbers. (You also might hire a calligrapher to write out these cards.) The cards may be on solid-colored paper or might be accented with the couple's initials, or a dried flower (e.g., daffodil for "regard") that echoes a flower in the table centerpieces. To create a friendly atmosphere

THE HEAD TABLE:

1. Bride
2. Groom
3. Bride's honor attendant
4. Best man
5. Bridesmaids
6. Ushers

among guests, use informal address (*Janet Riley* or *Mrs. Riley* instead of *Mrs. John P. Riley*. If two people have the same last name, however, be sure to include first names or initials.) Check your cards against a master guest list—to make sure you haven't omitted anyone.

Set the cards in alphabetical order on a separate table near the doorway. Or, post a seating chart with each guest's name and table number.

Place cards mark each seat at the bride's and parents' tables, but are optional elsewhere. At very formal weddings, and if you want to introduce specific guests to each other at each table, you might specify in which seat they will sit at their tables; set place cards on the folded napkin which rests on each service plate (or above the dinner plate). Write first and last names on both sides of the place card—to make it easier for guests who don't know one another to strike up a conversation.

Decide if you'll have a head table. Traditionally, the focus of the reception is the bride's (or head) table, where all the members of the bridal party sit on one side, facing the guests. The table is often elevated on a large platform called a dais, and covered with a long cloth of lace, damask, or linen. Keep decorations low—maids' bouquets and candles, or simple garlands of flowers, greens, and ribbons—so guests get an unobstructed view. You and your groom sit in the center of the table (groom on the bride's left, best man on her right). The matron or maid of honor sits to the groom's left. Bridesmaids and ushers sit in alternating seats on either side.

Attendants who are married to each other needn't be seated next to each other, or even at the same table, if the bridal party is large. If the wedding party is small, however, you might have the husbands and wives of attendants, your parents, siblings, clergymember and his or her spouse join the head table; or, arrange a few seated tables for the bridal party and their partners.

Plan special parents' tables if parents won't be seated at the head table. Traditionally, your mother and father, as hosts, sit at opposite ends of the parents' table. The groom's father sits at your

head-table etiquette

All eyes will be on you; set a good example.

- **Keep voices low—especially during reception announcements and rituals (e.g., clergymember's prayer or the toasts).**

- **Men should keep jackets on; women, shoes on—for the entire celebration.**

- **Women should not comb their hair or apply makeup at the table.**

- **Smoking looks out of place in bridal attire. No one should smoke when seated, posing for pictures, or standing in the receiving line. (Slip outside.)**

- **Avoid getting inebriated. Have someone escort a drunk attendant outdoors for a while.**

- **Remember to eat. You'll all need energy for the dancing, toasting, and socializing.**

mother's right, the wedding officiant to her left, the groom's mother to your father's right, and the wedding officiant's spouse or assistant, or another honored female guest, to his left.

Or, you might arrange two parents' tables, one for your folks and one for his. That will seat more guests at special tables. If parents are divorced, they can individually host tables.

Blessings

When all the guests are seated for the meal, your clergymember, a member of your family, or another honored guest may say a prayer. Be sure to arrange this ahead of time, since not everyone is comfortable speaking in public, spontaneously. At Christian weddings, the clergymember may rise to say grace. At Jewish weddings, a special blessing called the *hamotzi* is spoken over a large braided loaf of egg-rich bread called *challah* by the rabbi or two fathers, or any other honored guest. Pieces of *challah* are then passed to guests. The *sheva shevahot*, or seven praises, may be recited before the meal by female relatives and friends, to honor the bride's and groom's names, their abilities, and plans. These praises parallel the traditional men's Hebrew prayer, the *sheva b'rachot* (wedding grace after meals), recited after the wedding feast by the rabbi, cantor, and other male attendants or relatives. (In Orthodox and Conservative Jewish tradition, these prayers must be spoken by a man.) Guests should not leave until this ritual ends the meal.

toasting tips

- Prepare and rehearse.

- Record words on index cards.

- Don't exceed three minutes; keep it short and sincere.

- Stand to give or drink a toast; stay seated to receive one.

- Mention those whom you're toasting by name, your relationship to them, a thought about their future good fortune.

- Cite a favorite poem, quotation, joke, Scripture, song lyric.

- If you hear glasses clinking, it means everyone wants to see you and your groom kiss. After a few times, start a new tradition: kiss your father, brother; have them kiss another guest the next time the glasses clink!

Wedding Toasts

Traditionally, the best man makes the first reception toast to the bride and groom—anytime after the receiving line is over and everyone has been served a glass of champagne or other sparkling beverage. The band may get everyone's attention with a drumroll or fanfare. The groom rises to thank the best man, then toasts his bride and both sets of parents. The bride may then rise to make a toast, followed by parents, relatives, members of the wedding party, and friends. The best man can act as toastmaster, and might prepare a list of the order in which each person will make a toast. At the end of the toasts, the best man may read aloud any congratulatory letters or telegrams received (see Appendix, under Chapter 13, "Your Reception").

Sample best man's toast:

"Here's to Sharon and Gary. I wanted to come to their wedding so much, I introduced them! May their lives be full of the kind of happiness we are enjoying here today."

Sample groom's toast:

"Thank you Paul. You've been my best friend for twelve years, and I can't tell you how much it has meant for me to have you by my side through every major milestone. I thank you for introducing me

to my beautiful bride; I'm eternally grateful. I toast you, Lisa, for coming into my life and agreeing to share your own life with me. And I toast, and thank, your parents, for welcoming me into their family, and for giving us this incredible wedding. We'll always remember it. I also toast my own parents and family for their support and love over the years. And I thank all of you for coming to share this day with us."

Sample bride's toast:

"To my husband, the most wonderful man in the world. To my new family, with thanks for raising such a loving and supportive person. And to my parents, for all the love and strength they've given me. May we all have many, many more memorable days together."

The Wedding Cake

Since Roman times, when a thin loaf was broken over the bride's head to ensure her fertility, the wedding cake has been an important feature of the wedding celebration (see Chapter 2, "Wedding Customs"). In Victorian times, cakes became as frilly and elaborate as the bride's attire, decorated with roses, cupids, and garlands, often in the shape of romantic gazebos and cupolas. Today, bakers are equally innovative (see Appendix, under Chapter 13, "Your Reception"), varying the traditional white Bride's Cake with favorite flavors (orange, cherry, banana, chocolate, spice, carrot, hazelnut, mocha, marble, spice, Amaretto, cheesecake), fillings (mousse, apricot, blueberry, orange liqueur), icings (chocolate, mocha, vanilla, strawberry), and shapes and/or cake toppers reflecting hobbies, occupations, symbols (racquet, bicycle, golf cart, castle, scales of justice, top hat). Spotlight the wedding cake (and protect it from jostling) on a separate table covered with a white cloth and decorated with flowers, greens, or maids' bouquets. Below are tips for cutting the cake.

Cut the cake just before dessert at a luncheon or dinner reception; just after guests have been received at a tea or cocktail reception.

Use a ribbon-tied silver knife—a Heritage Cake Knife just received from your registry—with your initials newly engraved, or an heirloom knife (the one your parents used at their wedding).

The groom places his right hand over the bride's, and together they cut into the bottom layer.

Traditionally, the bride and groom feed each other a taste of the first slice as a symbol of their willingness to share a household. (No food fights!)

The bride serves her new in-laws their pieces, then the groom serves his new in-laws slices.

The rest of the cake is cut by the catering staff, or a friend designated in advance, then served to all guests. (It is bad luck for a guest to leave the reception without tasting the cake.)

cake innovations

- woven-basket icing
- spun-sugar swans, butterflies
- delicate sugar orchids, roses, anemones, lilies, pansies, daisies, etc., coordinating with the floral decor
- gum-paste flowers and beaded medallions echoing color and details of the wedding dress, color scheme
- elaborate lace and embroidery details in icing, echoing the wedding dress
- rainbow-hued pulled-sugar ribbons
- clusters of white chocolate, colored berries, grapes, cascading across latticework tiers
- icing baskets filled with sugar field flowers
- photograph of couple on ski slope, tennis court, reproduced on cake
- different flavor for every tier
- edible 22k-gold leaf for Art Deco weddings
- satellite stands display large wedding cake and several smaller cakes; some rotate, have fountains between tiers
- marzipan fruits and flowers; candy hearts; white or dark chocolate
- a cake with tiers shaped and decorated like festively wrapped packages

According to custom, the top tier of the wedding cake may be saved and eaten on the couple's first anniversary (the groom's cake may also be used for this purpose). Wrap cake carefully so it is airtight, and freeze. Or, to ensure it will still be tasty, freeze it to share on your one-month anniversary. Re-create a mini-cake for the first anniversary.

Tradition says a piece of bride's cake under a single person's pillow will lead to dreams of a future spouse. (The groom's cake may also be used for this purpose.) If the couple are not planning to save the top tier of the bride's cake for their first anniversary, they might ask the caterer to pack slices in decorative boxes to send home with guests.

creative cake toppers

- porcelain bridal pair
- porcelain figurines painted to resemble bride and groom in coloring, features, attire
- blown-glass ornaments
- electric lights illuminating golden bells
- a music box playing a favorite song
- animals in bridal attire (e.g., frogs, bunnies)
- famous cartoon couples (e.g., Mickey and Minnie, Kermit and Miss Piggie)
- regional symbols: cowboy and cowgirl; a couple in lederhosen (leather shorts with suspenders—often worn in Bavaria)
- a tree sapling—the traditional cake topper in Bermuda—to be replanted in the newlyweds' yard
- bridal figures holding the publications for which the bride and groom work

Cake Toppers

Plastic bride and groom figurines have been replaced by personalized, whimsical cake ornaments depicting a couple's occupations, hobbies, or how they met. Some examples: a miniature T-bird (representing a passion for antique cars), a bride and groom in tennis attire with tennis racquets, a blindfolded couple (if they met on a blind date!). Also popular: fresh flowers, especially at country or outdoor weddings; heirloom toppers from parents', or grandparents' cakes.

The Groom's Cake

Traditionally, the groom's cake is a one-layer dark fruitcake that accompanies the Bride's Cake, which is white (see Chapter 2, "Wedding Customs"). Groom's cakes today are often baked in the groom's favorite flavor, such as chocolate, and may be in the shape symbolic of his favorite interest or hobby—a fish or a football; a card with the Queen of Hearts (if he plays bridge); jogging shoes; an open book; a car.

The groom's cake can be sliced and served at the reception and festively boxed for guests to take home as favors, or, prior to the wedding, you might serve it for dessert at the rehearsal dinner. It also might be saved for the couple's first anniversary. (To preserve a fruitcake, wrap it in a brandy- or rum-soaked cheesecloth, seal in a tin, and store in a cool place until you're ready to eat it.)

Reception Dancing

Dancing adds a festive note to the celebration. Guests can waltz to an orchestra or pianist, swing to the sounds of a string trio, or rock to the tunes played by a disc jockey or a friend with a stereo. At a hotel or club reception, the area in front of the bride's table is usually cleared for dancing; at home, you might set aside one whole room or have a temporary dance floor laid down at the end of a large living room. For a garden reception, guests may dance on the terrace or on a temporary floor set up under a tent.

The first dance. The bride and groom's first dance as husband and wife is most often scheduled immediately after the first course, before the entrée is served. Guests can still be invited onto the dance floor as soon as they have been through the receiving line and passed into the reception banquet room. The bandleader will announce your first dance to clear the dance floor. (Although some couples opt to put all dancing off till after the entrée course, this can put a damper on the natural celebratory spirit that guests are eager to express.)

Ballroom-dance lessons. In preparation for the first dance, which will make you two the center of attention, many engaged couples are taking ballroom-dance lessons and practicing dancing to their favorite song. For your reception, you'll want to learn the basic steps of the waltz, fox-trot, and swing. (For fun, also learn the cha-cha, rumba, and tango!) Begin classes six months before the wedding; aim for two classes a week, and practice.

To find a dance studio, look in the Yellow Pages under "Dancing," and ask friends for recommendations. (Also see Appendix, under Chapter 13, "Your Reception," for sources.) Visit the studio, observe a class, and check out the studio's reputation with the local Better Business Bureau before signing up. Inquire about instructors' credentials (are they members of Dance Masters, Dance Educators of America, the Imperial Society of Teachers of Dancing?). Rent or

buy dance videos for home practice.

Ethnic dances. To get everyone onto the dance floor, many couples are asking their bands to play songs that reflect their heritages (see Chapter 14, "Wedding Music," for the "Wedding Reception Music" chart). In fact, many disc jockeys and bandleaders will play a recognizable line or circle dance such as the *horah* to get everyone out onto the dance floor. If a band doesn't know a particular song, taped music can be used. These lively dances can be done by young and old alike:

The Mizinke: Usually performed to the Yiddish song "*Die Mizinke Oysgegeben,*" this song is played at a wedding when the last child in the family marries. Originally played to honor a Jewish mother whose last daughter wed, today the custom is extended to the last son *or* daughter. *Both* parents are seated in the center of the dance floor and presented with bouquets, while guests swirl around them in a lively circle dance.

The Dollar Dance ("The Bride's Dance"): This is derived from an old Polish custom in which the men who dance with the bride fill her peckets with money or pin bills to her veil. The money may be given in lieu of a gift, or a dollar (or more) may be given for a turn around the dance floor. The bride today may put the money in a lacy bridal purse.

The Greek Handkerchief Dance: The

---

first-dance order

Here is one possible dance order to follow. Remember that it is not necessary to dance through an entire song before switching partners.

1. The bride and groom circle the floor to their favorite tune.

2. The bride's father cuts in and dances with the bride, while the groom dances with his mother-in-law. (If the bride's parents are divorced and it is awkward to choose a dance with a father or stepfather, all guests may be invited onto the floor then.)

3. The bride dances with the father of the groom while the groom dances with his own mother.

4. The bride dances with the best man, while the groom dances with the honor attendant.

5. The bandleader invites the other members of the wedding party onto the dance floor.

6. The bandleader invites all guests onto the dance floor.

Before the evening ends, you will probably dance with each usher, and your groom with each bridesmaid. It's also customary for the ushers to dance with many of the single women present, and to request a dance with each bridesmaid and both mothers.

- live statues that wink, blow kisses, fall off pedestals—to amuse and surprise guests

- fortune teller; tarot-card reader

- handwriting analyst

- mimes

- professional dancers who give a demonstration, a group lesson

- laser show in banquet hall or evening sky: aerial toasts penned on an electronic pad, laser animation of couple's courtship

- outdoors, a fireworks display; indoors, sparklers, fountains (obtain required permits from fire department; check insurance with banquet manager). (See Appendix, under Chapter 13, "Your Reception," for source.)

- "This Is Your Life" slide show; videobiography with home movies, snap shots shown on an opaque projector (fifteen minutes, tops)

- disposable cameras on each table, so guests can pose or snap their own candids

- colorful toasts

- interpretive dance or ballet

- piano show tunes

groom is linked to the bride by a handkerchief; others hold shoulders; the dancing weaves around the room.

The Horah: This Israeli folk dance is performed in a circle, with hands held. Dancers lift bride and groom up on chairs in the center; they hold a linen napkin between their hands.

The Tarantella: This lively Italian folk dance in 6/8 time is often danced by couples at weddings. It has quick hops and tapping foot movements.

The Grand March: Newlyweds at Italian weddings may link arms and lead attendants and guests in a lively march around the room, sometimes outside and around the building. They then form an arch with their arms. Two by two, the guests pass under their arms, then form another arch to continue the "bridge" longer. When all the guests have followed suit, the bridge disbands with the last two in line passing all the way back through to kiss the couple who started it all. All come back through until the bride and groom head the line.

Following the Grand March, a second receiving line may be formed beside a table laden with *bomboniere*—cake boxes, porcelain boxes, cookies, candied almonds, cigars, or other favors (see Chapter 2, "Wedding Customs," under "Italy"). This receiving line is a chance to say good-bye to the couple, who will dance their last dance and then depart.

Guests may also form a circle to watch the couple's last dance. The bride and groom pass through and say good-bye at the song's conclusion.

Reception Entertainment

Some couples elect to provide entertainment for their reception guests. You might feature a slide show of your childhood and romance; friends might stage a scene from a play or read suitable poetry, your college glee club might sing a rendition of "your song" or school song. You and your groom might even perform yourselves or write your own wedding song, with humorous lyrics, and sing it to a familiar tune. Or, you could hire a professional wedding entertainer, such as a mime, magician, comedian, or caricaturist to sketch portraits of guests. Some couples even arrange for fireworks or a laser show. If you hire an entertainer, be sure to review the entire act beforehand to make sure it is in good taste and likely to be appreciated by the many ages and personalities at your party. And no matter who's performing, don't let it run too long. Guests need a chance to eat, dance, and mingle on their own, as well.

Favors

Mementos will create a memorable wedding for your guests. Choose gifts and themes reminiscent of the unique style and regional location of your wedding.

Special Weddings. Give parents at a Progressive Wedding photographs of you two at each previous celebration. For a Sentimental Journey wedding, give parents previously compiled "This is Your Life" albums filled with photos from your birth to engagement.

Theme Weddings. If you have a Honeymoon Wedding, create breakaway table centerpieces of small, individually potted cacti in the Southwest; set leis at each place in Hawaii; shell necklaces on a tropical island. During a Long Weekend Wedding, place baseball caps at each place setting. A country theme? Set pottery mugs or small dried-flower arrangements at each place. Married on a boat? Give guests toy boats filled with perfume or candy; emboss matchbooks with anchors. At a Surprise Wedding, have guests break a piñata to release a grab bag of tiny treats.

Food Favors. Give guests a taste of your ethnic cuisine: Chinese fortune cookies, English fruitcake, Italian *confetti* (candy-coated almonds), German cookies, French pastries. Make the centerpiece a basket of loose fruit for all to sample.

Personalized Favors. Order monogrammed mints and set them at each place, in porcelain keepsake cups. Or, at a summer wedding, give each guest a beautifully folded paper fan, inscribed with romantic words that appear as the fan is unfolded. Another innovative idea? Write meaningful fortunes for each table of guests and either order or bake fortune cookies to tuck them into; the messages will amuse guests and start the conversation! Another meaningful keepsake? Ask the photographer's assistant to snap an instant photo of each guest or couple as they enter the reception room, then hang them on a "Photo Tree." Throughout the reception, or when leaving, they can find and keep their picture!

Ecologically and Socially Correct Favors. Give guests packets of seeds or tree saplings; they can plant them at home. Leave a note written in calligraphy on each table stating that "in honor of the wedding of George and Sue, a donation to a favorite charity has been made." Print programs or menu cards on recycled paper.

Floral Favors. Give each guest a small mini-wreath made of a symbolic herb (e.g., rosemary, for remembrance). Set a long-stemmed red rose at each place. Wrap linen napkins in floral sashes. Position votive candle holders with floating magnolia blossoms at each place.

Collectible Favors. Give guests figurines, decorative boxes. Or, near Christmas, select limited-edition ornaments engraved with the year.

Favors They Can Use Again. Put escort cards inside small picture frames or pewter or china card holders. Wrap candied almonds in lace or men's handkerchiefs, sashed with ribbons. For a Jewish wedding, order velvet or satin *yarmulkes* (skullcaps) that men will want to wear on future holidays; inside, personalize them with the names of bride and groom, the wedding date (so they'll always remember where they got it!).

ideas for favors

Below are just a few ideas. Your imagination is the only limit!

- tulle-wrapped candied almonds
- small boxes of chocolates
- chocolates personalized with the couple's initials
- bottles of wine with the bride and groom's own label
- small vials of a signature scent created by a perfumer just for the bride
- cakes of scented soap
- breakaway centerpieces
- a cluster of small bud vases filled with fresh blooms
- handpainted Easter eggs personalized with the couple's initials for a spring wedding
- initialed silver Mylar™ balloons and noisemakers for a New Year's Eve wedding
- bags of bagels and copies of the Sunday newspaper, distributed at the end of a Saturday evening wedding

- The bride turns and throws the bouquet over one shoulder. If you'd like to aim at a sister or close friend, face the group as you throw. (Tradition holds that the woman who catches the bouquet will be the next to marry.)

- The groom removes the bride's garter and tosses it over one shoulder to the bachelors at the reception; in some regions, the bride may toss the garter. (The man who captures it is destined to be the next to wed.)

Wedding Pranks

Part of the fun of a wedding is planning decorations for the couple's car, a "ribbing" sung to the tune of your college song, a funny telegram sent to the honeymoon hotel, or a groom who kneels at the altar to reveal the words "Help Me!" scrawled by his ushers on the soles of his shoes. But sometimes, in all the excitement, good judgment goes out the window. There is nothing funny about having your reservations changed from a double to a single room, your plane tickets canceled, or your car's paint job ruined by whitewash lettering. And no one likes an elegant country club reception to be interrupted by a rowdy group of friends determined to throw the groom into the pool. The best man should pass the word to the ushers: Play all the tricks you want at the bachelor party, but keep the fun under control at the reception.

The Bouquet and Garter Toss

Just before you leave to change into your going-away clothes, your bandleader, musician, or disc jockey may ask your bridesmaids and other single women to gather at a convenient spot for the throwing of the bouquet. If you wish to keep your bouquet, to be dried as a keepsake, you might have your florist make up a breakaway bouquet, a small arrangement that separates from the main bouquet for you to toss. Or, ask your florist to make up a small, separate token bouquet for tossing. (You can also have a bouquet made up with detachable flowers that you can remove before tossing and use as your going-away bouquet.)

The groom may next remove the bride's garter and toss it to a gathered group of single men. The lucky bachelor who catches it may then slip the garter onto the leg of the single woman who caught the bouquet (see Chapter 2, "Wedding Customs").

WEDDING MUSIC 14

The music you choose should reflect the style of your celebration and the personalities of you and your groom. Take the time to hire musicians and/or a disc jockey who will be responsive to your wishes and help to create a truly harmonious day.

Religious Ceremony Music

Inquire about the music policy at your house of worship. Some churches and synagogues will not allow musicians other than their organist or permit secular (nonreligious) music to be played during a wedding ceremony. For example, some churches do not allow "Wedding March (Bridal Chorus)," from Wagner's *Lohengrin*, composed to mark an ill-fated operatic union, or Mendelssohn's "Wedding March," from *A Midsummer Night's Dream*, written for the pagan wedding of the Duke of Athens to the Queen of the Amazons. Some religions will permit classical music and contemporary hits while others do not. (See Chapter 9, "Religious Rituals & Requirements.")

Protestant Weddings. It is acceptable to have both popular and religious music. It can be performed by the church organist, soloist, or choir, who will be familiar with wedding procedures and can offer a wide variety of selections from which you can choose. If you request something obscure or unusual, give the musician enough time to learn and practice the piece.

Catholic Ceremonies. Some Catholic clergy may ask that you refrain from playing popular music and instead choose religious selections and the hymns sung at regular Masses. A choir or, more often, a soloist may sing. Schubert's "Ave Maria" is a favorite ceremony selection; other possibilities may include César Franck's "Panis Angelius" and Mozart's "Ave Verum."

Jewish Ceremonies. Many Reform and Conservative weddings permit secular music, including the usual wedding marches. Orthodox rabbis, however, may prefer that couples use only traditional Hebrew music. The cantor traditionally chants the Seven Blessings and may perform other solo pieces, if requested. Ask the rabbi and cantor for suggestions on both traditional Hebrew songs and contemporary Israeli music.

Eastern Orthodox and Greek Orthodox Ceremonies. Eastern Orthodox and Greek Orthodox faiths allow only vocal music at wedding ceremonies.

Quaker Ceremonies. No music is allowed during wedding ceremonies.

Ceremony Choices

Ceremony music is usually performed by an organist and/or string quartet (two violins, a viola, a cello); a trio (a violin, a flute, a harpsichord); or a brass ensemble (trumpets, a trombone, a French horn, a baritone). Think about the songs you prefer, the mood you want to create (see Appendix, under Chapter 14, "Wedding Music").

Consult with the music director of the church or synagogue. He or she will be familiar with wedding music. Ask about the use of an organ, other keyboard instruments, and the policy of hiring a professional organist. You may have to pay the church organist whether or not you employ him or her (see "Hiring Musicians" section).

Add your own personal touch. Choose from current love songs, show and movie themes, folk and country ballads, classical works, or even the song played when you two first danced. (See "Wedding Ceremony Music" chart.)

Include the people you love. If friends' or relatives' talent is on the *professional* level, and they've performed in public before, ask one to play the prelude on the piano, another to offer a solo after the vows. (Some couples prefer to invite guests to perform at the reception, where the mood is lighter.) Thank these talented performers with small gifts at the rehearsal dinner or another prewedding event.

Think twice before singing yourselves. Even the most seasoned performers get wedding-day nerves. Consider whether you two want the stress of performing musically, in addition to walking down the aisle! It may be most effective for you to simply say your vows with clarity and confidence.

Hiring Musicians

Whether hiring musicians for the ceremony, cocktail hour, or reception, realize that some orchestras, bands, and soloists may be booked a year or more in advance. Begin your search as soon as the wedding date is set.

ceremony music timetable

- Prelude—soft instrumental music, vocal solos, performed during the thirty minutes when guests are being seated

- Vocal solo or choir piece—performed after the mothers are seated

- Processional—majestic pieces played while wedding party and bride walk down the aisle

- Ceremony—vocal or instrumental solo, hymns, or folk songs performed after the vows

- Recessional—triumphant piece played as newlyweds walk up the aisle as husband and wife, followed by wedding party

- Postlude—lively selection played as guests file out

Choose ceremony instruments and musicians. Ask the organist or clergymember about the acoustics in the house of worship. Ask them to refer you to local musicians. A string or woodwind quartet, a group of madrigal singers, a harpist, or a trumpeter will enhance the processional or recessional. Select instruments and tunes that are not too soft or too overpowering.

Get other referrals for ceremony musicians from friends, relatives, other newlyweds. Call local high schools, colleges, and symphonies for the names of string quartets and soloists. Contact the local musicians union (listed under "Musicians" in the Yellow Pages); union offices may provide videotapes of bands, direct you to musicians who meet the description of the style you prefer. If you want to include a band in your ceremony, ask your caterer, photographer, and florist for the names of those with whom they've enjoyed working. Ask for and check references from couples who have recently hired the musicians for their weddings.

Listen to the musicians perform. If you choose to hire a band, try to see a live performance or watch an audition tape. This will help you to evaluate the band's stage presence and will give you an overall feel for their style of music. Make sure you like the quality of instrumental and vocal performances, that the sound is not overpowering, and that it seems appropriate for a ceremony.

Give the ceremony musicians your musical requests. If you plan to include a contemporary or original song, provide the group with sheet music early enough so that they have time to learn it well.

Ask friends and relatives for reception-band referrals. Follow the same process detailed above when searching for ceremony musicians. Attend a wedding or other large party where the band is playing. At the very least, view a videotape. Notice how loud the sound is (it should not be overpowering), the dress and demeanor of the band members, the style of the bandleader when introducing songs, guests, or reception activities.

Discuss your tastes for dance music. Since your reception music should appeal to all guests, a versatile band is the best choice. Meet with the bandleader to discuss the type of music you want played—popular, jazz, Motown. Be as detailed as possible; if you like jazz, specify swing, familiar, or progressive jazz.

Give the bandleader a list of any special songs you want played. If songs are unusual, provide sheet music and lyrics, and allow sufficient time for the group to practice. Also prepare the bandleader with any introductions you'd like him or her to make (e.g., "This is the song that the bride's parents danced to at *their* wedding, thirty years ago"). Fill in the musicians on how and when the wedding party will be introduced;

when you want the first dance, father-daughter and mother-son dances played; when the best man will make his toast; if you'll throw the bouquet and garter.

Tell the bandleader what you do *not* want played. Some couples specify that they do not want a particular song played (e.g., *not* "The Hokey Pokey," or "The Farmer in the Dell"—played while the band sings "The bride cuts the cake…").

Ask if the musicians will bring their own sound system. If they will, check to see if the equipment is electrically compatible with the reception site, and where electrical outlets are located. If they won't, ask what they will require and find out the total cost for providing it. An extra generator is a must; more than one wedding has been without music when a generator has blown or failed to work. Plan where in the reception hall the band will perform and test the acoustics. (It's best to position a band at one far end of a tent or room—so sound isn't overwhelming.) If you want the band to provide continuous music, ask if they will also provide a guitarist, a violinist, a piano player, or bring taped music—compact discs (CDs) or cassettes. Do they own this equipment? If not, how much are rental fees?

Get everything for ceremony and reception musicians in writing. In a contract signed by you and countersigned by the band, specify all details (see "Music Contract Tips" box). Expect to pay a 50 percent deposit up front, with the balance due on your wedding day. Your only leverage if the vocalist or "star" of the orchestra whom you thought you booked does not show up, or the group deviates in any way from the service promised in the contract, is to decrease the balance due accordingly. (Bands do not expect tips or full meals, but since the average reception is four hours, it is courteous to offer snacks and sandwiches.)

Look for a harmonious working relationship. If the bandleader isn't responsive to your needs during the initial negotiations, look elsewhere.

Hiring a Disc Jockey

Today, many couples are hiring a disc jockey (DJ) to provide taped music for their ceremony and/or reception. DJs are often skilled at sensing what style of music will get each group of guests out onto the dance floor. (To help your DJ make sure the dance floor fills up as soon as the reception begins, enlist a group of college friends or spirited cousins in advance to get up and dance immediately. It will set an exuberant tone for the entire party.)

Is a DJ appropriate for a wedding? Yes. Taped music, CDs, or records played by a DJ are good alternatives when live music is not available, or when the reception site does

music contract tips

Specify the following points in a signed and countersigned contract:

- date, time, place

- equipment provided; rental fees

- names of specific musicians, vocalists, (DJ) to perform (you may pay a premium for "stars")

- backup system if band members become ill: Who will perform?

- hours musicians will play

- parts of wedding during which musicians will play (prelude, ceremony, cocktail hour, reception)

- all fees, overtime rates

- late-arrival penalties

- number and length of breaks

- if music will be continuous (ask for taped music, a soloist during breaks)

- musicians' attire

- if full meals are provided

not have a dance floor, yet you would like to provide background music. There are cassettes of wedding music, dance tunes, hits from the twenties and fifties (or any period), which can be bought or rented from many music stores. Or, ask your DJ to premix some specific selections on one long-playing tape. A DJ can play quality recordings for all segments of the wedding—prelude, ceremony, processional, recessional, postlude, receiving line, cocktail hour, reception.

Don't DJs show up at parties in jeans, wearing gold chains? As with any wedding-service professional, including musicians, you should list all of the points that will be a factor on your wedding day in a signed and countersigned contract (see "Music Contract Tips" box). Simply specify that you would like the DJ to wear formal attire.

How expensive is a DJ? In most cases, hiring a DJ will be less expensive than hiring live musicians. Most charge a set fee for a party. Specify this amount, as well as overtime rates, in your contract. Also allow for a tip at the end of the evening.

Will a DJ be familiar with wedding protocol? Maybe, but not necessarily. Ask for the names and phone numbers of couples who hired the DJ for their weddings. As when interviewing or auditioning wedding bands, ask to see videotapes of the DJ in action, or attend an event where he or she will be working. Is the DJ's manner of speaking pleasing to you? He or she will be your announcer for all wedding events, introductions. Always specify in your contract that the DJ you saw *will* be the DJ you get at your wedding. Never pay in full in advance, or you will have no leverage if a different DJ shows up. Specify in the contract who will be the backup if the DJ becomes ill.

How can I be sure the DJ is experienced? Anyone can buy equipment, tapes, CDs, or records and call himself or herself a DJ. That is why you must ask for referrals from friends, relatives, and other wedding professionals who may have worked with DJs in the past. You may find DJs listed under "Disc Jockeys and Entertainment" in the Yellow Pages, but check references before signing a contract.

Will the DJ bring his or her own equipment? Yes. Otherwise, why hire one? (You could borrow or rent the equipment and music tapes and ask a friend to stand at the controls throughout the celebration.) You *should* ask the DJ about his or her equipment, and ask if he or she has worked at your site. If not, visit beforehand to check electrical outlets. As with a band or orchestra, have an extra generator.

Will the DJ play what I want? DJs pride themselves on knowing what to play when—to get the crowd onto the dance floor. Although you want your DJ to have creative leeway, give him or her a list of songs to be played for the first dance, father-daughter dance, mother-son dance, cake cutting, bouquet and/or garter toss. Include groups and specific songs you want to hear during the reception.

disc jockey pluses

- variety of music
- original songs played as guests remember them
- minimal space needed for equipment
- continuous music
- skilled announcer

The Ceremony

The Prelude. The musical prelude should last about a half hour as the guests are seated. Wedding musicians (as well as the musical director at your house of worship) have a broad repertoire of beautiful classical pieces from which to choose: Ask to hear several possibilities and then pick your favorites. You might consider Bach fugues, preludes, inventions and chorales, as well as slow movements from concertos or sonatas by 19th-century composers such as Brahms, Chopin, Schubert, and Mendelssohn. Baroque chamber music for instrumental groups is also appropriate.

The Processional. A majestic selection is played while the wedding party walks down the aisle, followed by a regal piece played as the bride and her father proceed. (Some processionals, if especially uplifting, may be used instead for the recessional.)

Hymns and Solos. Today, contemporary rock songs may be blended with Broadway show tunes and religious hymns—performed with lyrics or as instrumentals. Check with your clergymember for any restrictions. Hymns are a great way for everyone to participate in the ceremony. When selecting hymns, remember to read through all the verses and eliminate the inappropriate ones. Your clergymember can lend you hymnals and offer suggestions.

The Recessional. The triumphant first notes of the recessional are heard shortly after the newlyweds kiss and begin to walk back up the aisle as husband and wife. The piece selected should be joyous and uplifting—in celebration of the new marriage.

The Postlude. Triumphant music continues as guests file out. (See the "Wedding Ceremony Music" chart for suggestions for each part of the ceremony.)

The Reception

Reception music may range from acoustic jazz for cocktails to electric rock for after-dinner dancing. Variety is essential (see "Wedding Reception Music" chart).

The Cocktail Hour/Receiving Line. Soothing background music is most appropriate at this time, perhaps soft piano music, a string quartet or jazz ensemble. Consider jazz selections by Duke Ellington or Miles Davis, or piano music by George Winston.

Special Dances. Throughout the reception, you may request special dances (e.g., the first dance; the father-daughter dance; the mother-son dance), ethnic line and circle dances, specific songs from various decades, and current hits. Give the bandleader a list of your requests at least two weeks before the reception.

WEDDING FLOWERS 15

Since the earliest days, brides have worn or carried flowers, and garlands and blooms have graced wedding sites. Flowers were thought to symbolize bounty, fertility, and their heady aroma was believed to ward off evil spirits (see Chapter 2, "Wedding Customs"). A formal wedding with all of the trimmings will make lavish use of decorative blooms. Even a bride marrying quietly or economically, though, will want to include floral flourishes as part of her bridal attire and wedding celebration.

Your Floral Agenda

Your wedding-day flowers should have the same creative touch as every other detail of your wedding (see Appendix, under Chapter 15, "Wedding Flowers"). The true path to satisfaction is to hire the right florist and establish a solid working relationship.

1. Know yourself. Are you a flower aficionada with definite ideas, or could you not care less—as long as they're pretty and on time? Do you want to indulge in the language of flowers, or do you prefer a more practical approach? Your personality will influence your needs.

2. Look everywhere for ideas. Consult flower books, party-planning books, decorating books, and bridal magazines, which frequently feature stories on bridal flowers. Visit parks and botanical gardens. Put together a scrapbook of information— photographs of your dresses, your sites, favorite colors, flowers, and decorative elements.

3. Choose a florist carefully and early in the planning process. Most florists have experience planning parties and can offer valuable advice, suggesting reception sites, even caterers. Visit shops, ask friends and family whose flowers you've admired for

cost-cutting tips

- Carry a mass of baby's breath; it looks grand and is priced right.

- Avoid wired, labor-intensive—more expensive—bouquets. Opt instead for a few full-blown peonies or a single hydrangea, simply bound with ribbon.

- Find your own antique or unusual ribbon, lace (at flea markets, in antique stores). Some florists have only a standard supply; your bouquet can look more elegant with special touches.

- Avoid scheduling your wedding on or near a flower-giving holiday; flowers can be much more expensive near Valentine's Day or Mother's Day.

- Utilize seasonal (more plentiful), local (less costly) blooms and flowering branches. Vases of fresh-cut garden rhododendron or magnolia are magnificent.

- Consider blossoming bulbs as table centerpieces: Trim small pots of miniature daffodils, hyacinths, with a bow of tulle.

- Select wedding and reception sites that need minimal decorating—a flowering garden or ornate room.

- Check to see if ceremony flowers can be shared with the bride whose wedding is before or after yours in your house of worship.

- Use ceremony arrangements at reception site.

- A single majestic arrangement is more impressive than a dozen minimal clusters.

recommendations. Also look in the Yellow Pages under "Florists" and write down names from bridal magazines and bridal newspaper supplements.

4. Make an appointment. Don't expect to walk into a busy flower shop and start discussing ideas. Choose a time that will give you a chance to interview the florist. Is she or he open to your ideas? Does he or she have interesting suggestions? Is the florist comfortable with your budget? Has she or he handled a wedding your size before? Does the shop service more than one wedding in a day? Do you feel comfortable with the florist and other staff members' attitudes?

5. Judge a store by its look and its staff. Are the flowers presented in an appealing manner? Do they appear healthy? Look for design flair. The shop decor will clearly signal the existence of a creative, inspired owner.

6. Ask to see photographs of flowers created for other weddings. The ability to design is essential, but so is a florist responsive to your ideas and preferences.

7. Determine the mood and style of your wedding. You'll want your floral plans to match your wedding. Will it be grand or casual, a holiday celebration or a summer fête? Will the ceremony be at a religious site with a reception elsewhere, or will the wedding and reception be at the same location? Describe the style of your gown and your attendants' gowns; bring along swatches of fabrics or photos taken during your fitting, swatches of linens for the tables at the reception. Before ordering, be sure no one in the wedding party is allergic to any particular flower or greenery (see Chapter 4, "Planning Your Wedding").

8. Establish a budget. Be realistic—it will eliminate wasteful replanning. Inquire about specific costs. Every good florist can work within any budget. Remember, though, even brides planning to spend very little on flowers can make a splash. Consider enlisting the help of creative friends or marrying in a garden at full bloom. (See "Cost-Cutting Tips" box.)

9. Reserve your date early. To avoid disappointment, book the florist up to a year in advance, especially if the florist or your wedding date is popular. If your wedding will be a grand celebration with a large flower budget, start specific floral planning at least three months in advance; you'll want time for multiple appointments with the florist to refine details. Less formal weddings are easily managed in eight weeks or less.

10. Sign a contract. A signed and countersigned contract or bill of sale should outline the services you expect from your florist (see "Flower Contract Tips" box). Be realistic. Flowers are perishable and not always available as requested. In an emergency, a florist should make only comparable substitutions.

Prayer Book Flowers

In a formal or semiformal wedding, the bride may choose to carry a flower-covered prayer book instead of a bouquet. This prayer book is often an old family Bible or a new book purchased for the occasion by the bride's or groom's parents. Cover the book in white silk or satin (to complement your gown). Choose any flowers to adorn the prayer book; white orchids, with a few smaller blossoms or ribbon streamers (to match the proportion of a long gown), are classic.

Bouquet Glossary

Bouquet—The classic bridal accessory. A cluster of blooms either handtied or anchored in a water-saturated oasis, sunk inside a plastic bouquet holder. Available in a wide variety of sizes and shapes.

Nosegay—A round burst of flowers gathered in a bouquet holder or handtied with ribbon; a small nosegay is a posy. In Victorian times, nosegays were always carried to social events.

Biedermeier—A small tight nosegay featuring concentric rings of varied colors and blooms; each of the rings in a Biedermeier is usually comprised of a single type of small blossom.

Tussie mussie—Handtied bouquet in which stems are tied together, then cut to a uniform, convenient-to-carry length and trimmed with ribbon. May be inserted into a silver, cone-shaped, tussie-mussie holder, popular in Victorian times (see Appendix, under Chapter 15, "Wedding Flowers," for sources). Tussie mussies of colorful herbs and flowers were once carried to ward off bad smells and disease.

Wired—Each individual bloom is wired to stand upright, or each bloom may be attached to a slender filament of wire with green tape to simulate a stem. These flexible stalks are manipulated to create a bouquet.

Cascade—A bouquet commonly anchored in an oasis, which acts as the support base. Blooms and greenery gracefully spill downward from the oasis along the front of the gown.

Composite—Individual petals of a flower or a cluster of individual blooms are wired or glued together to create a fuller, fanciful blossom on a single stem. A "glamelia" is a bloom handmade by a florist: Dozens of split gladiola florets combine, one inside the other, to create a camellia-like blossom.

Pomander—A lush blossom-covered globe that is suspended and held from a satin ribbon; an easy-to-carry option for child attendants.

Boa—A luxurious length of wired blossoms and greenery worn as a stole in lieu of a bouquet.

flower contract tips

Include:

- date, time of deliveries, and sites (e.g., your home for the bouquets, the house of worship for corsages, the reception site for table arrangements).

- amount and color of each type of flower (e.g., ten red roses) in each bouquet, corsage, boutonniere, and arrangement.

- acceptable substitutes within your budget if first choices are not available that week. (State that you must be notified to approve substitutions.)

- unacceptable substitutes (e.g., *no carnations, nothing purple*).

- numbers and sizes of altar and table arrangements.

- decorative items (e.g., garlands, wreaths, pew markers).

- expected condition of flowers (e.g., fresh and in bloom, not wilted).

- style and color of ribbons, balloons, vases, other accessories.

- name of person responsible for on-site setup that day (and backup person in case of emergency).

- total cost and payment schedule; deposit made.

- refund or cancellation policy.

The White Bouquet

All-white or all-cream bouquets have been traditional for weddings since Queen Victoria wed in white in 1840.

Classic. For texture, mix flowers in different hues of white and in various stages of bloom: tiny rosebuds newly picked, past-peak roses, or those in full bloom; diminutive snowdrops with full peonies. Add ivy, a symbol of fidelity, and other greens.

Modern. Today, in addition to combining white and near-white blooms (in ivory, champagne, creamy white, ecru, pure white) and varying textures, bridal bouquets may have small blossoms layered inside each other, creating one large, composite, new bloom. Cluster single flower stems of the same variety of flower (e.g., a mass of tulips) to create one lush blossom. Leaves can be gilded for a festive holiday bouquet.

classic white bouquet choices

- astrantia and freesia together
- camellias
- Easter lilies
- gardenias
- hyacinths and stephanotis together
- lilacs
- lily of the valley
- orange blossoms
- orchids
- poinsettias
- Queen Anne's lace
- ranunculus
- roses
- stephanotis
- stock, peonies,
- white violets

Floral Headpieces

Brides and bridesmaids have traditionally worn floral wreaths or crescents of orange blossoms or other light, symbolic flowers, such as stephanotis. These headpieces fit across the top of the head, or in a circle that rests on the crown. They may be held in place by small combs or hairpins; a veil may be attached. *At the reception*: The bride may remove her traditional veil and headpiece and replace them with a festive fresh floral wreath, which is easier to wear while dancing. Bridesmaids may wear a single bloom in their hair, held in place with a comb or hairpin (each maid should wear the flower on the same side of her head).

Bridesmaids' Blossoms

The bouquets that your attendants carry need not all look alike. Select one flower that *will appear* in each arrangement, with accent flowers varying. If bridesmaids will be in floral-print dresses, include at least one flower from the pattern in their bouquets. The honor attendant may carry a bouquet in a different shade or contrasting color. Below, other tips:

Shape and style. The bridesmaids' bouquets should complement the bridal bouquet, and also be in proportion to each woman's stature.

Classic choices. Anemones, carnations, chrysanthemums, daffodils, freesia, dried herbs mixed with flowers, holly, larkspur, lilacs, peonies, poinsettias, roses, sweet peas, wheat sheaves.

Innovations. Bridesmaids can carry baskets of blossoms in sunny hues. If each attendant is wearing a different-colored gown, perhaps select tulips in contrasting colors, tied with ribbons. For a Victorian wedding, select tussie mussies or nosegays. Order each bridesmaid's favorite flower (or birth-month flower) in her bouquet; all other flowers in their bouquets will match.

Accessories. Additional flowers may be ordered for attendants to pin in hair; floral hatbands, pendants, necklaces, or bracelets, for members of the family.

Children's Blossoms

The flowers your child attendants will wear or carry should charm them and enchant adults. Although traditionally little girls tossed rose petals as they walked down the aisle, these petals may cause guests (or wedding-party members) to slip. Order a miniature basket of blooms or a precious nosegay instead.

Shape and style. Order witty, diminutive, easy-to-hold arrangements. Add colorful ribbon streamers that will complement the wedding color scheme and the children's outfits.

Classic choices: Biedermeier bouquets of "Serena" roses and miniature grape hyacinths, French roses, lily of the valley, rosebuds, Victorian nosegays, violets.

Innovations. Select mini-nosegays, tiny basket arrangements, garlands of flowers and greens that will drape over children's shoulders as they walk down the aisle; trimmed with pretty bows that form handles, they can be hung by them at the altar when they arrive. Also consider floral balls, pomanders, floral hoops—to loop over little arms.

Accessories. Headbands, hair wreaths, single blooms for barrettes, bracelets, necklaces of dainty blossoms, sash trims for flower girls; pocket posies for jacket pockets of ring bearers.

modern white bouquet choices

- apple blossoms with blush tulips, peonies, lilacs
- dendrobium orchids
- jasmine
- "Serena" roses
- wild sweet peas

colorful accents

Add touches of color to an all-white bouquet:

- blue violets
- gloriosa lilies
- irises
- ranunculus
- stargazer lilies with red centers

Boutonnieres

The groom's, ushers', and fathers' boutonnieres are worn on the left lapel. To distinguish his position of honor, the groom should wear a different flower from that of the other men in the wedding. Boutonnieres should be small in scale and tailored, symbolic in meaning (see "The Language of Flowers" section). Consider a bud or tiny floret paired with baby's breath or greenery or one single bloom. The groom might first wear a bachelor's button (which symbolizes *celibacy*) and remove it as the bride reaches the altar. She might then remove a "pull-away" boutonniere concealed inside her bouquet, which she pins to his lapel at the altar as a loving gesture. Or, the groom might wear one flower found in the bride's bouquet.

Classic choices. For ushers, and fathers: White carnations or white roses. For groom, best man: Stephanotis, lily of the valley, freesia with greenery.

Innovations. Ranunculus, calla lily, phlox, gloriosa lily, bachelor's button, one red rose (love) paired with a white rose ("I am worthy of you").

The Language of Flowers

Indulge in the sentimental tradition of flowers. The very reserved Victorians coined the romantic meanings of blossoms, a clever pairing of blooms translated into a passionate "hidden" message between lovers.

aromatic flowers

Flowers perfect for potpourri, sure to leave a fragrant memory in your path:

- daffodil
- freesia
- gardenia
- grape hyacinth
- iris
- jasmine
- lilac
- lily
- magnolia
- rose
- stephanotis
- violet

More fragrant tips:

1. Add a drop of flower oil (to match bouquet) on pew bows.
2. Blend fragrant herbs—thyme, rosemary—into arrangements.
3. Place a bowl of fragrant potpourri on entry table.

amaryllis—splendid beauty, pride
bachelor's button—celibacy, single blessedness
blue violet—faithfulness, modesty (flowers hide beneath leaves)
bluebell—constancy
camellia—perfect loveliness, excellence
daffodil—regard
daisy—"Share your feelings," innocence
forget-me-not—true love, do not forget
honeysuckle—generous affection, bonds of love
ivy—fidelity, marriage
jasmine—grace, elegance, joy, amiability, attachment
jonquil—"I desire a return of affection"
holly—foresight
larkspur—levity
lilacs—first emotions of love
lily—gaiety
lily of the valley—return of happiness

mimosa—secret love, sensitivity
myrtle—love, remembrance
orange blossoms—bridal festivities, fertility, purity
peony—bashfulness
red carnation—"Alas, my poor heart!"
red chrysanthemum—"I love you"
red rose—"I love you"
red tulip—declaration of love
rosemary—remembrance
sweet pea—delicate pleasures, departure
sweet William—gallantry
thyme—activity
water lily—purity of heart
white camellia—perfect loveliness
white daisy—innocence
white lily—purity, youthful innocence
white rose—"I am worthy of you"
wood sorrel—joy, maternal tenderness
yellow tulip—hopeless love

The flowers in *your* bouquet can be selected for their specific meanings, or the first letter of each one can together spell out a word (his name, a message?). For example, select bachelor's buttons, orange blossoms, and bluebells (to spell B-O-B). Choose lilacs, oak leaves, violets, and evergreen (to spell L-O-V-E). Give your mothers small white bellflowers (gratitude) on wedding day; send them wood sorrel (maternal tenderness) from your honeymoon destination. Order your attendants blue periwinkle (early friendship) bouquets. Wear a blue violet (faithfulness, modesty) corsage as you leave for your honeymoon. Be creative and use flowers to make a personal statement. (See

Flowers in Season

SPRING	SUMMER	FALL	WINTER	ALL-YEAR
anemone	bachelor's button	bouvardia	amaryllis	alstroemeria
azalea	bells of Ireland	celosia (cockscomb)	cyclamen	baby's breath
camellia	blue lace flower	China aster	heather	calla lily
daffodil	clematis	chrysanthemum	helleborus	carnations
hyacinth	delphinium	dahlia	(Christmas rose)	cattleya orchid
hydrangea	eremurus	euphorbia fulgens	holly (ilex)	chrysanthemums
Iceland poppy	larkspur	hydrangea	narcissus	cymbidium orchid
jasmine	lilies	statice	(paper-whites)	daisy
lilac	phlox	yarrow	poinsettia	dendrobium orchid
lily of the valley	Queen Anne's lace			freesia
mimosa	rosemary			gardenia
pansy	sunflower			gerbera
peony	sweet William			gladiolus
primrose	zinnia			iris
ranunculus				ivy
sweet pea				lilies
tulips				lily of the valley
viburnum				nerine
violets				phalaenopsis orchid
				roses
				September aster
				snapdragon
				stephanotis
				stock
				tuberose

If you select flowers that are in bloom during the month of your wedding, they will be less expensive, more readily available, fuller, and heartier.

Because of new, improved nursery operations worldwide, many varieties of seasonal flowers are now available for longer periods of time or year-round. Consult your florist.

Appendix, under Chapter 15, "Wedding Flowers," for books with more on the language of flowers).

Ceremony Flowers

Discuss what altar decorations are permitted with your clergymember before you place your order. You may find that a simple chapel needs more decorations than an ornate cathedral. Ask if another wedding will take place the same day in your house of worship. You may be able to share the cost of altar flowers with the other bride. Also ask your florist to visit the site to generate ideas. Here are floral tips that range from inexpensive to "the sky's the limit." Consider designating one or two family members, or your florist, to move flowers to the reception site.

Have at least one vase of flowers on each side of the altar. Add several other arrangements if budget permits.

Attach dramatic sprays of flowers to aisle posts, instead of, or in addition to pew ribbons. Place them on every second or third pew, or on those pews reserved for special guests or relatives. Fasten nosegays of fragrant blossoms, such as freesia. Drape garlands of white tulle tied with large bows.

Place an eye-catching arrangement of flowers on each windowsill. This is especially lovely if the house of worship has plain windows.

Position a bank of ferns, palms, potted flowers to mark the section of the church needed for the ceremony. Use ropes of flowers mixed with ivy, laurel, or boxwood to partition the church or drape the altar rail.

Repeat the bridesmaids' flowers in the altar arrangements. It will create a unified theme.

Inquire about other altar decorations. Consider large urns filled with elaborate garden arrangements, set on pedestals or columns—on each side of the altar. Rent ficus trees in wicker baskets, or an arch fashioned of twigs, metal, or fabric, laden with twisting vines, fresh or silk flowers. For an evening wedding: Rent tall candelabra to stand on each side of the wedding party.

Ask your florist to visit an outdoor ceremony site in advance. Don't overdecorate if it's already beautiful. Include cuttings from the site's bushes and plants in floral arrangements. Liven up dull shrubs with bright blossoms, such as crimson azaleas, in clay pots. Set flowering branches of cherry blossoms and forsythia in large urns or vases.

Floral Styles

Formal—The bridal party's flowers are usually white, maybe finished with a gilded ribbon or petals. Identical bouquets, frequently wired, are carried by every bridesmaid. The bride's blooms are a grander version, featuring just one to three types of flowers, such as a lush clutch of lily of the valley. A lavish splash of flowers decorates all important areas of the wedding and reception sites, following a simple, elegant color scheme.

Semiformal—A wide range of bouquet options are favored. Handtied bouquets or baskets of colorful blooms—a potpourri of garden roses or vibrant striped parrot tulips—needn't be identical, merely compatible. Attendants may instead be garland-bearing children. An arch of garden blossoms marks the wedding site; a wreath hangs on the door, welcoming guests.

Informal—A posy or alternative floral accessory—a breast pocket filled with tiny blossoms, a hat brimming with blooms, a fragrant necklace or bracelet, a flower boa worn around the shoulders—is the bridal choice. The groom may opt for a pocket square in lieu of a boutonniere. A single, wonderful table arrangement or flowering plant is appropriate for intimate weddings.

Reception Flowers

Floral arrangements may be as simple or elaborate as your budget allows. Echo the wedding color scheme by repeating the flowers in your and your attendants' bouquets. Place centerpieces on dinner and refreshment tables, as well as on the cake table. Select anything from a few sprigs to arrangements of mixed blossoms. Repeat a few signature blooms throughout the wedding celebrations.

Make sure centerpieces don't obstruct conversation, views. At the head table, the wedding party will want to be able to see guests, and vice versa. Similarly, centerpieces on all reception tables should be low enough to make it easy for guests to meet and talk across the table. There is a trend today toward tall centerpieces (which fill up the space in a room with a high ceiling) with clear glass columns; the flowers spray outward. Long-stemmed flowers, such as roses, lilies, accentuate height.

Be creative. Use seasonal fruits or vegetables as containers, as well as accents. For an autumn wedding, use shiny red apples with their centers cored out as flower containers. (Place them in a basket or on a silver tray.) Also consider gourds and squashes in the same capacity. Sprinkle nuts, strawberries, or colorful fall leaves across a tabletop; use gilded pomegranates for holiday weddings. Strew flowers casually around the centerpieces, too.

Create a tropical paradise. Decorate tables with mini-pineapples (nonedible), pink dendrobium orchids, waxy red anthurium, large split monstera leaves. Choose flowers with sentimental meaning: the yellow roses he brought on your first date; red tulips from the park where he proposed.

Make blossoms twinkle. Brighten the reception with tiny, Christmas-style-lights that are intertwined among the flowers, in matching colors.

Consider topiaries in amusing shapes (e.g., animals, bicycles). They are increasingly popular as centerpieces—particularly for a garden wedding site or in a ballroom. They may also form the base of a *huppah* for a Jewish wedding.

Consider the color of table linens. Cream-colored linens offer the most flexibility. Stark white linens may wash out pastel flowers.

Consider a breakaway centerpiece. Guests may each take home a small potted plant or a bud vase as a favor.

floral dos & don'ts

DO create a visual backdrop for your wedding vows. Rented plants and columns instantly transform non-descript rooms.

DON'T overdecorate. Well-placed tasteful table arrangements impress without cluttering or overwhelming the view.

DO opt to carry a manageable bouquet. Heavy, awkward bouquets are impossible to clutch gracefully.

DON'T consider heat-sensitive blooms for summer weddings. Quick-to-wilt gardenias, lily of the valley, and wildflowers look limp before the "I dos" are said.

DO have flowers delivered before the ceremony well-misted and boxed with cellophane wrappings—to maintain moisture.

DON'T forget to assign a reliable friend to double-check flower arrivals and their condition—you'll be too busy!

Decorate the cake table with garlands or other small floral arrangements. You might also top your cake with more fresh flowers that match your bouquet.

Use floral screens or banks of ferns as backdrops for the receiving line. Flowers and greenery warm a room and create an inviting environment.

Florists may also rent other room or tent decorations. Inquire about draperies, statues, paintings, columns, large potted plants, etc.

Your Floral Keepsakes

Fragrant, beautiful mementos of your wedding day can be the legacy of your bridal bouquet and your groom's boutonniere.

Order a second mini-bouquet (of fresh or silk flowers) to toss at your wedding. Dry yours to create an aromatic, sentimental potpourri or bath oil. Or have an expert dry, preserve, and frame your bouquet *and* perhaps the groom's boutonniere (see Appendix, under Chapter 15, "Wedding Flowers").

Press petals from your bouquet. Use them to decorate thank-you notes and stationery for you, your parents.

Order thank-you arrangements for your parents. Have your florist deliver them the day after the wedding.

Arrange to have flowers sent to mark your first anniversary. It will be a festive surprise for you and your husband one year later, to receive a duplicate of your bridal bouquet!

PHOTOGRAPHY, VIDEO-GRAPHY, & PUBLICITY

16

You dream of your wedding for years, you plan it for months, then the ceremony and reception fly by in a blur. That's why it's important that your mementos—bridal portrait, photographs, videotape, and newspaper clippings—capture the spirit of your day. Here, how to ensure that you, your groom, and your families are left with enduring keepsakes you'll treasure for years to come.

Your Bridal Portrait

This posed wedding photograph is key—since it's the one that may be published in the newspaper and displayed in your home, and in the homes of relatives. Today, since many newspapers are publishing black-and-white or color photographs of couples, the two of you may make an appointment to go to the photographer's studio, in your wedding outfits. (While there, you may also have some lifestyle photos taken, in everyday clothes, which may be displayed at the reception and included in your wedding album.) Select an unobtrusive background for results that will stand the test of time. This is also a good opportunity to have a dress rehearsal for your wedding hairstyle; bring your headpiece to your hairdresser the day of your portrait shooting. Since precise makeup application is the key to a flawless look, consider hiring a makeup artist before your bridal portrait, and for your wedding day. It's an extra cost that's well worth the great photographic results you'll cherish for years.

When should I have my bridal portrait portrait taken? Most newspapers require that wedding photographs be submitted at least ten days before the scheduled publication date. To allow enough time, plan on having your portrait taken one to three months before the wedding (depending on when your gown arrives).

Where should I go? If the proper facilities are available, you can arrange to have your

wedding-portrait trends

- Portraits of bride and groom: Most newspapers now print engagement and wedding photos of couples. Let photographer know if groom will join you; groom should wear his wedding outfit, too.

- Color photos in newspapers: Some papers can print color portraits.

- Lifestyle shoots. Many couples are spending an afternoon with a photographer, posing on the beach, riding horses, playing golf.

- Lifestyle photos displayed at the wedding: Some couples have enlargements made of their lifestyle shoot, then display a few on easels, near the cake table.

- Lifestyle photos in wedding albums: Today, albums become "this-is-your-life" reviews. Many couples begin and end their albums with shots from their lifestyle shoot.

227

makeup for color photos

Color film intensifies bold shades. Makeup should enhance your natural look.

- Wear neutral shades: navy, olive, brown, or taupe.

- Avoid frosted shadow; the flash will make it look like tinfoil!

- Complement eye shadow with a smoky shade of liner smudged below the eye, which will give the effect of a shadow cast by bottom lashes.

- Remove stray eyebrow hairs that interrupt the natural curve of your eye socket. Brush brows upward with clear mascara, to hold in place.

- Highlight cheeks with soft color that enhances natural skin tone.

- Wear a natural lipstick shade. Apply; blot; apply; blot. Repeat till the buildup of color is a beautiful matte that won't need retouching.

makeup for black-and-white photos

Black-and-white film whitens pale shades, darkens rich, vibrant colors.

- Avoid red lipstick; it photographs black.

- Choose natural hues that enhance natural skin tone.

- Blend all makeup, eliminating any harsh lines.

portrait taken at your bridal salon during your final fitting. Ask your photographer to join you there. Otherwise, make certain that your dress will be ready in time for you to make a prewedding trip to the photographer's studio. The advantage of doing it there: You'll have the proper lighting and background.

What should I bring with me? Your bridal portrait should look as if it were taken on your wedding day, so bring along all accessories—shoes, slip, gloves, jewelry, headpiece, and prayer book (if you'll carry one). If you want to be photographed with your bridal bouquet, order a replica from your florist.

Should I pose any particular way? Your photographer will take several different shots of you in a variety of poses, then supply proofs. Choose one look for publicity purposes (some newspapers will work with color if it's sharply focused, though most require a 5x7-inch black-and-white glossy for their wedding columns). Then, perhaps select another pose for the portrait you'll display in your home, and give to your family. Order at least one black-and-white print for yourself, too; color may fade over the years.

Your Wedding Announcement

It's customary to publish the details of a formal wedding in your hometown newspapers. A morning wedding is sometimes written up in an evening paper the same day, but most wedding stories are published the day after the ceremony. Ask if your newspapers will print announcements the week after the wedding. You may have time to send in an actual wedding photo.

Decide on the publications to which you'll send your announcement. Many couples send the news of their wedding to their hometown papers, college alumni magazines, professional societies and clubs, and the newsletters of their church or synagogue.

Meet the deadline. Check with the lifestyle editor of your local newspapers in advance to learn exact requirements and deadlines. Some papers ask brides to fill out a standard form, or offer their own guidelines for writing the notice, requesting that information be submitted to the lifestyle editor ten or more days before the wedding. (Some papers may accept announcements two months in advance.) Others want telephoned confirmation that the wedding has actually taken place before they'll publish the news. Some papers charge a fee; others will print your announcement free of charge.

Follow the appropriate style. If your paper does not supply wedding-announcement forms, type the announcement, double-spaced, on an 8½x11-inch sheet of white paper (select nonerasable paper, so key facts won't accidentally be blurred). In the upper-right corner, list your name, address, and telephone number(s)—or those of someone in your family who can be called for verification and additional details. The date you'd like the announcement published should appear, as well. Keep a photocopy of the information you send.

Decide how much information to include. Read several announcements published by the paper to get a sense of the amount of information they will publish (see "Traditional Announcement Wording" section). Decide if you will include your ages, parents' occupations, stepparents' names and occupations, dress descriptions, names of attendants, whether or not the bride will keep her name, any unusual details of the wedding day (e.g., *The couple left for their honeymoon in a hot-air balloon*, or *The bride was walked down the aisle by her stepfather, James Connelly*.).

Include a photograph. Make sure it's a 5x7-inch or 8x10-inch glossy black-and-white print of your bridal portrait, or of you two together. Again, some papers will accept a color photo. Tape a typed line of identification to the photo's back, in case it gets separated from the story. Don't expect the picture to be returned. If you send photos to more than one local paper, you may want to submit different shots to each.

Package the photo and announcement carefully. Enclose the picture, announcement, and a piece of stiff cardboard in a Manila envelope and address it to the lifestyle editor. Mail it or drop it off.

Handle errors tactfully. Check your photocopy to see if the mistake was yours, then call the paper. Most can't rerun a whole announcment, but if it's a major error—it says you've married your brother-in-law—request that a correction be printed.

news tips

- Ask two people to proofread the announcement before sending it. Make sure names, locations, are spelled correctly.

- Keep a photocopy of the announcement in case it's lost in the mail or a question arises.

- Don't expect the newspaper to mail you a free copy when your announcement appears. Check newsstands and purchase one.

- Don't be surprised if your announcement doesn't appear right away. Some are printed only in weekend editions.

- Don't be disappointed if your announcement is abbreviated. If there is a major news event, space may be tight.

Traditional announcement wording:

Patricia Clark Butler, the daughter of Mr. and Mrs. Clifford Marion Butler of Atlanta, was married this afternoon to Mitchell Sullivan, a son of Dr. and Mrs. Paul Sullivan of Philadelphia, Pennsylvania. Msgr. Patrick Flynn of Birmingham, uncle of the bride, performed the ceremony in Trinity Church in Atlanta.

Ms. Butler is a teacher at Woodrow Wilson Elementary School in Atlanta. She graduated from the University of Virginia. Her father is a senior vice president at the advertising agency Glenn & Howard in Atlanta. Her mother is an art director at Sun Graphics in Atlanta.

Mr. Sullivan is an associate at the Atlanta law firm of Cody & Wallace. He graduated magna cum laude from Princeton University, where he was elected to Phi Beta Kappa, and received his law degree from Georgetown University. His father is a pediatrician in Philadelphia. His mother is a partner at Wales & Malloy, a law firm in Philadelphia.

If couples want careers emphasized:

Patricia Clark Butler, a teacher at

photo trends

- Disposable cameras, left at each guest's place setting, invite everyone to snap candids.

- Black-and-white prints are making a comeback in wedding albums. They add a dramatic, artistic tone to the wedding.

- Photo portfolios of over-sized black-and-white prints are being chosen by some couples, instead of the traditional smaller albums.

- Special effects, such as superimposed, retouched soft-focus images (rings on hands, candles, champagne glasses) are still requested by some brides for wedding albums.

- Some brides are requesting brown-toned sepia prints, or black-and-white photos that are handpainted after printing.

Woodrow Wilson Elementary school in Atlanta, was married this afternoon to Mitchell Sullivan, an associate at the Atlanta law firm of Cody & Wallace. Msgr. Patrick Flynn of Birmingham, uncle of the bride, performed the ceremony in Trinity Church in Atlanta.

Ms. Butler graduated from the University of Virginia. She is a daughter of Mr. and Mrs. Clifford Marion Butler. Her father is a senior vice president at the advertising agency Glenn & Howard in Atlanta. Her mother is an art director at Sun Graphics in Atlanta.

Mr. Sullivan graduated magna cum laude from Princeton University, where he was elected to Phi Beta Kappa, and received his law degree from Georgetown University. He is the son of Dr. and Mrs. Paul Sullivan of Philadelphia. His father is a pediatrician in Philadephia. His mother is a partner at Wales & Malloy, a law firm in Philadelphia.

If bride is keeping her own name:

First paragraph remains the same. Add:

Ms. Butler is keeping her name. She graduated from the University of Virginia, and is a daughter of...

If dress descriptions are included (50 words or less):

First three paragraphs remain the same. Add:

The bride, escorted by her father, wore an ivory dress of organza trimmed with Venise lace. Bands of matching lace edged her chapel train and veil. She carried a cascade of white roses.

If attendants' names are included:

The first three to four paragraphs remain

the same. Add:

Carla Butler, sister of the bride, was maid of honor. Bridesmaids were Gloria Geller and Linda Kerr of Atlanta, Gina DeGeorgio of Savannah, and Francis Demery of Buffalo, New York.

Arthur Clay of Birmingham served as best man. The ushers were Neil Butler, brother of the bride, Nathan Freeman of Short Hills, New Jersey, and Harvey Lyons and David Chan of New York, New York.

If parents are divorced and one parent is remarried:

First paragraph remains the same. Add:

Ms. Butler graduated from the University of Virginia. She is a daughter of Clifford Marion Butler and Jane S. Butler, both of Atlanta. Her father is a senior vice president at the advertising agency Glenn & Howard in Atlanta. Her mother is an art director at Sun Graphics in Atlanta.

Mr. Sullivan graduated magna cum laude from Princeton University, where he was elected to Phi Beta Kappa, and received his law degree from Georgetown University. He is the son of Dr. Paul Sullivan of Pittsburgh and Elizabeth S. Mason of Philadelphia. His father is a pediatrician in Pittsburgh. His mother is a partner at Wales & Malloy, a law firm in Philadelphia. The bridegroom is a stepson of Jonathan Mason of Philadelphia.

If a parent is deceased:

First paragraph remains the same. Add:

Ms. Butler graduated from the University of Virginia. She is a daughter of Jane Marion Butler of Atlanta and the late Clifford Marion Butler. Her mother is an art director at Sun Graphics in Atlanta.

Her father was a senior vice president at the advertising agency Glenn & Howard in Atlanta.

If a bride or groom is remarrying:

To the first two paragraphs, add:

Mr. Sullivan is an associate at the Atlanta law firm of Cody & Wallace. He graduated magna cum laude from Princeton University, where he was elected to Phi Beta Kappa, and received his law degree from Georgetown University. His father is a pediatrician in Philadelphia. His mother is a partner at Wales & Malloy, a law firm in Philadelphia. The bridegroom's previous marriage ended in divorce.

The bride's (or groom's) parents have divorced, and the bride (or groom) has adopted a stepfather's name:

Patricia Clark Butler, a teacher at Woodrow Wilson Elementary school in Atlanta, was married this afternoon to Mitchell Sullivan, an associate at the Atlanta law firm of Cody & Wallace. Msgr. Patrick Flynn of Birmingham, uncle of the bride, performed the ceremony in Trinity Church in Atlanta.

Ms. Butler graduated from the University of Virginia. She is the daughter of Mr. and Mrs. Clifford Marion Butler of Atlanta. Her stepfather is a financial consultant with Shearson Lehman Brothers in Atlanta. Her mother is an art director at Sun Graphics in Atlanta. She is also the daughter of Mr. Jeremy Wade of Dallas, Texas, an attorney.

Wedding Photography

Shoot for the best. A wedding is a once-in-a-lifetime occasion. If your photographs turn out dim and fuzzy, you'll never be able to precisely reenact the celebration. (The Fireman's Fund now offers an insurance policy called "Weddingsurance," which will reimburse a couple for the cost of reassembling the wedding party to retake wedding photographs if they do not come out or the film is stolen. See the Appendix, under Chapter 4, "Planning Your Wedding," for more information.) Though it may be tempting—and inexpensive—to enlist a talented friend or relative for the job, hiring a professional is the best insurance that you'll end up with quality wedding photos. Professional wedding photographers should have top-of-the-line equipment, correct lighting, as well as experience in quickly posing people for traditional portraits and reception-table shots. He or she should also have a quick eye for spotting a good candid shot; unexpected photographs are often the most precious mementos of your celebration.

Find a professional. Soon after you've set the date, start asking around for referrals (some photographers book a year or more in advance). Caterers, hotel managers, recently married friends, and the Yellow Pages are all good sources. Also, visit bridal shows where you can see samples of photographers' work. Then, set up appointments; meet with the person who will actually photograph your wedding. Remember, your

photo secrets

Meet with your photographer two weeks before the wedding to review details.

- Give him or her a list of attendants, guests, and family members to pose in formal portraits.

- List not-to-be-missed photos (e.g., your grandmother with all her grandchildren and great-grandchildren).

- Appoint someone from the bride's and groom's side of the family to cue the photographer in to who you want in photos (bosses, cousins, college roommates).

- Tell those you want photographed to remind photographer to snap them.

- Brief photographer about awkward family relationships (e.g., divorced parents, stepmother with whom you don't get along, gay siblings attending with partners).

- Discuss special events that will take place—religious customs, ethnic dances, a dance with your grandfather.

- Review site/clergy regulations. Some churches, synagogues, don't allow flashbulbs or altar shots during the ceremony. Some country clubs don't allow wedding couples on the green.

photo-contract tips

List the following in a signed and countersigned contract:

- name of the professional whose work you've seen, who will photograph the wedding

- name of photographer's backup (in case of emergency)

- backup equipment on site, in case of equipment failure

- number of assistants

- attire (tuxedos, suits)

- number of rolls of film to be shot

- all locations (e.g., bride's house, church, reception site) and addresses, arrival times

- date, time, hours to be worked (e.g., 11:30 a.m. to 6:30 p.m., so he or she is there for the cake cutting)

- what's included in package

- total cost and overtime fees

- cost for extra albums, prints, proofs

- time frame for delivery of proofs, prints, albums

- deposit and payment schedule (when balance is due)

photographer will be by your side for most of the wedding, so choose someone who makes you feel at ease, and whose work you admire. Look at sample wedding albums. Ask for references if you haven't been referred to the photographer by someone you know (see Appendix, under Chapter 16, "Photography, Videography, & Publicity").

Invite guests to snap candids. Photographs taken by family and friends can beautifully supplement professional shots. Relatives, especially, may have the chance to capture unusual candids (such as the bride waking up on wedding morning). *New trend:* Leave rolls of film or disposable cameras in a basket outside the reception room or on each reception table. Ask guests to drop the cameras or film rolls in baskets after the festivities.

Take some posed shots. Posed shots are a sure way to make sure that all guests are photographed. Some professionals specialize in this type of portraiture, staging most in the hour before the wedding. For the most natural results, the wedding party should be placed in comfortable positions: the two mothers and the bride looking at the bride's ring; the bride and groom signing the register; the best man shaking the groom's hand.

Request candid shots. Your photographer should also capture spontaneous action (the flower girl waltzing with her brother, a spirited bridesmaid kicking off her shoes). If this style especially appeals to you, choose a photographer who specializes in a photojournalistic or documentary-style approach.

Schedule reception time for photos. Whatever you do, don't make your guests wait around while you and your wedding party, take endless formal portraits. It will make every detail of your reception late! Have your posed shots taken as quickly and unobtrusively as possible. If you want to be photographed with your parents or bridesmaids, for instance, take these shots at home as soon as you finish dressing, or arrive at the wedding site an hour to an hour and a half early. Perhaps go directly to the reception site after the ceremony, before the receiving line, and pose for formal photos with your husband and the wedding party.

Get everything in writing. Your photographer should countersign a contract with you that puts in writing everything you've discussed (see "Photo-Contract Tips" box).

Wedding Videography

Videography captures the sights—as well as the sounds and movement—of your wedding day. To ensure a quality videotape, don't rely on a well-meaning relative or friend who offers to bring his video camera (see Appendix, under Chapter 16).

Hire a professional. Start your search for a videographer several months before the wedding; book at least twelve months before (as with photographers, the best ones are hired early). Ask your photographer, wedding officiant, and friends for recommendations. Contact candidates by phone and ask them about their packages, prices, and how you can review their sample tapes. (Some will mail tapes to you, others ask that you visit their studio.) When reviewing videotapes, note the look and sound of the tape—whether the music is clear; the voices audible; the colors bright, not muddy; the images clear, not grainy; the camera close-ups and pans smooth; the editing professional. Be sure the tape you're watching has been shot by the same professional you will hire, which will be written into a contract (see "Video Contract Tips" box).

Ask about the videographer's equipment. Technology has advanced significantly. The equipment should not be distracting to the day's events. There should be no bright, blinding lights.

Find the right package. Your videographer will work with you to choose the style of tape that suits your budget. Typically, packages include taping and editing the master tape, and perhaps a second copy. (The number of cameras used, as well as the length of the ceremony and reception—longer than four hours, for example—can affect the price.) Ask about special effects, such as freeze-frames and strobe techniques, and familiarize yourself with the editing styles available:

Romance/Nostalgia

This style may also be called a "stroll down memory lane" or a "reflection show." It may be the most costly, since it includes extensive editing and camera work. Accompanied by the couple's favorite songs, the video begins with childhood pictures of the bride and groom from family albums, then segues into a sequence of courtship and lifestyle shots of the couple together (e.g., in a park). After video footage of the ceremony and reception, the video ends with photos of the couple leaving, and may include honeymoon footage.

Documentary

This video style features the wedding day, alone, beginning with a behind-the-scene look at the wedding couple (e.g., the couple getting dressed, guests arriving). There may be extra editing costs, since videographers may shoot with two cameras. The groom may wear a cordless microphone, so that vows can be recorded and conversations captured. At the reception, guests may be asked to make a toast to your future, or may be interviewed by the videographer for their advice on marriage, family, anecdotes about your childhood or college days.

Straight-shot Format

The ceremony and reception are shot with one camera; there is no editing. The videotape is ready for your VCR at the end of the reception.

Animated Titles

During the introduction, the couple's

video-contract tips

List the following in a signed and countersigned contract:

- **name of the professional whose work you've seen, who will videotape the wedding**
- **name of videographer's backup (in case of emergency)**
- **backup equipment on site, in case of equipment failure**
- **number of assistants, cameras**
- **attire (tuxedos, suits)**
- **number of tapes to be be shot**
- **all locations (e.g., bride's house, church, reception site) and addresses, arrival times**
- **date, time, hours to be worked (e.g., 11:30 a.m. to 6:30 p.m., so he or she is there for the cake cutting)**
- **editing techniques (credits, music, etc.)**
- **what's included in package**
- **total cost and overtime fees**
- **cost for extra tapes**
- **time frame for delivery of wedding video**
- **deposit and payment schedule (when balance is due)**

budget-conscious tips

Talk to your photographer about ways to keep photo costs within your budget. Ask if:

- traveling to your home before the wedding will add to the cost. (If so, dress at the ceremony site.)

- the photographer can bring a backdrop to the reception and shoot your formal portrait there.

- paying an hourly fee will be less than a package.

- you can buy proofs, prints, without albums. (Order portraits to frame; use guests' candids for albums.)

- choosing fewer photos for an album will lower the cost.

- ordering smaller prints lets you afford more shots.

- photographer will keep your negatives for several years. You may order additional prints in the future.

photo gift ideas

- extra albums for parents
- 5x7-inch wedding portraits for your coffee table, desks
- 8x10-inch prints for your parents
- copy of wedding video for those unable to attend
- extra prints for parents
- framed prints of attendants: their thank-you gifts
- wedding candids slipped into holiday cards

names and wedding date are added to the tape with a character generator for a minimal (or no) fee. For a nominal fee, a sixty-second musical animation can be added to the introduction of the video, during which the couple's names and wedding date are written in script across a scenic background.

Plan in advance. Check with your officiant regarding policies on cameras and lighting equipment. Also, let your videographer and photographer know that they'll be working together so they can compare schedules and avoid clashes. Request that they both attend the rehearsal to discuss where cameras will be set up, any clergy restrictions on lights or tripods. As with the photographer, you should create a detailed list of reception events (e.g., the wedding party's introduction, the bride's dance with her father), and inform the videographer of any special events (e.g., your groom's dance with his mother). Ask a close friend to let the videographer know who key guests are (he or she may ask them to say a few words into the microphone).

Get everything in writing. As when hiring any wedding professional, you should put all details in a contract signed by you and countersigned by your videographer (see "Video-Contract Tips" box).

Prewedding News

In large metropolitan areas, the only advance publicity a marriage receives is the engagement announcement (see Chapter 1, "Your Engagement"). In many smaller communities, though, the activities surrounding an upcoming wedding make life-style-page news for weeks before the ceremony. Some papers report the details of showers and other prewedding parties; others publish the wedding plans a week or two in advance. Before submitting an item of this type, make sure your newspaper considers such information newsworthy. Then, follow the form used:

Traditional Prewedding News:
Plans for the marriage of Cynthia Joy Dumbrowski, daughter of Mr. and Mrs. Frederick Hugh Dumbrowski of Briarcliff Drive, and Ronald Lloyd Felker, Jr., son of Mrs. Ronald Lloyd Felker and the late Mr. Felker of Omaha, Nebraska, were announced today by the bride's parents. The ceremony will be performed on July 16 at the First Presbyterian Church of Lockport, with the Reverend Roland Saunders officiating.

Miss Dumbrowski will be attended by her sister, Mrs. Kevin McGovern of Lexington, Kentucky, matron of honor. The bridesmaid will be Jessica Kramer of Lockport. Leslie McGovern, the bride's niece, will be the flower girl. Dennis O'Connor of Omaha will be Mr. Felker's best man. William Harris of Lockport will be his usher.

The ceremony will be followed by a reception at the White Hills Lodge.

WEDDING GIFTS 17

The time-honored custom for those attending a wedding is to send a wedding gift to the bride and groom. Gifts help the couple furnish their home, mark the joyous occasion of the couple's marriage, and are lifelong symbols of the givers' affection.

Gifts may begin arriving at the bride's and groom's home(s) as soon as their engagement is public knowledge. Although engagement gifts are optional (see Chapter 1, "Your Engagement"), many friends and relatives will want to mark this occasion, as well. Shower guests will also be selecting gifts—for either a traditional women-only shower or for a co-ed shower (see Chapter 3, "Prewedding Parties"). Wedding gifts will arrive throughout your engagement months, and may be sent up to a year after the wedding.

If you've ever shopped for a wedding gift, you know how much time and thought is involved. As a bride, however, you can make the gift shopping and giving experience easy and fun for your guests, *and* you can even get what you want and need.

The Wedding Gift Registry

Many department stores, specialty stores, museums shops, and catalogs now have Wedding Gift Registries, which offer brides and grooms an opportunity to list their gift preferences in a computer. Guests will then be certain that they are selecting a gift that the couple will appreciate. They can request a printout and select a gift in person, or call and have the printout mailed to their home or office. If desired, the purchase can then be made over the telephone. Below are guidelines for registering.

Register early. List registry choices before prewedding parties or showers— about six to twelve months before the wedding. Since certain domestic items, such as linen patterns, might be discontinued seasonally, update choices closer to wedding day.

Ask how long your registry list will be kept in the store's computer. This time frame may range from three months to two years. Many couples find that they continue to receive items from their registry list for anniversary and birthday gifts.

Do some preliminary shopping. Both you and your fiancé should look through bridal and home magazines together and browse in registry departments, setting up sample place settings with china, crystal, and silver. Make some basic decisions before registering. When selecting china, for instance, narrow down the colors you both prefer. Decide if you prefer a white or ivory background. Consider border styles—do you prefer geometric, plain, or floral motifs? What type of entertaining do you enjoy— grilling outdoors for a crowd or candle-lit, intimate dinner parties; casual or elegant table settings—or both? Consider care of your tableware (is it dishwasher-safe?) and size (can both of you drink comfortably from cups and glasses?).

Make an appointment with a registry consultant. Try to shop during off-hours; call ahead and ask when the bridal department is least crowded. Monday mornings and evenings tend to be best; avoid one-day sales, holiday weekends, and lunch hours. Some bridal registry consultants will make appointments with brides in the morning, before the store opens. Set aside one to two hours for the consultant to guide you through the registry, help you coordinate table patterns, suggest other gifts to suit your lifestyle. She or he will also tailor the size of your gift list to fit the number of wedding guests invited, provide information on manufacturers (e.g., how long they take to ship merchandise, whether patterns and sizes are changed often). Later, he or she may notify you if your selections go on sale or will be discontinued. (For this reason, always notify the registry of any change of phone number or address.)

Don't register in a day. If you register in haste, errors and confusion for guests are the result. Give yourselves time to reflect. Choose tabletop items (china, crystal, and silver) one day, domestics (sheets, towels, bed linens, tablecloths, and napkins) another, cookware a third. Many brides visit the registry department alone to narrow down choices, then return with their fiancé to make final selections.

Use your imagination. Never again in your lifetime will you receive so many gifts, so why not use the opportunity to create your ultimate wish list! Today, couples register for everything from gas grills to computers; sporting goods and luggage to gardening tools; computers and stereo equipment to fax machines. If a store has a travel bureau, you can register for your honeymoon, using a gift fund. (Some travel agencies also offer this option; see Appendix, under Chapter 17, "Wedding Gifts".) Registries are

gift-receiving etiquette

- Register your gift preferences together.

- Ask relatives, attendants, and friends to spread the word about where you are registered.

- Suggest that your maid of honor send out a "wedding newsletter" to other attendants, shower guests, and wedding guests, listing where you are registered. (See Appendix, under Chapter 4, "Planning Your Wedding," for source.)

- Never print registry location on wedding invitations. It is acceptable to have shower hostesses enclose printed registry cards in shower invitations only.

- Keep all enclosure cards and accurate gift records. Buy a wedding-planning notebook or gift-record book from a bridal salon, stationer, or bookstore as soon as you get engaged.

also available at many art galleries, museum stores, hardware and home emporiums, mortgage banks (for home down payments), record or video stores, sporting goods stores, even a few antique stores. Some mail-order houses also have national registries (see Appendix, under Chapter 17, "Wedding Gifts").

Register for a variety of gifts in a wide price range. List high-priced items for guests who can afford them or who want to pool funds for group gifts, as well as less expensive items—measuring cups, kitchen gadgets, place mats, lingerie—for showers and guests on a budget.

Be descriptive. To prevent errors, include as much information as the space in the registry form allows: brands, model numbers, patterns, colors, and quantities. Go over the form with the registry consultant before leaving the store. Since errors may be made in keypunching, request that the store send you a computer printout of your registry list and check it against your own carefully compiled list for errors.

Avoid overlap. Don't register for the same items in different stores unless you want multiples, such as place settings. Even then, be sure that each store stocks the same-size dinner plate and the same soup bowl (some have handles) for the pattern you have selected. Unless the stores are linked by computer (as most department-store chains are), it will be your responsibility to keep track of purchases. Figure out what stores are convenient for guests. For example, register for linens at a bed-and-bath shop in your groom's hometown, silver in your parents' hometown, china in the city where you and the groom work, kitchen accessories in the city where most shower guests live, place settings and other basics in large department stores with many branches. If you will be moving to a new town after the wedding, perhaps register there; the gifts can be held for delivery until after you arrive.

Don't announce where you're registered, or your gift preferences, on or with the wedding invitations. This implies that a gift is expected. Family members, attendants, or close friends can spread the word to other guests in person, over the telephone, or perhaps through a wedding newsletter sent out by your maid of honor. If someone asks you what you and your fiancé need, mention where you are registered. Some stores may issue registry cards, which are appropriate enclosures for shower invitations (since the very reason for a shower is to "shower" the bride with gifts).

Keep an accurate gift record. First check attached paperwork to be sure you've received all the boxes and pieces sent. Save enclosed cards, invoices, tags, mailing labels (often the only proof of purchase and needed to make exchanges), and gift boxes (which have the store's logo). Devise an easy-to-use system (index cards, a notebook, a computer program, or wedding-planning book) to record gifts and notices that merchandise has been special-ordered or back-ordered. This will facilitate

your
gift
record

When a gift or special-order notice arrives, record:

- gift description
- your feelings about it (for reference when writing thank-you notes)
- name and address of sender
- store
- date of arrival
- date thank-you note is sent

Save card, paperwork, tags, mailing labels, and gift box.

writing your thank-you notes and keeping stores up-to-date on purchases. (Some wedding-planning books come with self-adhesive numbers with which to number your gifts so that they correspond with your guest list.)

Follow up with registry personnel. Contact the registry consultants every few weeks (more often when it's closer to wedding day) so that your computer list can be updated. Definitely call after every engagement party or shower. Visit the department once or twice to compare your computer printout to your gift list and correct any disparities. If most of your choices have been bought, go ahead and add more!

where to register

- department store
- specialty store
- museum store
- crafts store
- electronics store
- audio/video store
- gourmet/cookware store
- hardware store
- mail-order catalog
- art gallery
- bookstore
- computer store
- sporting goods store
- luggage/leather store
- home emporium
- giftware store
- travel agency
- liquor store
- mortgage bank

If a store you like does not have a registry, ask to speak to the manager; he or she may create one for you.

Personalized Gifts

Identifying your passions will help guests select original and useful shower and wedding gifts. This quiz is designed to help you register for gifts that will inspire your guests and their imaginations. (For more ideas, see Appendix, under Chapter 17, "Wedding Gifts.") Ask yourself questions like these before registering:

What is your favorite destination?
Sample answer: "The spot where we will spend our honeymoon: Italy."
Register for: Videotaped walking tours of your honeymoon destination, tableware made in Italy, Italian cookbooks, a cappuccino or espresso maker with sacks of savory fresh coffee beans, bottles of Italian aperitifs, CD's of Italian operas, and videos of films set in Italy.

What is your favorite way to entertain at home, together?
Sample answer: "Last year, we threw a Super Bowl party with finger food, plenty of beer, and a delicious, hearty chili."
Register for: Appetizer and casserole cookbooks, gift certificates from mail-order food companies, a pressure cooker (for large stews, chilis, and soups), a cheese grater, a vegetable chopper, a food processor, a set of beer mugs, and coasters emblazoned with the logo of a favorite team.

What are some of the best memories you and your fiancé share with guests?
Sample answer: "Staying up till three a.m. after a party, eating take-out pizza, and watching suspense films."
Register for: A pizza-making kit, a pizza cookbook, gift certificates to a local pizzeria, a potato-chip maker (the perfect complement), a video library of Alfred Hitchcock classics, a membership in a local video store, or a gift certificate from a video catalog.

What is your and your fiancé's secret food obsession?
Sample answer: "We love anything chocolate—particularly fudgy brownies."
Register for: A chocolate cookbook, a subscription to a food magazine, a great stainless steel cake/brownie pan, a pound of the best Swiss unsweetened baker's chocolate, a box of gourmet chocolates for instant gratification, a crystal or china candy dish.

How do you two like to spend your leisure time?

Sample answer: "He likes to hike. I'm an amateur photographer. And we both enjoy going to plays and concerts."

Register for: Hiking shoes, matching-backpacks; tents; sleep bags; canteens; guides to the outdoors; a new camera; a flash attachment; a telephoto lens; a camera bag; photo albums; frames in assorted sizes; subscription(s) to the opera, ballet, symphony, summer stock; Broadway show tickets; CDs or cassettes of favorite show tunes.

Couple's Gift Questions

Won't registering make us seem mercenary? No. Specifying gift preferences can make things easier for guests, especially for those not sure of your needs, taste, or decor. Some guests will send gifts of their own choosing, anyway. The registry is simply there to refer to, if they wish.

Will we have to tell guests how to use the Wedding Gift Registry? No. When the guest visits (or telephones) the bridal registry, the consultant will print out (or mail) a copy of your computer gift list. A listing of the floors on which each gift category can be found, and the prices of each item, are also often listed. With increasing frequency, long-distance or time-pressured guests are calling to request that the printout be mailed to them. They can select a gift at leisure, bill the gift to a credit card, and have it crossed off your list—avoiding duplication of gifts.

If a guest calls for my list, must he or she purchase the gift in that store? No. If a guest prefers to shop in their area and see the gift "in person," he or she can look for your pattern preferences anywhere. It will be your responsibility, however, to let the Wedding Gift Registry consultant know what items should be crossed off your list if you receive them from other sources.

How can we let guests know we prefer gifts of money? Don't ask for money directly. Tell your mother, siblings, and honor attendant your preference; they can spread the word to any guests who ask what you need or want. (Many couples who have lived on their own and have adequate furnishings and accessories would rather receive money to cover large expenses such as a home or car.)

What should we do with the money we receive at the reception? Carry a white bridal purse (usually made of white satin and lace, available at your bridal salon) to collect envelopes containing money and checks given to you at your reception. When you change into your honeymoon clothes or after you leave the reception, endorse the checks and on the back of each write the phrase, "For deposit only." Keep a list of givers and the amount of each gift. Then give all checks, cash, stock certificates,

gifts for remarriage

Although gifts are not required for a remarriage, expect that many guests will send them. Register:

- **at specialty stores (e.g., antique, sporting goods, stores; gourmet or wine shop; travel agency)**
- **for serving pieces to match your good flatware**
- **for a new china pattern (start fresh!)**
- **for small kitchen gadgets**

Send thank-you notes for each gift, expressing your appreciation for the person's continuing support.

filled in deposit slips, perhaps the key to your safety-deposit box, to a trusted relative or attendant, so that all can be deposited in the bank in your absence.

Is it appropriate to designate a particular charity to which we'd like guests to make a donation in lieu of buying a gift for us? Some couples today are passing the word through friends and relatives that they would prefer guests to contribute to a particular charity as part of or instead of a wedding gift. This is especially common among older and remarrying couples, who have already acquired many household possessions and are committed to a cause. Remember: *Don't* print your gift preference on your invitation. Some guests will prefer to give you a present anyway; accept it graciously.

It is also not unusual for couples to leave printed cards at each reception place setting, stating: *"In lieu of wedding favors, Jan and Marty have made a donation in your honor to (name of charity) to celebrate their marriage."*

What should we do with gifts brought to the wedding? Arrange in advance for a safe place for gifts at the reception site (perhaps in an attended coatroom?). Or, set up a table in a locked room or closet. Give two friends the key and ask them to collect and store the gifts as guests arrive. *Don't* open the gifts there. You could easily lose the cards, and guests who didn't bring gifts may feel uncomfortable. *Do* arrange for a friend to transport the gifts safely home after the reception.

At a Long Weekend Wedding (see Chapter 10, "Special Weddings & New Ways to Wed"), it's best to open gifts after the reception. If possible, open them in private (not in front of other guests). If you do open gifts in front of close friends or attendants, temper your reactions so individual feelings aren't hurt. When you receive a gift of money, do not openly acknowledge the amount.

Where, when, and how is a gift display set up? A gift display is not necessary, but is traditional in some parts of the country. It is often easier to leave your wedding presents out than to unpack them each time friends and relatives visit. You might arrange a gift display as soon as you receive presents, and leave it up until after the wedding, when you start to use them. Set your gift display up where visitors will be arriving, in a central location—your home or your parents' home. (In some parts of the country, gifts are displayed at the reception. Only do so if someone will stay there and watch them for you.)

Set gifts up on cloth-covered tables, perhaps adding flowers and greenery (perhaps in a new vase), ribbons from packages. Don't display gift cards next to presents, and avoid positioning a very costly item (sterling tea set) next to a less expensive gift (picnic plates and cups). Do group gifts according to category (silver, electronics, crystal), or create attractive groupings that mix textures and colors. Set out only one place setting of china, crystal, and silver, or one gift if there are duplicates. Similar items, such as candlesticks, can be scattered about the table. *Never* display broken items or monetary gifts.

gift-display tips

- Don't display gift cards next to gifts.
- Set out one sample tableware setting.
- Group gifts by category and value.
- Don't display duplicates.
- Don't display monetary gifts.
- Don't display broken gifts.

In some parts of the country, it is customary to host a special luncheon, tea, or bridesmaids' party to display wedding gifts. The gift display might also be viewed by guests during the reception, if it is at home. Or, the parents of the bride might leave it up the week after the wedding, so that friends and relatives can drop by to see it.

Gift Dilemmas

Throughout your engagement, you may encounter some sticky gift situations.

What should I do with duplicate wedding gifts? You will probably want to keep duplicates of many items—extra towels, sheets; breakable items, such as goblets; candlesticks and salt-and-pepper shakers, of which you'll use several on a formally set table for a large group.

If you do decide to exchange duplicate items, *don't* tell either guest about the exchange (and don't mention it in the thank-you note). *Never* ask the giver where a gift was purchased so that you can exchange it. If later asked about a gift's whereabouts, show the new gift to the giver.

We received a brightly colored serving dish that clashes with our pastel china. Should we exchange it?

Before returning any gift, consider the giver's feelings. If it comes from a close friend or relative who will be coming to your home and expecting to see the gift in use, it's probably a good idea to keep it, even if it remains hidden at the bottom of a closet until the giver visits. Think about future needs, too. That contemporary platter might be perfect as a vegetable platter at a summer barbecue.

If you do decide to return the gift for something you need more, bring it back to the store where it was purchased with any paperwork that was enclosed with it. Write the giver a thank-you note expressing appreciation for his or her thoughtfulness, and don't mention the exchange.

Is there anything we can do about gifts that arrive damaged? Check the wrappings to see if a store shipped the gift or if it was mailed by an individual. If the gift was sent by a store, call the store's customer service department to arrange for a replacement gift to be sent to you—at no charge. There is no need to tell the giver about the damage; request that the store not do so, as well.

If the present was mailed by the giver, check the package for a post office insurance stamp, indicating that the contents are insured against breakage. If a stamp is there, return the package to the gift giver with a note of explanation. He or she will be reimbursed by the post office and will probably send you a replacement gift. If the gift was not insured, however, don't mention the damage; the person may feel obligated to send another gift. Don't mention the damage in the thank-you note, and don't display the gift in your wedding gift display (see "Wedding Gift Protection" section and Appendix, under Chapter 17, "Wedding Gifts").

If the wedding is postponed or canceled, should the wedding gifts be returned?
When a wedding is postponed, send an announcement to the guests (see Chapter 5, "Invitations & Announcements"), and keep the gifts you've received. If the wedding is canceled, however, every gift—even those that have been monogrammed—must go back to the person who sent it. Send a note with each returned gift, expressing gratitude and explaining that the wedding will not take place. You do not have to give a reason for the cancellation.

I haven't received a gift from a close friend, whom I know would be sending one. Should I call her to make sure it wasn't lost? Don't call. Assume that if she sent a gift and hasn't heard from you, she will eventually ask if you've received it. At that point, she can follow up if the gift appears to be lost. (Traditionally, a guest has up to one year to send a wedding gift.)

How can I use a wedding gift that is chipped when the giver visits? Honesty is the best policy—and in this situation, the sincerest form of flattery. Tell your guest that you are very upset that the gift got chipped, but that it shows how much you have loved and used her or his beautiful gift.

Is it appropriate to serve a meal with sterling-silver items that have not been polished recently? No. Polish them before guests arrive. If you realize your oversight and guests are there, greet them, then quickly polish the silver in the kitchen.

Wedding Gift Protection

During your engagement months, the number of valuable personal possessions and pieces of jewelry that you own will increase dramatically. Talk with your insurance agent to be sure that you are adequately covered for theft or loss.

Take out wedding insurance. There is now a new insurance policy, called Weddingsurance, offered by the Fireman's Fund in Novato, California (see Appendix, under Chapter 4, "Planning Your Wedding"). For $95 to $129, besides protecting against other wedding-day disasters and disappointments, the policy will reimburse you up to $1,000 if wedding attire is damaged or stolen; up to $1,000 if wedding gifts are stolen or broken at the reception.

Take inventory of your new possessions and ask your insurance agent about adding more coverage. To protect against loss or theft of wedding gifts and wedding rings, pearls, watches, purchase an *endorsement* (additional coverage added to your homeowner's/renter's policy). Or, purchase a *floater* (a separate policy offering additional insurance). Both are usually good for the term of the contract—often one year.

Don't print your exact address in your newspaper engagement or wedding announcement. This will alert potential burglars that you will probably be honeymooning and the house will be empty the week(s) after your wedding.

Arrange for someone to guard wedding gifts at the reception. Don't leave them piled, unattended, in a corner of the reception-site lobby or banquet room. Plan in advance for the coat-check attendant to watch gifts, or for friends to store them in a locked room or closet.

Ask friends to safely transport gifts home. Since you will be leaving on your honeymoon, you'll want to be certain the gifts are not forgotten.

Tell police the dates you will be away. They may patrol the neighborhood more frequently in your absence.

Alert neighborhood crimewatch groups of your absence. Give neighbors departure and return dates of your honeymoon. They will also keep an eye on your house and notify the police if anything seems suspicious.

Make sure you have a burglar alarm. If you have been planning to install one, now is a good time to take action.

Use light timers that turn on, off, at different times. Other tips to make your home seem lived in: Stop delivery of mail, newspapers, packages. Ask a neighbor to collect circulars and restaurant menus.

Don't leave your keys under a mat, over the door, or in the mailbox. Thieves know where all the common hiding places are.

Thank-you Notes

You or your groom must send a personal, handwritten letter of appreciation for each gift you receive, even if you have already verbally thanked the individual. Perhaps the only exceptions to this rule might be gifts received from your groom and your parents, although they would surely treasure a written expression of your love and appreciation; it really is recommended that you write to them, too. Follow these guidelines:

Select your thank-you notes early. The most important thing about writing thank-you notes is to do it promptly—within two weeks of receiving a gift before the wedding; within a month of your return from the honeymoon if gift is received on wedding day; within a month if it is received afterward. The traditional wedding thank-you note is written in blue or black ink on folded notepaper in ivory or white. (Your stationer may recommend a type of folded stationery called *informals* for this purpose.) Today, however, it is common to select colored or decorated notes. Your name or monogram may be embossed on the note. Since you can use your married name or initials only after the wedding, you might order two sets of thank-you notes, one for after the wedding. (Or, you can use plain notes beforehand.) Your fiancé should also order thank-you notes for his own use before the wedding.

Don't use typed notes or printed cards. They appear too impersonal. Those who feel they can write only with the help of a word processor might draft their ideas on a computer, then handwrite the finished note on stationery. (If your computer draft turns into a series of childhood reminiscences, send it along inside the handwritten note. Your guests will be pleased to receive it!)

Keep careful records. As each gift arrives, along with the name and address of sender, jot down a description, your thoughts and feelings: *"yellow hand towels embroidered with pink tulips; remind me of Aunt Jane's garden; will look great in our powder room."*

Try not to let notes pile up. It's much easier to think about three or four notes at a time, rather than thirty or forty.

Categorize. Divide thank-you notes into manageable chunks. Separate your gift list into categories: your family, his family, mutual friends. Establish a system (e.g., you each write to your own family and friends). Next, subdivide these into smaller stacks (college friends, work friends, cousins, etc.).

Give some gift givers priority. Try to respond in the order in which you received the gifts; those givers will be most anxious to hear their gift arrived safely. Thank long-distance guests in writing for making the trip. Write quickly, too, to those who could not make the trip, but sent a gift. It's a nice gesture to enclose a wallet-sized wedding photo, as well.

Write notes together. Read to each other what you've written, as you sip tea on a rainy afternoon. Or, take your notes and list to a romantic country inn. Perhaps write five notes each morning as you eat croissants in your honeymoon suite.

Take notes, pens, and addresses with you each day. You may be able to squeeze in a few notes during your lunch break or in a doctor's waiting room.

Set up an inviting writing space. Clear a desk or a table, put out all the pens, paper, and supplies you'll need, and reserve the area for thank-you–note writing. Then you can slip over to your writing area and get started immediately without wasting precious time hunting for your pen or gift notebook. Put on a soothing classical or jazz tape, and sit in a comfortable chair.

thank-you–note tips

- Enlist your groom's help. He might write notes to his friends or family for items he's more familiar with (e.g., tools, the wok, etc.).

- It's acceptable to write one thank-you note for a gift given by a large group (8–10 or more). Thank each individual giver in person when you see them.

- Acknowledge gifts received before the wedding within two weeks of their arrival; within a month after the honeymoon for gifts received on wedding day; within a month of receipt afterward.

- Send printed gift-received cards (see Chapter 5, "Invitations & Announcements," for wording) if you expect to receive many more gifts than you can acknowledge during the expected time period. These *must*, however, be followed promptly by handwritten notes.

Create a routine and a reward system. A suggestion from time management experts: Set a reasonable goal and when you meet it, give yourself a reward. For example, you and your husband could agree to write five notes on weekdays, ten notes each weekend day. When they're done, you'll go out to dinner or rent a video you've been longing to see, perhaps snuggle in front of the fire. Even the process of checking off the notes you've finished, on your list, will give you a sense of accomplishment that will motivate you to do more. When you've completed all of the notes, splurge on an evening at the theater or an intimate dinner for two.

If that doesn't work, write for ten minutes a day. If penning a set number of notes each day seems tedious, devote just ten minutes to thank-yous. After you've written for the allotted time, decide whether you're inspired enough to continue for another ten minutes, and so on, until you're ready to stop. You'll accomplish more than you expected!

Do the hardest first. Get difficult notes—for gifts a bit out of the ordinary, or to distant relatives whom you don't know very well—done first. Or, alternate between difficult responses and those you're looking forward to dashing off.

Remember that writing is just the process of putting your thoughts on paper. It may help to sit back, close your eyes, and imagine using the gift—the sights, sounds, and feelings. (For example, serving your first Thanksgiving turkey on the platter sent by your aunt.) Or, think about the giver and all the fond memories you have of him or her.

Wording Thank-you Notes

Some of your notes will be easy to write, others will be more of a challenge. Each note should be warm and personal. Describe the gift and how you plan to use it. Add at least one thought besides "thank you" to the note. You might include an invitation to visit, a comment about the wedding, or a word about your new apartment.

Traditionally, only one person signs a note; mention your husband in the body of the note. You may sign notes to relatives and close friends with your first name only, but use your full name to people you don't know well. After the wedding, you may include your maiden name whenever necessary for identification (e.g., sign your name *Ann Smith*, *Ann Brown Smith*, but never *Mrs. John Smith*). If you will keep your maiden name after marriage, take this opportunity to let everyone know by signing your notes *Ann Brown*. Below are some examples:

Note to married couple. Traditionally, a note to a married couple is addressed to one person—most often, the wife, alone. The husband is referred to in the body of the note. (Today, you may address both, *Dear Mr. and Mrs. Smith*, if you prefer,

three-step guide to writing thank-you notes

- **Name the gift.** "Thank you for the beautiful crystal dish."

- **Describe how you'll use the gift or its attributes.** "John and I love how it sparkles in candlelight, and have already used it to serve after-dinner mints at our first dinner party."

- **Add a personal thought or two about your wedding, your relationship with the giver.** "I've known you all my life. It meant so much for me to have you there to share my wedding day."

but only one person still signs the note.)
Dear Mrs. Smith:

Thank you so much for the beautiful crystal vase you and Mr. Smith sent. Ann and I love the way it looks on the mantle.

We are both so glad that you were able to share our special day with us.

Sincerely yours,
Steven Jones

Thank-you for a monetary gift. Acknowledging a gift of money or a savings bond, stock certificate, is easy if you mention how you plan to use the money.
Dear Uncle Ed,

Thank you so much for the generous wedding check. It was a wonderful surprise. Steve and I have added it to savings earmarked for a car—and thanks to you, we're almost there!

We'll be driving down to see you soon!
Love,
Ann

Thank-you for a mystery gift. If you unwrap a gift that has an obscure purpose, refer to it by color and material.
Dear Mrs. Martin:

Thank you for the beautiful blue glass piece you and Mr. Martin sent. It was such a nice surprise to find it waiting when Ann and I came home from work. My mother always said you were someone who could brighten a day!

We're glad you could share our wedding.

Sincerely,
Steve Jones

Thank-you for a gift you're lukewarm about. There's no need to rave about a gift you don't like or plan to exchange.

You might mention appreciation for the trip the giver made to attend the wedding.
Dear Cousin Shirley,

Steve and I would like to thank you, sincerely, for the humidor. We'll think of you each time we use it.

Thank you again for traveling to share our special day.

Love,
Ann

Note when you haven't met the giver.
Dear Ms. Robbins:

Thank you for the set of pots and pans. Steve tells me that you are a wonderful cook, so I am sure that they are the best! I will think of you as I develop my own culinary skills!

I look forward to meeting you at the wedding.

Sincerely yours,
Ann Brown

When you don't care for a gift and can't return it. Find something nice to say about it or about the senders, anyway. You can always bring the gift out just when they visit.
Dear Bob and Jan,

Thanks so much for the gum-machine lamp! It is one of the most unusual gifts that we received—and we're sure it will be a conversation piece whenever we have guests.

Please come visit us soon!
Fondly,
Steve

Thank-you when you receive a group gift. When you receive a single gift from several relatives, attendants, or close friends, you should still write each one a separate note. However, if the gift came from a very large group (eight to ten or more)—your co-workers, perhaps—one thank-you note addressed to the group is sufficient. (Thank each sender in person, as well.)

Dear Jane, Jim, Susan, Bill, and Fred: (Travel Accounting Department):

Thank you for the place setting of china. Now Steve and I have service for seven—just the right number to have you all for dinner! How did you ever guess?

We appreciate your thoughtfulness. I can't wait to get back and show you our honeymoon snapshots.

With much affection,

Ann Smith

Monogramming Gifts

Monograms are initials, embossed or embroidered on silver, linens, or other items to give them a personal trademark. There was a time when almost every wedding gift bore a monogram when it arrived. Most brides today, though, will probably want gifts to be monogrammed after the wedding. This will give them time to decide if they will keep their maiden name after the marriage or design a contemporary monogram that includes both their husband's and their own first initials. *Also note*: Since most stores have a no-return policy for monogrammed items, you might want to request on your Wedding Gift Registry list, *"Please do not monogram."* Here's how to go about monogramming gifts:

Ask your Wedding Gift Registry consultant to help you choose an appropriate style. Options: A single initial (usually your husband's last name); your first and last initials *and* your husband's first and last intials; your first initial *and* your husband's first initial; the initial of his last name, large, in the center, with each of your first initials on either side.

Consider the style and size of the gift, and the space that will be filled by the monogram. A towel, sheet, or table cloth has ample room for any monogram. Silver flatware, serving pieces (cake knives, pie servers, soup ladles), on the other hand, will need your chosen monogram or a simplified version reduced.

Be careful to note if your joint initials spell out an offensive or humorous word. If your initials spell out a word such as *BAD, JAR, FUN, ICK*, etc., choose a monogram in which the last initial is in the center, larger than the other two: *bDa, jRa, fNu, iKc.*

Gifts for Attendants

It is customary to give each of your attendants a small gift as a token of appreciation and as a memento of your wedding. These need not be expensive, but should be items that will have lasting meaning. Traditionally, each bridesmaid and usher get an identical gift, but honor attendants usually receive something more special. Or, you may break with tradition and give each attendant a unique gift chosen just for him or her. Consider hobbies and lifestyles.

Gifts to your attendants are distributed before the wedding, usually at the rehearsal dinner. (Some couples prefer to present the gifts at a special party that is planned in the attendants' honor, and set the gifts at each place setting.)

Attendants may receive something to wear for the wedding (that might be monogrammed and engraved with the wedding date). Everyone in the wedding should receive a thank-you gift, including flower girls, altar boys, pages, ring bearers, and junior bridesmaids. When buying their gifts, consider items that they'll enjoy, which will be fondly remembered and also commemorate your wedding.

buy thank-you gifts for:

- bridesmaids and ushers
- honor attendants
- child attendants
- prewedding party hosts
- ceremony readers and soloists, musicians who are friends
- reception helpers (guest-book attendant, program and rice passers, spotter for photographer)
- friends who lodge or drive out-of-town guests
- parents
- each other

Gifts for Bridesmaids. Gloves; pearls; necklaces; earrings; shoes; bracelets; pins; pendants; heart-shaped lockets; charms; handbags; handkerchiefs; perfume bottles or atomizers; picture frames; pillows filled with potpourri—reminiscent of their bouquets; pewter cups, business-card or contact-lens cases; silver hair-combs, compacts, or makeup brushes; jewelry boxes; crystal bud vases; desk clocks; voice-controlled alarm clocks; topiaries.

Gifts for Ushers. Engraved money clips, business-card cases, pewter mugs, belt buckles, key rings, silver flasks, bar jiggers; pen-and-pencil sets; Swiss Army knives; wallets; leather pocket agendas with wedding dates marked; silver razors, comb-and-brush sets, bookmarks; pocket watches; cuff links; suspenders. The groom may also offer to pay for his ushers' accessories as a gift (e.g., cummerbunds, shirts, bow ties) when they rent their tuxedos.

Gifts for Children. Bride and groom dolls, teddy bears; flower-girl or ring-bearer books; tickets to the circus, zoo, a movie; gift certificates for ice-cream sundaes; necklaces or bracelets; cuff links; frames with wedding photos.

Thank-you Gifts

It is appropriate to give or send both sets of parents a gift to thank them for all they have done during the engagement months. Also thank any friend or relative who graciously hosted a prewedding party by giving them a gift. You might arrange for flowers to be delivered to parents the day after your wedding (prewrite cards). Send flowers to host/hostess the day of the party, or present a gift as you leave.

Gifts for Party Hosts/Hostesses and Other Wedding Helpers. Flowers; wine, fruit, or cheese baskets; decorative plants; scented soaps and bath products; mugs and gourmet coffees; notepapers; porcelain figures; paperweights; Christmas ornaments; collectibles (e.g., cups, thimbles).

Gifts for Mothers. Flower arrangements; perfume bottles or atomizers; silver compacts and makeup brushes; silver or enamel pillboxes, appointment books.

Gifts for Fathers. Cuff links, key chains, tie clips, pewter or crystal beer mugs, money clips, wallets, paperweights, electronic beepers, mobile phones.

Gifts for Both. Teacups; teapot or coffeepot; picture frames with wedding photos, photos of them with you as a baby; framed wedding invitations; leather-bound albums; engraved silver bowls or plates; clocks; champagne bottles and champagne flutes; spa gift certificates.

Gifts for the Bride and Groom

Although optional, it is traditional for the bride and groom to give each other a meaningful wedding gift in addition to the wedding rings. A wedding is also the time many parents pass down heirlooms—gifts with sentimental meaning.

Gifts from Parents to Newlyweds. Sterling-silver tea set; antique jewelry; a favorite rocking chair; a bottle of cognac or case of wine purchased the day the bride was born; a family Bible or crèche; furniture; a set of flatware; money for buying a home, a car, or a wall unit.

Gifts for the Groom from the Bride. Watch; gold cuff links; wallet; attaché case; sterling picture frame with wedding photo; camera; TV; CD player and favorite CDs; VCR and video-store membership; answering machine; calculator; wok, chop sticks; pasta machine, saucepan; salad bowl, chopping block, food processer; coffee mugs; beer mugs; shower massage; whirlpool bath; shower radio; breakfast trays; over-sized bed pillows; wool blanket; robe; lambs' wool slippers; skis; skates; racquets; golf clubs; fishing gear; luggage, luggage rack; sports bags; passport holder; money belt; car stereo; CB radio; cooler; pic-nic basket; stadium blanket.

Gifts for the Bride from the Groom. Pearls; earrings; pendant; necklace; bracelet; locket; leather handbag or luggage; sports bag; wraparound robe; gift certificate to a spa; breakfast tray; porcelain tea set; porcelain figurine; puppy; bicycle; jogging suit; health-club membership; sterling-silver compact, hairbrush and comb; ring holder; skates; skis; golf clubs; saddle, bridle, riding clothes; travel iron; travel hair dryer; croquet/boccie set; snorkeling gear; sailing gear; canoe; silver-plated key to new home; chilled champagne and chocolates in honeymoon suite; limousine waiting at airport for honeymoon return.

Ultimate Personalized Gifts. Fortune cookies with personal messages; framed love poem delivered on wedding morning; tape of favorite love songs from courtship—representing first date, first kiss, first dance, favorite romantic film; postcard from honeymoon sent to home address with message: "I love you!"; on wedding morning, request that his favorite song be played on favorite radio station; honeymoon booklet with coupons for "one back rub," "bubble bath for two," breakfast in bed," "dancing under the stars"; shadow box filled with courtship memories: matchbooks from restaurants, ticket stubs, pressed flowers from park where proposal took place.

Gifts That Reflect Your Heritages

There are many age-old traditions that you may choose to follow or adapt—to reflect various cultural, ethnic, and religious backgrounds. (Some are still customary!)

American Colonial

Women in the community sewed handcrafted items, such as samplers and quilts, for the couple.

Australian

Couples still receive congratulatory telegrams from faraway friends and relatives, and read them aloud at the wedding. Guests bring gifts to the reception.

Austrian

Brides received wooden tubs with the words *"Be Happy and Industrious"* painted on the sides. The tubs were to transport possessions to their new home.

Chinese

The bride's mother still fills a pocketbook with gold, jewelry, money, and valuables. Wedding gifts from guests are useful; money is the most popular. Gifts of gold, silver, are considered ostentatious; white, funereal. Red (the color of joy) wrapping paper is used.

England

Brides received brass warming pans inscribed *"Love and Live in Peace."* In Hertfordshire, England, a pig was a traditional gift from a father to his newly married daughter.

Fijian

The groom still may give the bride's father a whale's tooth, or something of great value—like himself.

French

Friends or family still present a special two-handled cup (the *coupe de mariage*) for drinking wedding toasts; have it engraved with your initials. Guests still send gifts to the bride's parents—with a note of congratulations *and* flowers to the bride on wedding day.

Hopi Indian

Community members still give cotton to the groom's father, to weave cloth for bridal garments.

Iroquois Indian

The bride and her mother brought maize cakes to her future mother-in-law's home, and the mother-in-law presented them with venison. This gift exchange constituted a marriage ceremony.

Italian

Guests still receive candied almonds wrapped in tulle or presented in porcelain boxes (guest favors called *bomboniere*) as a symbol of good fortune.

Japanese

The bride receives clothing, accessories, and food—in pairs (two measures of tea, two pairs of sandals). Her family gives identical presents to the groom—down to the exact number of fish in a picnic basket. Guests give money envelopes with gold and silver cords, and receive gifts back (one-third to one-half *their* gift value).

Jewish

The bride's mother still may give the groom a *tallit* (prayer shawl) of silk; the groom's mother may give the bride Sabbath candlesticks or a tablecloth. The act of espousal is sealed when the groom gives his bride something of value, usually a plain gold wedding ring.

Korean

Ducks and geese mate for life, so friends may give a live goose and gander, or a figurine, as a symbol of fidelity.

Mexican

Godparents participate in the wedding ceremony; give the couple rosaries, prayer books, or kneeling pillows.

Muslim

The bride and groom may give guests candy or eggs, representing a sweet and fruitful life. Guests may give crystal, silver, or china—*after* the wedding, and don't expect thank-you notes.

Nigerian

After marriage, a bride may give her family members old clothing. She wears the new garments and jewelry given to her by her husband.

Philippino

The groom's family may give old coins, symbolizing prosperity, to the couple.

Pennsylvania-German (Amish)

Neighbors still give the couple practical items (e.g., a *schrank*—a handpainted storage piece) for their new home.

Polish

To mark the bride's married status, her mother and grandmother may replace her wedding veil with a *babushka* (a triangularly folded kerchief) and an apron.

Scottish

Grooms may give their bride a silver teaspoon (a *wedding spune*), engraved with their initials and wedding date.

Southern Indian (Hindu)

The groom may present his bride with a jeweled string or necklace, called a *thali*, to wear throughout the marriage.

Swiss

Junior bridesmaids may lead a procession with handfuls of colored handkerchiefs. Guests "buy" handkerchiefs, with the money going to the couple.

Welsh

The bride may give her bridesmaids sprigs of myrtle from her bouquet. The maids plant them; the one whose sprig takes root will marry soon.

Anniversary Gifts

Picturing the years of marriage ahead, you may be thinking of anniversaries—and the gifts you will give each other to celebrate. If you request, your Wedding Gift Registry may keep your list of gift preferences current, for years of gift giving from your spouse or parents. You may want to hold a reaffirmation ceremony to celebrate an important anniversary (five, ten, or twenty-five years), or to mark a re-commitment of your love. Here is a list of traditional and contemporary anniversary gifts:

Traditional

1st: paper	16th: peridot
2nd: cotton	(deep yellow-
3rd: leather	ish green gem)
4th: linen	17th: watch
5th: wood	18th: cat's eye
6th: iron	(semiprecious
7th: wool	stone)
8th: bronze	19th: aquamarine
9th: pottery	20th: china
10th: tin,	25th: silver
aluminum	30th: pearls
11th: steel	35th: coral, jade
12th: silk	40th: rubies
13th: lace	45th: sapphires
14th: ivory	50th: gold
15th: crystal	55th: emeralds
	60th: diamonds

Contemporary

1st: clocks	16th: silver
2nd: china	hollowware,
3rd: crystal, glass	sterling
4th: electrical	or plate
appliances	17th: furniture
5th: silverware	18th: porcelain
6th: wood	19th: bronze
7th: desk sets	20th: platinum
8th: linens, lace	25th: sterling
9th: leather	silver
10th: diamond	30th: diamonds
jewelry	35th: jade
11th: fashion	40th: rubies
jewelry,	45th: sapphires
accessories	50th: gold
12th: pearls or	55th: emeralds
colored gems	60th: diamonds
13th: textiles, furs	
14th: gold jewelry	
15th: watches	

These are, of course, suggestions. Use your imagination and build on the traditional and contemporary gift choices listed. For example, a first-anniversary gift of paper could mean a magazine subscription, engraved stationery, or a stock certificate. Silver on the twenty-fifth anniversary could easily be a silver ice bucket or plane tickets to Los Angeles—and Hollywood—land of the silver screen. Feel free to interpret the traditional suggestions in a contemporary way: leather for a third aniversary could be anything from a stadium coat to an antique leather-bound book. A gift from the heart that reflects the love you've shared for another year is what matters.

WEDDING GUESTS 18

Wedding guests are invited to witness the wedding ceremony, wish the bride and groom happiness and prosperity at the reception, and join them in celebrating their new life as husband and wife. Each wedding style—whether a formal evening ceremony followed by a seated dinner or a surfside ceremony followed by an afternoon beach barbecue—calls for a particular kind of invitation response, gift, and style of dress. Here, a guest's guide to enjoying the festivities (see Appendix, under Chapter 18, "Wedding Guests").

Receiving an Invitation

Wedding invitations are typically mailed four to six weeks before the wedding date (eight weeks before—if the wedding is near a holiday). Whatever the R.s.v.p. date, it is courteous to reply promptly, in writing, so the seating plan can be worked out as early as possible and the final head count can be given to the caterer. How the guest responds depends upon the formality of the invitation.

An R.s.v.p. card acceptance:
Today, most invitations include a printed response card with a stamped, self-addressed, printed envelope. To help the wedding host keep track of replies efficiently, guests should fill out the card and return it promptly.
Mr. and Mrs. Joel Kageyama
____ will ____ will not attend.
Another alternative: a blank response card, for guests to write their own acceptance or refusal message.

An R.s.v.p. card regret:
Mr. and Mrs. Joel Kageyama
____ will ____ will not attend.
A guest may also slip a separate note in with the R.s.v.p. card, in the enclosed envelope, to add a more personal explanation or message of congratulations.

invitation dos and don'ts

Here, etiquette points for wedding guests:

DO let hosts know if an unexpected complication (e.g., an illness or out-of-country business trip) will make it impossible to attend the wedding, as planned. Write, telephone, or telegraph regrets to the hostess with an explanation as soon as possible.

DON'T assume that children and others who live with you are invited *unless* their names appear on the inside envelope (see Chapter 5, "Invitations & Announcements"). If the hosts address the invitation "Miss Marx," then they expect her alone to attend the wedding—not every member of her household.

DO bring young children if they are invited, but only if you or someone else can watch them closely during the ceremony and reception (ask the hosts if a baby-sitter will be present). Otherwise make arrangements to leave them at home.

DON'T ask the bride if you can bring a date or special friend along to a wedding unless the bride has requested a specific name or address for her invitation guest list (see Chapter 5, "Invitations & Announcements"). Space might be tight and your request could put the bride in an awkward position. (If you thought you would have a better time with an escort—who is not a longtime boyfriend—remember that weddings are wonderful places to meet new people!)

A formal acceptance:

A traditional, engraved invitation to a wedding ceremony and reception may arrive without a printed R.s.v.p. card. The guest is expected to send a written response to the wedding host promptly. It should be written on plain white or cream-colored notepaper in blue, blue-black, or black ink.

> *Mr. and Mrs. Joel Kageyama*
> *accept with pleasure*
> *the invitation of*
> *Mr. and Mrs. Ernest Carr Burke*
> *for Saturday, the fourth of April*
> *at half after four o'clock.*

It is not necessary to repeat the name of the bride and groom, but including the date and time indicates that they have been correctly understood. Including the location is optional. Wording and spacing should duplicate as closely as possible that of the invitation.

A formal regret:

> *Mr. Jean-Jacques DeLille*
> *regrets that he is unable to accept*
> *the kind invitation of*
> *Mr. and Mrs. Ernest Carr Burke*
> *for Saturday, the fourth of April.*

A regret does not repeat the time or the place, merely the date. It is not necessary to give a reason, but the guest may enclose a separate personal note to explain why he or she cannot attend the wedding and to wish the bride and groom a life full of happiness.

An informal acceptance:

A handwritten, contemporary, or personalized invitation calls for an informal, handwritten note on the guest's favorite stationery.

Dear Stephanie,

Rick and I are delighted to be included among the guests at Rochelle's wedding on the fifteenth of June at 11:30 a.m., at Central Methodist Church. We are looking forward to both the ceremony and the reception.

Affectionately,
Becky

An informal regret:

Dear Stephanie,

Charlotte and I regret that we will be away on the fifteenth of June, as my younger sister will be graduating that day. You know that nothing but a family celebration of our own could keep us from attending Shelly and Norman's wedding.

Please give Shelly and Norman our best wishes for their future happiness.

Fondly,
Gary

Receiving an Announcement

A wedding announcement does not obligate a recipient in any way; neither a gift nor a personal acknowledgment is necessary. When dear friends are involved, however, it is a thoughtful gesture to send a personal note of good wishes to the couple, and perhaps to their parents, as well. If announcement recipients *do* want to mark the news of the wedding with a gift, they can check with a parent or close friend to see where the newlyweds are registered.

Out-of-Town Weddings

Most invitations to out-of-town weddings include a map or other written directions to the wedding site. If they are not included, guests can request them from the bride's or groom's family. To avoid missing the ceremony, double-check the instructions received with the police in that city, or consult a road map.

Wedding hosts have certain obligations to guests who are traveling long distances to attend a wedding. (In return, guests should keep track of whoever entertained them and send thank-you notes, perhaps small gifts of appreciation.) Here are some traditional duties.

Wedding accommodations. The bride's family should recommend places to stay, and may reserve a block of rooms in a hotel for out-of-town guests (at a reduced group rate). The bride's family is not expected to pay for the accommodations of out-of-town guests, but should enclose printed information about available hotels with the wedding invitation. Guests can then call the hotel to make their own reservations.

Entertainment. Family or friends will probably host a welcome cocktail party or dinner for out-of-town guests (often the same night that the bride's and groom's families and the wedding party will be at the rehearsal dinner). Or, out-of-town guests may be invited to a get-acquainted breakfast the day of the wedding, or to a postwedding brunch the day after the wedding. At a Long Weekend Wedding, there will most likely be many gatherings hosted by friends and family members of the bride and groom. Some couples host a barbecue and pool party or a softball game: bride's team vs. the groom's team. If an itinerary of all of these outings is not included with the invitation, the wedding hosts should leave a schedule in each guest's hotel room, along with a welcome basket of fruit, candy, cookies, etc. It is also a thoughtful gesture to leave each guest a list of all other out-of-town guests staying in the same hotel, as well as the name and phone number of a friend or relative who lives in that town, and can answer any questions about the planned activities and logistics.

Sight-seeing arrangements. The wedding host(s) may also arrange a bus tour of a large city, a trip to a museum, or perhaps an afternoon of skiing or skating. Or, they may leave a list of suggestions in each out-of-town guest's hotel room, should guests want to explore on their own. The bride's and groom's families will appreciate being left free the day before the wedding, to finalize last-minute details.

Transportation. It is considerate for the wedding hosts to arrange transportation around town, at least back and forth to the ceremony and reception sites, for all out-of-town guests. Some couples arrange for a bus or trolley to transport all guests. Others arrange for limousines, or ask wedding attendants and other close friends to provide rides.

gift-giving etiquette

- Find out where the couple are registered.

- *Bring* a shower gift to a shower. *Send* a weding gift before or after the wedding.

- Send a wedding gift within one year of the wedding (within one month, though, is best).

- Ask the store to enclose a receipt for the item, omitting the price.

- Wrap the gift in a box with the store's name or logo.

- If mailing the gift yourself, insure the package to cover damages.

- Mail the gift to the address on the registry form or to the return address on the wedding invitation.

- Make monetary gifts payable to the bride *or* groom before the wedding; to *both* on wedding day or after.

- If you don't receive a thank-you note, wait at least one month after the gift was sent to ask if it was received.

The Wedding Gift

Always plan on sending a gift when you accept a wedding invitation (see "When Wedding Gifts May Be Optional" box). Below, some etiquette pointers for guests:

How much time does a guest have to send a gift? Traditionally, a gift may be sent up to a year after the wedding, but it's best to shop nearer to the event (within one month after the wedding), so the occasion isn't forgotten. The guest will also have the benefit of the choices on the bride's and groom's Wedding Gift Registry.

Where should the wedding gift be sent? Wedding gifts traditionally are sent to the bride at her home, or to the R.s.v.p. address on the wedding invitation. However, if the guest is a close friend of the groom's parents and wants them to see the gift, it is acceptable to send the gift to their home. Also consider the address that will be most helpful for the couple. If they will be relocating to another city, or already live in a city other than the site of the wedding, sending the gift to that address will give them one less item to move. Check with the couple's Wedding Gift Registry. There should be a preferred delivery address listed on their computer printout.

Can't a guest just bring the gift to the reception? In some geographic regions, this is the custom. However, making sure that the gift arrives at the appropriate home address before or after the wedding is traditional and *wise*. Otherwise, the bride and groom will have to worry about security (gifts can be lost, damaged, or stolen, and cards often get detached), as well as having the gifts transported home by their wedding party, family, or friends. If the gift is sent directly to the parent's or couple's home, it can be safely stored.

What is an appropriate wedding gift? Wedding gifts are chosen with the couple, not each individual, in mind (even if the guest is a friend of only the bride or groom). As a result, most guests choose gifts for the couple's home—china, silver, crystal, linens, glassware, housewares, and decorative objects. Guests may also consider theme gifts (e.g., everything to bake an apple pie, the groom's favorite dessert: baking apples, flour, mixing spoons, rolling pin, pie dish), as well as gifts that represent shared memories you have with the bride, groom, or both (e.g., a pasta maker, colander, pasta bowl and Italian cookbook from the friends who once whipped up lavish feasts with the bride). (For more creative gift ideas, see Chapter 17, "Wedding Gifts.") Whenever a couple have listed their their preferences with a Wedding Gift Registry, it makes it easier for guests to choose gifts they will truly appreciate. Expense need not be a criterion; most registries include items in a variety of price ranges. If you don't know the store at which the couple are registered, call the bride's or groom's mother, the maid or matron of honor, or the couple themselves. Many couples today register at stores that have branches all over the country, or they register at more than one store

when wedding gifts may be optional

Guests may choose to send a wedding gift as a token of congratulations and affection. It is not, however, absolutely necessary if you will not be entertained at a reception, or if it is second wedding. Optional gift situations include:

- When a group invitation to the ceremony is extended to members of the church congregation.

- When a wedding invitation must be refused because of a previous commitment.

- When the guest is attending the second wedding of the bride or the groom just a few years after attending the first. (If you wish to give something, remember the couple are combining homes, not creating one, and choose items they would not buy themselves. See Chapter 17, "Wedding Gifts."

(e.g., one for tableware, one for videos, another for sportswear, still others for hardware, gourmet foods, liquor, or books).

Should a guest order an item on the couple's registry list if it is out of stock, or a special order? How will they know a gift has been sent? If an item is not immediately available, the store will place an order with the warehouse and should send the bride a card telling her what was purchased, where, the name of the salesperson and buyer, the name of the sender, and the date it will be delivered. If the item ordered is discontinued, the bride should also be notified, by mail, and asked to make an alternate gift selection.

Is a monetary gift appropriate? To whom should it be made payable? Money is a suitable and always appreciated wedding gift. This may take the form of a check, cash, gift certificate to a favorite store, contribution to a travel (honeymoon) or mortgage registry fund (see Appendix, under Chapter 17, "Wedding Gifts"), U.S Government Bond, or stock certificate. Before the wedding, checks are made out to the bride *or* groom (based on with whom the guest is related or most friendly) and are sent (in a wedding card—some have special compartments for checks) to that person's home. On wedding day or after, make the gift payable to *both* the bride and groom; if you wish, present it personally to the couple at the reception.

When can a guest expect to receive acknowledgment of their gift? For gifts received before the wedding, thank-you notes should be sent by the bride or groom within two weeks of their arrival. For gifts received on or after the wedding, thank-you notes should be sent within a month of the honeymoon (see Chapter 17, "Wedding Gifts"). If several months have passed since the wedding and the couple still have not acknowledged receiving the gift, it is understandable that a guest might be concerned about the gift's safe arrival. It is appropriate to phone the store from which the gift was sent to make sure it was actually delivered. Or, the guest might ask the post office to trace the package (always keep insurance receipts for any gifts mailed). If the gift seems to have been lost or damaged, replace it, enclosing a note of explanation to the couple. If all appears to be in order, the guest must decide whether or not to ask the couple about the present's arrival; it may be awkward to check on the gift's status without implying to the newlyweds that their manners are amiss. A casual remark made during conversation with them (or their parents), such as, *"How's that warming tray working out?"* may bring you exactly the reassurance you need. This should be followed by a thank-you note.

Are guests expected to send other prewedding gifts, in addition to a wedding gift? Engagement gifts are optional, even if a friend or family member receives an invitation to an engagement party (see Chapter 1, "Your Engagement"). Many guests do, however, choose to give the couple a congratulations present. If a guest accepts an invitation to a shower, however, a gift is mandatory. After all, the purpose of a shower is to shower the bride and groom with the items needed to set up a home together.

Dressing for the Wedding

General guidelines. Wedding guests dress as they would for almost any other social event held at the same hour and season (see Chapter 7, "Guide to Wedding Clothes" chart). Traditionally, it has been taboo for women guests to wear black (perceived as too funereal) or white (the distinctive color reserved for the bride). Today, however, it is acceptable for a woman guest to wear a black cocktail or evening dress to a formal evening reception. At a black-and-white wedding, the bridesmaids, mothers, and flower girl wear black or black-and-white dresses, often with red, silver, gold, or other colored accessories. A guest's outfit that is black may also include colored accessories, such as a red stole, shoes, and purse. It is also becoming more acceptable for women guests to wear white—especially if the wedding is a snowball wedding (bridesmaids, mothers, and flower girl all wear white dresses). So as not to draw attention away from the bride, women guests in white dresses should wear bright or pastel shoes and a matching purse; a woman in a white suit should also wear a bright or pastel silk blouse and belt, perhaps a colorful patterned scarf around her shoulders.

Very formal and formal evening. Traditionally, an engraved invitation to an evening wedding indicates very formal (white tie) or formal (black tie) attire for the wedding party. Although this does not mean that all male guests must dress at the same level of formality, many hosts today, will print "black tie" or "black tie invited" on the invitation, to let guests know that the wedding will be formal and that black tie (tuxedos) will be appreciated. Although "white tie" is seldom printed on the invitation, to let guests know that the wedding will be *very* formal and that white tie (tails) will be appreciated, the information can be spread by word of mouth. At a *very* formal evening wedding, women are expected to wear long dresses; at a formal evening wedding, long dresses or very dressy cocktail clothes are called for.

Formal daytime. Before 6 p.m., women guests wear dressy short daytime dresses in floral prints or solid colors, or elegant cocktail suits. Men wear dark suits.

Informal (daytime or evening). Traditionally, women wear street-length dresses, luncheon or festive suits, depending upon the time of day. Men wear suits or a blazer and tie. At a non-traditional wedding, perhaps one held in a meadow with a barbecue afterward, however, "casual clothes" might be specified, particularly if the reception will include an activity such as a softball game or swimming. When in doubt, call the bride, her mother, the groom's mother, or anyone involved in the wedding preparations. Then help spread the word by telling other guests what is intended. Always be guided by the bride's mother, who may advise guests that bare-shoulder looks are inappropriate for that particular house of worship.

Ceremony Procedures

When should guests arrive at a wedding? One may not be "fashionably late" to a wedding. Guests without pew cards should arrive at the site of the ceremony thirty minutes before the time printed on the invitation, even earlier for a very large wedding, to allow ample time to be seated by the ushers. People with reserved seats (pew cards) should arrive about twenty minutes before the ceremony begins. Guests arriving later than ten minutes before the ceremony should seat themselves quietly in the rear if ushers are no longer seating guests. If the wedding procession is already under way, guests should remain in the rear of the church or synagogue until the wedding party reaches the altar, then seat themselves (unless an usher is stationed at the back to seat latecomers). Travel arrangements should allow for inclement weather, traffic delays, finding an out-of-the-way church or synagogue.

On which side should guests sit? When guests arrive at the church, synagogue, or ceremony site, they'll be met in the vestibule by an usher who will ask if they are a friend or relative of the bride or the groom. In Christian weddings, the groom's relatives and friends are seated on the right side of the altar (the same position the groom will be in as he faces the altar); the bride's relatives and friends on the left (where the bride will be). The reverse is true for Jewish weddings: the groom's relatives and friends are seated on the left side of the altar; the bride's on the right. A friend of both bride and groom is seated in the best available spot. The usher will extend his right arm to a female guest and escort her down the aisle to her seat; if she has a male escort, he walks a few steps behind. Sometimes the usher will simply say, *"Please follow me,"* and lead the way down the aisle, so a couple can walk together. He may let guests know that both families are sitting together in a spirit of unity; in this case, he will show the guest to the best available seat.

Is it appropriate for guests to talk before the ceremony? It is customary for guests and ushers to have a polite conversation in a low tone as they proceed down the aisle (see Chapter 6, "The Wedding Party"). Once in their seats, during the playing of the prelude, quiet talk with other guests is permitted until the wedding procession begins.

Are guests expected to participate in all religious ceremony rituals? A printed wedding program explaining all religious customs or details may be distributed by ushers to guests as they enter the church or synagogue (see Chapter 8, "Your Wedding Ceremony"). It is not necessary for guests to carry out unfamiliar rituals, especially if they are of a different faith and feel uncomfortable doing so. It is polite, however, to

guest ceremony tips

- Arrive 30 minutes before the ceremony begins.

- Tell the usher whether you are a friend or relative of the bride or groom.

- Take the usher's right arm (if you're a female), or follow behind (if you're a male), to pew indicated by the usher.

- Wait to file out of sanctuary after the recession until ushers direct your pew to leave.

- Pass through the receiving line—if it is directly after the ceremony—introducing yourself and stating your relationship to the couple.

follow the lead of the families seated in the front pews. Guests may stand when the families stand (in some religions, when the bride proceeds down the aisle), but may remain seated when others kneel. In Orthodox or Conservative Jewish congregations, all men cover their heads; married women may also choose to do so. It would be polite for a Christian man to accept the *yarmulke* (skullcap) and a married woman, the lace handkerchief with hairpin, distributed at the door. Women may also wear a hat; check with the bride's relatives to determine what's proper.

The bride and groom may request certain personalized rituals to be part of the ceremony—such as congregational hymn singing, or handshakes, and a brief greeting with the guests seated nearby. Guests should enter into the spirit of the occasion.

Is there a proper way to exit the sanctuary, after the wedding party walks up the aisle? After the recession, guests remain in their seats until the ushers have escorted the families of the bride and groom, including the grandmothers and other close relatives, out of the church or synagogue. Frequently, the ushers will indicate the time to leave by returning to stand at the sides of each pew, beginning at the front of the sanctuary, signaling guests to file out row by row. Should you need directions to the reception site, restrooms, and so on, the ushers are the best people to ask. If the receiving line is scheduled for right after the ceremony (often positioned in the vestibule of the house of worship or in the hallway of the hotel or banquet hall), guests will file out in an orderly manner, moving down the receiving line and greeting the newlyweds, their parents, and attendants (see Chapter 13, "Your Reception").

Reception Rituals

Must all guests walk through the receiving line? Yes. This is an excellent opportunity for each guest to greet and hug or shake hands with the newlyweds and their families (fathers and attendants may circulate), wish the couple well, and share the joy of the occasion (see Chapter 13, "Your Reception").

Is there any receiving-line etiquette of which a guest should be aware? If a guest does not personally know the bride's mother, he or she should introduce himself or herself to each person in the line. It's customary to make some remark about the wedding, the bride, or the newly married couple, depending on how well the guest knows the people involved: *"Hello, Mrs. Atkins. I'm Indira Shakib, Glenda's old friend from music camp. I really did enjoy the violin solo."* It was once traditional to congratulate the groom and to wish the bride happiness—since the groom "caught" the bride. Today, however, both husbands and wives will be happy to receive congratulations from their guests.

It's considerate to move quickly down the line so that others are not kept waiting. Women wearing gloves may remove them to shake hands, if desired.

When should guests sign the guest book? Once past the receiving line, guests sign the guestbook (or Bride's Book), which may be positioned near its end. Sometimes, the bride may position the guest book on a table in the room where the cocktail hour is held, or near the cake table in the reception room. Or, a bridesmaid or friend of the bride or groom may circulate throughout the cocktail hour and reception, asking guests to sign the guest book (see Chapter 13, "Your Reception").

Where do guests go after the receiving line? If there is a cocktail hour, guests go directly to that area. Or, the receiving line may be positioned in a corner of the room where cocktails are being served. If the receiving line was held in the church or synagogue vestibule, or on the steps, ushers will point the guests to the reception site. If the reception is to include a seated meal, guests may pick up an escort card with their name and table assignment on it from a table set up in the entry area of the reception site.

How will guests know when to take their seats in the reception room? Usually, the banquet manager or the waiters will personally approach guests and ask them to make their way into the reception room. At a seated luncheon or dinner (buffet or waiter service), guests should proceed to the table indicated on their escort card. At that table, place cards may indicate where they are to be seated. If the celebration is buffet service with unspecified seats, guests may proceed to the buffet line, then choose a seat at one of the unreserved tables. At a tea or cocktail reception, guests may serve themselves and circulate, introducing themselves to one another whenever necessary.

When is it appropriate for guests to begin dancing? At a very large reception, the father of the bride may see to it that dancing is well under way before the couple appear on the scene for their traditional first dance with each other and with their parents. At most weddings, however, the bride's father, a member of the wedding party, or the bandleader introduces the newlywed couple for their first dance after the receiving line and the cocktail buffet are over, and the couple have entered the room where the dinner will take place (see Chapter 13, "Your Reception"). After several stanzas of the song, the bride and groom may dance with their parents; next, the wedding party, and finally, all guests will be invited to join in the celebration. The band may wait, at the couple's request, to begin the music and dancing until the main course has been served, although this decision is not the best way to facilitate the mixing and meeting of guests.

What is the appropriate etiquette for guests' participation in the best man's toast? After the wedding party take their places at the bridal (or head) table, the best man will make the first toast, followed by a thank-you toast from the groom, and often the bride. Then other relatives and friends (probably the fathers and mothers first) may rise to make a good-natured toast to the couple. Every guest should rise and drink

guest reception tips

- If at the reception site, pass through the receiving line introducing yourself and stating your relationship to the couple.

- Introduce yourself to guests at your table, talking briefly to the person on your right and left, then to others at the table.

- Join other guests on the dance floor when invited to dance by the bandleader, or by friends.

- Rise and drink to each toast made to the couple at the reception.

- Dance and participate in the bouquet toss, or the garter toss—if you are single.

- Thank hosts before leaving the reception, and write a thank-you note the next day.

every toast (but not necessarily finish the glass), whether his or her beverage preference is champagne, iced tea, or ginger ale.

What are the other festivities that guests can expect at a wedding? Guests should enjoy themselves, which will make the party a success. They should talk to the people seated at their table (splitting their attention equally between the persons seated to their left and right, then talking to others at the table, introducing themselves and getting to know their table mates). If they are invited onto the dance floor for an ethnic dance or for a big-band swing medley, they should comply, and also should clear the dance floor when the time comes for the cake-cutting ceremony, as well as for special dances for the bride and her father, and the groom and his mother. Single female guests should gather together if asked to catch the bride's bouquet; single male guests should gather if asked to catch the bride's garter, removed and thrown by the groom.

When is it acceptable for a guest to leave the reception? Wedding receptions have no specified length, although four hours is about average. Traditionally, guests remain at least until the the bride and groom change, say good-bye, perhaps throw the bouquet and garter, and leave the reception. Today, however, most couples are choosing to stay until the party ends. (After all, many wedding guests travel from all over the country to see them, and the couple want to visit with them as long as they can.) If the couple do not seem to be in a rush to leave, it is acceptable for guests to depart any time after the cutting of the cake. (It is considered bad luck if a guest does not have at least a *taste* of the wedding cake!) Before leaving, guests should find a member of the bride's immediate family and thank them. (A guest might say, *"Thanks for a really enjoyable evening, Mrs. Atkins. It was a beautiful wedding."*) If a guest is not able to personally thank the wedding hosts, he or she should write the next day (perhaps phone, if a close relative or friend) to say that he or she had a wonderful time. Eventually, the wedding hosts will signal the end of the reception by ending the music (a last dance will be played), closing the bar, and preparing to leave themselves. (For more tips, see Appendix, under Chapter 18, "Wedding Guests.")

GOING AWAY

Traditionally, the bride and groom have been the first to leave the reception; their departure has signaled to guests that it is appropriate for them to leave, as well. However, today many couples live far away from the town in which they grew up, and many guests have traveled long distances to help them celebrate. Because of this, newlyweds often choose to stay till the end of the reception, continuing to visit with their guests.

If you do decide to linger, have attendants pass the word to your guests that the tossing of your bouquet is not a sign of your imminent departure. If you do not make a dramatic exit, it is appropriate for guests to begin to leave any time after the cutting and serving of the cake (see Chapter 13, "Your Reception").

Leaving the Reception

To leave your reception in the traditional way, about a half-hour before it ends, shortly after cutting the cake, the bride throws her bouquet, and the groom throws the bride's garter. (It's optional to have the single man who catches the garter slip it onto the single woman who catches the bouquet). The bride and groom then leave the room with their honor attendants to change into traveling outfits and dash out amid a shower of rice, birdseed, or potpourri (see Appendix, under Chapter 2, "Wedding Customs"). The couple leave in their getaway car, decorated by the ushers. Guests usually leave shortly after. Below, a going-away timetable:

Enjoy a last dance, about a half-hour before you leave (after cutting the cake). Begin saying good-bye to your guests.

Have bridesmaids pass the word that you are about to toss your bouquet. Ask the bandleader to announce what's going on to guests and play a musical fanfare. Single women should gather at a picturesque spot—under a balcony or at the bottom of a stairway.

With your back to the group, give the bouquet a good toss over your shoulder. Or, you may face the group and toss the bouquet to your sister or special friend. Tradition says that the woman who catches the bouquet will be the next to marry.

Stage a garter toss, if desired. The groom removes the garter from the bride's leg and either the bride or groom tosses it to the assembled group of single men. The recipient (who, legend has it, will be the next to wed) may then place it on the leg of the woman who caught the bridal bouquet.

Leave the room with your honor attendants to change into your going-away outfits. Your maid or matron of honor, or another friend or relative, should help—by making sure your going-away outfit is ready in a comfortable changing area, by unfastening hard-to-reach buttons, and by seeing that your wedding dress and accessories are safely stored while you are on your honeymoon. (The best man should assist the groom, take responsibility for returning his formalwear.) The going-away outfit can be a suit, dress, or pants ensemble suitable to your destination. Even if you're just going camping, wear something more stylish than jeans or sweatpants. It's a festive custom to wear a corsage of flowers or carry a miniature of your bridal bouquet (perhaps a pull-away bouquet detached from your

flowers before you toss them).

The best man will make sure all honeymoon luggage is safely stored in the getaway car. He will keep practical jokers away from the car, and make sure that no decorations obstruct the driver's vision or hamper his hearing. He will also hand the groom the car keys and plane or train tickets. While you're on your honeymoon, he and the maid or matron of honor can also assist by depositing endorsed gift checks.

Say a special good-bye to parents. Have attendants notify them that you are about to leave, so you have a chance to thank them and bid an affectionate farewell. When your groom has said his own goodbyes, he should come for you and thank your parents.

Dash to your getaway car under a shower of rice, seeds, or potpourri. Your child attendants and younger guests will enjoy distributing packets of rice, millet seed, safflower seed, birdseed, or potpourri for guests to toss in your direction. (Rice and grains are symbols of fertility and bounty and have been used in weddings for centuries; see Chapter 2, "Wedding Customs").

When your parents are ready to leave, they will signal the band to stop playing, and the bar to close. Guests take the cue and begin to leave. *Note*: Some families decided to pay the band overtime and keep the celebration going an extra hour. That's why it's important to write the overtime fee into your contract. Or, continue the party at a nearby home.

Staying at the Reception

Many brides and grooms choose to remain at the reception until the end, much as they would do if hosting a dinner party. Since many guests may feel they have to stay until you make a traditional departure:

Have attendants pass the word that you two will stay till the reception ends. Guests will then know they need not wait for your departure before leaving.

After the cake cutting, make a thank-you toast. Thank your guests for coming, and tell them that you two will be the last to leave because you are staying to visit longer with all of them.

When the party is over, the two of you can slip away in your gown and formal-wear or change into something more comfortable, depending on your plans. Some couples enjoy arriving at their wedding-night hotel in wedding attire; others prefer to arrive discreetly.

Attending Postwedding Parties

If you have organized a Long Weekend Wedding, with several parties scheduled throughout the weekend for long-distance guests, your wedding will probably not be the last occasion where you will see your friends and relatives. If this is the case:

Plan to leave the wedding reception whenever you wish, but show up at all other parties during the weekend. Pre- and postwedding parties during the weekend will allow you time to visit with all your faraway loved ones. You may not wish to stay for the entire length of time, but do show up at each one. The postwedding brunch (the morning after the wedding) is often when the newlyweds say a final good-bye before leaving for their honeymoon.

Decorating the Car

It's part of wedding lore: The bride and groom drive off in a car festooned with streamers, crepe paper, tin cans that clatter against the pavement, old shoes, flowers, and "Just Married" written in big letters on the back (see Chapter 2, "Wedding Customs"). Exactly how—and when—is the newlyweds' car bedecked? The light-hearted task of decorating the car belongs to the ushers, who do this job while you are enjoying your reception. If you will leave on your honeymoon in a borrowed or rented car, be sure to have your groom pass this helpful information to the ushers, so that decorations will be kept to a minimum. To keep decorations safe, also have your groom discuss these guidelines with the ushers:

car-decorating tips

Ushers must decorate carefully so as not to damage the car or obscure vision for driving:

- Avoid using tulips, or other flowers that may not hold up.

- Use masking or floral tape, or shoe polish. Avoid using glue, cellophane tape, rubber cement, paint, which can cause damage to the car's paint finish.

- Don't write or drape streamers, balloons, across windows; obstructed views are dangerous.

- If it looks like rain, steer clear of colored crepe paper, which might bleed.

- Be sure it's the right car!

creative getaways

Here, other unique ways to exit:

- hot-air balloon
- dogsled, skis
- horse and sleigh
- horse and buggy
- horseback
- canoe
- water or ski gondola
- rowboat
- sailboat
- motorboat
- riverboat
- bicycle built for two
- motorcycle
- fire truck
- Rollerblades
- antique car
- mobile home
- trolley
- cable car
- antique car
- helicopter
- in costumes, with musical serenade

Start with a "getaway kit" from party stores. These kits include crepe paper, signs, balloons. Perhaps wrap the car up as a gift with a big bow on top. Paint the newlyweds' first names and "Just Married" on a sign or write it with white shoe polish (which washes off with water—test it on a small area, first!) on the hood. Hang the cake topper in the window.

Check with limousine companies before the wedding. If you've hired a limousine, ask if they provide decorations.

Ask your florist to bedeck the car in advance. Many will provide special floral tape that won't mar the body of the car and metal clips for stringing garlands. Consider encircling the car with a garland of inexpensive blooms, such as carnations or the more flamboyant dendrobium orchids, that extends from the center hood to the trunk. Or, form a rainbow-style arc of colorful blossoms across the top of the windshield, leaving a clear view; a train of flowers and streamers that trail behind.

Renting a Limousine

For many couples, the stylish getaway vehicle of choice is a chauffeur-driven limousine. Contact an established, reputable limousine firm—your wedding is one day you can't afford a reckless or late driver, an unsightly or unsafe car.

Book a limousine six months before the wedding. Ask friends for recommendations; or find companies from the Yellow Pages under "Limousine Service" and ask them for references. To be sure you're dealing with a reputable firm, call the National Limousine Association (NLA) (see Appendix, under Chapter 19, "Going Away") and ask if the company is a member. (The NLA requires members to have proper licensing and insurance.) Call the local Better Business Bureau and Consumer Affairs Department to see if any complaints have been registered against the companies you're considering.

Visit several companies. Read their insurance policy; is it valid, up-to-date? Ask to see their license, NLA logo.

Examine the cars. Do they have livery plates? This means they are properly licensed by the state or municipal agency. Look for a sturdy steel body (not fiberglass); shatterproof windows (marked with a visible stamp); seat belts in back and front seats. What is the make, model, year of cars?

If there are few cars, or you're told the cars are out, it may mean the company doesn't own their vehicles. If they're renting them from other firms, this may increase your chance of not getting what you ask for, or being left waiting on wedding day.

Meet the driver. Ask to see his or her driver's license; the back should indicate how many points (moving violations) there are against his or her driving record. Has the driver had any serious accidents? Inquire about his or her driving record. Specify how he or she should dress. Ask for a driver who knows the area. (Send written instructions, maps, and phone numbers to the company one month in advance.) *Note*: Never ride with a driver who appears to have been drinking or using drugs, and don't offer your driver a drink when celebrating.

Decide how many cars you'll need. Traditionally, one limousine transports the bride and her father to the ceremony site, while one or more limousines (or sedans, which seat two in back comfortably, one in front) transport your bridesmaids and mother. Additional cars (or sedans) can drive members of the groom's family, and ushers. After the ceremony and reception, the bride and groom ride in the limousine in which the bride and her father arrived. (A *formal limousine* seats four people, so the maid of honor and best man *could* join the newlyweds. A *stretch limousine* allows for six to ten people.)

Cost-cutting tips: Most companies have a one- or two-hour minimum. Don't keep a limousine on call; you'll just pay for the driver's waiting time during the reception. Instead, hire one limo to take you to the ceremony and reception; another for leaving the reception. Or, just hire two limousines: one each for the bride's and groom's families. Ask attendants to drive their own cars to the ceremony; later, the two limousines can shuttle attendants from ceremony to reception and back. Also ask about special wedding packages, the different cars available (e.g., a luxury stretch limousine costs more to rent than a corporate stretch limousine). Are extra amenities—sunroof, bar, tinted windows, VCR, TV—necessary after the reception? Finally, let companies know you're comparison shopping; ask if there are any considerations they can extend.

Sign a contract or letter of agreement. Once you choose your limousine company, get the details in writing, either in a standard contract or a letter you write and have the company manager sign. Read the fine print. The bill may be based on a minimum number of hours and may or may not include the standard fifteen percent gratuity; ask. Put down the smallest deposit possible (twenty to twenty-five percent) to minimize loss if the firm goes out of business, or provides inadequate service. If balance is due on wedding day, assign an attendant to deliver it. (Allow extra cash for gratuity—if service is great.)

limousine-contract tips

Include the following:

- total cost—deposit; balance (is gratuity included in fee?); payment schedule; extra fees for tolls, parking, travel time, overtime, cleaning up (rice, spills)

- date and times

- pickup locations, destinations, whether drivers should wait at each site or return

- make, model, year, color, license-plate number of car

- amenities—decorations, TV, VCR, stereo, FM-radio, bar, air conditioner, champagne, sunroof, phone, umbrellas

- cancellation and refund policies (what happens if the car breaks down? if features contracted for are missing? if you or they must cancel?)

- driver's name; backup driver in case of emergency

- driver's attire (suit and tie, tuxedo, or uniform?)

- driver's duties—buff car before reception, assist elderly guests

- safety guarantees (e.g., the car will be steel-sided, not fiberglass)

Having Your Friends Drive

Friends can help drive out-of-town guests, elderly guests, or the wedding party to the wedding and ceremony sites (if you choose not to use a limousine company). Thank your drivers by paying for a tank of gas, a car wash, and perhaps give each a gift (e.g., theater tickets, engraved key rings).

Contact local rental-car firms. Consider renting cars for friends to drive. Car rentals are usually on a twenty-four-hour basis. Several cars of the same model and color will add a more uniform look to wedding vehicles. Be sure to familiarize your drivers with times, passengers, and locations.

Perhaps rent a mini-van to transport the wedding party; an English double-decker bus for out-of-town guests. Inquire about renting sports cars, antique cars, for yourselves and the wedding party. Remember, however, that sports cars may lack trunk space. Antique cars may have a diminished speed capacity;

budget in extra time to get from home to ceremony, ceremony to reception!

(You must be twenty-one to rent a car; twenty-five to rent some specialty cars. A driver's license is required, as is a major credit card—it will be punched in on a credit slip—as insurance that you'll return the car and pay the fee. For exotic cars, a loss/ damage waiver—which says the renter pays for any damage done to the car—may be mandatory; standard auto insurance won't cover damage to a very expensive car. (Some credit cards do cover auto insurance when the card holder rents a car; ask if this is true for your card.)

honeymoon spicers

- breakfast in bed
- flowers placed on pillow at turndown
- room service and candlelight
- champagne lunch on a balcony
- bubble baths with candles
- coupons for sexual favors (written out by one partner for the other)
- love notes in bottles found on the beach
- love notes tucked in towels

The First Night

Years ago, weddings were in the morning, followed by a simple lunch or even breakfast, giving the newlyweds a chance to get a good start on honeymoon travels. Now wedding receptions are later and longer, and many couples stay till the end. Since most newlyweds leave on flights the next morning, they spend their first married night together in a hotel room or at home. If you and your groom have been living together, the idea of returning to the comforts of your own apartment before leaving on a trip can seem appealing and practical, months before wedding day. On your wedding day, though, you are likely to want to make your first night of marriage festive—and special. Even if you are in familiar surroundings, be carried over the threshold, as brides have been for centuries (see Chapter 2, "Wedding Customs"), surround yourselves with flowers, candlelight, and champagne.

Sexpectations

It will be hard to face the most meaningful sexual encounter of your lives right after the emotional roller coaster of your wedding and hours of traveling. If something wonderful happens the first night, great! If you just collapse into bed and pass out, that's okay, too. Realize that this is just the first of many nights together, or the continuation of what is

already a satisfying relationship.

The second day of your marriage may be filled with the excitement of exploring your honeymoon resort. You may overdose on hiking, tennis, beach walks, sailing, sumptuous buffets, dancing.

By day three, you'll finally realize that you're married. You'll both unwind, relax, and have time for hours of leisurely time together.

Traveling Together

You may envision your honeymoon as non-stop bliss, but like any trip it can have its ups and downs. If you anticipate the quiet or tense moments and handle them with humor and understanding, your honeymoon will flow smoothly.

Different styles. You have two bulging suitcases with every possible outfit; he seems to get by on a tote bag with a few shirts and changes of underwear. You insist on getting to the airport at least an hour before your flight leaves; he likes to dash in a few minutes before departure. While these travel-style differences may drive you crazy, try not to criticize. Compromise: Maybe you can make do with one sweater instead of three; perhaps getting to the airport with time to spare isn't such a bad idea.

Scheduling standoffs. He always wants to be doing something: golf, tennis, windsurfing. You treasure long walks holding hands, two-hour lunches, leisurely interludes in bed. A honeymoon doesn't mean you have to be together constantly. Now, and in the future, you won't always want to do the same things at the same time. Talk things out and reach compromises: He might windsurf while you shop; then meet for lunch to share your experiences.

Disappearing dialogue. What if you're at a romantic meal and can't think of anything to talk about? Don't worry. Quiet companionship is fine, too. At home, you're apart most of the day, so there's catching up to do. After a few days and nights together, you may not have dozens of things to tell each other. Why not invite another couple you meet to join you for a meal or a drink. This is the beginning of married social life.

honeymoon tips

- Purchase the lowest refundable fare if plans are tentative.

- Book *nonstop* flights—no stops or plane changes (*direct* flights land at airports along the way; *connecting* flights require plane changes—more chance for missed flights, lost luggage; *charter* flights are a bargain, but might be delayed, canceled.

- On a cruise, ask about cabin sizes, prices; if beds are doubles or bunks.

- If renting a car, reserve early for the model of choice; specify *automatic* or *shift*; ask about hidden expenses (e.g., rate per mile, insurance, tax, gas, one-way rental). Will car insurance, credit-card limit cover rentals?

Honeymoon Travel Plans

It's never too early to start planning your honeymoon—the best travel buys go quickly, and many popular destinations are booked a year in advance. Shortly after your engagement, set time aside to discuss your dreams, your time frame, your budget. Compile travel articles from BRIDE'S and travel magazines, consult guidebooks (borrow from the library till you know where you're going), and review newspaper travel sections. Once you've narrowed your destination choices to two or three, it's time to call or visit a travel agent (at least nine months before the wedding). He or she can guide you through the rest of the planning—from plane tickets and hotel reservations to rental car.

How do we find the right travel agent? Your best bet is a personal recommendation. Also scan the Yellow Pages for members of the American Society of Travel Agents (ASTA), or contact ASTA (see Appendix, under Chapter 19, "Going Away"), for a list of members near you. Remember that some agencies have specialties: cruises, ski packages, adventure trips. Look for someone who is experienced, who will listen to your needs, and shop around for the best rates.

Can we just leave everything to the travel agent? A travel agent can simplify things a lot for you, but she or he is not a mind reader, and you must take some responsibility for yourself. Meet with the agent in person and set the budget, detail the types of sports and leisure-time pursuits you both enjoy, whether you prefer city or country-side, luxury resort or quaint inn, sight-seeing or relaxing. Also make decisions early enough to take advantage of lower airfares, and packages. The agent can book airline, cruise, or train tickets, accommodations, car rentals, sight-seeing tours, package deals. Once your trip is booked, you should ask the agent for a written room confirmation from the hotel (which you should carry with you) and itinerary; reconfirm your own flights before you leave and before you return.

What's the most important item in our travel budget? Your hotel and/or airfare. After you decide on the total sum you can spend, make a list of all it must cover: plane tickets, hotel, meals, rental car, cocktails, tips, gifts. Research all costs before you go, from the price of a taxi between airport and hotel to the cost of a helicopter ride, sailboat rental, tennis lessons, admissions fees to museums or clubs. In most cases, you will save time and money by working with a travel agent (their services are usually free to you—they are paid commissions by airlines and hotels).

Will we need special travel documents? Ask your travel agent to fill you in on the requirements for your destination. If you plan to travel to a foreign country (except Canada, Mexico, and some parts of the Caribbean), you'll need a passport. You can apply for passports at county clerk's offices, authorized post offices, or federal passport offices. Each of you should bring along proof of citizenship (birth or natural-ization certificate), proof of identity (driver's license), two identical 2x2-inch head-shot photographs, and cash or a check to pay the fee (about $42). Allow about a month to receive the passport. In lieu of a passport, Mexico and some Caribbean countries now require just a photo ID—usually a driver's license and perhaps one other proof of U.S. citizenship, such as a voter-registration card. Other destinations, such as Jamaica, may require proof of citizenship (e.g., a birth certificate, voter-registration card), instead of a passport. Check the requirements of the country you are traveling to, as well as those of any other countries you may visit.

A passport cannot be obtained in your married name before your wedding. Travel-er's checks, international airline tickets, and visas should be issued in your maiden name. Hotel reservations and domestic airline tickets, however, can be reserved in your married name. Carry a copy of your marriage license with you just in case someone questions discrepencies. For instance, in some countries, a couple traveling together may not be allowed to share a room without proof of marriage. Mention this to

*honeymoon
budget
tips*

- Investigate off-season rates.

- Ask about special rates available (e.g., because hotel is under construction, it's hurricane season).

- Consider package tours.

- Book hotel, airfare/cruise, car rental at same time—and early.

- Turn in frequent-flier miles early; leave time to receive discount coupons.

- Check exchange rates.

- Use travel discounts available through professional memberships.

- Watch out for offers that seem "too good to be true."

- Mention that you are honeymooners.

your clergymember if you will have to arrange to photocopy the marriage certificate after the ceremony. With proof of your marriage, you can visit the local American embassy and have your passport adjusted to indicate your new marital status.

Immunizations against diseases may be required or recommended if you're traveling outside North America, Hawaii, the Caribbean, or Europe. Ask your doctor or call the International Travelers Hotline, Quarantine Division/Travelers Health Section of the Centers for Disease Control in Atlanta, Georgia, or Travel Health Services in New York, New York (see Appendix, under Chapter 19, "Going Away"). While this may seem like a lot of paperwork, your travel agent will help by finding out exactly what documents you need and what the deadlines are.

Should we buy trip insurance? It's always a good idea. If bad weather delays your flight and the ship sails without you, you'll be reimbursed. If a broken bone sidelines you from a white-water rafting adventure, you'll also be glad you bought trip insurance, which covers you against trip delay or cancellation, as well as for lost, stolen, or delayed luggage. It also provides emergency assistance—even medical evacuation. First, confirm the coverage provided by your home policy and through credit cards. Then, contact your travel agent or a reputable insurance company if you need additional insurance (see Appendix, under Chapter 4, "Planning Your Wedding").

How do we turn frequent-flier miles into a honeymoon trip? If you've been stockpiling frequent-flier miles (a minimum of twenty thousand on any one carrier), at least one of you can probably fly for free, perhaps with a discount on a rental car or hotel, too. Ask your airline or travel agent about blackout dates and other restrictions.

Is it true we can save money in the off-season? In the off-season, hotels discount their rates by as much as forty percent, and may offer off-season bargain packages (with meals, sight-seeing excursions, rental car) that are unavailable at other times. In the Caribbean, Mexico, and Florida, the low season is summer (generally April 15 to November 15). Even though these tropical resorts can be delightful in June, it's in winter (high season) that travelers will pay top dollar for sun and sand. In subtropical Bermuda, where winters can be cool, low season extends from fall until spring. *Note*: Hawaiian honeymoons are in demand year-round; resorts there generally do not offer seasonal rates. Going to Europe in March or October may be less expensive than in July. Ski resorts, off-season, provide great horseback riding and mountain climbing; contact chambers of commerce to inquire about regional events and arts festivals.

How can we cut costs when planning our honeymoon? Consider a travel agency with a wedding registry; then guests can make gift donations toward your trip (gift cards will not list monetary amounts). (See Appendix, under Chapter 19, "Going Away".) Also ask your travel agent about prepackaged tours, which include airfare, hotel, food, and sight-seeing. With so many hotels now vying for your business, there are often special rates that may be available at any time. Cruises are also a good value; they include food, entertainment, several destinations (see Appendix, under Chapter 19, "Going Away"). Decide early and take advantage of early-booking bonuses (e.g., cash discounts, free rental cars, extra land tours). Traveling off-season will also stretch your budget (see "Honeymoon Budget Tips" box). For greater discounts, book airfare, rental car, and hotel at one time. Also check your organization memberships, which may lower your car and hotel rates; tell your travel agent which alumni groups, professional organizations, groups such as the American Automobile Association (AAA), you belong to. Turn in your frequent-flier miles early, since it can take four weeks to receive discount-ticket coupons. And wherever you travel, tell hotel management that you're honeymooning; they may upgrade your room, or offer champagne, chocolates, etc.

Is it vital to be right on the ocean, or could you save significantly by staying in a hotel with a short walk to the beach? Could you save money by renting a condo with a small kitchen and having some of your meals there? Also have your travel agent ask if the hotel is offering any special rates. Often, if a resort is under construction, it will offer lower rates during the duration. If you don't mind the inconvenience, it can be a cost-effective way to honeymoon.

If you travel abroad, check exchange rates first. Change only a small amount of money before you go; you'll get the best exchange rate at a bank once you arrive. (*Note*: Hotels offer the *least* favorable rate of exchange.) To get the allure of foreign destinations right here in the United States, investigate weekend packages offered by city hotels. Some chains feature theme rooms—you might sleep in an igloo with a faux bearskin rug!

Honeymoon Travel Checklist

Nine to twelve months before wedding: With fiancé, find a travel agent, discuss honeymoon plans, make airline and hotel reservations.

Three months before wedding: Get passports and other documents; make a copy of each and pack them separately. Get any inoculations required by your destination. Research doctors who speak English in your host country (see "Honeymoon Health" section). Finalize all reservations. Shop for any clothes you'll need for the honeymoon.

Ten days before wedding: Pick up all tickets, transfer coupons, hotel confirmations, sight-seeing vouchers, etc., from travel agent. Read them carefully right away so the agent will have time to correct any mistakes. Buy traveler's checks; make copies and pack separately. Refill prescriptions and pack in original bottles *with* prescriptions.

Three days before wedding: Pack suitcases. Reconfirm overseas flights. Domestic flights can be reconfirmed twenty-four hours in advance.

Honeymoon Health

It's your worst nightmare: sick on your honeymoon. Fortunately, most travel-related illness are short-lived, and many can be prevented.

Don't drink the water. To head off traveler's diarrhea and the nausea, cramps, and other symptoms that result, avoid tap water and ice in certain tropical areas (such as Mexico), and in rural areas of many foreign countries. Stick with bottled water, hot coffee or tea, sodas or other bottled beverages. Bring along an anti-diarrhea medicine, such as Imodium or Lomotil, just in case.

Make sure meals are served piping hot. Since contaminated food can trigger stomach problems, be sure meals are served hot. It's fine to eat breads, peelable fruits, but avoid melons—which may be filled with water to increase weight—and avoid raw vegetables, guacamole, and dairy products. To stave off digestive disorders, take two Pepto-Bismol tablets (or another anti-nausea medication) with meals, plus two at bedtime (you can safely take this dosage for up to three weeks).

Use a sunscreen. While you may think you look better with a little color, it's very easy to overdo sun exposure in tropical climates, even if you're just out shopping. Use a sunscreen with an Sun Protection Factor (SPF) of 15 or more, and a pair of UV-protective sunglasses in any warm-weather spot. Try to stay out of the sun during the time of the day when rays are strongest (between 11 a.m. and 3 p.m.). Schedule museum visits, van tours during those hours.

Soothe "honeymoon cystitis," what is medically called a urinary-tract infection. Since this infection is more common during periods of increased sexual activity, such as a honeymoon, ask your gynecologist to prescribe medication, and pack it, just in case. (Common symptoms are burning during urination, and increased frequency of urination; in bad cases, blood in the urine.)

Prepare ahead for motion sickness. Island-hopping or cruising? Pack anti-nausea pills, such as Dramamine, Bonine, or Travel Garde acupressure cloth wristbands to help prevent motion sickness from ruining the trip.

Guard against bugs. If you plan to golf, or will be in humid climate, bring along insect repellent to ward off mosquitoes.

Guard against allergies. Pack any allergy medications you normally take in their original bottles. The newest prescription antihistamines do not cause drowsiness and won't interfere with honeymoon activities.

If you become ill while traveling abroad, ask your hotel, the U.S. embassy or consulate, for a referral of a doctor who speaks English. Before you leave, write to the International Association for Medical Assistance to Travelers for a list of doctors overseas (see Appendix, under Chapter 19, "Going Away").

portable medicine chest

Drugs made overseas may vary in strength and quality from those back home. Pack your own:

- prescription medications in original bottles (to avoid customs hassles). Pack in carryon for safety; take all prescriptions with you.
- cold remedies
- antiseptic
- anti-itch ointment anti-bacterial ointment
- extra birth control
- pain relievers
- bandages
- thermometer
- spare eyeglasses
- bug spray

Travel Dilemmas

I want to go to the beach; he wants to ski. What should we do? The secret is compromise. Will he settle for water-skiing? If he's firm about downhill skiing, try to work in some of your favorite things, too. Agree that you'll ski mornings, then spend the afternoon together shopping, hot-tubbing, getting to know your fireplace. Or, do a "sea and ski" honeymoon—one week in a warm climate, the next week at a ski resort.

My fiancé wants to plan a surprise honeymoon for me, but I'm worried I won't pack the right things. Any ideas? Make sure the surprise doesn't go sour; ask him to tell you what type of destination you're heading for (tropical island, big city, etc.), what temperatures to pack for, how formal or casual it is. Or, have him confide in your maid of honor, who can steer you in the right direction.

We're honeymooning at my parents' Florida condo, which fits our budget. How can we make the trip special? With the money you'll save, try to make this a completely different honeymoon. Why not travel by train—a romantic journey? Once you arrive, arrange an elaborate beach picnic, fill the place with a rainbow of flowers, eat out every night. Rent a convertible! Put a "Do Not Disturb" sign on the door!

What if we lose our plane/train/cruise tickets? Tickets are as good as cash, so act quickly. Call your travel agent—he or she may be able to get new tickets delivered, even to your hotel. If you're already at the airport, airlines will ask you to file a lost-ticket claim, buy new tickets, and they will refund your money within ninety days if no one finds and uses the originals. (It's wise to keep a copy of your plane tickets. Then you can call the airline and report the specific ticket number lost; airline officials may be able to intercept the ticket if someone tries to use or change it, although it is difficult to monitor ticket usage on domestic flights.) If you have proof of purchase (e.g., a credit-card receipt), an airline ticket-agent or his or her manager may re-issue the tickets for you (each airline's policy varies).

On Amtrak, and all trains, tickets are viewed like cash; if you lose them, they're gone! (You'll have to repurchase them at full cost.)

For cruise tickets, find the company representative at the pier. Since a room has been reserved in your name, if you provide identification, he or she should be able to issue a new ticket with little trouble.

What if we miss the plane/train/boat? Phone ahead, if possible. Airlines will re-book you on the next available flight, even on another airline, and accept the tickets you hold. (If you had nonrefundable tickets, there might be a nominal additional fee.)

Amtrak and most railroad companies will book you on the next available train.

An agent of a cruise line or the local port authority will tell you whether it's possible to charter a launch if the ship is still in sight, or how to fly to meet it.

What if our luggage doesn't show up after our flight or in our room on a cruise?
Some luggage mishaps can be prevented by attaching indestructible identification tags on the outside of bags; enclosing identification cards inside luggage, as well; making sure luggage is tagged for the correct destination by the airline when you check in. Also get to the baggage-claim area promptly to minimize the likelihood that bags might be stolen off the carousel. (Tie ribbon to the handles to ensure that they're easy to spot.)

If your luggage doesn't show up on the carousel, tell the representative in the baggage office at the airport and present your luggage-check tags. You'll be asked to fill out a form describing the pieces to help airline personnel conduct a search. In nearly all cases, the bags will arrive on the next flight or within twenty-four hours; the airlines will transport them to your hotel. If they still don't turn up, you'll need to describe the bags' apprearance clearly; the airlines then tap into a computerized network that matches stray bags with their owners. If the bags still don't surface, you'll need to describe the contents in detail; the airlines will reimburse each individual $1,250. (You must provide sales slips for any big-ticket items lost.) The airlines will also provide varying amounts of money to cover any expenses you incur while buying the necessities you need.

While it's rare that cruise companies lose luggage, report any missing bags to the ship's purser. Slip-ups can occur with air-to-sea transfers. Personnel from the ship can search the airport for passengers' luggage as soon as it's reported missing. Use the color-coded luggage tags provided by your cruise company. If there's a delay in getting luggage to you, the cruise company should provide funds to enable you to buy essentials; if bags are never located, they will reimburse you $300 per person.

What if we arrive at a hotel and they don't have a room for us? Here's where it helps to have a written confirmation of your reservation. When you present a confirmation number, the hotel is obligated to find a way to accommodate you—either by upgrading you to a better room or by finding you a room at an equivalent hotel nearby and providing transportation to it.

What if the room is not what we wanted? (There are twin beds, no view, it's too dark, or too cold.) Call the assistant manager or front desk, tell him or her the problem, and ask politely but firmly to be moved. In many cases, you can be moved or the problem fixed. It can't hurt to add that you are honeymooners.

What if the resort is not the way it was described in the brochure? Brochures alone may not tell the true story. Rely on personal referrals from friends, a travel agent, or a reputable magazine. For example, *on the water* might mean a waterway separates hotel and beach. *Traditional* may translate to dated, not quaint. *Deluxe* may be the smallest room, while *junior suite* and *grand-luxe* are more spacious. Ask for specifics on room size, view; on-site facilities; location of beach; restaurants; nightlife.

Also be aware that new resorts and hotels may need up to a year to perfect operations. Research the site carefully before you book. Are rooms fully furnished? Are electricity, hot water, connected? Are sports facilities operating smoothly? Are restaurants open? Similar to working with any contractor, the date of project completion may often be behind schedule; expect up to a six-month delay. Do check if the hotel is offering any special low rates during construction; you should not have to pay full price for diminished services.

When traveling, it's always wise to budget several hundred dollars extra to allow for emergencies where you have to change hotels. (The general rule is to allow at least ten percent extra for the unexpected—the dress that needs dry-cleaning, the muffler that needs repair, the illness that necessitates a doctor's visit. For this reason, too, it's also wise to leave with all of your credit-card bills paid, so that you have the maximum credit limit available to you. Often, a credit card gets a couple through an unpleasant situation; new accommodations can be billed to your account. (Before you have to pay the bill, previous reservations canceled or altered will be credited to your account.) Billing your honeymoon accommodations to your credit card will also give you recourse if there is a problem during your stay.

What if one of us gets seriously ill? Many hotels have doctors on call (English-speaking in foreign countries) who can come to your room. Some credit-card companies can also put card holders in touch with local physicians. If you have a pre-existing health problem, such as diabetes or asthma, you may want to research doctors and health facilities and consult your own doctor before you leave (see " Honeymoon Health" section).

What if we lose our passports? Look around very carefully, then report the loss to the nearest U.S. embassy, and they will instruct you. It will help to have your passport number, date, and place of issue in a safe place, separate from your passport. It also helps to bring along a photocopy of the passport, packed separately from the passport.

What if we run out of money? A hotel may agree to send all or part of your bill home. Hotels can often cash checks for small to moderate amounts.

If you're in a foreign country and funds are getting low, call your hometown bank and arrange for an international draft in the local currency. You may also be able to use automatic-teller (ATM) cards around the world.

How to Pack

Less is more when packing for a honeymoon. You won't want to be burdened with too much luggage. (Remember, you *can* do laundry while traveling.) To get the most into the least space, follow these tips (see Appendix, under Chapter 19, "Going Away"):

Pack heavy things first. Place shoes, hair dryer, travel iron, next to the hinge of the suitcase.

Make a layer of no-wrinkle items. Pack jeans, sweaters, underwear. Fill empty spaces with socks or panties. Stuff belts and jewelry into shoes.

Pack everything that requires careful folding next. Layer in dresses, slacks, skirts, and blouses. Make as few folds as possible. Put plastic bags between layers to cushion against wrinkles; the bags can be used on your trip home for damp swimsuits, dirty laundry.

Pack a collapsible suitcase. This will be useful for carrying souvenirs home.

Pack the items you'll need first, last. On top of your suitcase, pack your nightgown, toiletry case, perhaps shorts and T-shirt, a dinner outfit.

Travel Protocol

There used to be a strict code of etiquette for behavior aboard ships, trains, and airplanes. Today, however, common courtesy is the only thing you really need observe (see Appendix, under Chapter 19, "Going Away"). And, pay attention to the following:

Air travel. Allow plenty of time for travel to the airport, checking luggage, and re-checking seat assignments (you'd hate to be seated three rows apart on your honeymoon!). Also make any requests early for vegetarian, salt-free, or kosher meals. (To get your honeymoon off to a sparkling start, you might also request on-board champagne. Tip skycaps, curbside attendants, taxi drivers, for each bag they handle (see "Honeymoon Tipping" chart).

If your flight is delayed or canceled, which in turn affects your connections, or if your luggage is lost, ask to see a special-service representative and ask him or her to arrange lodging, a new flight, money for replacement clothes.

Train travel. On overnight train trips, tip the porter each night for making up your berth and for wake-up calls.

Cruise lines. It's customary to find out where you are seated for dinner as soon as possible and to request any table changes within two days after arrival; tip the steward for this service. On board a commercial ship, except for captains and doctors with professional titles, all personnel are addressed as "Mr.," (or "Miss," "Mrs.," or "Ms.").

Hotels. Your groom may sign the register for you both, although the hotel may ask for the first names of the husband and wife ("Mrs. Shirley Moore" and "Mr. Russell Moore"). Don't be afraid to say you are newlyweds; you may get special treatment (complimentary champagne or cocktails, fruit, candy, or flowers).

Tip the bellman for carrying suitcases to your room. Any problems with the room should be directed to the assistant manager or manager at the front desk.

carry-on items

Don't check essential items! Pack them in a carry-on and take them with you on the plane—just in case other luggage is lost or delayed. Include:

- tickets and copies
- passports, visas, other proof of citizenship (and photocopies)
- driver's licenses (and photocopies)
- address book
- itinerary with phone numbers
- hotel, car-rental confirmations
- cash for taxis, tipping, small purchases
- traveler's checks, major credit cards (write numbers down and pack separately)
- birth control, prescription drugs
- good jewelry (pack the minimum)
- camera, film
- house (car) keys
- change of clothes, underwear, socks
- swimsuit, coverup, sunscreen
- glasses, sunglasses, contact-lens case, solution
- copies of all documents, numbers of traveler's checks, credit cards, separately.

Honeymoon Tipping

WHOM TO TIP	HOW MUCH TO TIP	WHEN TO TIP
AIRPORT		
Porter	$1.00 per bag	Delivery of luggage to check-in or curb
SHIP		
Cabin/Dining Room Stewards	$2.50–$3.00 each per day, per person	End of voyage
Busboy	$1.50–$2.00 per day, per person	End of voyage
Bar & Lounge Stewards	15–20% of bill	With each bill
TRAIN		
Redcap	$1.00 per bag	When service is performed
Cabin Steward	$5.00 per person, per night	Each night
Dining Car Waiters*	15–20% of bill	Each meal
HOTEL		
Bellboy	$1.00 per bag, plus $1.00 for hospitable gestures—opening windows, turning on lights	When service is delivered
Chambermaid	$1.00 for each service (minimum $5.00 per couple, per week)	Each time service is delivered (a new maid may be assigned)
Doorman	$1.00 per bag; $1.00 for hailing taxi	When service is delivered
Headwaiter	$5.00 per week for special service	Upon first visit
Waiter	15–20% of bill when no service charge; 5% of bill with service fee	Each meal
Room-Service Waiter	15–20% of the cost of the meal (excluding the room-service charge)	Each meal
TAXI		
Driver	15–20% for good service	Completion of ride
INSTRUCTORS		
Water Skiing, Horseback Riding, etc.	15–20% of bill (unless they own the business)	End of lesson
GOLF		
Caddie	30% over the caddie fee with good service	End of 18th hole
BUS		
Tour Guide	$5.00 per couple, per half day	End of ride

*When meals are included in fare, tip of $5.00 per person, per day is acceptable.

Often, the housekeeping department can handle requests for smaller things, such as extra pillows, towels, blankets, hair-dryers. Unless service is included in the total bill, leave a tip each day on the pillow for the person who straightens up your room. (Because staff assignments rotate daily, waiting until the end of your visit to tip in a lump sum means the appropriate people may not be remembered.) However, if service is included, extra tipping is not necessary until the end of your stay.

To save time when checking out, you can call the front desk in advance to have them prepare your bill; call the bell desk when your luggage is ready and a bellman will appear shortly to help. Double-check the room—any balconies or terraces, and bathroom—to make sure you have all your belongings.

Foreign countries. Master the native words for "please" and "thank-you"; it may improve the service received. Always tip in the local currency. Ask if restaurants include gratuities in bill.

Honeymoon tipping. Decisions about tipping can be embarrassing and confusing. (See "Honeymoon Tipping" chart; factors such as quality of service and the economy of the country you visit should be considered.)

Coming Home

Once again, you may want to repeat the wedding custom of the bride being carried over the threshold of her new home by her husband (see Chapter 2, "Wedding Customs"). This custom dates from a time when it was thought that carrying the bride would prevent the evil spirits that lurked around doorways from entering through the soles of her feet. Carrying the bride over the threshold ensured future good luck.

The threshold gift. Jewish parents or close friends of the married couple may observe the tradition of the *threshold gift*. Candles, bread, and salt are brought to the new home to express the wish that there may always be light, joy, and plenty to eat in the home.

Visiting around. In the Amish community, newlywed couples spend the first several months of married life visiting family and friends. Indeed, some non-Amish couples tack a few extra days on their honeymoon to visit relatives or friends who couldn't attend the wedding.

Newlywed Checklist

Once you're home from your honeymoon and ready to start married life, you'll find that there are still some postwedding plans and tasks to take care of. Some of these things can be delegated to friends and relatives. Others can be accomplished during the first few months. Settle in and follow this checklist:

Say thanks for wedding help. Call or write to attendants, clergymembers, others who made your wedding special.

Write thank-you notes. Every gift should receive a prompt handwritten thank-you note, even if you thanked the giver at the wedding (see Chapter 17, "Wedding Gifts" and Appendix, under Chapter 17).

Preserve your wedding dress. Have your gown, veil, and headpiece professionally dry-cleaned (see Chapter 7, "Wedding Clothes"). Inquire about various storage methods with those who specialize in wedding-dress care (see Appendix, under Chapter 7, "Wedding Clothes," for source).

If you'll change your name once you're married, change it on all documents, if you haven't already done so. (See Chapter 4, "Planning Your Wedding," "The Name Decision" section.)

Update financial records. Deposit wedding-gift checks, bonds, stock certificates (if not already done by attendants). Pay outstanding wedding bills. Discuss a home budget, savings plan, checking accounts (joint or separate?). Set up a home-filing system.

Evaluate insurance needs. Health, car, and life insurance may have be adjusted to reflect your married status. Have wedding gifts appraised and insured. Consult insurance agent if necessary.

Unpack, exchange, and store wedding gifts. Consider giver's feelings before exchanging gifts.

Select photographs, review video. Have any film taken at wedding and on honeymoon developed. Review photographer's wedding proofs; review wedding video to determine edited length and special editing techniques. Choose photos for wedding album and order wedding prints for yourselves, relatives, and friends. Put other photos in albums.

Invite family and friends to your home. Plan some time shortly after your honeymoon to get together with attendants, friends, and family members to show them your honeymoon photos and video, your home with their wedding gifts on display. (Bring back some duty-free Caribbean rum for piña coladas; French chocolates to share your honeymoon magic.) Don't delay these gatherings; even if there are still a few unpacked boxes, everyone will want to see you and share your happiness!

REAFFIRMATION

Reaffirming your wedding vows is a memorable way to pledge your lasting commitment to one another all over again. The reaffirmation, while solemn, is not a legal act, so this time you won't need a license, certificate, or blood test. If you want the reaffirmation ceremony to be in a church or synagogue, however, you will need a clergymember to sanction your vows. While the reaffirmation may include many elements of your first wedding, the emphasis now is on the two of you and the personal things that have made your marriage so special.

Why a Reaffirmation?

There are many reasons couples decide to reaffirm their marriage vows, and each will influence the style of the reaffirmation service and celebration.

The first ceremony was a civil ceremony, or the couple eloped. Perhaps this was due to religious differences, pregnancy, or a difficult divorce. Now, days, months, or even years later, wanting their religion's blessing of their earlier marriage, they may find their church more accepting, even eager to create a private chapel service or to include their reaffirmation in a Sunday church or Friday evening synagogue service. Friends and family will attend this time.

The couple wish to mark a milestone in their relationship. On their fifteenth—or fiftieth—anniversary, they are proud to announce that they still want to be married to the person their spouse has become. Or, perhaps they want to mark the birth of a long-awaited child, a long-strived-for graduation. This couple can repeat the same vows they spoke long ago, or write new ones that express how their feelings have grown, with new words about family, health, and their

Today, it is not uncommon to read announcements of reaffirmations in newspapers. Tips for reaffirming couples:

- Call the lifestyle editors of local newspapers to ask if reaffirmation news should be submitted on the standard wedding announcement forms.

- If not, write the news up as a press release, telling why the decision was made to have a reaffirmation, how it was planned. If reaffirmations are uncommon in that area, it may be reported as a feature story.

- Include the same details found in a wedding announcement (see Chapter 16, "Photography, Videography, & Publicity").

- Add the number of years married, names of children, and that it is a reaffirmation of marriage vows. Include the text of the reaffirmation vows used.

senses of humor. The ceremony might resemble a wedding before a congregation in a church or synagogue, with their children included. Or, the clergy can visit the couple's home for a private ceremony, followed by a gala celebration. Another option: A reaffirmation at the site where you met (a ski lodge?); invite close family and friends.

The couple are finally able to afford the "wedding of their dreams." Perhaps when they first married, it was wartime, or money was tight. Invitations might be extended to those who attended the original ceremony and to any new friends or family members with whom the couple would like to celebrate.

The couple recently overcame hardship. Perhaps an ill child has recovered, or one spouse has returned home from serving overseas—and they would like to reaffirm their commitment to one another and to their family. Or, maybe a couple separated for a time and considered divorce, but have now decided to reconcile. These couples might invite those who helped them through their difficult period, encouraging them to now join in toasting happy times. Or, a couple might feel that their reaffirmation is a ceremony they'd like to share only with one another, stressing the strength of their love in their vows. Following the ceremony: a romantic dinner for two at a favorite restaurant.

The couple's children wish to host a reaffirmation for their parents. Often, in honor of a milestone anniversary, the couple's children and grandchildren plan and host a reaffirmation ceremony and reception for their parents. The celebration may be a formal ceremony and seated reception, similar to their original wedding, or it may be the big wedding they never had. It may also take place at home, as a cocktail party or backyard barbecue. Some families plan their reaffirmation ceremonies during family-reunion weekends.

Reaffirmation Questions

How soon after our first ceremony can we renew our vows? A reaffirmation, or "Service of Blessing," as it is sometimes known, can take place anytime after a wedding—two days or twenty-five years later.

Can music be part of a reaffirmation ceremony? Yes, as can poetry, Scripture readings, a blessing of the original wedding rings or new reaffirmation rings. The couple will want to select music for the processional and recessional, perhaps a few popular songs that are meaningful to them. Include meaningful touches such as the lighting of a Unity Candle (see Chapter 10, "Special Weddings & New Ways to Wed"), or the sharing of a cup of wine. Distribute a flower to each member of the congregation. Ask married couples in the pews to rise and renew their vows with you, or, later, to witness the planting of a tree to symbolize the ongoing life of your love and marriage.

Must a reaffirmation ceremony be presided over by a clergymember? Any authority figure may officiate at a reaffirmation, since unlike the actual wedding, this is not a legal function. For those who see renewal of their vows as a religious commitment, a clergymember is the right officiant. A judge might appeal to those who want someone who represents the community to give sanction to their vows. At the family reunion, the patriarch of the clan might preside. A military commander might fill the role for a couple in the service; for a faculty pair, the college president.

How far in advance should planning for a reaffirmation begin? Allow up to twelve months to plan a gala reaffirmation (the same amount of time needed to plan a wedding); less time for a simpler celebration.

How much money should be budgeted for a reaffirmation? Expect to spend money on the details you didn't have at your first wedding—or on those you want to repeat—such as bouquets, centerpieces, a photographer, and now also a videographer to record the event, a seated dinner and band for dancing after the ceremony. As when planning a budget for a wedding, the celebration can be as simple or elaborate as you choose. A reaffirmation at home on a Friday night, with a home-cooked meal, will be less costly than a seated dinner reception at a hotel.

Is it necessary to have a wedding party? Attendants are unnecessary at a reaffirmation ceremony, but some couples choose to invite their original bridesmaids and ushers back to reprise their roles. Many couples also have their children and grandchildren escort them down the aisle, stand at the altar, perform a reading during the ceremony, or make sentimental toasts at the reception.

Reaffirmation Preparation

If the couple want a religious reaffirmation, they should visit with their clergymember. Their feelings about the service, vows, music, and readings will be discussed. They'll see existing services and receive guidelines for writing their own.

In some churches and synagogues, reaffirmations may be an annual event. Couples come together at an annual reaffirmation ceremony, often during a weekly worship service, to rededicate themselves to their marriages. All couples in the congregation celebrating an anniversary are invited to participate.

The couple might consider attending an enrichment program for couples. A program such as this may help strengthen and renew their relationship. Worldwide Marriage Encounter, Inc., is an interfaith organization dedicated to keeping married love alive. During two-day weekend retreats (held away from home), husbands and wives learn to

reaffirmation sites

- a church or synagogue
- a home
- a scenic location (the beach at sunset, a mountaintop)
- a park, garden
- a sentimental location (the art gallery where the couple met, the chapel visited on the couple's honeymoon)
- a historic building (an elegant mansion)
- a vacation spot (camping with friends)

share the intimate, truthful feelings they may find hard to talk about back home—everything from how much money to invest in savings to how often they make love. At the end of every weekend, all couples are invited to renew their marriage vows. For many, these weekends spark a desire for public reaffirmation. (See the Appendix, under Chapter 20, "Reaffirmation," for marriage-enrichment programs.)

Reaffirmation Invitations

Compiling the guest list. The reaffirming couple should review their wedding guest book, Christmas card list, and address book to be sure they are not forgetting any guests. If missing an address, they might send an invitation to a mutual friend with a handwritten note stating, *We'd love to send an invitation to Gene and Judy Shaw—do you have their address?* The couple should be sure to include guests who missed their first wedding (a baby was born, someone was overseas in the service). If children wish to invite a few friends to this family celebration, the reaffirming couple should agree; it shows they're proud, too!

Selecting the invitation style. Personal handwritten notes are appropriate if the guest list is small; cheery, colorful invitations are suitable if the celebration style is festive (e.g., a summer barbecue). If the reaffirmation will include a formal ceremony and seated meal, printed or engraved cards are preferred. Couples might personalize their invitations with a reproduced original wedding photo or their own thoughts, in verse, on renewing their vows.

Reaffirmation invitation:

The honour of your presence
is requested at the reaffirmation
of the wedding vows of
Mr. and Mrs. John David Smith
Saturday, the eighth of March
nineteen hundred and ninety-four
at three o'clock
All Saints Church
New York, New York

Simplified reception card:

Reception
immediately following the ceremony
The Plaza Hotel

Kindly respond
860 Park Avenue
New York, New York 10021

Invitation issued by children:

The children of
Daniel and Sarah Patterson
request the honour of your presence
at the reaffirmation ceremony of their
parents
Saturday, the twentieth of June
nineteen hundred and ninety-four
at six o'clock in the evening
Bethany Memorial Church
201 Main Street
Bethany, West Virginia

R.s.v.p.
Jan Patterson
21 Highland Avenue
Wheeling, West Virginia 26003

Reaffirmation Attire

The attire of the remarrying bride and groom depends on the style and formality of the ceremony and celebration. It is perfectly acceptable for a remarrying couple to invite their original wedding party back for the reaffirmation ceremony, or to include new persons who have played meaningful roles in their married life. Select bridesmaids, ushers, even honor attendants. The couple's children—young or grown—may fill the roles of attendants or carry the guest book, pour punch, pass out wedding programs.

THE BRIDE

The original dress. If repeating the same vows or returning to the original wedding site, the reaffirming bride may choose to wear her original wedding gown (a dressmaker might make alterations, if necessary; see Chapter 7, "Wedding Clothes," and Appendix, under Chapter 7.) The dress can be updated with accessories— a new strand of pearls (a gift from the remarrying groom), a flower boa, a new headpiece.

A new dress. A traditional new bridal gown may be the choice for the remarrying bride who once eloped. Or, she may choose a stylish cocktail dress or a formal evening dress. Depending on the style of the ceremony, the dress may be floor-length (without a train), ballet-length, or skim the knee…and be white, pale peach, ecru, or dusty rose.

The headpiece. This accessory should be simple. The remarrying bride should consider a charming hat, demure pillbox, floral wreath, or combs with tiny blossoms. A wedding veil is not worn because it has long been a traditional symbol of virginity.

The flowers. Fresh blooms are a refreshing addition to a reaffirming bride's ceremony attire. For an island reaffirmation, she might wear colorful leis; for a garden ceremony, she might carry an armful of bright field flowers or a colorful handtied bouquet. New innovations: pocket posies in suits, floral bracelets or boas, floral hatbands (see Chapter 15, "Wedding Flowers").

The accessories. A remarrying bride may complement her dress with the pearls she received from her groom on their wedding day; the diamond eternity ring received on a milestone anniversary; a locket with photos of her children; and, of course, her wedding ring, which will be blessed again if the reaffirmation is a religious service.

THE GROOM

The original formalwear. The reaffirming groom may choose to wear his original tuxedo, suit, or military uniform (a tailor can make alterations). It can be updated with a new tie or bow tie, cummerbund, and pocket handkerchief.

New formalwear. If the reaffirmation ceremony is before 6 p.m., for a semiformal or informal ceremony, the remarrying groom may wear a dark suit and tie or blazer; for a formal ceremony, a gray

reaffirmation gifts

Gifts should not be expected for a reaffirmation, although many guests will probably want to give the couple a memento to mark the happy occasion. The reaffirming couple may:

- Register for items not received the first time around (a completer set to their china pattern, or a soup tureen) at a local department store's Wedding Gift Registry (see Chapter 17, "Wedding Gifts").

- Register at specialty stores for leisure-time gifts (golf equipment, picnic accessories).

- Stress that this is a celebration of love by suggesting (by word of mouth, not in writing) that in place of gifts, friends might make a donation to a favorite charity in the couple's names.

stroller, waistcoat, striped trousers, shirt, and striped tie; for a very formal ceremony, a cutaway coat, gray striped trousers, gray waistcoat, and wing-collared shirt with ascot. If the celebration is after 6 p.m., for a semiformal ceremony, he may wear a tuxedo or dinner jacket; for a formal ceremony, a tuxedo; for a very formal ceremony, white tie—or a full-dress tailcoat, matching trousers, white waistcoat, wing-collared shirt, and white bow tie.

The accessories. The remarrying groom may complement his reaffirmation outfit with gifts of jewelry his wife has given him over the years—cuff links, his engagement watch, a new coordinated bow tie and cummerbund.

The flowers. The remarrying groom should always wear a fresh floral boutonniere on his left lapel.

THE ATTENDANTS

Bridesmaids' original dresses. Those bridesmaids who still have their original bridesmaid's dress might have it altered for the occasion. They might also update

the dress with new accessories—jewelry, shoes, flowers.

New maids' dresses. Women attendants might wear any short or long elegant dress, luncheon or dinner suit. The remarrying bride should ask them to wear dresses of similar length, style, and perhaps color.

The ushers' original formalwear. Those ushers who bought and still own their original outfits may choose to wear them (see "The Groom" section). They might update cummerbunds, bow ties.

New ushers' formalwear. The men's attire should complement the reaffirming groom's (see "The Groom" section).

Children's attire. Children should wear their best outfits, or pehaps have a new outfit for the occasion (similar to what a flower girl or ring bearer might wear).

Children's flowers. Fresh, colorful nosegays and boutonnieres will add to the spirit of the day, and make children feel even more special.

Reaffirmation Vows

Meaningful vows are the focal point of the recommitment that a couple make.

Write original vows. This will ensure that what the reaffirming bride and groom say will be exactly what they feel. It will also help to make their relationship healthier by forcing the two of them to address any long-buried issues. They might mention the qualities they most love about each other, describe the things they have created and shared together, mention any hardships overcome, make pledges relating to patience, make note of a sense of humor, the ability to communicate, and any other items most valued in their marriage, stating, *"I promise you, the man I have loved so long, to be* *more open about my feelings, to share equally with you the care for our children, Denise and Samuel, and to respect your personal needs and beliefs. I understand that marriage for us means working toward an ever richer companionship."*

Thank family and friends. Being acknowledged for what they've contributed to the couple's relationship will make guests feel as if they are a vital part of the ceremony. Perhaps make references to hardships overcome, and how guests have helped.

Alter the traditional marriage vows for a reaffirmation ceremony. Have the clergy-member use the words *"renewing their promise in the presence of God"* in the service. Or, look into the revised marriage services many faiths now offer. Almost every faith celebrates reaffirmation. Some churches have created standard services. Look in *The Book of Common Prayer*, from the Episcopal faith, for "The Blessing of a Civil Marriage"; this ceremony is for couples previously married in a civil ceremony who want to reaffirm their vows in a religious ceremony. The Methodist church uses several services from *A Service of a Christian Marriage*, including "Renewal of Vows," "The Blessing of a Civil Marriage," and "Anniversaries of Marriages." In a reaffirmation ceremony, couples may repeat their original vows, use their church's or synagogue's traditional wedding-ceremony vows, or alter the vows to reflect that the ceremony is a reaffirmation. For example, when the clergymember asks, *"Do you take this woman/man?"* you might answer, *"I did and I do,"* or *"I still take..."* Or, the clergymember might say, *"William, you have taken Joan to be your wife. Do you promise to love her, comfort her, honor and keep her, in sickness and in health; and, forsaking all others, to be faithful to her as long as you both shall live?"* Guests might be asked *"to uphold these two persons in their marriage."*

Reaffirmation Rings

Similar to a wedding ceremony, the reaffirmation ceremony is a time when the clergymember will ask for the couple's original wedding rings, or the new ones they may wear in the future. These rings will be blessed before the reaffirming bride and groom present them to each other with a pledge of love (e.g., *"We have lived and loved as we promised long ago in the presence of God, and our past and future are a circle unbroken...like the ring, with which I renew my pledge to you of never-ending devotion."* The couple might ask the clergymember to also bless the gifts that will be given to their children to commemorate the day—a gold charm, locket, birthstone ring.

The Reaffirmation Reception

The party can be any style—a candle-lit dinner for family or a large cocktail party.

reaffirmation-ring ideas

- an anniversary ring (usually a band of diamonds, meant to be worn alone or as a complement to the original wedding band)

- a gemstone ring (precious stones set with the birthstones of the husband and wife, as well as each child)

- an eternity ring (with a diamond or other precious stone for each year together)

Food can be creative. A reaffirmation reception can feature finger foods ("dinner by the bite") and drinks; a hearty buffet of favorite family recipes; or a seated dinner with traditional ethnic dishes (see Chapter 4, "Planning Your Wedding"). Some classic touches, such as champagne for toasts and a festive reaffirmation cake, should be included. Perhaps, the couple might use their original wedding-cake topper again!

Delegate planning tasks. This time, the two of you may be the hosts and may be making the arrangements yourselves. It might be a more carefree celebration, though, if you rely on wedding professionals, such as a wedding consultant (see Chapter 4, "Planning Your Wedding"). As hosts, you'll spend time with each guest and oversee hospitality details. Don't hesitate to delegate some responsibilities (e.g., writing out place cards, making a list of must-take photos) to children, relatives, and friends.

Include wedding traditions. A receiving line should be included at a large reaffirmation to ensure that the couple have a chance to greet every guest. The reception can include some—or all—of the traditional wedding customs: the first dance, toasts, the cake cutting. Throwing the bouquet may not seem as appropriate; the couple might choose another way to pass on their "good fortune" to guests. They might present them with symbolic favors—rooted sprigs of forget-me-nots (signifying true love), or ivy or veronica (meaning fidelity) to take home and plant.

Don't forget decorations. The reaffirmation site might be trimmed with fresh, colorful floral arrangements and nostalgic items (e.g., enlarged pictures of the couple's original wedding—with space around the borders of one special photo for all guests to sign; place cards printed with the couple's engagement photo).

Plan to have keepsakes, mementos. Since the reaffirming couple will want to cherish the memories of this special day, they should hire a professional photographer and/or videographer to record all the happy moments. Everyone will have fun leafing through the original guest book; don't forget to provide another for guests to write new messages, good wishes, humorous recollections.

reaffirmation favors

Guests will appreciate a token to remember the reaffirmation. The reaffirming couple might consider:

- a picture of their family
- a CD with "their song"
- a scroll with an inspirational passage that has shaped their marriage
- a videocassette of their ceremony

A Second Honeymoon

A reaffirming couple may take a celebratory trip, either directly after the reaffirmation or in the near future. All of the preparations and the excitement of the occasion will rekindle romance, and romance is good for marriage! It might be just the right time for the reaffirming couple to take the trip they've always dreamed of—back to visit the ancestral sod in Ireland; or, it may just be a chance to splurge for a weekend at an elegant resort. They should give themselves a little private time and space to reflect on all the joy they've rediscovered.

APPENDIX

1. YOUR ENGAGEMENT

American Gem Society (an association of fine jewelers dedicated to consumer protection)
5901 West Third Street
Los Angeles, CA 90036-2898
(213) 936-4367

Cultured Pearl Associations of American and Japan
c/o Tele-press Associates
321 E. 53rd Street
New York, NY 10022
(212) 688-5580
(Contact for pamphlets, information.)

Gembureau (colored gemstone information)
609 Fifth Avenue
New York, NY 10017
(212) 688-8452

Jewelers of America
Communications Department
1185 Avenue of the Americas, 30th Floor
New York, NY 10036
(212) 768-8777; (800) 223-0673

Jewelry Industry Council
8 West 19th Street, 4th Floor
New York, NY 10011
(212) 727-0130

The Diamond Information Center
825 Eighth Avenue, 36th Floor
New York, NY 10019-7498
(212) 474-5193
(Send for information about carats, appraisals.)

2. WEDDING CUSTOMS

American Folklife Center
Folklife Reading Room
Library of Congress
Washington, DC 20540-8100
(202) 707-5510

BRIDE'S Little Book of Customs and Keepsakes, by the Editors of BRIDE'S. New York: Clarkson N. Potter, 1994. (800-426-9922, Dept. 526046)

Caprilands Herb Farm (environment-friendly confetti, such as rose petals, potpourri; "Wedding Herbs" booklet)
534 Silver Street
Coventry, CT 06238
(203) 742-7244

Jumping the Broom: The African-American Wedding Planner, by Harriet Cole. New York: Henry Holt & Co., 1993.

The Bride—A Celebration, by Barbara Tober. New York: Longmeadow Press, 1992. (1-800-322-2000, Dept. 708)

The Celebration Book of Great American Traditions, by Wicke Chambers and Spring Asher. New York: Harper & Row, 1983.

Yaffa Productions
143 West 120th Street
New York, NY 10027
(212) 840-1234
(African-American cultural resources, musicians)

3. PREWEDDING PARTIES

A&M Shower Traditions
1227 North Linden Street
Oak Park, IL 60302
(708) 383-2080
(Romantic Secrets, shower game with invitations)

Bridal Showers: Fifty Great Ideas for a Perfect Shower, by Sharon E. Dlugosch and Florence E. Nelson. New York: Perigee/Putnam, 1987.

Entertaining, by Martha Stewart and Elizabeth Hawes. New York: Clarkson N. Potter, 1982.

4. PLANNING YOUR WEDDING

American Association for Marriage and Family Therapy
1100 17th Street, NW, 10th Floor
Washington, DC 20036
(202) 452-0109

American Ethical Union
2 West 64th Street
New York, NY 10023
(212) 873-6500
(Contact for referrals to local affiliates for listings of officiants who perform interfaith ceremonies.)

American Rental Association (owners of party-rental and party-supplies stores nationwide)
1900 19th Street
Moline, IL 61265
(800) 334-2177
(Call for referrals, "Party Rental Guide")

Association for Couples in Marriage Enrichment (A.C.M.E.) (for premarital counseling)
P.O. Box 10596
Winston-Salem, NC 27108
(800) 634-8325

Association of Bridal Consultants
200 Chestnutland Road
New Milford, CT 06776-2521
(203) 355-0464
(Call for consultants in your area.)

BRIDE'S Shortcuts and Strategies for a Beautiful Wedding, by the Editors of BRIDE'S with Kathy C. Mullins. New York: Perigee/Putnam, 1986.

BRIDE'S Wedding Planner, by the Editors of BRIDE'S. New York: Ballantine Books, 1990.

Computer Creations (Newsletters, programs, maps, invitations.)
P.O. Box 11414
Torrance, CA 90510
(310) 530-4575

Harry Forrest (Quaker marriage certificates)
500 Park Avenue
Cinnaminson, NJ 08077
(609) 829-6486

Insurance Information Institute
110 William Street
New York, NY 10038
(212) 669-9200

International Special Events Society (ISES)
(professionals in the party-planning field)
6133 Bristol Parkway, Box 3640 Culver City, CA 90231-3640
(800) 543-4116

Interpersonal Communication Program (for premarital counseling; check with your local church)
7201 South Broadway, Suite 11
Littleton, CO 80122
(303) 794-1764

Judaic Creations (toasting cups, *ketubahs*, and other ceremonial items)
340 East 74th Street, #6C
New York, NY 10021
(212) 772-0223

Jonathan Kremer/Kesset Press (*ketubahs*)
35 East Athens Avenue
Ardmore, PA 19003
(215) 642-6711

Love and Tradition: Marriage Between Jews and Christians, by Egon Mayer. New York: Plenum, 1985.

Marriage Contract: Spouses, Lovers & the Law, by Lenore J. Weitzman. New York: Free Press, 1981.

Mixed Blessings, by Paul Cowan with Rachel Cowan. New York: Doubleday, 1987.

National Caterers Association
P.O. Box 4510, Dept. B
Akron, Ohio 44310
Hotline for brides planning weddings:
(800) 837-2569
(Call for referrals to caterers in your area.)

National Easter Seal Society
230 West Monroe
Chicago, IL 60606
(312) 726-6200
For the hearing impaired: (312) 726-4258
(Contact for information on making your wedding site accessible to the disabled.)

National Judges Association
42 Little Horn Road
Westcliffe, CO 81252
(800) 654-3099
(Contact for referrals to non-attorney judges who perform civil wedding ceremonies.)

PAIRS (Practical Application of Intimate Relationship Skills) (for premarital counseling)
PAIRS Foundation
3705 S. George Mason Drive, Suite C8
Falls Church, VA 22041
(800) 477-2477

Places: A Directory of Public Places for Private Events & Private Places for Public Functions, by Hannelore Hahn and Tatiana Stoumen. New York, NY: Tenth House Enterprises, Inc. For information on ordering:

Places
Box No. 810
Gracie Station
New York, NY 10028
(212) 737-7536

Planned Parenthood (Federation of America, Inc.)
810 Seventh Avenue
New York, NY 10019
(212) 541-7800
("Facts about Birth Control" brochure available.)

PREPARE™ (premarital counseling; contact clergymember or
send self-addressed, stamped envelope to:)
PREPARE
P.O. Box 190
Minneapolis, MN 55440-0190

Rabbinic Center for Research and Counseling
128 East Dudley Avenue
Westfield, NJ 07090
(908) 233-0419
(For fee, will send related articles, plus list of rabbis
who will perform interfaith marriages.)

Registry of Interpreters for the Deaf
8719 Colesville Road, Suite 310
Silver Spring, MD 20910
(301) 608-0050

Robert Francis Company
6927 Ludlow Street
Upper Darby, PA 19082
(800) 548-7797
(Liturgical banners, posters, program covers.)

SIECUS (Sex Information and Education Council of the U.S.)
130 West 42nd Street, Suite 2500
New York, NY 10036-7901
(212) 819-9770

***The Down-The-Aisle Directory: The New York Metropolitan Tri-
State Area***. New York: MRS Publications, Inc., 1993.

The People's Place Gallery/Good Enterprises (Amish marriage certificates)
Main Street
Intercourse, PA 17534
(717) 768-7171

United Marriage Encounter (for engaged couples)
Larry and Nancy Rodgers
211 So. Indiana
Mason City, IL 62664
(217) 482-5368

Weddingsurance (insurance coverage for wedding gifts, photography, wedding clothing, cancellation, illness)
Fireman's Fund
Association of Program Managers
55 East Monroe Street, Suite 3300
Chicago, IL 60603
(800) 428-1419

5. INVITATIONS & ANNOUNCEMENTS

Arlene Segal Designs (creative, upscale invitations)
20350 NE 16th Place
North Miami Beach, FL 33179
(305) 651-8283

Crane & Co., Inc. (Write for free brochure on ordering tips.)
"Wedding Invitations and Announcements"
Crane & Co., Inc.
30 South Street
Dalton, MA 01226

C. R. Gibson Company (wedding invitations, thank-you notepaper, other stationery needs, gift items)
32 Knight Street
Norwalk, CT 06856
(203) 847-4543
(Offers "The Bride's Planner," a purse-sized orga-
nizer; contact for information on ordering and fee.)

Rexcraft (Order free color catalog of invitations.)
Rexburg, ID 83441
(800) 635-4653

Society for Calligraphy
P.O. Box 64174
Los Angeles, CA 90064
(213) 380-5957
(Contact for referrals to calligraphers.)

The Social Secretary (computerized calligraphy and printing
service in 500 stationery, party, and card stores nationwide)
(212) 956-2707
(Call for a listing of stores in your area with the service, and for information on "Perfect Calligraphy," a
software package for your computer.)

Washington Calligraphers Guild
P.O. Box 3688
Merrifield, VA 22116-3688
(301) 897-8637
(Contact for referrals to calligraphers.)

6. THE WEDDING PARTY

For the Flower Girl/ For the Ring Bearer (two books detailing roles and activities). For information on ordering and cost, write:
Jacqueline Beverly Hills,
P.O. Box 7840
Beverly Hills, CA 90212
(213) 536-9080; (800) 444-7753

That's Only the Down Payment: A Survival Manual for the Father of the Bride, by Michael M. Warren, M.D. Galveston, TX: Ledero Press, 1992. ISBN: 0-96277775-2-8. (For information on cost and ordering, write: Dr. Michael Warren, U.T. Box 35099, Galveston, TX 77555-5099 or call: 800-444-2524.)

7. WEDDING CLOTHES

American Formalwear Association
401 North Michigan Avenue
Suite 2400
Chicago, IL 60611-4267
(312) 644-6610
(Send self-addressed, stamped envelope to receive their free pamphlet, "Your Formalwear Guide.")

Dressing the Bride, by Larry Goldman. New York: Crown Publishers, Inc., 1993.

International Fabricare Institute
12251 Tech Road
Silver Spring, MD 20904
(301) 622-1900
(Your member [IFI] dry cleaner can contact this organization for wedding-gown care problems or for help in restoring an antique wedding–gown.)

The Wedding Dress, by Maria McBride-Mellinger. New York: Random House, 1993.

8. YOUR WEDDING CEREMONY

American Bible Society (suppliers for Today's English Version of the Bible)
P.O. Box 5656, Grand Central Station
New York, NY 10164-0851
(212) 408-1200

BRIDE'S Little Book of Vows and Rings, by the Editors of BRIDE'S. New York: Clarkson N. Potter, 1994. (800-426-9922, Dept. 526046)

I Do: A Guide To Creating Your Own Unique Wedding Ceremony, by Sydney Barbara Metrick. Berkeley, CA: Celestial Arts Publishing, 1992.

Marriage in Christ (ceremony, blessings), available from:
The Liturgical Press
Saint John's Abbey
Collegeville, MN 56321-7500
(612) 363-2213

Marriage Vessel and the Rose (special ceremony)
Westport Allen Center
Clergy Services
706 West 42nd Street
Kansas City, MO 64111
(816) 753-3886

The New Wedding: Creating Your Own Marriage Ceremony, by Khoren Arisian. New York: Vintage Books, 1973.

With These Words I Thee Wed: Contemporary Wedding Vows for Today's Couples, by Barbara Royster Eklof. Holbrook, MA: Bob Adams, Inc., 1989.

Write Your Own Wedding: A Personal Guide for Couples of All Faiths, by Mordecai L. Brill. Hampton, New Jersey: New Win Publishing, 1985.

9. RELIGIOUS RITUALS & REQUIREMENTS

Assemblies of God
1445 Boonville Avenue
Springfield, MO 65802
(417) 862-2781

Beth Din of America (Jewish/Orthodox)
275 Seventh Avenue
New York, NY 10001
(212) 807-9042

Church of Jesus Christ of Latter-day Saints (Mormon)
50 East N. Temple
Salt Lake City, Utah 84150
(801) 240-2205

Evangelical Lutheran Church in America
8765 West Higgins Road
Chicago, IL 60631
(312) 380-2700

Greek Orthodox Archdiocese
    10 East 79th Street
    New York, NY 10021
    (212) 570-3500

Jewish Wedding Book: A Practical Guide to the Traditions and Social Customs of the Jewish Wedding, by Lilly S. Routtenberg and Ruth R. Seldin. New York: Schocken Books, 1987.

Presbyterian Center, News Services Office
    100 Witherspoon Street
    Louisville, KY 40202
    (800) 872-3283

Rabbinic Hotline (Jewish/Conservative)
    c/o Jewish Theological Seminary
    Department of Communications
    3080 Broadway
    New York, NY 10027

The New Jewish Wedding, by Anita Diamant. New York: Summit Books, 1985.

Together For Life: Special Edition for Marriage Outside Mass, by Joseph M. Champlin. Notre Dame, Indiana: Ave Maria Press, 1988.
    (Note: There is a regular edition for the wedding within the Roman Catholic Mass and a special edition for marriage outside Mass.)

Union of American Hebrew Congregations (Jewish/Reform)
    838 Fifth Avenue
    New York, NY 10021
    (212) 249-0100

Unitarian Universalist Association
    25 Beacon Street
    Boston, MA 02108
    (617) 742-2100

10. SPECIAL WEDDINGS & NEW WAYS TO WED

BRIDE'S New Ways to Wed, by the Editors of BRIDE'S with Antonia van der Meer. New York: Perigee/Putnam, 1990.

Office of the Chief of Army Public Affairs—New York Branch
    133 East 58th Street, 15th Floor
    New York, NY 10022-1236
    (212) 688-7572
    (Or contact the nearest military installation—base administration office or chaplin—for military wedding requirements.)

Old Print Factory, Inc. (Victorian ornaments, fans, sachet holders, favors, stationery, marriage certificates)
    P.O. Box 498
    New Baltimore, MI 48047
    (313) 749-9498; to order: (800) 325-5383

Service Etiquette, by Oretha D. Swartz. Annapolis, MD: Naval Institute Press, 1988. For information on ordering and fee:
    U.S. Naval Institute
    2062 Generals Highway
    Annapolis, MD 21401
    (800) 233-8764

Wedded Bliss: A Victorian Bride's Handbook, by Molly Dolan Blayney. New York, London, Paris: Abbeville Press, 1992.

Weddings Southern Style, by Beverly Reese Church. New York: Abbeville Press Publishers, 1993.

11. REMARRIAGE

A Hole in My Heart: Adult Children of Divorce Speak Out, by Claire Berman. New York: Fireside/Simon & Schuster, 1992.

Family Medallion (Contact for information on medallion and ceremony, plus cost)
    Westport Allen Center
    Clergy Services
    706 West 42nd Street
    Kansas City, MO 64111
    (816) 753-3886

The Second Time Around: Why Some Second Marriages Fail While Others Succeed, by Dr. Louis H. Janda and Ellen Mac Cormack. New York: Carole Publishing Group, 1991.

The Stepfamily Foundation
    33 West End Avenue
    New York, NY 10023
    (212) 877-3244

12. UNEXPECTED SITUATIONS

Better Business Bureau of Metropolitan New York
257 Park Avenue South
New York, NY 10010
(212) 533-6200
(Send for wedding advisory material; contact for ordering information and fee.)

Better Business Bureau of Washington, D.C. (national office)
(202) 393-8000

Consumer Information Center (Call for free pamphlets.)
General Services Administration
18 & F Streets, N.W., Room 142
Washington, D.C. 20405
(202) 501-1794

13. YOUR RECEPTION

BRIDE'S Little Book of Cakes and Toasts, by The Editors of BRIDE'S. New York: Clarkson N. Potter, 1993. (800-426-9922, Dept. 526046)

Cake Decorating for Any Occasion, by Cile Bellefleur Burbidge. Radnor, PA: Chilton Book Co., 1978.

Dance Educators of America (Contact for referrals for local dance teachers.)
85 Rockaway Avenue
Rockville Centre, NY 11570
(516) 766-6615

Dance Masters of America (Contact for referrals for local dance teachers.)
P.O. Box 438
Independence, MO 64051-0438
(816) 252-0111

Fireworks by Grucci
1 Grucci Lane
Brookhaven, NY 11719
(516) 286-0088

Imperial Society of Teachers of Dancing (Contact for referrals for ballroom dance instructors.)
U.S. Ballroom Branch (USISTD):
c/o Step in Time School of Dance

Lorraine Hahn
366 Easton Road
Warrington, PA 18976
(215) 491-9696

Sara Lee Wedding Cake
325 West Huron, Suite 315
Chicago, IL 60610
(Send self-addressed, stamped envelope for free brochure on creating your own wedding cake with Sara Lee pound cakes.)

Toastmasters International (Contact for local referrals for toastmasters, masters of ceremonies.)
23182 Arroyo Vista
Rancho Santa Magarita, CA 92688
(714) 858-8255

Toasts, by Paul Dickson. New York: Crown Publishers, Inc., 1991.

Wedding Cakes: A Pictorial Preview (cakes that can be duplicated by your own baker; contact for information on ordering and fee) Cal-Mex Supply Company
279 Third Avenue
Chula Vista, CA 92010
(619) 422-4241

Wilton Book of Wedding Cakes, ed. by Eugene T. Sullivan and Marilynn C. Sullivan. Woodridge, Illinois: Wilton Enterprises, 1971.

14. WEDDING MUSIC

American Federation of Musicians
1501 Broadway, Suite 600
New York, NY 10036
(212) 869-1330

American Society of Composers, Artists and Publishers (Contact for information about songs, reprinting.)
One Lincoln Plaza
New York, NY 10023
(212) 595-3050

"BRIDE'S Guide to Wedding Music" (CD or cassette)
New York: Angel Records, 1993. To order, call:
(800) 550-6555, Ext. E.

Cantor's Assembly (Conservative)
Jewish Theological Seminary
3080 Broadway
Suite 613
New York, NY 10027
(212) 678-8834

"Nancy Cook's Music Programs" (booklet and newsletter)
P.O. Box 18626
Washington, DC 20036
(202) 223-6856

The Complete Wedding Songbook, Milwaukee: Hal Leonard Publishing Corp., 1987

The Golden Book of Wedding Songs
P.O. Box 35
Oradell, NJ 07649

The New Complete Book of Wedding Music
Hansen House
1820 West Avenue
Miami Beach, FL 33139
(305) 532-5461

Transcontinental Music (a division of Union of American Hebrew Congregations—Jewish/Reform; has published specially commissioned music for weddings)
838 Fifth Avenue
New York, NY 10021
(212) 249-0100

15. WEDDING FLOWERS

Ann Plowden, Inc. (preserving bouquets, boutonnieres, in frames or under glass)
33 Cary Avenue
Milton, MA 02186
(617) 696-3559

Bridal Flowers, by Maria McBride-Mellinger. New York: Little, Brown and Company Inc., 1992.

BRIDE'S *Little Book of Bouquets and Flowers*, by The Editors of BRIDE'S. New York: Clarkson N. Potter, 1993.
(800-426-9922, Dept. 526046)

Cazenovia Abroad (tussie-mussie holders for nosegays)
67 Albany Street

Cazenovia, NY 13035
(315) 655-3433

Flowers, by Malcolm Hillier. London: Dorling Kindersley, 1988.

Flowers for All Seasons (four volumes: Summer, Winter, Spring, Fall), by Jane Packer and Elizabeth Wilhide. New York: Fawcett Columbine,1989.

Teleflora (Free brochures, wedding guidebook, available at Teleflora florists.)
12233 West Olympic Boulevard
Suite 140
Los Angeles, CA 90064
(310) 826-5253

16. PHOTOGRAPHY, VIDEOGRAPHY, & PUBLICITY

Association of Independent Video Filmmakers
625 Broadway, 9th Floor
New York, NY 10012
(212) 473-3400

International Professional Photographers Guild
7900 Jerome Avenue
St. Louis, MO 63143
(880) 333-5725

Professional Photographers of America, Inc. (wedding photography planning)

1090 Executive Way
Des Plaines, IL 60018
(708) 299-8161
(Kit available; includes a directory of member photographers all over the world.)

Wedding Photographers International
1312 Lincoln Blvd.
P.O. Box 2003
Santa Monica, CA 90406
(310) 451-0090

17. WEDDING GIFTS

Arbor National Mortgage Inc. (Call to register or get more information)
Arbor Home Bridal Registry
615 Merrick Avenue
Westbury, NY 11590
(800) ARBOR91

Consumer's Resource Handbook (for handling problems, inquiries regarding gifts or purchases; free from:)
United States Office of Consumer Affairs
Consumer Information Center
Pueblo, CO 81009
(719) 948-3334

Crate & Barrel (Call for registry and store information.)
(800) 967-6696

Gift of a Letter, by Alexandra Stoddard. New York: Doubleday, 1990.

Gifts that Make a Difference: How to Buy Hundreds of Great Gifts Sold Through Nonprofits, by Ellen Berry. Dayton, Ohio: Foxglove Publishing, 1992.

Liberty Travel Honeymoon Registry (Guests receive gift certificates; contact for nearest office in your area.)
Liberty Travel/ATT: Leslie Lafferty
69 Spring Street
Ramsey, NJ 07446
(201) 934-3778

National Bridal Service (800 members: small gift shops, fashion and tabletop stores nationwide)
3122 W. Cary
Richmond, VA 23221
(804) 355-6945

National Housewares Manufacturers Association
6400 Shafer Court, Suite 650
Rosemont, IL 60018
(708) 292-4200

The Art and Etiquette of Gift Giving, by Dawn Bryan. New York: Bantam, 1987.

The Complete Guide to Buying Gems: How to Buy Diamonds and Colored Gemstones with Confidence and Knowledge, by Antoinette L. Matlins and Antonio C. Bonanno. Woodstock, Vermont: GemStone Press, 1988.

The Greatest Gift Guide Ever, by Judith King. White Hall, VA: Betterway Publications, Inc., 1982. Distributed by The Berkshire Travelers Press, Stockbridge, MA.

Williams-Sonoma (Call for store and registry information.)
(800) 541-1262

With Thanks & Appreciation: The Sweet Nellie Book of Thoughts, Sentiments, Tokens & Traditions of the Past, by Pat Ross. New York: Viking Studio Books, 1989.

18. WEDDING GUESTS

Charlotte Ford's Book of Modern Manners, by Charlotte Ford. New York: Fireside/Simon & Schuster, 1982.

Letitia Baldrige's Complete Guide to a Great Social Life, by Letitia Baldrige. New York: Doubleday, 1987.

Miss Manners' Guide to Excruciatingly Correct Behavior, by Judith Martin, New York: Galahad Books, 1991.

The Amy Vanderbilt Complete Book of Etiquette, by Nancy Dunnan and Nancy Tuckerman. New York: Doubleday, 1994.

19. GOING AWAY

Adventure Travel North America, by Pat Dickerman. New York, NY: Adventure Travel Guides, Inc., 1991.

American Society for the Prevention of Cruelty to Animals (A.S.P.C.A.)
Education Department
424 East 92nd Street
New York, NY 10128-6899
(212) 876-7711
(Send self-addressed, stamped envelope for free booklet on traveling with pets.)

American Society of Travel Agents (Send self-addressed, stamped envelope for free list of members.)
1101 King Street
Alexandria, VA 22314
(703) 739-2782

Amtrack (National Railroad Passenger Corporation)
400 N. Capital Street, NW
Washington, DC 20001
(202) 484-7540; (800) 872-7245

Aviation Consumer Action Project (Offers passengers' booklet; contact for information on ordering and fee.)
"Facts & Advice for Airline Passengers"
P.O. Box 19029
Washington, D.C. 20036

Better Business Bureau of Metropolitan New York (Travel packet available for fee.)
257 Park Avenue South
New York, NY 10010
(212) 533-6200

BRIDE'S Honeymoon Travel Guide, by the Editors of BRIDE'S with Sally Kilbridge. New York: Perigee/Putnam, 1988.

Citizens' Emergency Center (Contact for up-to-date information on foreign travel.)
United States Department of State
Bureau of Consular Affairs
(202) 647-5225/5226)

Cruise Lines International Association (Send self-addressed, stamped envelope for free booklet.)
"Answers to the Most-Asked Questions about Cruising"
500 Fifth Avenue
Suite 1407
New York, NY 10110
(212) 921-0066

European Travel Commission (Send self-addressed, stamped embelope for free brochure)
"Planning Your Trip to Europe"
630 Fifth Avenue
Suite 565
New York, NY 10110
(212) 307-1200

International Association for Medical Assistance to Travelers (Travel packet available; contact for information.)
417 Center Street
Lewiston, NY 14092
(716) 754-4883

International Travelers Hotline (information on disease control, by country)
Department of Health and Human Services
Public Health Services
Centers for Disease Control
Quarantine Division/Travelers Health Section
Atlanta, Georgia 30333
(404) 332-4559; or, fax: (404) 332-4565

Luggage and Leather Goods Manufacturers of America, Inc. (free pamphlet available; send stamped, self-addressed business-size envelope)
"Traveler's Guide to Luggage: How to Choose It and Use It"
350 Fifth Avenue
Suite 2624
New York NY 10016
(212) 695-2340

National Limousine Association (Contact for local referrals of members.)
1300 L Street, NW
Suite 1050
Washington, DC 20005
(800) NLA-7007

The Consumer Reports Travel Letter (Contact for details on subscribing.)
P.O. Box 53629
Boulder, CO 80322
(800) 999-7959

The Great Weekend Escape Book, by Michael Spring. New York: E. P. Dutton, 1991.

"Tips for Travelers" (Contact for free brochures on various foreign regions)
United States Government Printing Office
Washington, DC 20402
(202) 783-3238

Travel Health Services (information on disease control, by country)
50 East 69th Street
New York, NY 10021
(212) 734-3000

20. REAFFIRMATION

ENRICH™ (Contact your clergymember or send a self-addressed, stamped envelope for information on marriage-enrichment program for married couples.)
ENRICH
P.O. Box 190
Minneapolis, MN 55413
in Minnesota: (612) 331-1731; nationwide: (800) 331-1661

Jewish Marriage Encounter (for married or engaged couples; call for referral to a group in your area)
Bob and Barbara Kamholtz, International Directors
1800 Everett Place
East Meadow, NY 11554
(516) 538-7766

National Marriage Encounter (for married couples; send self-addressed, stamped envelope)
Chuck and Sandy Ogg
4704 Jamerson Place
Orlando, FL 32807
(800) 828-3351

Reaffirmation: Renewing Your Marriage Vows and Values, by Susan Lane and Sandra Carter—with Ann Scharffenberger. New York: Harmony Books, 1982.

United Marriage Encounter (for married couples)
P.O. Box 209
Muscatine, IA 52761-0209
nationwide: (800) 334-8920

Worldwide Marriage Encounter (for married couples; weekends presented in 12 faith expressions and several languages; contact for a group in your area)
1908 East Highland Avenue
Suite A
San Bernardino, CA 92404
(909) 881-3456

Marriage Laws

STATE	AGE WITH PARENTAL CONSENT MALE	FEMALE	AGE WITHOUT CONSENT MALE	FEMALE	PHYSICAL EXAM & BLOOD TEST FOR MALE AND FEMALE — MAXIMUM PERIOD BETWEEN EXAM AND LICENSE	SCOPE OF MEDICAL EXAM	WAITING PERIOD BEFORE LICENSE	LICENSE VALID
Alabama*	14a	14a	18	18	—	Venereal Diseases	—	30 days
Alaska	16b	16b	18	18	—	V.D.	3 days,k	—
Arizona	16b	16b	18	18	—	—	t	—
Arkansas	17c	16c	18	18	—	s	—	90 days
California	no age limits		18	18	30 days,k	s	—	30 days
Colorado*	16b	16b	18	18	—	V.D.,q	—	30 days
Connecticut	16b	16b	18	18	—	V.D.,q	4 days,k	65 days
Delaware	18c	16c	18	18	—	—	—	30 days,w
Florida	16a,c	16a,c	18	18	—	V.D.	3 days	30 days
Georgia*	no age limits		18	18	—	V.D.	3 days,u	30 days
Hawaii	16d	16d	18	18	—	V.D.	—	—
Idaho*	16b	16b	18	18	—	V.D.,q	—	—
Illinois	16	16	18	18	30 days	V.D.,n	—	60 days,x
Indiana	17c	17c	18	18	—	V.D.,q	72 hrs.	60 days
Iowa*	18b	18b	18	18	—	—	3 days,t	20 days
Kansas**	18b	18b	18	18	—	—	3 days,k	—
Kentucky	18b,c	18b	18	18	—	—	—	—
Louisiana	18b	18b	18	18	10 days	V.D.	72 hrs.,k	—
Maine	16b	16b	18	18	—	—	3 days,t,k	90 days
Maryland	16c,f	16c,f	18	18	—	—	48 hrs.,k	180 days
Massachusetts	14e	12e	18	18	60 days	V.D.,q	3 days,t	—
Michigan	16c,d	16c	18	18	30 days	V.D.	3 days,k	—
Minnesota	16b	16b	18	18	—	—	5 days,k	—
Mississippi	17	15	21	21	30 days	V.D.	3 days,k	—
Missouri	15d, 18b	15d, 18b	18	18	—	V.D.	—	180 days
Montana***	16	16	18	18	—	V.D.,q	—	—
Nebraska**	17	17	19	19	—	V.D.,q	—	—
Nevada	16b	16b	18	18	—	l,s	3 days,t	90 days
New Hampshire	14e	13e	18	18	—	l,s	3 days,t	90 days
New Jersey	16b,c	16b,c	18	18	30 days	V.D.	72 hrs.,k	30 days
New Mexico*	16d	16d	18	18	30 days	V.D.	—	—
New York	14e	14e	18	18	—	p	—	60 days,k,x
North Carolina	16c,u	16c,u	18	18	—	m	—	—
North Dakota	16	16	18	18	—	—	—	60 days
Ohio*	18b,c	16b,c	18	18	30 days	V.D.	5 days,k	60 days
Oklahoma*	16c	16c	18	18	30 days,k	V.D.	—	30 days
Oregon	17	17	18	18	—	—	3 days,k	—
Pennsylvania*	16d	16d	18	18	30 days	V.D.	3 days,k	60 days
Puerto Rico*	18b,c,d	16b,c,d	21	21	—	V.D.	—	—
Rhode Island*	18d	16d	18	18	—	V.D.,q	—	—
South Carolina*	16c	14c	18	18	—	—	1 day	—
South Dakota	16c	16c	18	18	—	—	—	20 days
Tennessee	16d	16d	18	18	—	—	3 days,v	30 days
Texas**	14e,g	14e,g	18	18	—	—	—	30 days
Utah*	14	14	18h	18h	30 days	V.D.	—	30 days
Vermont	16b	16b	18	18	30 days	V.D.	1 day,k	—
Virginia	16a,c	16a,c	18	18	—	V.D.	—	60 days
Washington	17d	17d	18	18	—	r	3 days	60 days
West Virginia	18c	18c	18	18	—	V.D.	3 days,k	—
Wisconsin	16d	16d	18	18	—	V.D.	5 days,k	30 days
Wyoming	16d	16d	18	18	—	V.D.,q	—	—
Dist. of Columbia*	16a	16a	18	18	30 days	V.D.	3 days,k	—

*Indicates 1987 common-law marriage is recognized; many states only recognize such marriages if entered into many years before.

♦ Marriages by proxy are valid.

♦♦ Proxy marriages are valid under certain conditions.

(a) Parental consent not required if minor was previously married.

(b) Younger parties may marry with parental consent and/or permission of judge. In Connecticut, judicial approval.

(c) Younger parties may obtain license in case of pregnancy or birth of a child.

(d) Younger parties may obtain license in special circumstances.

(e) Parental consent and/or permission of judge required.

(f) If parties are at least 16, proof of age and consent of parents in person is required. If parent is ill, an affidavit by the incapacitated parent and a physician's affidavit to that effect required.

(g) Below-age-of-consent parties need parental consent and permission of judge.

(h) Authorizes counties to provide for premarital counseling as a requisite to issuance of license to persons under 19 and persons previously divorced.

(k) Waiting period may be avoided.

(l) With each certificate issued to couples, a list of family-planning agencies and services available to them is provided.

(m) Mental incompetence, infectious tuberculosis, venereal diseases and rubella (certain counties only).

(n) Test for sickle cell anemia given at request of examining physician.

(p) Tests for sickle cell anemia may be required for certain applicants. Marriage prohibited unless it is established that procreation is not possible.

(q) Rubella (for female). In Colorado and Wyoming, rubella for female under 45 and Rh type.

(r) No medical exam required; however, applicants must file affidavit showing non-affliction of contagious venereal disease.

(s) Required offer of HIV test, and/or must be provided with information on AIDS.

(t) Parties must file notice of intention to marry with local clerk.

(u) Unless parties are 18 or over, or female is pregnant, or applicants are the parents of a living child born out of wedlock.

(v) Unless parties are over 18.

(w) Residents before expiration of 24-hour waiting period. Non-residents formerly residents, before expiration of 96-hour waiting period. Others 96 hours.

(x) License effective one day after issuance, unless court orders otherwise.

Source: Gary N. Skoloff, Skoloff & Wolfe, Livingston, NJ; as of May 1, 1993.

Reprinted with permission from THE WORLD ALMANAC AND BOOK OF FACTS 1994. Copyright 1993 by Funk & Wagnalls Corporation. All rights reserved. The World Almanac is an imprint of Funk & Wagnalls.

INDEX